POOR LITTLE RICH BOY

(and how he made good)

Authors: Gwen Morgan and Arthur Veysey
Cartoons by Joseph Parrish
POOR LITTLE RICH BOY
(and how he made good)

First Edition, 1985

Commissioned by the DuPage Heritage Gallery, Wheaton, Illinois

Published by: Crossroads Communications
Manufactured in the United States of America

Library of Congress Catalog Number: 85-70124
International Standard Book Number: 0-916445-10-0

Other Books By—

Gwen Morgan
Cicero and the Silver Drums

Arthur Veysey
Death in the Jungle

Gwen Morgan and Arthur Veysey
Halas by Halas

The Chapters In
"A Great Life And An Adventurous One"

Cartoons
By Joseph Parrish

Introduction

For a half century, as reporter and literary editor for the Chicago Tribune, I talked with a parade of personages from poets to presidents. Almost all sought publicity. Some believed their future depended upon what the public knew or thought about them. Others craved to see their names in print.

Col. Robert R. McCormick was a rare exception. Although he lived in a fishbowl and was concerned with the great dramas of the world, he shunned publicity. He was a very private person. In the absence of readily available facts, speculation arose and, when the Colonel continued silent about himself, congealed into rumor and then hardened into fable and legend. Foes deliberately created and spread falsehoods. Few people sought understanding.

It was inevitable that someone should undertake a biography. Perhaps no persons are better prepared to take on the challenge than Gwen Morgan and Arthur Veysey. Their years abroad as correspondents brought them hours with the Colonel in his last years and, more important, they developed their ability to seek truth. Fortunately, for the past ten years they have lived in the place the Colonel loved best, his country home, Cantigny. His interests surround them; his books are piled high before them. People associated with him come, often from distant places, to review and renew their impressions. From Cantigny, Gwen and Arthur ranged afar asking, "What was the Colonel really like?"

They have separated fact from fiction. Skillfully and without prejudice, as all biographies should be written, they have brought out of the mist of fable and legend a living man.

Fanny Butcher

Foreword

In Search of The Colonel

This book grew out of a request by the DuPage County Heritage Gallery that we produce for its historical records and publications a book about Colonel Robert R. McCormick, the combative editor of the Chicago Tribune for 45 years. The Gallery listed him among DuPage's great men, basing its claim on the fact that his 500 acre estate, Cantigny, is in the county.

Almost at once we were confronted with a teasing question: Why did the Colonel and his wife Amy abandon the comforts and pleasures of the rich suburbs along Lake Michigan and come 30 miles into the corn country, scorching in summer, freezing in winter, short of the graces of wealthy long-established communities? The answer surprised us. It also gave us a vital clue to the Colonel's character and the shape of his life.

We, as foreign correspondents for The Tribune, had known him during his last annual visits to Europe. We had flown around Africa with him in his converted B-17 Flying Fortress bomber. We found him patient, mild, shy, quiet, courteous.

But we knew him when he was off duty and relaxed. What was he like in action, daily speaking his mind in plain words? Was he the dictatorial, unswerving, prejudiced autocrat, his mind firmly locked into the 14th century, as his enemies declared? Why was he so opposed to government expansion, so dedicated to keeping America out of the Second World War—until the Japanese bombed Pearl Harbor? What prejudices and principles did he inherit from his grandfather Joseph Medill, a founder of the Republican party and a discoverer of Abraham Lincoln? What did the Colonel learn from his father Robert Sanderson McCormick,

ix

American ambassador to Emperor Francis Joseph, Czar Nicholas and the president of republican France? Was the Colonel right about his mother?

For the answers we had to look beyond Cantigny and DuPage County. Then more questions cascaded upon us. We knew from going with him to his English school, Ludgrove, that he did not hate his days there with Winston Churchill's cousin. Was it at Groton that he first began looking down on Franklin "Frank" Roosevelt, a junior schoolmate? Why on returning to Yale for the 50th reunion of his class of 1903 did he sign a nostalgic songbook, "From Rubberfoot"? How did he meet Amy Irwin, daughter of America's earliest Congressional Medal of Honor winner and wife of his cousin? Why did Chicago Republican bosses choose him at 23 to be an alderman and, two years later, to preside over Chicago's biggest engineering project? How did he become a colonel? What did he do in the Great War? When did he become fascinated with airplanes and radio? What took him into the Canadian wilderness? And come to think of it, how did he acquire control of the Chicago Tribune and build it into the country's first integrated newspaper enterprise, employing 20,000 dedicated men and women? How did he get along with his elder brother Medill and his Patterson cousins, Joe who so well understood the everyday New Yorker and Cissy who at the Washington Times-Herald "would rather raise hell than vegetables?" Why did he jerk his niece Bazy from Washington after only two years?

Each question led to another and to another and still more. The search for answers led us happily back to Tribune men and women who had come to see us during our 29 years abroad. The story of life at Cantigny came easily. Since 1975 we have lived at Cantigny as director of the Robert R. McCormick Museum and as general manager. Our guides are alert for comments that may identify among the quarter million visitors each year someone who had lived or worked at Cantigny.

The Tribune has not sought any editorial control over this book nor opened its records during our three-year search for the truth about the Colonel.

Gwen Morgan
Arthur Veysey

Cantigny, 1985

About the Authors

ARTHUR VEYSEY, graduate of the University of Colorado, began his newspaper career on the Denver Post. After stints in Scottsbluff, Nebraska, and Omaha, he joined the Chicago Tribune in 1943 and was sent to the Southwest Pacific as a war correspondent. He covered a dozen invasions, wrote a column "GI Pacific," did broadcasts for Mutual, was on the Missouri for the Japanese surrender, reported the return of the British and Dutch to Southeast Asia. In 1946 The Tribune sent him to Europe as a roving correspondent based in London. In 1949 he was named chief of the London bureau. Although responsible for coverage of British news, he continued to travel often to Scandinavia, the Lowlands, France, Spain, the Middle East doing the Israel-Arab wars on one side or the other, occasionally to Russia and Eastern Europe, twice to Viet Nam, many times to Africa. He made a sentimental journey through the Southwest Pacific 20 years after the war. Some of his Viet Nam pieces were collected in a book, "Death in the Jungle," published in London.

GWEN MORGAN, Smith College graduate, began her newspaper career with William Allen White on the Emporia Gazette. After brief periods on Kansas City and Omaha newspapers, United Press in 1943 made her a Washington correspondent covering State Department and White House stories with numerous exclusive interviews. In 1946 the Chicago Tribune sent her to Europe as a roving foreign correspondent based in London. Her canvas was wide—international conferences, national elections, revival of Western Europe, economic developments, catastrophies, personalities, Queen Elizabeth's continuing story including her accession, coronation and foreign tours, Queen Juliana's coronation, Pope Paul's election and coronation, the Eichmann trial in Jerusalem, Pope John's Ecumenical Council, deaths and funerals of Pope John, King George VI, Queen Mary, Duke of Windsor, Pope Pius XII, Jacqueline Kennedy's state visit to India and Pakistan, only correspondent at the burial of Winston Churchill, the Viet Nam Peace Talks and Treaty in Paris, where she was named chief of the bureau in 1972. Her story of Queen Elizabeth's drumhorse Cicero became the book "Cicero and The Silver Drums," published in London.

Each author has received Beck awards for excellence in foreign-correspondence. They collaborated in writing "Halas By Halas," the autobiography of George Halas, owner of the Chicago Bears and a founder of the National Football League. They married in 1946.

About the Artist

JOSEPH PARRISH, former political cartoonist, served on the Chicago Tribune editorial board for 34 years.

1. Bertie
1880—1893

"It's a boy."

The doctor may have held out the baby to the young mother and, if he made that natural offer, she may have turned away and said something like, "Oh no!" But more probably she flared into an angry rage and said something like, "Damn, damn, damn!"

Such a word was not flung out by properly reared young ladies in 1880, but Katharine Medill McCormick, called Kate, had good reason to be shocked. Three years earlier, on May 16, 1877, she had delivered her first child, a son whom she named Joseph Medill McCormick and presented to his grandfather, Joseph Medill, as heir to his fast-growing newspaper, the Chicago Tribune, burgeoning in power and wealth.

The heir produced, Kate waited for the coming of a daughter. The child arrived on January 17, 1879. Kate named her Katrina and bathed her with tender love. The sun shone with new glory for Kate. Life sparkled. Then after six months, abruptly and with little warning, Katrina was snatched from her. The death shattered the mother. Despair and bitterness consumed her. "She has become unhinged," awed friends told one another. The only healing, Kate slowly reckoned, could come with the gift of another daughter, another Katrina. On July 30, 1880, the doctor held forth the third child and announced, "It's a boy."

The pronouncement staggered Kate but a second revelation, that Kate would have no more children, destroyed hope and poisoned her life. There never would be a Katrina.

The finality could have made Kate think again about the second son and have led her into accepting him and cherishing him and expecting that a mother's love would heal her depression, bury her frustration, open her heart to the boy and that she would hold him close and tell him he was dear to her.

1

But Kate at 27 was not that kind of woman. The resolute, steadfast, independent spirit of her Scotch-Irish ancestors, so vital for accomplishment and so effective in overcoming difficulties, had twisted within her into self-centered willfulness. What Kate wanted, Kate got. How dare anyone, even God, deny her? Kate's answer to a rebuff was to explode; she had learned that sound and fury gained her the goal. . .but not this time.

The doctor waited a month before he filled out the birth certificate and then wrote Robert Sanderson McCormick as the name of both father and son. But a christening cup was inscribed Robert Grigsby McCormick, Grigsby being the family name of the baby's paternal grandmother. Not long after the birth the parents visited Scotland, home of the McCormicks, and there Kate learned that she shared with Sir Walter Scott an ancestor named Rutherford. She substituted that sonorous name for Grigsby. For several years, perhaps in thoughtless desperation, perhaps in self-delusion, she sometimes addressed the boy as Katrina, dressed his soft auburn-brown hair as though he were a girl and decorated him with more bows and frills than were the fashionable attire for little boys. Grandfather Medill called him Bobby and playmates called him Bertie.

The doctor gave the birthplace as Joseph Medill's house at 101 Cass Street, a short carriage ride from the Chicago Loop, but that too was an error. Sixty years later, Colonel R. R. McCormick told friends, with laughter showing through his brown eyes, that more people visited his birthplace than that of Abraham Lincoln. By then his parents' town house at 150 Ontario Street had become a popular supper club.

Chicago in 1880 was sprouting fortunes with the showy abandon of dandelions in May. The McCormicks were among the first and most industrious in gathering the wealth. Cyrus McCormick's new works, rebuilt south of the river after Mrs. O'Leary's hay set the town alight in 1871, spewed forth onto the newly broken midwestern prairies two or three thousand reaping machines each month. Profits approached a million dollars a year, the annual average collective wage for 1,500 men. Cyrus brought in artisans who over four years erected, embellished and over-embellished a mansion for his young wife, Nettie, grandiosely taking as his model both the Paris Opera and the Louvre.

Robert Sanderson McCormick did not share in the golden harvest. His father, William Sanderson McCormick, and uncle, Leander McCormick, had come to Chicago in 1849 from the

2

McCormick plantation, Walnut Grove, in western Virginia at the urging of their elder brother Cyrus, who needed Leander to manage the steadily expanding works and William to keep the books. William came reluctantly, leaving his heart in the soft Virginia valley. He and his wife Mary, daughter of "Squire" Grigsby, made a sentimental journey home each year. William watched Chicago flood outward as trains and boats brought fortune seekers from the East and land-hungry immigrants from Europe. Land that could be bought for a few dollars, or even a few cents, increased tenfold, a hundredfold, a thousandfold, and more.

Buy land, William told Cyrus. Let's put all profits into land. Cyrus said no, insisting that every penny was needed to add to the works, to hire more men, to make more reapers. William put his own funds into land but resented Cyrus' domination. Other pains developed. Why did Cyrus boast he invented the grain reaping machine? Cyrus knew their father, Robert McCormick, was the genius and had given years to mastering the problem. The father, not Cyrus, should have the glory and honor for ending the painful task, as old as man, of cutting grain, bent double, with a blade. Also, their sister Amanda recalled that Cyrus had promised their dying father he would share equally with his brothers and sisters any profits from the reaper, but he was taking much more than his share.

By 1865, William had enough. He sold his partnership to Cyrus and Leander and, recognizing a weakness, signed himself into the state mental institution. In a few months he died of cholera. He was 50. His son was 15. The widow, a believer in education and culture, detested the rough ways of tough Chicago. She sent her son to the University of Virginia and then to Europe. By the time the son came of age, William's land investments had multiplied in value, giving young Robert an inheritance of $400,000. Young Robert, eager to be equal with his ultrarich McCormick cousins, joined a commodity partnership and commuted between Chicago and St. Louis. Markets were bad and Robert's judgment was worse. His inheritance seeped away.

Then he met Kate. She had been in Europe with her parents, Joseph and Katharine Medill, and her sisters, Nellie—a year younger and already a rival—and little Josephine. Kate, 21, tall, slender, selfish, spoiled, willful, with a temper as hot as her red hair, had been smitten with the cosseted life of the rich Europeans. She envied their comforts and parties, their self-confidence, their arrogance. Some day, she determined, she would marry a young man, handsome, suave, rich, and together they would enjoy the good life of aristocratic, self-indulgent Europeans. On coming home, she saw him, young, handsome, suave, only somewhat rich but with very rich relatives. He kissed her hand and proposed marriage. She accepted, but first he must ask father. The swain presented himself to Medill. The editor-publisher, a warrior who put the end of slavery above the unity of his country, was irate. His daughter marry the son of a slave owner, a Democrat, a deceitful Copperhead not revealing his true, deadly intentions? Never!

But on June 8, 1876, Kate Medill and Robert Sanderson McCormick were married. With much of the bridegroom's inheritance gone, the newlyweds were unable to build or buy a home. They rented a narrow row house, one room wide, three stories high, distinguished only by a bow window running up the facade. Chicago's haughty society relegated the couple to the category of "the poor McCormicks." Medill relented far enough to give McCormick an assignment as Tribune literary editor and Kate fiercely set her course on making her firstborn the heir to The Tribune, all of it. To certify her claim, she spoke to the boy and of the boy as "Medill." For the younger son, she didn't give a fig; he could manage for himself. An early photograph shows Kate holding Medill close to her side, her right side, their arms linked, eyes speaking mutual admiration. On her left, Bertie stands alone, apart in a wilderness, isolated, hands in pockets, looking at the stars. The quarantine into which Kate had placed him with her first words spoken on his birth was solidifying into a wall around a boy untouched by love.

Bertie and Medill were assigned a room at the top of the house and, as was the custom in socially busy families, meals were sent up on trays. Some late afternoons, plump Aunt Nellie joined the boys during the evening high tea. The Colonel remembered her visits only for her eager gobbling of leftovers.

Cyrus died when Bertie was four. His widow, Nettie, recognized Bertie's aloneness and, perhaps wanting to make up for his mother's lack of love, often invited him to stay overnight with her. Nettie Fowler McCormick early had learned how to deal with willfulness. When Cyrus, 48 and accustomed to having his way, proposed marriage, Nettie, only 21, wrote her demurral: "Problems may arise between us because of your lack of proper appreciation for the opinions of others, a self-confidence that brooks no denial, a resolute determination to overcome every ob-

4

stacle, a hardness and blindness of purpose that will not quit."
Cyrus persisted. Nettie consented only after they drew up a
mutual pledge: "If either of us makes an abrupt charge, the other
is not to reply in the same strain but is to direct the attention
calmly to the real point." Nettie signed "N" and Cyrus added his
"C." They locked away the pledge.

Bertie, instead of opening his heart to Great Aunt Nettie, resented her affection and crisply rejected her tenderness. "She
tried to adopt me," he said a long time later when he realized his
self-inflicted loss. Would the rejection become a pattern in his
life? Would he deny himself the comfort of friendship and the re-

wards of love, freely given and received?

From the start Bertie grew faster than other boys. Kate need not search to find his red-brown hair rising above a meadow of little boys. But, awkward as a day old colt, he could not run as fast as other boys, or throw a ball as far or as true. His sight was fuzzy and his hearing dull. When boys chose up sides to play a game, Bertie was apt to be the one accepted without enthusiasm after all the others had been picked. The ignominy reinforced the shyness which made him stand back. His favorite companion was the son of a neighborhood lawyer who had accused his wife of adultery. Bertie did not understand the nature of the crime but he recognized that the boy was an outcast, like himself. The two boys became expert with slingshots against birds. One day they clambered onto a church roof and whipped pebbles against windows of the adjoining hotel. They advanced to guns, making stray dogs their targets. Now and then Bertie played with sons of rich, young McCormick cousins. A Cyrus grandson gave Bertie a ride on a penny farthing bicycle. They ran over a dog. Sixty years later the Colonel had not forgotten the pain-filled yelp.

When Bertie was seven, someone threw a bomb at police trying to break up a union meeting, killing one and injuring 66. Police arrested seven union leaders, including a man who lived not far from Bertie's home. Angry working men demanded revenge, some shouting for revolution and teaching the making of bombs. Armed police patrolled the streets. For days Bertie and other boys were locked in their homes. As tempers eased, Bertie joined the other boys shouting taunts at the neighbor's wife scurrying along the street. As a man, he regretted his cruel behavior and, in self-justification, explained, "We shouted from fear." As years passed, the Colonel often preached the need to overcome fear, intending the advice as much for himself as for others.

Medill and Bertie were entered in the University School for Boys, the city's most fashionable, not far from the lake shore. The headmaster, Eugene C. Coulter, admitted only boys "of gentlemanlike conduct, with habits of purity, interest, industry and enthusiasm." Enrollment was kept to 99 and no class had more than seven students. All of the first 11 graduates went on to university. The five story, very solid, dignified building of stone and brick had a bowling alley and manual training shops in the basement and, on the top floor, a gymnasium presided over by a Yale graduate. The master's room was embellished by a copy made in England for the school of a Parthenon frieze showing a

6

battle between Greeks and Amazons. The headmaster emphasized, for health-conscious parents, that each boy had 250 cubic
feet of often-changed air, that fireplaces heated classrooms and
that light came over the left shoulder. The school drew boys from
Prairie Avenue mansions to the south and Ashland Avenue to the
west. Girls attended the older and larger Dearborn Seminary.
Since 1883, a Chicago law required all children to attend school
at least 12 weeks a year.

When Bertie was nine, Abraham Lincoln's son Robert Todd
Lincoln, who with his mother had come to Chicago soon after the
President's assassination, was appointed by President Harrison
to be United States minister to London. Lincoln handled law
matters for The Tribune and, conscious of The Tribune's support
for his father, asked Bertie's father to come to London as second
secretary on his eight-man legation staff. The position paid
poorly but Kate knew, she just knew, that she could wangle
enough money from her father to permit her and her husband to
live in the style she wished in the capital of the British empire.
Her dream was coming true.

The McCormicks and the Lincolns together crossed the Atlantic on the steamer *City of Paris*. With the McCormicks were their
sons, Medill and Bertie. The Lincolns had with them daughters
Mary, 20, and Jessie, 14, and 16-year-old son Abraham Lincoln
II, called Jack. The newly appointed naval attache, Lt. Cmdr.
William H. Emory, entertained the boys with tales of how he rescued the Arctic explorer, Gen. Adolphus Greely, but not before
the General, the Colonel remembered, reputedly had eaten one of
his men. The army attache, Capt. E. L. Zalinski, stimulated young Bert's creative mind with a description of one of his
inventions, an air gun which hurled dynamite at an enemy ship.
Bert took photographs with his farewell gift, a Kodak camera
which had just come on the market, but none of his photographs
survives in the family albums.

In London the McCormicks rented a Mayfair townhouse on
Brook Street between Grosvenor Square and Hyde Park. Bertie
saw Queen Victoria ride in her carriage from Buckingham Palace
to the park and noticed that the central pair of gates, closed to
ordinary folk, opened for her. People cheered and threw their
hats into the air. "Like a comic opera," he said later. The Colonel, when being driven through Brook Street on the way to Cla-
ridge's Hotel on one of his last trips to London, asked the driver
to move slowly. The Colonel studied the houses. "There, that's

it!" he said. He asked the driver to stop. "I wonder if it has changed," the Colonel said. A knock brought a woman to the door. Told that an American who lived there as a boy wished to pay a visit, the woman invited the Colonel to enter. The Colonel wandered from small room to smaller room. "The library, Father worked here. . .the dining room, we had a china cupboard there . . .upstairs. . .the drawing room. . .Mother served tea to the ladies here. . .up more stairs. . .Mother and Father had the large room on the front. . .Medill and I had the small room on the back, when we were at home from school. . ." He seemed happy with the memories.

Bertie and his elder brother were entered in a boarding school outside London. The Colonel remembered the headmaster's wife as a "lovely lady" but said the headmaster was unpleasant, hogging the fireplace, the only source of heat. The boys complained to their parents. After a short time, the boys were moved, Medill to Harrow, where Winston Churchill was a pupil, and Bertie to Ludgrove, 15 miles from central London near the battlefield of Barnet where, Bertie soon learned, Warwick the Kingmaker was slain in the Wars of the Roses. There were only 50 or so boys at Ludgrove.

A Scotch-Irish boy, Shane Leslie, a cousin of Winston Churchill—their mothers were the New York Jerome sisters—learned Bertie was an American and sought him out. "We shook hands warmly in view of our mutual American blood," Leslie recalled. Here began a casual friendship which was to last their lifetimes.

Ludgrove's headmaster, Arthur Dunn, was remembered by the Colonel as "a splendid, kindly man." Similarly, Leslie said Dunn and his wife "considered us to be their boys as much as their own children; she was sweet as summer to small, homesick boys." To Dunn, there were only two sins—scruggishness, which meant loafing and slacking, and the slightest breath of anything thought to be indecent. One day a master asked Leslie the name of the weapon the Irish used to hit one another over the head. The boy replied, "A bloody hawthorne." Never, never, Leslie was told sharply, must he use that adjective.

The headmaster had been an all-England soccer captain and expert cricketer. Bertie found the sports exciting but, tall, spindly and ungainly, he was not chosen for school teams. He did boast later that he was one of the few Americans who appreciated the niceties of cricket.

The school owned one of the first bicycles made of wood, called a bonecrusher, propelled by the rider pressing toes against the ground. The Ludgrove vehicle was too big for the boys but Bertie discovered that if another boy helped him mount the vehicle atop a hill, he could ride it to the bottom.

The masters taught the glories of Britain and her past but when addressing the young American added that he always must remember his loyalty lay with America. To Ludgrove and its masters, the Colonel attributed his own strong patriotism.

The English boys hazed one another but never the American. They respected the American flag he hung from the wall over his bed and shared with him food that came in wicker hampers from their homes. "At the time," he commented late in life, "English boys were brought up much better than Americans." But there is no record that any schoolmate took him home during a school break, an experience which could have provided an opportunity for the lonely young outsider to develop the easy comradeship that binds brothers and sisters and friends growing up together. The three years at Ludgrove encased Bertie more solidly in his solitary shell.

Shane Leslie had lived in France. Leaving Ludgrove for a holiday, he kissed his favorite master. "A shout of wild derision followed me as I fled," he recalled. "I learned that, unlike other Christians, Englishmen are not to be kissed." In later years Leslie, then Sir Shane, was guest of the Colonel in Chicago. Leslie was firmly Irish in sentiment. He also favored the kilt. As he set off to walk through the Chicago Loop, the Colonel dispatched his driver to protect the baronet from remarks by raw Chicagoans amused by the sight of "a man in a skirt."

"I have often been asked," Sir Shane recalled, "to explain why the editor of the Chicago Tribune frustrated English propaganda in the Second World War." Many people who considered the Colonel anti-British put it down to hostility generated in his English private school. "Wrong," Sir Shane continued. "I can say he was happy under Arthur Dunn."

But the Colonel's father, Sir Shane added, had at least one reason for hard feelings about Britain. According to Leslie, the then British foreign secretary, Lord Salisbury, did not receive the father at his country estate, Hatfield. "It was later said," Sir Shane commented,"that one cup of tea at Hatfield in the last century could have changed the status of Britain in Chicago journalism in the present century." McCormick was only a second secretary at the legation and the snub could be considered only a triviality, something of no consequence. But it was a foretaste of a vicious course of action by a British foreign service officer that was to ruin the father's diplomatic career, enough to give the son an acute awareness that action by one individual can determine the fate of another, as well as the course of a nation or alliance of nations.

The Colonel and Mrs. Dunn corresponded until her death. She remembered him as a "a very nice boy" and kept two pictures of him. After the Colonel became known in Britain as anti-British, newspapers taunted her for defending the Colonel. "I don't care a pin," she said.

One summer afternoon in 1952, the Colonel, on his annual European visit with Mrs. McCormick, said he would like to visit Ludgrove. By then, the school had moved to a fine old country estate near Wokingham, in Berkshire. After a telephone call to the headmaster, the McCormicks rode in a rented Rolls Royce through the richly green countryside. The headmaster led the Colonel to a long corridor walled with wooden tablets bearing, in gold, the names of all the students since the school opened in 1882. A star after a name identified the student as having gone into the navy, army, foreign or colonial service. "They helped build the empire," the Colonel, touched, remarked to the headmaster. Later, driving from the school, he tartly added that Britain, by regarding men in commerce or business as second class citizens, had itself become a second class nation.

*   *   *   *   *

In the late eighties parents often dressed sons in sailor suits. At a German spa with his parents, Bertie was so dressed. The ribbon on his cap bore the name of a British warship. The Prince of Wales, later King Edward VII, walking with his cousin, the German Kaiser, said, "Ah, a nice little English boy." "I am not an English boy," Bertie said with vigor. "I am an American." The Kaiser laughed. The angry boy told his parents and the next boat from New York brought a ribbon bearing the name of an American warship, a gift from Commander Emory.

Bertie was impressed by the strange outfit Lincoln wore as American minister when going to Buckingham Palace to present his credentials to Queen Victoria—black silk stockings over pink silk stockings, black shoes with silver buckles, black satin knee breeches, ruffled white shirt. The boy forgot the cut of the coat.

10

At the time he accepted court costume as part of diplomatic life and watched his mother practice walking backwards without tripping over her long train, a peril inherent in presentations at Buckingham Palace. Later, the Colonel looked upon it all as "folderol" and something to be shunned by Americans. Thirty years passed before an American ambassador, Chicago's Charles G. Dawes, challenged the royal dress code by attending court in morning coat and striped trousers. In The Tribune, John J. McCutcheon drew an understanding cartoon. The ambassadorial mind—depicted in a circle over Dawes' head—saw the Marietta, Ohio, home folk laughing at photos of their man wearing silk knee pants. The royal mind—shown in a circle over King George V, kindly smiling, crowned and seated on his throne—imagined Dawes to be knock-kneed and not wishing to expose the handicap. "A matter of form!" the cartoonist commented.

Bertie decided early that dress conventions evolved from royal need. "Look at the Prince of Wales," the Colonel commented about the portly man who later became King Edward VII, saying he invented the cutaway to look slimmer while his father, Prince Albert, a slender man, invented the double-breasted frock coat to look broader. In his time, the Colonel favored London clothes: suits from Henry Poole, shoes from Lobb, hats from Lock. On a visit to his London tailor, he ordered a belted Norfolk jacket and plus fours. "But, sir," the Poole cutter said, "no gentleman wears that kind of attire today." The Colonel's wordless stare sent the cutter scurrying for his long out-of-date pattern books.

Young Jack Lincoln developed a carbuncle, the Colonel recalled, and died, alerting young Bert to the transitoriness of life.

At 11, Bertie went with his mother to the French Riviera. The sea fascinated him. With a new chum, he set off in a small sailboat. Beyond the horizon lay Africa. Africa! The Foreign Legion! Prancing Arab horses and sword-wielding blood-thirsty Arabs! Let's go to Africa, the boys said. But before they were over the horizon, a faster boat overtook them and its skipper ordered them back to France. The wide, wide world must wait.

That same summer, Bertie was sent to live with a French couple, both teachers, at their home in Versailles, to become fluent in French, a task that later served to shape his life. He was intrigued by the wife's often dosing herself with arsenic. Why, he asked, did she not die? He could find no answer. A young English marquess preempted the head of the table. Bertie found him discourteous. "He expected deference," the Colonel recalled. "He did

11

not get it from me." At a Paris circus, he thought he made a friend of an American black performer called Chocolat, until Chocolat talked him out of his only five-franc coin. At an Ostend restaurant he saw a flashy woman sparkling with jewels. "Who is she?" he asked. His mother did not reply. From others the boy learned she was one of three "fancy ladies." Sixty years later the Colonel recited their names, Liane de Pougy, La Belle Otero and Cleo de Morode, mistress of the king of Belgium.

He was considered, at 11, self-sufficient enough to return to his British school alone: a train from Versailles to Paris, a carriage to the Gare du Nord, a train to Calais, the channel steamer to Dover, a train to London, a carriage to Charing Cross and a train to Barnet where the school carriage waited.

About this time Kate's younger sister, Josephine, came to London for a long visit with Kate and her husband who took pleasure in the company of the gentle 25-year-old woman. Josephine had inherited her mother's "weak lungs" and during an expedition to Paris with Kate, she became desperately ill and died. After a funeral in Paris, the body was sent to Chicago for services in the Medill home. Letters and cables sent daily to the Medills in California during the short illness did not reach them until after the Chicago burial.

In 1890, the U.S. House of Representatives authorized Chicago to be host to the ninth World's Fair, honoring Columbus' discovery of America 400 years earlier. Chicago won the prize over New York and St. Louis. Paris also planned a fair. Medill was one of 45 Chicagoans to pledge support to a venture expected to cost 30 million dollars, a regal sum. Soon Grecian palaces in lath and plaster rather than marble were rising in a swamp along Chicago's South Shore.

In London Second Secretary McCormick was appointed European representative for the Fair. Eight extraordinarily fine, detailed water color paintings by a Chicago artist, John R. Key, let the American give Europeans a taste of the delights that would be served up in Chicago. The Fair, planned to open in the spring of 1892, was delayed one year. The McCormicks came home in time for the opening. The paintings were slipped carefully into an expertly crafted wooden case, stored in an attic and forgotten.

2. The Inheritance
1820—1890

A child's inheritance is often reckoned in cash, securities and real estate, in a business or profession, in social position, all easily tabulated. But an accounting must consider also traits of character, convictions, prejudices. Are they products of heredity or of environment? That question can be left to professors, but an examination of these traits is essential in shaping a study of an extraordinary life. To recognize a man, one also must look at his forebears.

Love did not weave tight bonds around the resolute, often obstinate Medills and McCormicks. Kate's grandparents, William Medill and Margaret Corbet, had become unwelcome in their homes in Ireland after their marriage. William's father, of French Huguenot stock tempered in Scotland, was a Presbyterian minister in Belfast, a biblical scholar and author of a book about the Apocalypse. Margaret's father, an English army officer and member of the (Episcopal) Church of England, was stationed in Belfast to help subdue the Irish Catholics. Looking back more than a century and a half, one must stretch credulity to understand how two dedicated Protestant families could give up son and daughter to sectarian obstinacy while both families were engaged in a bitter and often bloody struggle with Catholics who wanted all Protestants delivered to hell or at least deported from the green island so cruelly rent by mortal hate in the name of immortal love.

In 1819, William and Margaret joined other Scotch-Irish families seeking a kindlier, happier future. They sailed across the Atlantic and up the St. Lawrence, settling on a rocky bit of ground on the south shore in New Brunswick. There the first son, Kate's father Joseph, was born April 6, 1823. At the time, the region was considered part of the new nation of the United States of America, but after the Medills moved to the softer, more fertile fields

13

of Ohio, a boundary commission placed New Brunswick in Canada, thereby depriving Joseph Medill, the Colonel commented with mock sorrow two generations later, of the right to seek the presidency.

Farm chores did not please young Joseph. He eagerly ran three miles to borrow books from a neighbor. In time, the parents suggested the bookish boy become a minister and Joseph dutifully strode five miles every Saturday to read Latin and logic with a minister in Canton. The youth examined the life of a rural pastor, listening to the woes of his flock, comforting his sheep, preaching brotherly love, forbearance and forgiveness, living poorly on often begrudged charity. The prospect did not fit Joseph's aggressively independent spirit. People were interesting to watch and to wonder at but not to serve. The Bible always had been at hand, but more to his liking was Gibbon's account of the Roman empire. Looking around, the youth was fascinated by the rise and fall of his neighbors. Some were carried steadily ahead by their intelligence, education and diligence or drifted miserably because of their stupidity, incompetence or laziness; while others, without concerted action of their own, were whisked to power and fortune or, contrarily, despite their best efforts, were smashed to smithereens. Life could be generous; life could be cruel; no one should expect life to be just.

Young Medill plucked episodes from the tiny world around him, turned them this way and that until they formed themselves into stories and sent them to newspapers and magazines. He pondered how laws and customs might be changed for the betterment of the citizens and the nation. He found flaws in both national parties, Democrats and Whigs, and, with the jaunty conviction of youth, sent his opinions to Horace Greeley, editor and publisher of the nation's leading Whig newspaper, the New York Tribune. Sometimes Joseph's pieces were printed, and sometimes editors sent kind notes, encouraging the novice to imagine for himself a place among the political and literary giants. Happy and fortunate was young Medill to have found his propensity and career before gaining the vote.

But editors rarely sent enough money to replace the paper and ink. Medill turned away from his destiny and looked for a more financially rewarding mode of life. Above the rural humdrum surfaced the lawyers. They were independent; they had power; people respected them, even feared them. And they prospered! A Canton lawyer let 21-year-old Medill sit on one of his chairs and read his books. After two years the name Joseph Medill, Advocate, appeared on the Tuscarawas county legal notice board. The brand new advocate joined a partnership in New Philadelphia and enjoyed sitting with his new brothers-in-law, listening to their tales of clever victories, watching small dramas unfold in courtrooms, meeting as an equal with town elders and politicians visiting from Columbus. Advocacy was pleasant, but few people would seek advice from a youngster who could cite no important legal successes. Those who did take a chance with him considered a chicken or a few eggs fair recompense. What to do?

At this time of indecision, fate produced an overgrown lout of a pupil and directed him to beat up the teacher. No more of this, the teacher said, and left town. Medill offered himself as a substitute, and was accepted. The bully stared impudently at the new teacher, his arms no thicker than the bully's wrists, and sneered a challenge. The new teacher said, "Let's go outside," removed his jacket and pounded the bully to the ground, becoming, he recalled later, a Greek god to the boys. "As for the girls," he said, "I married one of them."

She was Katharine Patrick, and unwittingly she was to bring Medill back to his destiny. Her Scotch-Irish, Belfast-born father, James Patrick, was justice of the peace in New Philadelphia and owner-editor of the local paper, the Advocate of Tuscarawas. Early he had selected for Katharine, his sixth child, a career which he considered honorable, pleasant and safe. He taught her the craft of setting type without error and the art of comprehensible composition so she could assist him in his livelihood and look after him when his faculties failed.

Children tend to accept without question conditions imposed strictly and early in life by their parents. Sit up straight, girl; she sat up straight. Eat your porridge, girl; she ate her porridge. Stay with me always, daughter; yes, father, dear father, the girl said and thought no more of her future. It was settled, until along came Joseph Meharry Medill, red-haired, fiery, burning with ambition. He devoted longer and longer hours in her father's print shop, learning from her the intricacies of producing a newspaper. One day he commanded Katharine, Marry me. Yes, dear Joseph, she said, but first you must speak with father. The judge-editor was alarmed by the threat to his own well-being but did not wish openly to refuse his daughter permission to marry. The Bible offered a tactic. Just as Jacob had to agree to delay his marriage to Rachel, Medill was told by Judge Patrick, yes, he could marry

15

Katharine—after he proved he could support her properly. Wait for me, Medill demanded of Katharine, and strode off.

Fate now had its hand firmly on Joseph Medill. The eager suitor borrowed $500 from his father, bought a newspaper in Coshocton, a tiny community 11 miles distant, and recruited as unpaid labor his younger brothers, William, James and Samuel, all eager to escape from the family farm. The paper's name, The Democratic Whig, displeased Medill. Whig had been a proud political name since the 17th century when troublesome Scottish Presbyterians turned an ancient Gaelic word for cattle thief, hung on them by the Catholic Stuarts, into a badge of honor. In time, Whigs became the British party of reform. In Colonial America Whigs demanded liberty from England, but, as issues changed, would not declare themselves on slavery. Disgruntled Whigs became Free Soilers or Know Nothings. Medill proposed that citizens wanting to end slavery should organize a new party and call themselves Republicans. He changed the name of his paper to The Republican and, after Whigs carried only four of the 31 states in the 1852 election, he wrote to Greeley about the need for an anti-slavery party. Greeley replied he would be saddened to have the Whig party vanish but he could see no possibility for its revival, so he wished Medill well with the party and the cause.

Medill, ready for a bigger audience, sold the Coshocton paper, bought one in Newark, sold it, and, bringing in a moneyed partner, Edwin Cowles, thereby setting that family on the road to riches, began a paper in Cleveland which, after a false start, he named The Leader, reflecting the goal for the paper and for himself. The paper thrived. Three years after Judge Patrick had stated his terms, Medill returned to New Philadelphia to claim Katharine. The Judge's principles did not allow him to say no, but his selfishness, his concentration on his own well being, did not let him say a gracious yes. Scotch-Irish tempers exploded. The two men spoke harsh words, cruel but true. Katharine did not know what to do. Up spoke Medill. Come, he commanded. The young woman, probably in tears as she looked over her shoulder at her father, left home forever. On September 2, 1852, she and Medill were married. He was 29; she was 23.

Katharine wrote frequently to her father, urging him to come to Cleveland and meet his granddaughters Kate, born July 11, 1853, and Nellie, christened Elinor, born January 30, 1855, but he ranked his anger and pride above the comfort he could have given his daughter and the joy he could have received from the granddaughters and stayed apart. Not for 10 years did Medill write one word to his father-in-law.

For Katharine, life continued unaltered. In New Philadelphia she had waited upon her father and accepted his words implicitly. Now in Cleveland she equally waited upon her husband and governed her actions by his words and moods. She loved her daughters, but Medill took most of her effort, perhaps leaving her less able for the increasingly difficult task of furnishing their minds, shaping their characters and teaching them the importance of consideration for others. Soon tuberculosis began draining her small store of energy. Medill, immersed in organizing the new Republican party, in writing pieces for The Leader, and in tending to his expanding business, had scant time or thought for the girls. They soon were to learn, when entering a room, to speak to him only after he had acknowledged their presence and spoken to them.

In 1855 Medill was 32 and ready for the big time. His forceful stand against slavery and his work for the new party had made him known far beyond Cleveland. One day a visitor arrived from Chicago. He, Captain James D. Webster, and two others were floundering around trying to run a newspaper founded eight years earlier when Chicago could count only 18,000 citizens. The paper, The Tribune, campaigned against booze, Catholics and all foreigners and was harassed by six rivals. Webster asked Medill to come to Chicago and become managing editor of The Tribune. Medill made the 11-hour journey on the new train. He was dismayed by The Tribune's junk printing plant and appalled at the town's 541 saloons and 110 brothels. He scampered back to Cleveland, but he was haunted by the promise of expansion he noticed in Chicago, and promise tantalized Medill. Almost every month a new railroad sent its tracks from Chicago out into the newly broken prairie. Medill liked the paper's name. Had not Gibbon written about Romans appealing to a tribune when seeking redress from imperial decrees? Medill turned again to Greeley. "Go to Chicago," the New York editor replied, "Buy The Tribune. If you need a partner, look up Dr. Charles Ray."

Medill sold his share of The Leader to his partner and set off for Chicago. Ray, alerted by Greeley, met him there. Ray, a medical doctor with a soul pledged to politics, had tasted the delights of political newspapering in Galena, Illinois, and in Springfield, capital of Illinois. The pair bought The Tribune, Ray promising to sell later to Medill for $40,000 if Medill so wished. Medill fetched Katharine, she protesting at having to leave the relatively elegant metropolis of Cleveland for a crude shanty town up to its ankles in stinking mud. Medill rented a house and, to help with the little girls, hired a German maid who spoke no English and thus was powerless in directing the children. Soon Katharine persuaded her husband to buy a house on high ground to the northwest, away from the mud and stench of the lake front. Medill's three brothers came as did Edwin Cowles' brother Alfred to keep the books and in time become a partner.

Medill praised the mayor, Levi Boone, relative of frontiersman Daniel, for trying to close the saloons on Sunday, stopped giving the paper to advertisers and went off to Washington for several weeks, his wife remarking, "My dear, you must be demented." Medill helped persuade the new Republican party at its first national convention in Philadelphia to consider for the vice presidency a country lawyer, Abraham Lincoln, admired by Medill for "hurling thunderbolts at the foes of freedom." The party passed by Lincoln but nominated him for the Senate two years later and The Tribune reported his debates with Stephen Douglas word for word. In 1860, the Republican party gathered in Chicago and Medill, shouting denunciation of supporters of slavery and whispering promises to delegates, helped gain the presidential nomination for Lincoln.

Medill had come easily to his position that slavery was evil and must end. Not so with Cyrus McCormick, who had come to Chicago eight years before Medill to build the town's first large factory for manufacturing the revolutionary grain reaper. McCormick looked upon slavery as inhuman but, as a son of a slave owner and himself once a slave owner, he would not condemn the practice nor the practitioners. He believed slaves would be freed gradually as the reaper and other machines reduced the need for their sweat, whereas an abrupt end to slavery would destroy the economic base of the South and the majority of Southerners therefore would resist abolition, by arms if necessary, destroying the Union.

Cyrus McCormick bought two Chicago papers, The Herald and The Times, merged them and preached that the Union must be preserved. Abolitionists sneered that such words emanated from devious men who deceived with false arguments and, like the copperhead snake, struck without warning.

Medill pounced on McCormick with the journalistic invective

so popular at the time, writing that McCormick, "like all poor white trash of Virginia, left that state a better friend of slavery than the slaveholders." Such darts wounded McCormick. He proposed North and South send delegates to a national convention and work out a compromise. Few responded; Chicago opinion was rising against slavery and the South. The McCormick paper lost money and after two years Cyrus sold it, but neither he nor Medill ever sought to close the breach between them.

Lincoln promised during his campaign to try to prevent war, but within weeks of his inauguration Southern guns shattered Fort Sumter. In the morning, the American flag appeared on the Tribune masthead. The flag is there today. Medill demanded the North send men to fight for the Union. Before dark President Lincoln called for volunteers. William and James Medill and 10 other Tribune employees replied, but in the first week of the war only 500 men volunteered from Chicago, a city of 110,000 and the nation's ninth largest. Medill warned that the war could not be won with volunteers and prodded Lincoln to draft 300,000 men. Medill sent reporters to live with the troops and told women how they could help win the war. Military blunders made Medill wonder if the war could be won but did not weaken his Scotch-Irish resolve. He demanded commanders "wage war fiercely" and was not silenced as death lists lengthened and included the name of his brother William. Captain Webster, who had enticed Medill to Chicago, became a general.

By late 1864, few volunteers were coming forward and thousands of young men were evading the half-hearted draft. Lincoln asked Illinois to send 5,500 more men. Medill travelled to Washington and told the President Illinois could not spare so many men nor should it be expected to do so. Lincoln's cold stare froze his long-time friend. You wanted the war, Lincoln said; now provide the men. Medill returned home and Illinois provided the men. Medill worked for Lincoln's re-election and was disgusted when Vice President Andrew Johnson was drunk at the inauguration. A month later Medill's editors wrote a headline:

Terrible News
Abraham Lincoln Assassinated
at Ford's Theater

A stunned Medill moved his support to Johnson, trying to blot out the inauguration disagreeableness by commenting that perhaps Johnson had suffered from an upset stomach and merely had taken a little brandy to settle indigestion. Medill suggested that General Lee "do penance by breaking rocks and toting paper for The Tribune."

* * * * *

Chicago drew people throughout the war. With peace, the river of settlers became a flood, 20,000 a year. A man could walk off a lake boat from the East, find a job by noon, and, working 10 hours a day six days a week, earn $50 a month. The Tribune printed 50,000 copies a day. Medill talked about Chicago's becoming the greatest city in America or—why not?—in the world.

For Medill, the road ahead should have been clear and bright but the feistiness which made him such a provocative, successful editor struck him down. It happened this way. In 1858, Medill and his partner, Dr. Ray, had merged their Tribune with their most formidable rival, The Democratic Press, the city's oldest newspaper, founded 14 years earlier than The Tribune, taking in the Press owner, William Bross, as a partner. Three years later, in 1861, the partnership was incorporated with 2,000 shares valued at $100 each. Medill and Bross received 430 shares each, Ray and John L. Scripps, another early partner, 420 each and Alfred Cowles 300. Scripps was elected president. During the war, Ray differed with Medill over editorial policies and left the paper but kept his stock. Scripps sold his shares to an ambitious newspaperman, Horace White, who had advanced quickly from reporter to Washington correspondent and saw himself as the future editor. The liberal White and the conservative Medill differed over tariffs. Cowles and Bross, alienated by Medill's constant determination to have his own way, supported White, reducing Medill to a minority of one.

Medill, only 42, was weary and cantankerous, racked with constant rheumatic pain despite a hypochondriac's swallowing of potions and pills. His hearing was almost gone. "He's deaf as an earless snake," a disgruntled staff member commented. Medill resorted reluctantly to an ear trumpet. Katharine, weakening from tuberculosis, yearned for warm, dry air. Unexpectedly, she became pregnant. After the birth of her third child, Josephine, in 1866, she told her husband there must be no more children. Life had become too difficult. Medill resigned the managing editorship to White and wandered about the nation, writing pieces for The Tribune, seeking relief for his pains and for his wife's cough. There was a rumor he intended to buy a Louisiana plantation,

21

but California became his favorite retreat, Katharine seeking help in a sanitarium in Redlands. Now and then Medill told other stockholders he would either sell to them or buy them out at $500 a share, five times its value only five years earlier, setting The Tribune's value at one million dollars.

In 1869, The Tribune erected a quarter-million-dollar building at Madison and Wabash. Medill long had worried about a holocaust sweeping through the clutter of wooden buildings — their construction, he said, was "criminal carelessness." The Tribune's directors considered the new structure to be fireproof and did not insure it. Chicago's Great Fire came in 1871, gobbling the two-year-old Tribune building. Medill, happening to be in Chicago, found a small printing plant beyond the charred zone and The Tribune did not miss an edition. "Cheer up," The Tribune directed. "Chicago will build again, bigger and better." It did, The Tribune leading the way.

The Republicans presented Medill as their candidate for mayor, calling him Fireproof Medill. He was elected to public office for the first time, also the last. He took firm command of city hall, put police on a 12-hour day to make the streets safe and built a fire alarm tower and a public library to which Queen Victoria contributed books. When he proposed the city raise the license fee for the 3,000 saloons and close them on Sundays, his popularity dried up. He resigned and took his family to Europe, seeking hot springs for his rheumatic bones and dry air for his wife's lungs and writing home that the United States is "the freeest, happiest, most glorious country on earth."

Early in the winter, letters from home indicated that Cowles and others would part with enough stock to give Medill a majority ownership. He hurried home and offered $450 a share. Cowles wanted $550. On November 1, 1874, Medill agreed to buy 600 shares at $500, devoting his entire savings, mortgaging his house and borrowing from Marshall Field, already the city's premier merchant, at 10 percent for five years. At 51, Medill achieved his life's ambition. His 1,056 of the 2,000 shares gave him unchallenged control of The Tribune.

Mrs. Medill and the three daughters came home from Europe in the spring. Kate saw young Robert Sanderson McCormick and slowly overcame her father's rejection of a Copperhead son-in-law. Barely had that tempest calmed when her sister Nellie brought home a marriage proposal. Again Medill was irate. What, another daughter marry another Copperhead? Never,

22

JOSEPH
MEDILL

REPUBLICAN PARTY

never! Without gaining her father's approval Nellie married Robert Wilson Patterson, Jr. He was 28, she 23. The bridegroom's father, a leading Presbyterian minister, had come to Chicago in 1840 from Tennessee. A Democrat and a sympathizer with his native South, the minister had not received Medill's accolade because of his soft attitude toward slave owners. The end of the Civil War did not ease Medill's strictures, nor did the Rev. Dr. Patterson's success in gathering Chicago's elite into his Second Presbyterian church nor his helping to found the summer colony and college at Lake Forest—"A quiet retired village with a fine moral and spiritual tone"—on a wooded bluff beside Lake Michigan north of Chicago. The minister had sent his son and namesake to the Lake Forest College and then to Williams in Massachusetts. Young Patterson returned to rough, tough Chicago with a degree in classical literature, a key to no doors. The son began to study law but, drawn to newspapering, found a job on a politically minded sheet blatantly calling itself The Copperhead Times, a stout enemy of The Tribune. Soon he moved to another Tribune foe, The Interior, as managing editor. In 1873 his skill and use of words earned him the position of night telegraph editor on The Tribune. Proving himself intelligent, efficient and careful, he was promoted in two years to night editor with responsibility for putting the paper to bed. The next year he began courting Nellie beyond the sight and hearing of Medill, to whom he had yet to speak the first word.

By defying Medill's denial of Nellie's hand, Patterson may have assumed he would be fired but his craftsmanship and, yes, his demonstration of independence and competence earned Medill's approbation. On January 6, 1879, a son was born and, by christening him Joseph Medill Patterson, Nellie challenged Kate to a bitter rivalry for succession to The Tribune that was to continue throughout their lives and bring anguish and problems for the sons. A daughter followed in two years. She was christened Elinor for her mother but her brother Joe called her Sissy. She changed Elinor to Eleanor and Sissy to Cissy. Neither mother gave the sons cause to love her. "My mother hated me," Colonel McCormick commented late in life. He also said, "My mother and aunt were real bitches."

* * * * *

The fire rid Chicago of a curse citizens had brought upon

24

themselves by building flimsy structures of wood and providing little more than water barrels and buckets to check flames from an out-of-hand bonfire, an overheated stove, or a kicked-over lantern. But a more deadly curse—"the fever"—continued to torment the city day and night. That curse also was self imposed.

Along the shore of Lake Michigan, nature built over the centuries a low strand of sand and mud a half-mile or a mile wide that, acting as a dike, held back water, draining toward the lake from the rolling land to the west. Midway along the strand, the water long ago had broken through to the lake. Southerners would have called the trapped water a bayou but Chicagoans called it a river although the flow, from the north and from the south and out to the lake, was so slow that if a man dropped his hat into the water he need walk only a few steps to retrieve it an hour later. The cut through the dike provided a welcome anchorage for lake boats. Citizens drew water from the river and dumped their waste into the river and wondered why so many people, including an early Tribune partner and Kate's father-in-law, died of cholera but did not suspect that the river water was the cause. Medill imagined Chicago was being persecuted by sunspots. For fastidious citizens who faulted the water for the peculiar taste and bad odor, entrepreneurs laid pipes of hollowed logs from the lake and for a fee delivered "pure" water to the homes. Other entrepreneurs, also for a fee, carried waste from the households to the river in triangular conduits made by nailing three planks together. Most of the filth settled on the river bottom forming a thick mattress of gas-exuding ooze. Newcomers smelled the river long before they saw it. Medill wrote editorials saying the river must be cleansed.

The rival Times commented: "Chicago is enveloped by a solid stink. The river stinks. The air stinks. People's clothing stinks. There is no other word. Stink reaches the infinite and becomes sublime in the magnitude of odiousness." Citizens long had proposed that the city send its waste into a barge canal completed by the army in 1839 to connect Lake Michigan with the Mississippi, but met a problem. Barges could be towed up the canal and through locks but sewage would not flow uphill and no one could make sufficiently large pumps to lift it. Citizens organized associations and appointed committees, talk clattered back and forth, delegations visited Springfield and Washington. For 30 years nothing happened. Then, on August 2, 1885, when Bertie was five years old, nature intervened. A mighty burst of thunder clouds dumped six inches of rain on Chicago. Water flooded into the river and far out into the lake, to the most distant intake and beyond. In the morning Chicagoans turned on faucets and out came yesterday's waste. Within days fever swept through the city with a deadliness beyond that of the fire. Joseph Medill demanded action now. A young lawyer, Richard Prendergast, appalled by 700 deaths in seven days, led a citizens' action committee of doctors, businessmen, lawyers, engineers, bankers, preachers, city officials, and, yes, editors led by Medill. The power wielders demanded the state legislature authorize the creation of a sanitary district which would sell bonds, deepen the river and dig a canal to the Des Plaines River, the nearest tributary of the Mississippi. Northern Lake Michigan would continue to drain into the Great Lakes and the St. Lawrence to the Atlantic, but southern Lake Michigan would drain into a reversed Chicago River, through the canal, to the Des Plaines River and on through the Illinois and the Mississippi Rivers to the Gulf of Mexico.

The Illinois constitution, written at a time of public protest about the shenanigans of railroad and canal builders, stated no public money could be used for either enterprise. Prendergast circumvented that legal block by describing the waterway not as a canal but as a channel, although it would, by happenstance, be big enough to carry barges and river boats. Another block appeared as residents along the Des Plaines and Illinois Rivers poured invective upon the legislature for allowing Chicago citizens to empty their privy pots on them. For two years, rival lobbies shouted at each other and at the legislators. Prendergast, recently retired as county judge and amassing a fortune from fast-rising real estate values, orated eloquently. Medill testified before a Senate-House committee and, in the words of a Tribune historian, "exerted his influence to the utmost." So did other men of consequence, and the legislature voted the Sanitary District into life.

The local Democratic and Republican party machines saw a rich opportunity and, departing from the customary winner-take-all rule, agreed to divide the jobs and the contracts. Each party chose four men and both parties nominated all eight, assuring their election. Each party nominated its own man for the ninth seat but agreed that the winner would not upset the board's equilibrium. The maneuver to move in on the new civic project enraged Republican Medill, Democrat Judge Prendergast and other members of the action group which had brought about the creation of the District. The group nominated a non-party slate of six, including the Judge who, in the words of a rising Democrat, Edward F. Dunne—he was a cousin of the Judge's wife—"roasted both parties until they became cinders." The voters elected the non-party ticket plus three Democrats. The Board chose the Judge as its president.

Prendergast brought in New York City's chief engineer, Rudolph Hering, who designed a waterway 36 miles long, 24 feet deep, at least 160 feet wide, through which lake water would flow at a pace of a mile and a half an hour. The engineer wanted more speed to reduce the possibility of waste settling in the channel, but the army demanded the slow rate to help the upstream movement of barges and boats. The water, before entering the Des Plaines River, would race through turbines creating 30,000 horsepower. Who could use so much electricity? Gas lighted buildings and streets, horses pulled trams, steam drove trains and machinery.

The District drafted horses from miles around but soon steam-driven shovels clawed into shattered rock, high pressure hoses washed away clay, cable buckets and trains carried off the spoil. In a few months, the science of earth moving advanced more than in the previous 20 years. Engineers came from afar to study "the Chicago method."

* * * * *

In London Second Secretary Robert Sanderson McCormick and Kate did not suspect that the efforts of the Judge and Medill to clean up the Chicago River would so affect the career of their ten-year-old second son, Robert, busy mastering the bone crusher at Ludgrove.

* * * * *

Joseph Medill was 67 in 1890 and old beyond his years. For 17 years he had been the majority stockholder and his increasingly harsh words were still law at The Tribune, but gradually he had passed power to his son-in-law, Nellie's husband Robert Patterson. Each October, Medill took Katharine to California to ease his rheumatics and her consumption, but every day he sent a telegram or letter to Patterson. In summer, Medill occasionally came to The Tribune office and plant, speaking only to Patterson. Medill had learned to trust Patterson's intelligence and judgment. When Patterson rejected a Medill command, events soon proved him correct, Medill wrong. Patterson shared Medill's creed that a newspaper must be independent. Echoing Medill of 40 years earlier, and to be echoed by Medill's grandson Bert 30 years later, Patterson declared: "A good newspaper cannot have friends. Nor should it have other irons in the fire, leading to possible conflicts of interest."

In the printing shop, each letter had to be picked individually from a case and placed in a holder, the stick. How much more quickly the task could be done and how much paper could be saved, Medill and Patterson agreed, if only words did not have so many unnecessary letters. They began a campaign for simplified spelling, citing as an example: "Silent leters wich are uterly useless are dropt in speling this adres to save space and sho what a great degree of simplification might be adopted."

They found few converts, but The Tribune continued to push the reform even after linotypes eliminated handsetting. Medill opposed introduction of the machines because they would eliminate jobs, but Patterson convinced him The Tribune had to mechanize if it were to remain competitive.

Alfred Cowles, Tribune president since 1861, died in 1889. The other major stockholder, William Bross, stood bareheaded at the grave in a cold rain, caught a chill and died. Their heirs happily took over the delightful chore of collecting dividends, no questions asked, no advice given. Patterson was harassed only by his sister-in-law Kate. As Medill's health failed and Patterson's power swelled, Kate increasingly saw Patterson as the most troublesome obstacle in her effort to gain The Tribune for Medill, her elder son. She must prevent Patterson from slipping in his son Joe ahead of her son. Alternately wheedling and blustering, she must lead her father into writing a will favoring her son in the distribution of his Tribune stock.

*　*　*　*　*

The McCormicks returned from London in 1893 to a Chicago grown in the 13 years since Bert was born from a half million to more than a million, becoming the nation's second city and changing dramatically. Multiplying land values produced quick fortunes but the new rich were learning that more of everything is not necessarily better. No host tried to restage the 1880 forest feast for 500, including Medill, his daughters and sons-in-law, at which waiters brought oysters, turtle steaks, terrapin, frog legs, roast deer, antelope, buffalo and 14 other woodland critters so unfortunate as to be considered tasty, 52 kinds of fowl. Cyrus was also there with his 55-inch waist.

True, Potter Palmer, who in 1875 had spent three and a half million dollars to support his boast that his hotel was the epitome of luxury and magnificence, now had spent a million raising his wife's idea of a Rhine castle along the lake shore. A New England Puritan, Samuel Nickerson, who sprouted his fortune by making booze and expanded it as a banker, devoted half a million to building a mansion aptly called the marble palace.

But Stanford White, a disciple of Pericles, was opening clients' minds to the ancient simple elegance. One convert was Nellie. Ever since Kate had gone to London and drawn richly on their father's purse despite his ceaseless demands that she curb her extravagance and stop trying to keep up with the Grosvenors, Nellie had harassed Medill to engage White to design for her a clean-lined Italian palazzo in Chicago. Soon copycat wives were abandoning their demand for a cupola and insisting instead on a piazza. A son of Leander McCormick discovered English painters and purchased a Gainsborough and a Reynolds. Kate brought home a portrait of "pretty, witty" Nell Gwyn, who so charmed King Charles II. The court artist, Sir Peter Lely, painted her with the gown below her bosom.

Most housewives darkened windows with heavy drapes but Medill insisted that sun be let into his airy home, on which he had spent merely $100,000. Windows reached almost to the floor. Medill placed his tip-down desk against a side wall, bringing the sunlight over his left shoulder. An artist picturing him at work made the editor's wastebasket overflow, spilling unsatisfactory manuscripts widely on the floor.

No longer need a family have in the basement a clanking dynamo to enjoy the magic of light coming from a glass bowl fastened to a wire. In winter coal-fed furnaces floated warm air up into the bedrooms. The telephone was no longer a toy. The home of every family of quality had hot water and cold water on tap. In the butler's pantry at the home of Perry Smith, a railroader, one faucet produced iced champagne on special days. Every family aspired to having its own front door and a thin ring of grass between the house and the surrounding tall, spiked, iron fence.

To gain this benefit, most businessmen were willing to travel an hour by carriage, tram or the new commuter trains—20 miles for a dime. Busy streets were paved with wooden blocks, kind to horses' hooves. Million-dollar commercial buildings were popping up from the Chicago mud and, with land selling for $3,000 a front foot, builders built as tall as the soggy earth would tolerate. One structure soared ten stories.

At Marshall Field's, The Big Store, the merchant ordered his clerks to "give the lady what she wants" and brought goods from all parts of the world. Fashionable women discarded the bustle of coiled rings, horse hair or old newspapers, but still confined the waist with whalebones in every seam, filled out the skirt with at least five petticoats and insisted that the little seamstress in her attic stitch miles of lace on gowns. The cloth top of the high button shoes must match the gown. On going to call, a lady required one coachman to announce her arrival and another to open her carriage door. On New Year's Day, newspapers announced names of ladies who would be home to receive visitors. The rich maneuvered to be among the 6,000 listed in the The Elite Directory. Etiquette books sold by the tens of thousands, advising against drinking anything from a saucer, feeding the dog at the table, scratching the head during dinner and never, never blowing cigar smoke in a lady's face. Chewers could eject tobacco juice if the aim were true. The elite already had ceased using a knife to convey food to the mouth.

The Latin School superseded Bert's University School. Erudite ladies joined The Fortnightly Society, in 1893 already 20 years old, and took turns reading literary papers. Robert Todd Lincoln, on coming home from Europe, expanded his wealth by doing legal jobs for George Pullman's sleeping car enterprise and the flourishing electricity trust but amused himself plotting movement of stars and solving algebraic equations. A Leander McCormick heir wrote books insisting that a man's appearance revealed his character. The Dial welcomed poets but the editor said, "Good books written in Chicago are no more plentiful than snakes in Ireland." Fourteen newspapers competed for readers with Medill's Tribune. Sullivan's new Auditorium Theater was preferred by some Chicagoans to Milan's Scala and 2,500 slightly hesitant men and women crowded in to see and hear the naughty Oscar Wilde.

Chicago built an Art Institute, and ladies with taste and money were to wall it with glorious French impressionist paintings ignored by established collectors. Catholics, one-third of the citizens, could choose among 200 churches. Protestants maintained one church for every 300 of their faithful. Rich men routinely kept mistresses with the unspoken tolerance, if not permission, of their wives. The county built a vast columned Grecian temple of health and staffed it with doctors and nurses who worked medical miracles.

Baseball fans acclaimed the White Stockings as world champions and considered the stars worth their $2,000 season pay but management differed and slashed the scale. Players struck, bringing about a new club composed of sandlot beginners. Fans belittlingly called them the Colts or the Cubs. Horse racing enticed gamblers but politics was the most popular sport, election rallies drawing thousands. To keep his daughter Alice happy at home on summer afternoons, Field's credit manager, H. N. Higinbotham, head of the World's Fair, built a tennis court. Young men wanting to cut a figure dashed about town on bicycles at the mind-blowing speed of 15 miles an hour. Daring girls quickly followed, cutting short and dividing their skirts or, oh my, adopting the flounced black knickers flaunted by Mrs. Bloomer.

But a third of Chicago citizens lived packed often ten to a room in stinking shacks, big and small, vulnerable to fire, without water and sanitation. Half of Chicago's babies died before they could walk. Wages had surged from a dollar a day after the Civil War to a dollar and a half a day. "Exorbitant," Pullman said, and cut the pay to $1.30, setting off the strike creating the riot, bringing the armed police and locking Bertie indoors.

* * * * *

Medill considered selling The Tribune, but Kate asked him not to do so. She wanted The Tribune's help in getting an ambassadorial post for her husband.

* * * * *

President Grover Cleveland pushed a button, and half a million people poured into the Fair. How Bertie's eyes devoured the miraculous splendors! Strings of electric lights! Boats driven by naphtha across silky lagoons! The 265-foot-high Ferris wheel! Krupp cannon, the most massive killer ever built. A torpedo. Little Egypt and her fluttering belly. Girls in short hair! Boys with

31

cuffed trousers and the chant that was fresh in the Colonel's mind 60 years later, "Roll up your trousers as far as they go, for it's raining in London, in London, you know." Columbus' descendant, the Duke of Veragua, came from Spain. So did replicas of the *Santa Maria*, *Nina* and *Pinta*. Paderewski impressed. Sousa's band thrilled. An actor playing the role of Hiawatha placed a deer at the feet of a beautiful Minnehaha. Of course there were fireworks. Two automobiles raced toward Evanston, 15 miles away. Neither arrived.

Excusion boats took Fair visitors northward along the lake, into the slow-moving Chicago River busy with ships, and then into the lower reaches of the new canal. Had any Fair soothsayer possessed an accurate crystal ball, she could have told Bertie she saw the canal as a central part of his life.

A fierce debate arose over the division of power between state and federal governments. The precise issue was whether the Fair could open on Sundays. Blue law advocates obtained an injunction from a federal court prohibiting the Sabbath opening. Medill said the state, not the federal government, should control entertainment on Sunday. The state legislature, agreeing with him, passed a law authorizing the Fair to open. A superior court sided with Medill and threw out the federal court injunction. Later the Colonel was to examine suspiciously any encroachment of the federal government on the states. The Fair opened on Sunday. Alas, not enough people came that day to pay expenses. The economy, not politics, not morality, proved to be the dictator. The Fair closed on Sundays.

By autumn, the Fair had paid its debts. The directors planned a mind-bursting final day but a lawyer, disgruntled at not getting a city job, killed the mayor, Carter Harrison, and the ceremonies were dropped. When the gates closed, 27,477,218 persons had come to the Fair. The rival Paris fair had drawn 28,149,353, but Chicagoans claimed "our Fair" would have been the more popular had not "some petty clerk" in the federal government recorded a decision that the Fair would close at the end of October and written down the date as the 30th, forgetting that October has 31 days. There was talk of reopening the next summer but a winter fire destroyed several of the lath-and-plaster structures. Later, the most popular structure was rebuilt in stone—at the Colonel's suggestion—and now houses the Museum of Science and Industry. Another replica placed near Chicago's Loop is the home of the Field Museum of Natural History.

The Fair's classical buildings influenced architects and builders. The Public Library and Art Institute set standards for quality rarely met in civic buildings. Not far from the Fair site, John D. Rockefeller's millions enabled the University of Chicago to build a modern Gothic campus. Chicagoans boasted of having the most powerful electricity plant, the finest orchestra, the biggest apartment house, the largest department store. Think big, planners advised. Teenage Bert accepted the creed and made it basic in his life.

* * * * *

Kate and Robert Sanderson McCormick, at loose ends, missed Europe and made long trips there. They preferred Washington to Chicago, although McCormick accepted appointment to the Library Board and later its presidency.

Bert lived with his grandparents during school vacations if they were in town. The ailing grandmother, sensing the youth's loneliness, sent him to The Tribune with instructions to her husband to take Bert to lunch. Instead, the grandfather gave Bert a dollar and sent him next door to the John Thompson restaurant where a dollar bought a feast for the fast-growing boy but did not provide the more deeply needed companionship.

On visits to The Tribune, young Bert caught sight of prominent Chicagoans. Of course there was Joe Leiter, son of Marshall Field's early partner, Levi Leiter. Joe was to try to corner the wheat market, trapping meat packer P. D. Armour who had been selling short. Armour offered to settle but Joe demanded, as the Colonel remembered the drama, "his full pound of flesh." The weather intervened, delayed the winter freeze, kept the Great Lakes open for shipping until the latest recorded date and let Armour bring from Canada enough grain to thwart young Leiter. Leiter paid his son's losses of ten million dollars by selling land. The Colonel never forgot Field's comment: "It pays to have a good cash balance in the bank." Young Leiter continued his extravagant ways. Once when he was running out of money he cabled his father: "Need 40,000 dollars." "For what?" the father cabled back. Joe's reply was brief: "For Joe."

Bert was fascinated by Coxey's army ambling toward Washington led by a girl on a white horse. The jobless marchers, on reaching the capital, skirmished with police. The Colonel later blamed the jobless for inciting the police into arresting Coxey for walking on the grass, a charge that amused the adult McCormick, who rated Coxey as "a sentimentalist."

To the youth, Pullman was "extraordinary." He was building sleeping cars by the hundreds and operating them as part of long distance trains on all major railroads, overcoming competition from the Vanderbilt railroad group who had their own car, the Wagner. Bert admired the way Pullman's strong personality had helped force Chicagoans to jack Loop buildings out of the mud. But he shared his grandfather's disapproval of Pullman's arrogance toward his own employees, leading to strikes and riots in the summer of 1894. In Bert's mind the riots produced a personal disaster. His grandfather was deeply troubled by the labor unrest and devoted much time to trying to bring peace. The overwork brought on a heart attack. His wife nursed him, overtaxing her body, already weakened by her long fight against consumption. Katharine died in October 1894 at Elmhurst. Medill overcame the heart attack but sharply cut back on his duties and lengthened his periods in California.

3. Odd Boy Out
1893—1899

Bert followed his brother Medill and cousin Joe to Groton. His classes included Latin, Greek, English, mathematics, history, government and religion. After "exile" in Ludgrove he expected to be one of the gang, but his enthusiasm for Groton soon vanished. He found himself scorned as a Midwesterner by boys from "old" Boston and New York families. The youth's protective shell hardened. Again, as at Ludgrove, there is no record of any Groton boy taking him home and introducing him to members of his family. He was shy with girls. Frightened may be a more accurate description. His mother called him "a late bloomer." Invited to a dance, he was a wallflower; he had not learned to dance.

Bert complained to his father about his classmates' derogatory attitude.

"You tell them," the father replied, "that they are descended from Boston tradesmen while you are descended from Virginia gentlemen." "I did not understand," the Colonel commented much later, "but the stand must have been effective because the headmaster called me in and told me that Groton discouraged sectional arguments although the headmaster did not object to Easterners assuming superiority." The Eastern belittling of Midwesterners was paid back manyfold after the Colonel became editor of The Tribune. Boston colonials, the Colonel said, elected as their governor the colony's only gentleman, William Bradford. Virginia drew several gentlemen from England but they, in the absence of nobility, he said, developed into a self-conscious aristocracy adorning themselves with silk and lace, earning the ire of the great preacher of equality, George Mason. The Colonel wrote off New York: "Were that city destroyed, with it would go all subversive elements in our country."

Bert respected the Groton headmaster for his splendid sense of honor, "never doubting a boy's word until the boy was proved to be a liar, whereupon the boy was expelled." The headmaster was a puritan but Bert found him also to be pragmatic. The fact that one boy's sister was a "notorious lady" did not disqualify him from enrollment. The headmaster, McCormick recorded later, admitted two boys whose mothers had been mistresses of the school's founder. One day the Latin master caught a student using a crib. The boy was expelled. The event frightened Bert. His grandmother, shortly before her death, had sent him a crib. He remembered it lay in full view on a table in his room. Bert took the book to the headmaster and explained how he came to have it. The headmaster handed it back. "Put it in a drawer," he said. "It might tempt other boys." When grown, the Colonel thought translations helpful in learning a foreign language. In Paris in 1917 as a member of General Pershing's staff, he found that reading a French novel in both the original and in English improved his fluency in French.

As the Colonel remembered Groton's version of American history, all heroes were New Englanders, apart from Washington and Lincoln. The choir master told Bert he had a poor voice, so the Groton choir had to do without him, but he forever happily joined anyone in belting out songs. The English master told him he could not write, so Bert ceased working for the school paper and for 20 years attempted no writing for publication. Then the unique experience he was to have with the Russian army on the eastern front early in World War I forced him into print.

Math was easy. He and another boy tied for first place in geometry. The master arranged a runoff. Bert quickly solved the problem and, with several minutes to spare before the paper was due, he redrew his worksheet triangle for neatness' sake. He miscopied the angle lettering and the prize went to the rival. Bert thought he had been cheated, but he commented years later that the loss of the prize was much more than compensated for by the lesson he learned to be careful in all things.

Groton heightened the sense of high patriotism Bert had developed at Ludgrove. As at Ludgrove, Groton's alumni fought for their country, although the Colonel once told a radio audience Groton must have been disappointed with the way the sons of Franklin Delano Roosevelt turned out. FDR was one class behind Bert. They were aware of each other but did not become friends. For the remainder of his life the Colonel addressed letters, even those to the White House, to "Dear Frank," while signing himself "Robert R. McCormick."

Bert developed pneumonia in the winter of 1894. With his elder brother he was sent south to Thomasville, in the Georgia pine woods, where Grandfather Medill was wintering after his wife's death. It so happened that Mark Hanna, the Ohio Republican politician credited with making and breaking presidents, had rented a house there to introduce the Ohio governor, William McKinley, to the national and state political figures before running McKinley for the presidency in 1896. Hanna brought his daughter Ruth. She found Bert's older brother Medill good company. In weeks, Medill proposed; she accepted, but marriage was still far away. He was 17, she just 13.

Bert and other young guests sat apart at dinner, but he was very much aware of the political dealing going on. He noted that McKinley had one flaw—he was bankrupt. Hanna and others paid his debts and guaranteed McKinley's nomination "in the usual manner," the Colonel recalled, by lining up delegations. For delivering the Illinois delegation, Charles G. Dawes was designated controller of the currency. The Colonel never saw cause to change his teenage conclusion that presidential candidates are chosen by a few men. Hanna raised such a large campaign fund that he overcame one of the most effective of American orators, William Jennings Bryan. Bert did not hear Bryan speak, but he did hear a recording made on an early Edison phonograph of Bryan's fiery "Cross of Gold" speech which caught the nation's attention.

Bert used his recuperation to learn how to shoot accurately. "You must hit with your first shot," he was told by his father. "You won't get a second shot." The father said he had learned that lesson in a duel but gave no details. The father took Bert and other boys to a shooting gallery. Each time a boy missed a shot, he had to pass the gun to another boy. Quail was a favorite Georgia bird for shooting. Bert found crows the most difficult target. He tried trapshooting but decided that exercise impaired his ability to hit birds. The clay disc, he found, slowed as it flew, whereas a bird gained speed as it rose. The boy scorned the use of decoys as "not much different from shooting sitting ducks." Later, as a soldier, he found marksmanship to be of little practical benefit. Very few soldiers were killed by aimed bullets; machine guns and shrapnel did the killing. However, on leaving the army, the Colonel continued to recommend that soldiers learn to shoot well. The ability bolsters a soldier's confidence.

37

He learned to ride and to throw knives. He experimented with Robin Hood's bow and arrows. One day he lay on his back, pulled his knees tight against his chest, placed the bow across the soles of his shoes, and pushed outward with his legs. The bow arched almost double, much more deeply that he could achieve by holding the bow in his hand. He loosed an arrow. Away it zipped. Through the woods. Across a garden. Into an open window. He never tried that again. Of that winter, Bert's startling memory was of Mrs. McKinley seized with epilepsy during a dinner.

In the nineties yacht racing was popular with the wealthy. The season peaked with the America Cup race. One summer Bert watched from shore as the British sailed into an early lead, but on the last lap the Americans drew level and, with people ashore cheering, crossed the finish line first.

Another summer Bert rode and hunted on a Montana ranch. He helped to drive cattle. One day a bull disrupted the herd. A cowhand lassoed the bull, staked him tightly to the ground and moved off. Bert saw the animal was doomed to a slow death. He rode back and cut the bull loose. The cowhand challenged him but drew back from a fight. "I was bigger," the Colonel reminisced.

Another summer he and his brother camped in the Michigan woods, taking firecrackers to frighten off animal intruders. One night a fire erupted not far away. The two brothers ran before the flames. Years later the Colonel returned to the area and found the woods had been replanted with fruit orchards. "An improvement," he noted.

One summer Great Aunt Nettie engaged a young man to teach Bert the basics of electricity. The pupil developed a profitable business installing doorbells in neighboring houses. "Much more rewarding than mowing lawns," the Colonel recalled. He and the boy next door rigged a telegraph line between their bedrooms. The understanding of how electricity functions helped the Colonel take on much bigger tasks in his later careers.

An evangelist caught the boy's attention. The Colonel didn't remember his words but never forgot he wore wings.

* * * * *

In 1895, Judge Prendergast's five-year term at the Sanitary District ended. Pernicious anemia had weakened him, and his

38

ceaseless effort to find new ways to move dirt and to check politicans' old ways of filching money and jobs had exhausted him. Several of the independent members had resigned. Early in 1892, he had bought a farm on a knoll 30 miles west of the Loop. The soft, rolling, Irish-like countryside was crisscrossed with belts of oaks, maples, walnuts, and its meadows were knee-deep with prairie grasses and flowers. Near a cluster of larches he built a white clapboard house, and there his children could romp and ride, shoot and swim, laugh and shout, free of coughs and fever. But the Judge's wife died that year after giving birth to their sixth child, a girl named Margaret. The Judge went home to Ireland, sought out a kinswoman and brought her to his house in Chicago and to the farm to run the household and help look after the children, of whom the eldest was only nine years old. They called her Aunt Mary.

The Judge did not accept renomination. He wanted to get away from the city, from the smell and fever, from the finagling politicians, from never satisfied citizens. The farm offered solace. But he needed a good neighbor. He persuaded his campaign ally, Joseph Medill, to buy a farm called Red Oaks on the adjoining knoll. Medill saw little use of such a place for himself but assumed that the farm would sooth his elder daughter Kate, out of sorts because of the fine town mansion he had just built for her younger sister Nellie. Kate's husband could seclude himself with his books; the boys could hunt in the woods little changed since the last Indians were driven out 40 years earlier.

The railroad passed only a mile to the north, offering a choice of 32 trains each day, capable of delivering passengers downtown in 43 minutes, the first to be in their offices at 6 a. m., the last to return home just before midnight. The fare was 25 cents. In the county seat, Wheaton, three miles away, a thousand dollars bought a cottage, ten thousand a turreted mansion. A family lived well on a hundred dollars a month. Medill approved of Wheaton citizens' strict Protestant manners and morals, permitting no saloon keeper nor liquor dealer to open shop. The flag flew high, churches abounded, a college trained preachers. The marvel of electricity was coming. A booster wrote, "Wheaton is halfway to heaven, a tip-top town."

But that was not how former Diplomat Robert Sanderson McCormick and Kate rated the slow community. After their fine London house, the Red Oaks farm house was a hut. Medill asked one of the architects of the Public Library and of the Art Institute, C. A. Coolidge of Boston, to build a country home on his knoll. The architect demolished the farmhouse and set the new residence farther back from the road, already a main thoroughfare between Chicago and the West, flanking the house by the great oak to the east and clump of venerable elms to the west. Coolidge was a master of the proportion, restraint and craftsmanship which ancient Greeks exhibited in creating the most beautiful building of all time, the Parthenon.

Coolidge's design was elegant. An open portico rising to the roofline, supported by four Corinthian pillars, gave prestige to the facade that sheltered the front door and its carved balcony. To the left of the central hall and staircase which rose two floors to the attic was the generous sitting room, about 20 feet by 30 with two sets of French doors leading to a large porch, so essential during the Illinois summer. To the right was a dining room, somewhat smaller, with kitchen below and, off it, a porch for the servants. Behind the hall was a small library with a bow window and that astounding invention, a telephone, its wire carried on a string of poles reaching to Chicago. Upstairs were the family sitting room flanked by two bedrooms and a bathroom, three more bedrooms and another bathroom. Tucked into the attic were the servants' five bedrooms and bathroom. A back stairs led to the kitchen, scullery, laundry, furnace and storeroom in the basement. For cool evenings, each important room had a fireplace to supplement a torrent of hot air rising from a coal-fired furnace through floor grills and drifting up the staircase to the rooms above. In summer the two porches offered refuge from the heat. By late evening, a breeze almost always crept out of the cool woods, frolicked across the pastures and lakes and refreshingly swept into the house. By leaving solid doors open and closing only louvered doors, sleepers let the breeze pass through the bedrooms unhindered.

In designing the interior, the architect borrowed from the Adam brothers, those Scots who in turn had borrowed from Inigo Jones and the Greeks and given such elegance to so many of Britain's great country houses. The central staircase and hall were made bright with delicately wrought leaded sidelights and a fanlight that would honor the finest Georgian house on any London square. By night, lamps, candles and fireplaces cast golden light and shimmering shadows. A windmill raised well water to a tank standing on tall stilts behind the house. Pipes carried well water into the house and barns. Often the tank drained faster than the windmill could pump and then someone had to drive the cattle each day to the DuPage River—a stream really—three miles to the west, and bring back casks of water for the cows. Much of the timber was cut at a mill in the woods. The Colonel liked to tell visitors the building cost $15,000. Medill changed the name from Red Oaks farm to Beaumont but the re-christening was ignored. Medill seldom went to the country home and soon gave it to Kate. Bert and his brother rode horses and shot birds and small game in the woods. Their nearest neighbors were the Prendergasts.

*   *   *   *   *

On the Tribune news staff in the nineties were two ingenious, energetic, youthful newspapermen, James Keeley and Edward Scott Beck. Keeley, a Briton, had come to the United States at 14. He told many versions of his crossing but one account seems probable: his father abandoned his wife who dispatched the boy to friends in Fort Leavenworth, Kansas. For years, the boy told everyone he was an orphan.

He did odd jobs before hawking papers on trains. From passengers he heard about happenings he considered more interesting than many events reported in the papers he sold. He began sending items to papers, which gave him cash in return. An easy way to make money burst upon the youth. He would become a newspaperman and turn chat into cash. In 1889, at 21, he came to Chicago. Patterson hired him as a night police reporter, traditional task for a recruit. Keeley's vision roamed far afield. He convinced Patterson a war was about to break out among Wyoming cattlemen over a fence dispute. Take a look, Patterson said. Keeley, on arrival at Buffalo, Wyoming, telegraphed an exciting account of a gunfight. The Tribune printed it on the front page. During the next two weeks, Keeley sent 11 more accounts of gunfights, all carried on the front page. By then, other newspapers were dispatching reporters who arrived in a blizzard and learned the only telegraph line was out of action. Perhaps the snow and wind were responsible for the breakdown. Perhaps Keeley had cut the line while on his way to send his final dispatch, reporting from a telegraph office many miles on the rail line back to Chicago that peace had come to Wyoming.

Keeley outworked, outscooped, outwrote all reporters. He also was effective in directing reporters, who considered him unfair

41

and mean and, noting his sharp, darting eyes, called him Bird, but confessed that he knew the job.

In 1895, Patterson made Keeley, then 27, city editor in charge of the local news gathering staff, and three years later advanced him to managing editor, in charge of all news operations. The city editor task was assigned to Teddy Beck, a good-humored Hoosier educated at the University of Michigan, erudite, mild in temper, correct in manners. When Keeley battered reporters, Beck soothed their feelings. When Keeley fired, Beck rehired. Together they were the ideal team. Patterson could concentrate on Tribune business operations and on fending off Kate.

Keeley delighted in the unusual. He was charmed one day when a young Englishman arrived in his office bearing a dispatch from Lord Northcliffe, the London press magnate. Keeley wrote a reply, called a Tribune copy boy, Jimmy Durkin, and told him to deliver the message to Northcliffe in London. And make sure you get there in less time than The Times' copy boy needed to reach Chicago, Keeley added.

The '80s and '90s brought solid growth to The Tribune. At the beginning of the century's last decade as one of 15 dailies in Chicago, it printed 50,000 copies daily and aggressively sought news, with bureaus in Washington, New York, Boston, Cincinnati and Milwaukee and, soon, London.

To test the efficacy of a new Pasteur vaccine against cholera, The Tribune sent a man to Paris to be inoculated before going to Hamburg, considered the most heavily infected city in the world. He survived. The Tribune assigned liquor-loving reporters to enter "institutes" operated by a former army doctor, Leslie Keeley, who claimed that his treatment based on chloride of gold "restored dipsomaniacs to health, reason and sobriety" and blocked any "lapse into debauchery." The Tribune published Dr. Keeley's reports, but did not accept one line of advertising. A woman reporter went to India with Mary Leiter, Joe's sister and wife of Lord Curzon, newly appointed viceroy of India. A Tribune man went with Peary on a search for the North Pole. An entire squad hurried to the Klondike to report that gold rush. Richard Harding Davis described the coronation of the Czar for The Tribune, Mark Twain reported Queen Victoria's diamond jubilee, Lord Randolph Churchill wrote about the growing dispute between Britain and the Boers in South Africa. Sir Edwin Arnold warned from Tokyo that Japan was becoming a tough business competitor and was building a strong military force to challenge Britain and the United States in Hawaii, where Queen Liliuokalani had been deposed. Britain considered annexing the islands. Medill said if any country acquired Hawaii, that country should be the United States. Britain, he muttered, is "the greatest land grabber in history." The United States, he reminded, was a nation of 70 million people and "should stop pursuing a timid policy when confronted with threats from other nations." Both remarks must have burned deeply into Bert's inquiring mind.

In 1897 The Tribune celebrated its 50th anniversary with a special issue predicting that by 1997 Chicago would be the greatest city in the world, surpassing New York, considered by Medill not a true American city. Chicago's 10 million people, the paper foretold, would live in buildings 60 or 70 stories tall; cemeteries would be parks; sewage would be carried by tunnels to farms; boats from Europe would travel up the St. Lawrence River, through the Great Lakes to Chicago, then along an enlarged canal to the Illinois River and on down the Mississippi to New Orleans and the Gulf of Mexico; Canada must join the United States; the American president must be limited to one term and the income tax, levied at two percent on incomes over $4,000, must disappear.

On the night the *Maine* was blown up, February 15, 1898, Bert was in Washington waiting to call on Assistant Secretary of Navy Theodore Roosevelt the next day and be shown models of American warships. Bert remained in the capital to hear Senator William E. Mason of Illinois advocate war with Spain. Medill joined the clamor. "The American people," he wrote, "demand war on Spain, the yellow dog among nations. There is no price to be put on American lives. America must fight." The Tribune sent a reporter to Cuba. Back at Groton, Bert found opinion against war. "A kindly old gentleman" asked him if the "western war fever" were not caused by hopes of army pensions. "New Englanders," the Colonel commented later, "quietly ensconced in their little group, had always opposed expansion of the country and held a totally different view from the pioneers who had endured many hardships to make the American nation."

In late April, Spain and the United States were at war. McKinley, with only 27,000 regular soldiers, called for volunteers. Scarlet fever kept Bert at Groton. His brother remained at Yale. On May 1, Admiral Dewey stormed into Manila Bay and sank all 11 Spanish warships there. Aboard his flagship was a newspaper-

43

man named Edward Harden, a one-time book critic for The Tribune, giving himself a world cruise after arranging with the New York World to receive any interesting news he came upon. The World had agreed to share the report with The Tribune. Dewey transferred Harden and two other newspapermen to a ship returning to Hong Kong for supplies. Picture the trio scrambling into the Hong Kong cable office, pushing each other aside and shoving pieces of notepaper toward the operators, each demanding his dispatch be moved first. The operators chose Harden's copy. He had attached a note asking his story be transmitted at the top rate of $5 a word. The cable reached The World at 3 a. m. The presses there were already stilled and the staff had gone home, but Keeley had decreed that The Tribune's man in New York must remain on duty until the Chicago presses stopped one hour later. The New Yorker forwarded the cable. In Chicago two editors slapped together an extra that was on newsstands when the earliest risers left home for work. Keeley telephoned the White House, roused President McKinley and gave him the news of America's most nearly complete naval victory up to that time. Dewey's sailors occupied the Spanish naval base of Cavite and the Admiral told the President he could take Manila but lacked men. The army dispatched a small band of regulars and volunteers westward and another, including Teddy Roosevelt's Rough Riders, to Cuba. On July 1, the Rough Riders charged up San Juan Hill led by Roosevelt on horseback. Seven weeks later Dewey's reinforcements took Manila. At the end of the year, Spain ceded Cuba, the Philippines and Puerto Rico to the United States.

The stream of events rolled over and around the growing Robert McCormick, shaping his character, his beliefs, principles and prejudices, his dreams.

*   *   *   *   *

Medill looked upon Tribune employees as an extended family. On New Year's Day of 1890, he had invited them and their families to a holiday dinner. The party was repeated every New Year's until 1908. By then there were so many employees the dinner lost its personal air. The Tribune gave each employee a gold coin in 1911. During the 1920's the Colonel reinstated the New Year's party and continued it until the strike in 1947 by printers proved they did not consider themselves part of a team and put a crack in the Colonel's heart.

Medill established The Tribune as a friend, perhaps a kind of outspoken uncle, to its readers. He boasted it was partisan, but independent. He sided with the working men against the Rockefellers, the Vanderbilts, the Swifts, but detested aggressive labor leaders, especially Eugene Debs. Dictators, he called them, a word that was to come easily to grandsons Bert and Joe. He fought the street car barons, the gas lords, the electricity gougers and the politicians who gave them the opportunity to rob the people. A foe replied that Medill "has a lot of character, most of it bad."

When his statehouse reporter, Frank Nevins, was jailed for refusing to tell who whispered that a legislator accepted a bribe, Medill said the prosecutors should jail him, not the reporter, who hurried to the nearest bathhouse to rid himself of jail fleas, and worse.

Medill condemned smoking. He railed against drunkenness —"the most important topic to engage the attention of intelligent men and women." For women readers, he bought descriptions and drawings of the Paris fashions. For men, The Tribune introduced the new game of football, then gaining popularity in eastern colleges, and an old Scottish game, new in the United States, called golf. Scores ranged from 81 to 117 in the first national golf tournament, held at the Chicago Golf Club in Wheaton near Red Oaks Farm. Medill looked upon boxing as damaging to competitors and degrading to spectators but carried blow-by-blow accounts of the Corbett-Fitzsimmons' match. He brought from England the Marquess of Queensberry to comment on American sportsmanship. Highbrow pages told of inventions— the x-ray which let doctors look through the human body and Edison's device which made photographs move. The Tribune predicted the phonograph would let a person, merely by turning a crank, listen to an entire novel read by rich-voiced actors, but wished failure for Edison's aerophone that carried a voice through the air. Just think, The Tribune mused, of an angry wife's diatribe following a fleeing husband for ten miles.

Medill forecast electricity would replace gas for lighting, causing gas company stocks to collapse. The Tribune printed the entire text of the revised New Testament—116 pages, set by 96 men in 12 hours—and denounced as a devilish hoax a version printed earlier by a rival. Medill backed the new Art Institute and Public Library, serialized the latest works of Robert Louis Stevenson,

Rudyard Kipling, Guy de Maupassant. For the less erudite, he printed comics in color. Every Monday morning he devoted a full page to resumes of Sunday sermons. He demanded Chicago raise itself from the mud and clean up its air and that America stop killing its young with firecrackers, a campaign waged for 20 years. He said women were injuring themselves by wearing tight corsets but the $15-million-a-year industry was too persuasive for him. A newspaper, Medill said, succeeds only if it is talked about. People like contests and prizes, so he gave awards for the best news stories by students and to the first girl who could wear a mock Cinderella's glass slipper.

* * * * *

Late in 1898 fire destroyed Medill's Los Angeles home and almost enveloped the partly invalided Medill. He retreated to Texas, to San Antonio and the Menger Hotel. Doctors did not declare him ill, but he rarely left his rooms. He said he did not need someone to be with him, but before Christmas 18-year-old Bert left Groton to go to his grandfather's side and remained. Every morning Bert brought his grandfather the newspapers and every afternoon he went to the cable office with Medill's urgent instructions to Patterson and to the post office with a packet of non-urgent news items marked "Must JM."

One day Medill noticed that his grandson was reading an A. Conan Doyle historical romance, "The White Company." Medill drew from a shelf the memoirs of Ulysses Grant and told the boy to read that. Medill settled back with the appropriated Conan Doyle book and, on finishing it, said it was the finest Conan Doyle work he had read.

The grandfather's switch of books lighted Bert's curiosity about the American Civil War and the heroes of the United States. In future years he was to become a Grant expert. His book, "Ulysses S. Grant, the Great Soldier of America," was published in 1934 followed 16 years later by a volume of related battles in which Grant did not take part, "The War Without Grant."

Tell me more about Great Uncle William, Bert must have asked, opening the grandfather's deep memories of his brother. To the adventurous youth, Great Uncle Willie was a hero, not the make-believe heroes of the Frank Merriwell stories which the boy had gobbled up, but a hero of real life, a hero of family flesh and blood, a part of history, the kind his classmates at Ludgrove knew so well. Willie was a small man, five feet five or so, "of genial, kind-hearted, generous nature" who, in his brother's eyes "willingly gave his life to protect his country from evil men who held other human beings in bondage and who, to preserve their devilish profit, would destroy the nation." Willie, volunteering on the first day of the war, was, with 59 other Chicagoans, enrolled in the Chicago Dragoons being assembled for manning Fort Defiance near Cairo, Illinois, where the Ohio River meets the Mississippi. General McClellan, Lincoln's first commander-in-chief, touring posts and forts, saw the Dragoons and rated them so highly that he ordered them east as his bodyguard. The Dragoons, Bert learned, met the rebels at Philippi, at Buchannon, at Rich Mountain, at Beverly, fighting dismounted, Indian style, darting from tree to tree, killing 200; at Carrick's Ford, killing a general and capturing 1,200 "graybacks" but letting the beaten forces escape when the commander halted the pursuit. "Our general is too cautious," Private Medill wrote home. "He lacks boldness and enterprise. If I were a general, I would strike vigorously, now."

Their three-month term up, the Dragoons returned to Chicago and were mustered out of service. William immediately asked the army to let him raise a company of cavalry. All right, the army said, if you can do it in two weeks. He needed 12 days. The men unanimously elected William their captain. The company was assigned to the 8th Illinois Cavalry. The Eighth's 1,164 troops paraded before the White House and then were sent to a low, wet, winter camp while McClellan considered how to overcome the rebel stronghold at Manassas in Virginia.

"We started marching toward Manassas on March 10th," William wrote to his brother Joseph. "We camped 10 miles from the fearsome place. Each man considered himself a martyr. Tomorrow the battle would begin. 'Boots and Saddles' sounded. Forward we started, every minute expecting to run into a concealed battery. At nine, a halt was ordered. My lieutenant galloped up and cried out: 'The rebel army skedaddled two weeks ago.' Incredulity was on every man's face. That we felt sheepish you may well imagine. Here was an army of almost a quarter million held at bay by a handful. We began to lose faith in our commander. All the stories you have read about the strength of Manassas are bosh. We could have crushed them like an eggshell anytime in the last four months. Manassas will go down in history as the biggest humbug on record."

Captain Medill's company harried the retreaters. Again the command called off the pursuit. The troopers scouted to within sight of Richmond, but the army did not attack. "All we do is dig ditches and die of fever," the Captain reported. "McClellan has waited too long. Mark my words." The Captain said the Confederacy drew its support from the forced labor of four million slaves. "We must knock away this great pillar of their edifice; else we shall never succeed in putting down the revolt," he wrote.

For the remainder of 1862 the eager 8th Illinois skirmished, raided, scouted but never challenged the rival army. The small encounters demonstrated to Captain Medill that the saber was no match for a pistol. He discarded his sword and bought two pistols.

On New Year's Day of 1863, President Lincoln published his Emancipation Proclamation. That same day, Captain Medill's company entered every plantation in its area and told a thousand "contrabands" they were free. Some joined the Union army. By nightfall, not one slave remained in all of King George county.

Skirmishes continued. In the spring, a fever seized Medill. "I cannot submit to this fever," he wrote home. "I shall mount my horse and rejoin my regiment if it takes two men to hold me."

His regiment met J.E.B. Stuart's raiders in Aldie Gap. Medill came side to side with a giant reb horseman. The giant raised his saber. "Surrender," he cried to Medill. The small Medill raised a pistol. "Don't shoot, I surrender," the giant cried, lowering his saber. The giant identified himself as commander of the 11th Virginia Cavalry. "Size confers but little advantage on the battlefield," a comrade wrote home. In June enthusiastic advance units of General Lee's Confederate army, moving boldly northward into Pennsylvania, collided near Gettysburg with scattered forces of the Union army, now under Meade. Neither general intended a showdown, but neither general could pull back. Both generals hurried in supporting forces.

Medill, now a major, was ordered to hold the right flank, harass the enemy and protect the infantry. Rebel cavalry cut off a Union brigade but Medill's troopers attacked and cut open an escape route. An official account states: "The 8th Illinois gave great annoyance to the enemy." On July 2, the armies met. The combat was deadly. The rebels broke. They fell back. Medill's troopers pursued, capturing 2,000 "grayback" soldiers and taking 800 army wagons. To the south, across the escape route, flowed the Potomac. The river was in flood. Medill was exhilarated, certain that the river would trap the rebel survivors of the Gettysburg disaster, that the Union pursuers could round them up by the riverside and that the war soon would end. A scout reported to Medill that the graybacks were building a bridge near Williamsport. He led his troopers into a woods near the bridgehead. The men dismounted, tied their horses, took their carbines and advanced in the Indian fashion they had found so effective. They came out of the woods. There, in a field, were the bridge builders. The troopers formed a long line abreast. Medill borrowed a carbine.

"Come on, boys," the Major shouted. The men walked into the field, shoulder to shoulder, firing between steps. Off to one side was a large barn. Behind it a force of rebel soldiers had been resting, unseen by the troopers. They ran out, formed lines and fired. A bullet smacked into Medill's right shoulder, "making a frightful hole and lodging near the backbone." He collapsed. His men carried him into the woods. The Union men, now heavily outnumbered, ran back to await the arrival of more troops. None came. Medill called off the attack. His men carried him a few miles to a church where a surgeon pronounced the wound mortal. The Major, in agony, was carried by wagon to Frederick City and left to die in an army hospital. A telegram brought his brother Joseph from Chicago. On the sixth day the Major asked for news of the bridge. Which troop had destroyed it? No one, he was told; Lee had escaped. "I wish I had not heard that," the Major said. "I am going to die without knowing that my country is saved and the slaveholders' accursed rebellion is crushed. The capture of Lee's army would have ended the war in 60 days. Now it may drag on for years. Cowardice and weakness let the rebels escape."

The news that Vicksburg had fallen was little comfort.

"There is more danger," he told his brother, "from division in the North than from the rebellion and foreign intervention. Let the free people of the free states stand together and in the end they will reclaim every seceded state."

He asked that he be buried in his dress uniform in Chicago's Graceland cemetery directed by Thos. B. Bryan, Esq., "a true-hearted man and a zealous and devoted friend of the soldier."

On the tenth day of fever and pain, Major William Medill died. The record states: "The same fearless heroism that carried him in triumph through many a fearful contest with his country's foes stood by him when he was brought face to face with the king of terrors." The Major was buried in Graceland.

The story of Great Uncle Major William Medill carried many lessons for young Robert McCormick—a citizen's ranking nation above self, a patriot's eagerness to fight for his country and for principle, the needless loss of life brought on by indecisive, weak commanders and political leaders, the inefficiency of armies in not giving the men the best equipment, the perils of disunity. For all of the Colonel's life, there, high above ordinary men, shone William Medill, a gallant ancestor whose name must not be sullied by any failure in duty. Yet, by adhering to Great Uncle Willie's beliefs, reasoning and standards, the Colonel was to come to the brink of being formally accused of treason in wartime.

*   *   *   *   *

During the early months of 1899, soldiers were coming home from Cuba. In Texas, they were received coolly. The South, young Bert was aware, was against the war, "because it was fought by Union soldiers." The talk at Groton, too, had been against the war. The European powers had advised the United States to stay out of Cuba. In San Antonio one night an opera troupe gave a special performance for the returning soldiers. The band played "The Star Spangled Banner;" the soldiers stood, but of the civilians only Bert arose. He was puzzled. The Civil War had been over for 34 years. Looking back after the Second World War on the 1898 war in Cuba, the Colonel concluded that the blowing up of the Maine "furnished President F. D. Roosevelt with the idea of provoking the Japanese to attack Pearl Harbor" as the best way to unite Americans for war.

The curious boy questioned the soldiers about the war. A lieutenant, Frank McCoy, who later became a general, told him that the Americans overcame the more numerous Spanish troops because of the rapid-firing Gatling gun. The words stuck in his mind, but the army command did not recognize the power of automatic weapons until the American Expeditionary Force arrived in France in 1917.

Few Americans objected to America's acceptance of sovereignty of the Philippines. But when, in February, Filipinos began defying American troops and administrators, a vigorous debate erupted. Some Americans said, "Turn them loose; let them find their own way." Others said, "Show them who is the master." In mid-March, Medill composed a strong telegram to President McKinley demanding the United States assert its rule and start assimilating the islands. Bert carried the message and an equally fierce editorial to the cable office.

That same day, Medill's sons-in-law, Robert Sanderson McCormick and Robert Patterson, left Chicago by train for San Antonio. In the morning, Thursday, March 16, 1899, young McCormick brought the papers as usual into his grandfather's room. "What's the news this morning, Bobby?" Medill asked and said no more. A maid brought coffee. The grandson left. Medill settled back with the papers. And died, a few days short of his 76th birthday. His personal physician, Dr. Toras Sarkisian, officially reported that the immediate cause of death was heart failure and the underlying cause was a long existing heart lesion. Two San Antonio doctors confirmed the diagnosis.

San Antonio was still very much a wild west frontier town. Any man who considered himself upright carried a gun. Bert had so equipped himself. There was a shooting almost every night. That night there was a shooting in a saloon. The Colonel, in his later writings and broadcasts, said he was involved in the affair and, for a time, was uneasy, but no serious consequences followed. More than a half century after the incident, Dr. Theodore Van Dellen brought his son, Teddy, to visit the Colonel. After the doctor's examination, the Colonel asked Teddy to stay behind.

"Teddy," he began, "did I ever tell you about the shooting in San Antonio on the day Grandfather died?"

Teddy said no he hadn't.

So the Colonel told Teddy this story:

The evening of his grandfather's death, Bert went to a saloon. Of course he wore his gun. He found an empty place at the bar. "What will you have, son?" the bartender asked. "A sarsaparilla, please," the tall, thin, very obviously young man replied.

A tough cowhand standing at the bar a few feet away, looked up from his drink and said, "Sonny, in this bar everyone drinks whiskey. If you get a sarsaparilla, I'll shove it down your throat."

The bartender was amused. "Well, son," he asked, "what will you have?"

"A sarsaparilla, please," the youth said.

The cowhand lunged. He may have pulled his gun, in earnest or in jest. Bert drew his gun and fired once. The cowhand slumped to the floor. Blood seeped through his shirt. Obviously he was dead. No one in the bar moved.

51

The bartender spoke. "Son, you better get out of here," he said. "Quick."

Bert strode toward the door. "You better get rid of that gun," the bartender called after him.

The next morning the youth went to the undertaking parlor and asked to see his grandfather. The undertaker led him into a room where the body was laid out in a casket.

"I'd like to be alone with my grandfather for a few minutes," Bert said.

"Of course," the misunderstanding undertaker said and left the room. The youth looked around to make sure all doors were closed. Then, with one hand he gently lifted his grandfather's back and, with the other, took the gun from his pocket and slipped it under the body. He lowered the body, straightened the disturbed clothing and casket lining. He stayed with his grandfather for some time and then left, pausing to thank the undertaker.

The Tribune obituary was limited to two columns. It praised Medill for his "fearless integrity" and for building a paper with an international reputation.

A Tribune historian reflecting on the first 75 years of The Tribune, described Medill as "a curious combination of austerity and aplomb, not showy but sternly persuasive, not caring for popularity but universally trusted, never evading duty, adopting as his idol common sense and thus a lover of Benjamin Franklin and Abraham Lincoln, a driver, a practical printer unafraid of experiments, a sense of humor behind the formal exterior." Medill, the historian commented, believed in the destiny of Chicago and regarded a newspaper as "a grand work, demanding all of the skill and fortitude that good minds and honest hearts possess." Medill had instructed his editors: "Put your protest of a wicked deed in your report, not in an editorial six pages removed." The summation could have been written equally truly a half century later by or for Medill's grandson, the Colonel, although by then journalism professors and other sideline coaches were preaching that news columns must be pure of the writer's opinion, a human impossibility.

Medill concluded: "I want The Tribune to continue to be after I am gone as it has been under my direction, an advocate of political and moral progress and in all things to follow the line of common sense."

The funeral was held at the Medill residence in Chicago on

March 21. Chicago courts closed. Flags were lowered to half mast. The casket was taken to Graceland cemetery. There it lies, undisturbed.

Medill's will, written in 1892, divided his personal estate between daughters Kate and Nellie after bequests of $1,000 each were paid to old-time Tribune employees. In the final settlement, the executors turned over to each daughter $371,196.38. A bitter legal squabble arose between the sisters when executors gave Nellie an extra $275.39 to reimburse her for Illinois inheritance taxes she had paid whereas the executors had paid Kate's tax for her before the settlement.

The major part of Medill's fortune rested in his holding of 1,056 of the 2,000 shares of Tribune stock valued for inheritance taxes at $1,106,681.12 although he had turned down an offer of six million. The will decreed his stock should be held in trust for the two daughters and the income divided between them but, exhibiting understanding of their refusal to work together and to put sense above passion, wisdom above willfulness, Medill decreed control of the stock would lie with the sons-in-law, Robert Patterson and Robert Sanderson McCormick, and William G. Beale, his lawyer. The trust arrangement also reduced inheritance taxes, eliminating the necessity of selling stock and diluting ownership. The three trustees were given the right to sell the stock but Medill advised them not to do so. "Managed with discretion, economy and ability," Medill wrote, "The Tribune cannot help continuing indefinitely to be a lucrative property; our family is really founded on it. Therefore, if you regard and respect my wishes, you will all stick together in retaining control of this great organ of popular opinion. Do not venture stock as collateral for any speculation. It will afford employment for such of my grandsons as develop journalistic taste and capacity. This is important for the family."

For the next two generations the trust arrangement, guarded assiduously by the Colonel, maintained the Medill legacy intact.

*　*　*　*　*

That year, 1899, Judge Prendergast, Medill's neighbor at Red Oaks and his ally in setting up the Sanitary District, died. He was only 44. His eldest son, John, was 15 and little Margaret seven. Relatives considered dividing the six children and taking them into their own homes but the children said no, thank you, we will stay together. John would become the man of the family and owner of the farm; "Aunt Mary" would remain, darning socks, kissing away bruises, chiding and admonishing. Swedish maids would do the chores. The Judge's fortune of $600,000 would more than pay the bills. The relatives accepted the decision and arranged to look in often. Ed Dunne, on his way to becoming mayor and later governor and a benefactor to Bert McCormick at critical times, served as trustee.

Kate opened her heart to little Margaret. On pleasant summer days when at Red Oaks, Kate rode in her carriage to the Prendergast knoll, picked up Margaret, drove to the station, rode the train into Chicago, took in the current Keith vaudeville show, feasted on cherry pie at The Fair Variety store and came home, the carriage meeting them at the station. More than 80 years later Margaret still could taste the tart cherries and remember the love she had for Kate. She also remembered a day when Kate told her, "Child, you must wash. Your fingers are dirty," and the little girl had replied, "That's not dirt. It is earth. I have been working in the garden." In Margaret, Kate saw a reflection of her own lost Katrina, and in Kate, Margaret saw a reflection of her own lost mother. The bond between the two families was not to die with the Judge.

4. Rubberfoot
1899—1903

In the autumn of 1899 Bert enrolled at Yale, still following his brother Medill and cousin Joe. For what career should he prepare? He did not know. For a while, excited by exploits of explorers, he had considered such an adventurous role for himself until Dewey's triumph in Manila Bay diverted his dream; then he would be an officer in the United States Navy, blow more enemy ships out of the water and keep America's shores safe, but Annapolis Naval Academy doctors said his eyes were not up to the tasks.

The Tribune did not enter his dreams; Kate had not weakened in her assignment of that future to her elder son nor had Nellie slackened her efforts to gain the prize for her Joe.

At 19, Bert was a confirmed loner. He was unhappy in his loneliness and determined that at Yale he at last would become one of the boys, even if the time and effort demanded by companionship would interfere with his studies.

Heeding his mother, Bert enrolled as R. Rutherford McCormick. Rutherford? What kind of name was that? The hooting boys transmuted it to Rubberfoot. Bert accepted the name with good humor, just as a sun tanned youth from Atlanta let himself be called "Nigg."

Yale encouraged its students to mix. President Arthur Twining Hadley later told the Colonel he believed a college's main purpose was to take in boys and send out men, giving the students along the way as much book learning as each could absorb. The President tried to shatter cliques brought into the college from prep schools or home communities. Freshmen, arriving early in New Haven, were thrown together at mixers, with wrestling as an adhesive. Most freshmen were grouped into one dormitory, Pierson House.

Yale had no college dining rooms. Students organized them

selves into "eating joints," choosing one boy, usually one of the 20 or so earning their way through college, to be manager and excusing him from contributing his share of the cost. A frugal eating joint cost $4.50 a week; the University Club assessed $8. Rubberfoot joined the University Club. In his junior year, he was treasurer and bookkeeper—unpaid. The task brought him a lesson which, later, he said was more valuable than anything he learned in classes. His personal account and the club's account were kept in the same bank. He marked with a rubber stamp the checks used to pay club bills. Going through his accounts at the end of the year before handing in his books, he discovered he had given a club check to his tailor. He was aghast. The lesson was clear: One cannot be too careful when handling other people's money. The lesson was, in time, passed to Tribune employees.

Boys met in the evening at Tontine's or Mory's. Rubberfoot didn't care for Tontine's, put off by the thick smoke and smell of ale, but he enjoyed Mory's, especially the enthusiastic collegiate singing. The Spanish American War had filled youths with patriotic fervor and produced enough songs to exhaust an evening. Traveling minstrel shows brought the songs with endless verses telling the joys and sorrows of Negroes, Irish and Jews. (The class had 10 Jews and 18 Catholics.) A student from Hawaii brought "Boola Boola"; it became a McCormick perennial favorite. And how often someone broke into Yale's own "Bright College Years!" One day in 1917 in Paris, the Colonel offered up that Yale song at a dinner. The French were aghast. The melody was similar to that of a German patriotic song.

A Mory tradition concerned a six handled pewter mug known as The Velvet Cup. Tradition demanded that only one of six boys may call for the cup, which the waiter filled with a mixture of champagne, ale and designated liquors. The cup was handed around and any boy who let it touch the table had to order a refill. Sometimes everyone refused to accept the cup and the possessor had to pay for the refill. Rubberfoot, in time, was chosen one of the six.

The operetta Florodora came to New Haven. Students packed the theater. A boisterous lot, they joined in the singing and shouted collegiate contributions to the script. What to do? Call the police? That would challenge the students. So the six girls who made up the sextet and performed the hit song of the show invited six seniors to tea. A hint here, a hint there, and the next night the six seniors stationed themselves throughout the theater and no Yale boy ever again interrupted the show. From New Haven the cast left for a world tour. The company invited the six helpful seniors to come along as far as Hartford. Rubberfoot thought the entire school went to the station to see the company depart. On the platform of the observation car were the six seniors, huddling happily with the six girls. At Hartford the boys decided they would continue on the tour until they ran out of money. They scrounged jobs and loans to get back to school.

Three secret senior societies flourished at Yale, Scroll and Key, Skull and Bones, and Wolf's Head. Rubberfoot was drawn into the Scroll and Key. The secret societies, the Colonel commented later, made a few collegians feel successful and many others feel unsuccessful but they did develop discipline. No member could reveal his membership or the group's activities.

At sports McCormick, six feet four—only one student was taller—and thin as a pencil, joined the cheering section. Basketball was yet to be invented. Only the boat crews had paid coaches. The football teams were taught and inspired by the father of football, Walter Camp, but his livelihood came from a clock factory. The team had its own training table serving champagne and ale. Old time gridiron greats returned to work out with the team but the greatest of them all, Frank Hinkey, never was invited. "The team could not be subjected to his demoniacal violence," the Colonel later explained. College morale rose and fell with the success of the team. High spirits carried an occasionally inferior team to unexpected victories. Defeats depressed collegians all week and a bad season, all winter. An error on the field brought shame. A boy who fumbled did not return for a class reunion until many years later.

In his senior year Rubberfoot discovered polo. He liked the excitement and the challenge. The pony supplied the physical dexterity. Although oversized, he decided to make polo his sport, a decision that demanded he must eat carefully or no polo pony could carry him.

Yale students delighted in politics, national and local. Every torchlight parade had its student contingent. The school encouraged political activities, arranged debates and brought prominent men to speak, sometimes with unhappy results. William Jennings Bryan, the spellbinding William Jennings Bryan, came expecting to spellbind the students. They hooted. He was not amused.

One weekend, a local politician heard that Rubberfoot was organizing a group to break up his political rally. The man swore out a complaint and a judge ordered Rubberfoot's confinement in jail for the weekend. A helpful policeman sent word ahead he was on the way to arrest him, and a helpful student hurried Rubberfoot onto a boat and then to his family's home in Greenwich. The boy told his younger sister that Rubberfoot was a wanted man and no one must give away his presence, building such a picture of Rubberfoot the Desperado that the sister, after dinner, locked up the family silver, packed her nightdress and fled to a neighbor's house to sleep safely.

*　　*　　*　　*　　*

On a visit to New York, Bert saw Admiral Dewey come home, a lone figure in white on the bridge of a warship. He was paraded up Broadway and there was talk of his becoming president. Quickly political aspiration died, but Dewey did remain a national hero. Forty-four years later, the Colonel was to think kindly of the presidential aspirations of another American military hero, General Douglas MacArthur, and saw those, too, fade away.

The American venture into the Philippines drew collegiate attention to China. Ever since the Japanese defeat of China in the dispute over Korea in 1894, European nations had been grabbing for political advantages and financial gains in China. The Boxer murder of missionaries fired young emotions. To Bert, the most memorable incident was the storming by an international force of the gates to Peking. As the Colonel recalled it, a Japanese soldier ran up to a gate and placed a small bomb, a petard, but a Chinese defender came out and removed it. Another Japanese placed a second petard and, with bayonet fixed, stood guard over it until the bomb exploded, killing the Japanese and opening the gate. American gunners tried to blow open another gate but their shells went cleanly through the planks without shattering them. An American lieutenant, Charles Summerall, walked up to the gate, studied it, and marked with chalk the position of unseen crossbeams. The gunners aimed at the chalk marks, the gates tumbled, and Americans were first to enter Peking. In the Colonel's memory the day had an unpleasant postscript. The British controlled the cable and British censors eliminated the Summerall heroism, leaving the world to praise Japan alone. The lieutenant years later was to come strongly into the Colonel's life.

New Haven was a boys' town. The only visible girls were considered "on the make" and thus were shunned. Students met "nice" girls at one another's homes on weekends or vacations. Serious romances were few and the boys looked upon the rare wedding as "time for conviviality and the loss of a friend." Rutherford meticulously heeded his mother's frequent cynical advice: Don't dally with a poor girl; you may have to marry her.

The two big social occasions were the junior and senior proms. Girls came from afar, welcomed with bouquets of violets. Dancing continued all night and in the morning the boys went to classes in evening wear. Few students had cars. The opulent rented horse breaks. Rubberfoot avoided the proms. He still had not learned to dance. He was graduated from Yale without having taken a girl to a dance.

Freshmen lost their lowly status on Washington's birthday. As a final penance, the Colonel remembered, each freshman wore a top hat and served as a snowball target for upperclassmen. Seniors considered themselves, he said, "lords of creation, blessed with eternal youth."

Oh yes, studies. Rubberfoot's grades were mediocre and would have been worse had not a professor told him: If you want to graduate, you had better play cards less and study more. He found French easy. He liked the practical aspects of physics, mechanics and geology, things that might be useful. He adopted, totally for his lifetime, the economic and political philosophy of the legendary Yale Professor William Graham Sumner that government must lift from "the forgotten man" tax burdens imposed by good-intentioned but wrong-minded schemes "designed to make people happy and support loafers." Less government, the professor preached, is better government, and being rich is no crime. The Colonel never doubted the Sumner principles.

A geology professor seized the examination papers of all boys sitting in the back row when he spotted a crib. Rubberfoot was in that row. After class he went to the professor, told him he never used a crib and asked him to recover his paper and read it. The professor agreed, reread the paper and found it wanting. The flunk stood. Again Rubberfoot appealed, arguing that the professor was ruining his reputation because everyone would think he had cheated. The professor changed the flunk to a pass and quipped: "You would make a good lawyer." The remark tore into young McCormick's mind. Perhaps he should become a lawyer? The whim hardened into a goal after a Supreme Court justice visiting Yale talked about the great lawyers of America's past and their service to the country. Bert wrote to his father saying he had decided to remain at Yale and earn a law degree. The father approved of the degree but said his son's future lay in Chicago and he should study law there, at Northwestern University. Bert, ever dutiful, agreed, and fate nudged Robert Rutherford McCormick toward his destiny.

* * * * *

The Colonel followed the life of Elsie Farrell, the girl who saved the family silver and herself from Rutherford the Desperado. She married a Spanish count named Torlonia and had a son. A divorce followed. When the son was of age, the King and Queen of Spain proposed that he marry one of their daughters, spurned by noble Spanish parents because of the royal family's tendency toward hemophilia. Elsie accepted for her son. The couple were married and produced healthy children. "Elsie's plebian blood overcame the royal taint," the Colonel explained. After the Count died, Elsie joined the Catholic church, with the King and Queen as sponsors. "Elsie had the reputation of being beautiful and dumb," the Colonel told a radio audience. "Beautiful she was. Dumb she was not."

5. Siren Songs
1900—1905

The new century began a new era at The Tribune. No longer did each day bring a telegram, note or visit from Joseph Medill. Robert Patterson was in full control, answerable only to the directors. He had been named a trustee in Medill's will but, in reality, he was still a hired hand. He owned one share of stock and had to accept the unpleasant fact that he was merely holding The Tribune for the next generation of Medills. Which grandchild would win the succession? For 20 years Kate and Nellie had connived, each to advance a son. Now the decision was near.

Kate's first son, proudly flaunting his middle name of Medill, came home from Yale in the spring of 1900 to take a place on The Tribune that his mother expected would lead him to the top. Patterson assigned him to the press room at the police headquarters, the usual baptismal font for cub reporters on big city papers. The pay was three dollars a week, hardly tips for a young man with a rich allowance from his mother and equally rich tastes. Kate was not pleased. Yes, her son should start at the ground floor. But the basement?

Within a year Patterson promoted the cub grandly, sending him as a foreign correspondent to the Orient to report the efforts of William Howard Taft to set up an American administration in the Philippines, newly wrested from Spain, and then to cross to China where the Empress had decreed death for all foreigners. Kate was content and, with her son seemingly set on the proper course, she was ready to return to Europe. At this critical time, a senator from Illinois who had cause to render a service to The Tribune and its owners proposed to President McKinley that Kate's husband be appointed minister to either Belgium or the Austro-Hungarian empire. McKinley, also beholden to The Tribune, chose Vienna. Kate was jubilant. Was not the Viennese court the most brilliant in Europe?

61

Nellie, jealous Nellie, needed an effective base from which to thrust her daughter, Cissy, home from Miss Porter's school in Farmington and Miss Hersey's in Boston, into Society where she would meet the right man. In Washington newcomers were welcome if they had enough power and cash. Nellie engaged Stanford White to create a mansion there on DuPont Circle. Her husband, content to have her out of town, sought peace and quiet in the Chicago Club, a male sanctuary.

* * * * *

Medill McCormick was barely over the western horizon when Patterson's son Joe came home from Yale to begin soaring, on his mother's insistence, up The Tribune hierarchy. Joe and Medill had developed an intense mutual dislike, young Patterson considering young McCormick something of a pompous prig and young McCormick, flourishing his middle name as a scepter, considering young Patterson, happy to be known as just plain Joe, something of a slob in thought and manners. Editor Patterson, showing even-handed justice, sent Joe to the police station press room but at $15 a week, augmenting the $10,000 a year Joe received from his mother. Joe said later he regarded his reportorial assignment as play acting. Joe liked girls, and girls liked him.

One morning when Bert was home on vacation from Yale, Patterson sought him out and said, "I don't want you to lie to me, Bert. Tell me truthfully, was Joe with you last night?" Bert protectively said, "Yes, Joe stayed the night." The father snapped: "I knew you would lie. Joe was home last night." The Colonel, relating the incident years later, said "I never could forgive Patterson for tricking me."

Joe became engaged to a Chicago society girl. As time neared for Medill to come home from China, Joe left for China to report events there, not for The Tribune—his father must have noted his lack of dedication—but for The Tribune's rival, William Randolph Hearst. Rubberfoot was still at Yale.

* * * * *

Kate loved Vienna from the instant she stepped from the train. The Empire was dying, but the court was obsessed with parties. Kate leased a palace which had been the home of Baroness Marie Vetsera adjoining the castle of Crown Prince Rudolph of Hapsburg, son and heir of the Emperor Francis Joseph. Rudolph had gone back and forth over the stone wall separating the two estates until one day in 1889 he and the Baroness were found dead at Mayerling, his hunting lodge outside Vienna.

Kate spent heavily from her $150,000 a year income, redecorating and refurnishing and giving balls, dinners and parties while her husband established himself firmly with the Emperor. The Colonel later enjoyed telling how the court, following strict protocol, had sent a carriage drawn by four horses to bring United States Minister McCormick to the Emperor for the presentation of his credentials from the President of his youthful republic. During the audience Francis Joseph found McCormick such good company that, on his departure, the Emperor instructed his aide: "Call for Ambassador McCormick's carriage and six!" With seven words the Emperor raised McCormick's rank, although the State department needed almost a year to confirm the imperial promotion.

The first summer Rubberfoot's parents were in Vienna, he went with a dozen other Yale boys on a hunting expedition by ship in Hudson Bay, visiting Eskimo and shooting caribou, seal, polar bear and walrus. One day he tried to pull a dead walrus into a rowboat and almost swamped the boat, vastly underrating the weight of the walrus. The crew needed a winch to get it aboard. On his 21st birthday Rubberfoot killed one polar bear and chased another across the ice, caught up with it and killed it, only then realizing how foolish he had been. Suppose the bear had turned on him? Suppose he had slipped and broken a leg? Who would have come to his rescue? In recalling the incident much later the Colonel said, "The Tribune's good luck had seen me through."

He had the skin cured. Fifty years later it still was serving as a library rug, much favored by erring household dogs.

That summer Commodore Robert E. Peary was coming home from another exploration in his long effort to reach the North Pole. Rubberfoot's newspaper instinct surfaced. He arranged with the Yale boys' skipper to return to his base at St. John's, Newfoundland, on a route which might intercept home-bound Peary so Rubberfoot could get the first story of the expedition and cable the news from St. John's before Peary could reach New York, giving The Tribune another world scoop. Alas, the ships passed out of sight of each other.

The next summer, 1902, the parents insisted Bert join them in

Vienna. He slept in the Baroness' suite and one day climbed over the wall into the castle yard. As he dropped to the other side, he realized the ground was lower there. Despite his six feet four, he jumped many times before he succeeded in gripping the top edge of the wall, enabling him to climb back. "I hadn't stopped to think that Rudolph had help," he later explained. One day police arrested him for picking a flower in a public garden to give to a visiting girl. He identified himself as the American ambassador's son. The police let him go and the next day two officials came to the embassy and apologized for the action of the police. Ridiculous subservience, the Colonel later commented.

He accompanied his father to Constantinople and with two other young men swam the Hellespont between Europe and Asia, a rare feat in those days and considered dangerous. He saw the Sultan pass in a carriage on his way to prayers in the mosque and was surprised that the next carriage conveyed ladies from the harem, all unveiled. He watched Turkish soldiers march with precision before their Japanese instructor.

In Paris on his way home, Bert and a friend rented a hot air balloon, floated up from the Bois de Boulogne and down to a farmer's field. The farmer and his neighbors provided a celebration feast and gave Bert the bill. The Aero Club of France elected him to its membership. College pals obtained a police permit authorizing them to parade Rubberfoot, the daring aeronaut, up the Champs Elysees.

*　*　*　*　*

Also that summer of 1902, Cissy went to Vienna for a long visit. She was 21. Nellie had paused before accepting the surprise invitation to her daughter from her detested sister Kate. But unsisterly feelings were smothered by the prospect of a daughter's being presented at the imperial Austro-Hungarian court and, glory of glories, meeting a baron or a count or a duke or a prince who of course would be smitten with Cissy's beauty and sparkle and give her a title in exchange for her money. In Vienna Cissy became the target of guards officers and young noblemen. One night at a dinner dance, a tall man with long curling hair and waxed upturned mustache walked boldly up to her and introduced himself.

"Count Josef Gizycki, mademoiselle," he said. Telling later of the moment, Cissy said she went cold. Unlike most other men at the ball, the Count was not in uniform and was old enough to be her father.

Kate, in her role as a good aunt, set out to learn about the Count. His paternal Polish title was real, dating back nine centuries; his mother, from an Austrian family not quite so old as the father's but respected, had been lady-in-waiting to the Empress. The Count's Polish estates reached for miles. Money? No one knew for sure. He spent as though his purse were imperial. For ten years he had been an officer in the Austrian cavalry and once had taken part in a horse race from Berlin to Vienna, a distance of 350 miles. He seemed to know everyone of importance in every court.

Beware, beware, matrons told Kate, he is no good; he lives only for women, horses, gambling and drink; he is charming, yes, but selfish and cruel; he's not a fit man for your pure young American girl.

"He's after you only for your money," Kate told Cissy. "I'll tell him you don't have a cent."

Cissy laughed. The Count took her deer hunting, to Salzburg for music, on picnics. They raced horses. He dazzled her. Their lovers' chat, a mixture of childish English and French, avoided serious talk.

In September, Ambassador McCormick was transferred to St. Petersburg. Cissy went along. The Count followed. He was as much at home in St. Petersburg as in Vienna. His castle had been within Russia since Russia, Germany and Austria had divided Poland, that sad country.

Kate wrote to Nellie telling her everything bad she heard about the Count. Nellie scoffed. Kate, Nellie argued with herself, was exaggerating, perhaps even making it all up. Certainly Cissy was a better judge of the Count. A countess! Cissy a countess! The prospect pleased her.

Cissy's father was practical. Is the Count solvent? Had he mortgaged his castle and lands? Replies were ambiguous.

Cissy stayed in St. Petersburg all winter. One sharp night when the snow crackled under the sleigh runners, she went with the McCormicks to the Hermitage for a reception given by the Czar. Police in great coats and servants in red capes met the sleighs. Guardsmen lined the halls and stairs of the imperial palace. Cossacks guarded the ballroom door. A courtier with a silver-tipped wand led the trio to their places, the ambassador in one line, the two women in the other. The doors opened. The Czar and Cza-

65

rina entered. The Czar progressed before the men, the Czarina before the women. She asked Cissy how she was enjoying St. Petersburg. Cissy was wordless. Kate replied for her.

Cissy went home in May of 1903.

* * * * *

For Robert Patterson, the new year of 1903 posed problems. True, Nellie was frequently in Washington and Kate was at the far side of Europe but even across those 4,000 miles he could feel Kate's insidious campaign to remove him from The Tribune to make way for her son. Medill came home from China and puttered about The Tribune. For nine years he had been engaged to Ruth Hanna. Now, with Kate far out of sight, Ruth, a tall, slender, brown-eyed girl, spoke more forcefully about Medill's need to break from his mother and find his real future, with her, in politics. On June 16, 1903, Ruth 22, and Medill 26, were married. President Roosevelt's daughter Alice, Ruth's best friend in the Capital, was maid of honor. The President was not invited, but came. He was photographed with arms around two pretty girls, but, the Colonel remembered long later, friends destroyed the photographs before they could reach the newspapers. John D. Rockefeller was a guest; a Rockefeller daughter had married a son of Cyrus and Nettie. Bert was introduced to Rockefeller, with no further consequence.

Medill told his mother he would like to buy into his grandfather's former paper, the Cleveland Leader. She, surprisingly at first glance but not so on close inspection, supplied the money. To Kate, the move would expedite her son's rise in journalism. He instantly would become a major owner and editor of a prominent newspaper and gain experience enabling him in a few years, in a very few years, to come home and assume command of The Tribune. Then she would push Patterson into oblivion and her life's ambition would be achieved.

Ruth saw the Cleveland adventure in a precisely contrary light. In Cleveland she and Medill would be at the heart of Republican affairs in Ohio, a state with clout in national politics. Her father's connections, his wealth, estimated at 12 million dollars, and her instincts would speed Medill along the boulevard to the Senate and the presidency. Ruth had grown up assuming that one day she would live in the White House. Nine winters earlier in the Georgia pine woods her father, Mark Hanna, had

66

advanced successfully his protege McKinley into the presidency with the expectation that, in 1900, McKinley would demand Hanna join him on his reelection ticket and, after another four years, would transfer his supporters and the presidency to Hanna. But in 1898 upstart Teddy Roosevelt had collected a band of rough riding cowboys and romped up San Juan Hill behind Col. Leonard Wood into the hearts of the American public and the vice presidency. Hanna could hope Roosevelt's glitter would dim before 1904 but on September 6, 1901, a crazed Pole who believed in anarchy—fellow believers had killed a czar and a shah—did his self-assigned duty to help rid the world of all rulers and shot McKinley dead, whereupon Roosevelt assumed the presidency with such dash, bashing the robber barons at home, carrying a big stick but walking softly abroad, that his re-election in 1904 was guaranteed. Hanna's dream died. But not Ruth's. If she could not enter the White House as a daughter, well, why not as first lady?

Medill's move to Cleveland gave Joe Patterson an open road at The Tribune. Joe had come home from the Orient unwell and the nice society girl fiancee tartly had cancelled the engagement. Soon, at a dinner, he sat next to a sparkling girl, Alice Higinbotham. Her father had risen to be head of Marshall Field's. Small, black-haired, Alice was delicate in feature but not in spirit, as Joe learned after a quick marriage. Alice enjoyed dressing up for balls and dinners and theater parties and garden games. Joe did not. He believed Chicago's new rich to be leading empty, idle lives. They disgusted him; the hunger and squalor of laboring men and women appalled him. He inserted in The Tribune a supplement entitled "The Workers' Magazine" designed for "the man who works with hand and brain." Such views were not welcome at the rich, powerful Tribune. The supplement must go. He must go. His father, without telling him, whispered to Republican leaders the suggestion that Joe be given a seat in the state legislature and they, again recognizing a half century's debt to The Tribune and their need for the paper, obliged. Joe went to Springfield. Life at The Tribune became a bit easier.

* * * * *

Bert was graduated from Yale in the spring of 1903. At the turn of the century rich young men were expected to see something of the world before taking up a profession. Panama was in the news. A few clever people there had declared their bit of jungle independent from Colombia and Roosevelt had dispatched marines with orders to get there before Colombian soldiers could arrive. To protect the new republic, he said. Bert wanted to hear for himself the rebels' story, to see the big ditch and to learn why the French had been beaten in their effort to hack a canal across the narrow rocky spine that joined two continents. He had no notion of following brother Medill and cousin Joe into matrimony. He could see little in Medill-McCormick-Patterson marriages that could entice him out of his shell and into the company of women. He was, by his own statement, still a virgin.

Bert rode a small freighter to Costa Rica and another to Panama, rented a horse, rode the length of the half-finished Culebra cut, marveled at the three-mile-long mountain of dirt and rock the French had extracted. Everyone he questioned applauded the revolution and the support given by Theodore Roosevelt. Young Bert approved of the keep-out notices coming from Washington. At 23, Bert already was the staunch supporter of America first, last and always. The United States, he said, must finish the canal and keep it always. The canal would be vital to America's future. Yes, that meant the new republic of Panama must do as America says but, he reasoned:

"I am afraid that we must except strategic places from the rule that people should have the government of their choice. Big nations cannot have their existence threatened by little nations. Self-preservation is the first law of nature. The principle of free government must come after it."

He also excepted Suez, Gibraltar and the Dardanelles.

Bert puzzled over the cause of yellow fever, cited by the French as reason for their failure to complete the canal. As Bert came home on a Norwegian freighter, the fever seized a sailor. Why the sailor? He had not gone ashore. "The fever could be carried by a mosquito," the captain told Bert. Later, medical research confirmed this guess.

It was all valuable preparation for the future but of that Bert had no hint.

In the autumn, Bert dutifully enrolled at the Northwestern University Law School. He had come home to Chicago, but where was his home? He joined the rivulet of rich lonely men to the Chicago Club and made that male bastion his base. For a time he had a small bachelor apartment in the Pullman Building, furnishing it expensively. For a while he shared an apartment with George Potter, described by the Colonel as "an orphan and a fine, generous normal person," who later killed himself. As years passed, the Colonel sometimes was troubled with the idea of suicide. In mid-life he listed two acquaintances who chose death when love turned bitter, two to avoid bankruptcy, two to escape from homosexuality, one because of the torment of arthritis. Pain alone, he thought, could justify suicide.

*　*　*　*　*

Among the young Chicago set was a girl of Irish descent, lively, witty, kind and, of course, beautiful. Her father, Edward Martyn, born in Galway, christened her Elizabeth, but early, because of her large luminous eyes seemingly leading into a happy soul, she was renamed Hazel. Her gaiety, loveliness and warmth drew Bert. Long later he confessed he lost his heart to her. Here was his salvation, an impish leprechaun who could shatter the wall hardening around him and, caring for him and being cared for by him, could draw him out into the world. But Bert did not dare court her. He did not dare speak to her of his feeling toward her. The opportunity faded when the mother took Hazel to Europe to ripen the girl's artistic talent. Hazel quickly was scooped up by a portrait painter named John Lavery, more than old enough to be her father. The mother, alarmed, sent not for Bert but for a young medical student who hurried to Europe, brought Hazel home, married her and three months later died of pneumonia. Six months later their daughter was born. Mrs. Martyn took her daughter and her granddaughter to England. Appendicitis brought her near death, but Lavery produced doctors who saved her life. Mrs. Martyn consented to the marriage of Lavery and Hazel. Almost instantly, the rich and famous paraded into the Lavery salon. Were they honest, they had to confess they came more to enjoy Hazel's conversation than have yet another portrait painted. A duke sent pearls. "Return them," Lavery ordered. Winston Churchill was fascinated by the technique of painting. Hazel taught him all she knew, setting him on the road to considerable prominence as an artist.

"Always remember you are Irish," her father often had told her. She remembered the advice as Irish hatred of English rule broke into bloody rebellion.

Hazel listened to the English and the Irish, to peacemakers and to warmakers. Gradually, she brought persons of opposing con-

69

victions together at small dinners and softened their prejudices. Michael Collins, one of the most energetic of the Irish rebels and certainly the most handsome and romantic, fell in love with Hazel and declared his feelings in verse.

After terrible years of strife, the basis for a solution of "the Irish problem" was worked out in the Lavery salon. During this period Collins wrote:

"A thousand ships launched Helen, poets relate. Yet Hazel is content with ships of state."

Collins and other rebels wanted to free all of Ireland, whereas the solution left the six Ulster Protestant counties part of Britain. "Take what you can now and get the rest later," Hazel urged Collins. Collins signed the treaty.

"I have signed my death warrant," he told Hazel. Indeed, companions turned on him. One night in Ireland, as Hazel and Collins returned from a dinner, assassins ambushed the car on a country road. Collins pushed Hazel to the car floor and fell over her. Both lived, but ten days later the assassins struck again as Collins drove away from a dinner with the Laverys and George Bernard Shaw. This time the assassins did the job thoroughly. A poem from Collins to Hazel, stained with blood and found in his pocket, was sent to her. The verses said:

Cucugan I call thee, Cucugan the Dove.
Because of thine eyes and the voice that I love,
Cucugan I call thee.
Hast thou no fear, little bird, little love,
I am an eagle and thou art a Dove.
Hast thou no fear of me?
Wild in my nest in the mountain above,
Wilt thou fly there with me, lovely White Dove?
Shall my wings carry thee...

The Irish leaders asked Lavery to paint a portrait of Hazel as the ideal colleen and, as Collins had wished, put the painting on the banknotes. "That way," said President William Cosgrave, "you will be sure the Irish people will always carry her picture next to their heart."

The Colonel followed Hazel's adventures silently from afar until she died in 1935. Nearly 20 years later, in his own last years, he asked Gwen Morgan, a London correspondent for The Tribune, to go to Ireland, visit his old Ludgrove schoolmate, Sir Shane Leslie, and write Hazel's story. He did not mention his own early love.

In Chicago, McCormick cousins abounded, 40 or more. Now and then Bert called on Edward Shields Adams—his mother was Amanda McCormick, sister of Bert's grandfather William. Ed had married the daughter of an heroic army surgeon. She, Amie Irwin, 12 years younger than Ed and eight years older than Bert, sensed Bert's aloneness and felt his need for a mother or big sister. Or perhaps a wife? Soon Bert was staying for the night, or weekend.

* * * * *

Bert occasionally rode the Cannonball Express of the Aurora and Elgin electric interurban line to the Chicago Golf Club station 30 miles west of Chicago near the handsome country summer home his grandfather Medill had built and given to Kate. The line supplied a parlor car, with waiters providing powerful drinks and stimulating food. Abraham Lincoln's son Robert and Bert's father were early Chicago Golf Club presidents. Golf had little appeal for Bert, who could not master the game. For members, golf was only part of the attraction. Families made the club their summer resort, building homes on its perimeter or renting cottages on the club grounds or houses in Wheaton raised for summer rental at rates high enough to pay off the mortgage of the owners who occupied them the remainder of the year.

The club was considered fast. Years later, the Colonel, while driving into Chicago, pointed to an attractive house in Wheaton and said, "That's where I lost my virginity." The mentor was a young wife from Chicago Golf. The Colonel did not say how long the association continued but he did add, with some delight, that the lady became one of the established matrons of prim, pure, non-alcoholic, church-strong Wheaton society. After many years, her husband fell ill and was believed to be dying. The wife gave away his clothes. He recovered. Ho, ho, ho, the Colonel laughed.

* * * * *

The Chicago Democratic machine was creaking and cracking from corruption, patronage and disagreement over what should be done about street cars. Republicans saw opportunities. In the

71

spring of 1904 a Republican manipulator on the rise, Fred Busse, a rich coal merchant, perhaps with a nudge from Robert Patterson but certainly aware of the need for The Tribune's continued support, proposed that Bert become the party's candidate for alderman from the 21st ward just north of the Loop, taking in both the lakefront Gold Coast residences and the Rush street saloons.

Bert found Busse "an extraordinary character with tremendous force and personality but with little control over his appetites." Busse said Bert's chances of election were good, although he would have to campaign vigorously. The seat was held by Honore Palmer, son of Potter Palmer, knee-deep in gold from real estate and hotels. Mrs. Palmer, the lively Bertha Honore, cultivated the Gold Coast vote, giving a party in her lake front mock castle. Voters were impressed but perhaps not in the manner she expected. Guests told Bert the Palmer mansion reminded them of the Everleigh Club, the city's most luxurious house of prostitution. To Gold Coast families, Bert promised a beach and a new bridge across the Chicago River to connect the lake front and the Loop.

Mrs. Palmer had her son photographed as a waiter carrying a tray and she herself worked the Rush street honky-tonks from her carriage, halting outside the swing doors. Bert entered the saloons boldly, announced "Call me Mac," and bought drinks all around, including a large rye whiskey for himself. The Democratic ward boss, "Hot Stove" Jim Quinn, orchestrated Democratic snickering about a silk stocking candidate seeking votes from men who wore cotton socks or no socks at all. Bert won. The new alderman was joined soon in the council chamber by Ed Dunne, the relative of Judge Prendergast who had applauded the Judge and Joseph Medill for their campaign to clean up the Chicago river. Dunne was elected mayor and, although a Democrat, was ready to form a working arrangement with the grandson of the Judge's ally and neighbor.

*   *   *   *   *

How quickly the prospect changed for Robert Patterson! Such a short time earlier he had been plagued by an excess of bothersome, quarrelsome Medill grandsons. He now had The Tribune to himself, Joe in Springfield, Medill in Cleveland, and Bert in the

72

council, studying law and starting on a political road leading to
the governor's mansion.

* * * * *

Count Gizycki wrote to the Pattersons asking for Cissy's hand.
"Show me your books," her father replied. The Count sent accounts, all solidly in the black—and false. Nellie, wishing to inspect the Count herself, took Cissy to Paris, met the Count there
and found him charming. To make certain he was serious, she
sent Cissy on a round of European resorts with a poor relative.
Sometimes the Count followed, sometimes not; chasing an American girl around Europe was hardly his sport. After Nellie and
Cissy returned home for Christmas, the Count carried on the
courtship by post. In February of 1904, Nellie sent a cable agreeing to the marriage. The service would be in her Washington Du
Pont Circle house. The Count was Catholic, Cissy Presbyterian.
It was decided a Catholic priest would preside. The couple would
proceed by train to the Waldorf Astoria in New York, sail to Europe and enjoy the resorts for two months; then he would take
her to his castle.

The Count left Du Pont Circle alone immediately after the service, saying he would meet the bride at the station. Cissy later
told how in New York he sent her to her room for three hours,
strode in and, without a word, destroyed her virginity and left
her to cry from fright, bewilderment and pain. The next two
months in western Europe had deliriously happy moments and
periods of pure hell. A confused Cissy awaited her homecoming
to her dream castle. It would be moated, turreted, beamed; kind
maids and butlers and gardeners and hostlers would love her and
serve her. She found a wooden structure, battered, cold, damp,
windows dirty and bare, chairs sagging, dust everywhere. The
Count pointed Cissy to one room and went on to his own. She
thought she would surprise her husband by going to his room.
She did indeed surprise him, catching him with his hair in curlers, his mustache in wires. She fled to her own room and there
came upon pictures and hairpins left by the most recent occu-
pant. What had she gotten herself into?

* * * * *

In Chicago and in the state capitol at Springfield, the big issue

74

of 1904 arose from the rapid spread of streetcar lines and the swelling purses of franchise holders. Want a franchise, do you? All right, how much will you contribute to the mayor, the alderman, the party? Not enough; others offer a lot more; think about it and come back. Efficiently mulcted, streetcar spoils could buy elections and keep the party in power. Rivals seeking the power and the spoils ranted against the misuse of civic services, but good citizens assumed that the turning out of the party in office merely would hand over the spoils to a different set of equally greedy people. Some citizens, including Joe Patterson, said the only cure could come with the city's taking over the streetcars. Mayor Dunne also argued for public ownership, but some citizens surmised that Dunne was willing to give up kickbacks from franchisers if he could get his hands on hundreds of streetcar jobs. Want to be a motorman? All right, how did you vote? Democrat? That's good; how many votes can you deliver? How much will you kick into the kitty? Rich spoils ebb but powerful patronage flows on.

Good citizens saw a middle way. Although Bert had inherited from Grandfather Medill a deep prejudice against expansion of government, he and other councilmen came together in a reform movement, proposing that streetcars remain in private hands but the city should obtain low fares and good service and share the profits. Bert became a member of the council's transportation committee and helped to write a compromise ordinance to produce the three goals. The committee pushed the ordinance through the council. The Mayor vetoed the measure but the committee organized a referendum and won. When a loser publicly accused the committee of dishonesty, Bert wrote a resolution condemning him and forced it through the council. The tall, silk-stocking freshman was making a name for himself as a stud-booted fighter and a rare politician interested in efficient government instead of spoils and patronage. His figure, looming above others, was always visible. His strong, low, gruff voice cut clearly through the debate. The accent, cast at English boarding schools and honed at Groton and Yale, let everyone know the words came from him. His dress could be individual. One day, when a polo match ran long, he hurried into the council chamber in jodhpurs. He "felt no prick of conscience for being rich."

Not so Joe. He thought that as a matter of principle public transportation should belong to the public, not the traction barons favored by the Republican masters. In Springfield he demanded a better life for the forgotten little man who rode the streetcars to his sweaty, poorly paid job. Joe ignored the Republican whip and, while lawmakers threw inkwells and chairs to reinforce insults, Joe voted with the Democrats and helped turn their public ownership bill into state law. The Republican managers asked Joe how he could do such a thing, especially after they had brought him to Springfield to please his father. The revelation shattered Joe. He resigned from the legislature, from the Republican party and from The Tribune. Ambassador McCormick wrote jubilantly from Europe that Joe's defection sealed the position as heir to The Tribune for his elder son Medill.

* * * * *

In St. Petersburg Ambassador McCormick had a problem of much wider consequence than his niece Cissy's souring romance. The Manchu empire of China was breaking up and the European powers plus Japan were grasping for privilege, plunder, profit and power amid the ruins. The American annihilation of Spain's Pacific fleet in Manila harbor, leading to the American occupation of the Philippines, had alerted Americans to opportunities and perils in the Far East. The China coast offered enough trade to satisfy the western European powers, but Russia and Japan were heading toward a confrontation over colonial aspirations in Manchuria. Japan had seized the Chinese fortress of Port Arthur but had lost it to the Russians who needed an ice-free terminal for their Trans-Siberian Railroad. To protect the port, the Russians also had taken Sakhalin Island from Japan. That nation refused to accept the losses and began building a modern army and navy, conscripting one young man out of five. Britain signed a mutual protection treaty with Japan; France signed with Russia but was losing to Germany its influence in St. Petersburg.

The Czar's army of three million, rising fast to 15 million, was the biggest in the world. But was it loyal? How firm was the Czar's rule? What were his intentions in the Far East? Would the rivalry for Manchuria involve western European powers and America?

For Ambassador McCormick the answers did not come readily. He rarely saw the Czar and never had a serious talk with him. Whispered confidences of the gaggle of grand dukes surrounding the Czar could not be trusted. Political leaders planned and plotted but had no power. The McCormicks gave dinner parties in their rented palace and went to diplomatic receptions. Ambassador McCormick reported to Washington vaguely that the Czar's rule was absolute, the peasants worshipful, the army loyal, the economy growing, but the reports were far short of information wanted by President Theodore Roosevelt and his secretary of state, John Hay.

Teddy Roosevelt's mind, since boyhood, had roamed the world. Early he had written a book about the sea war of 1812. He had resigned as assistant secretary of the navy to organize the Rough Riders and charge up San Juan Hill to glory. Since becoming president, he had destroyed German aspirations in Venezuela and British claims in Alaska while making friends and admirers of both Kaiser Wilhelm and King Edward.

It so happened that in the summer of 1903, the British foreign office sent a witty, caustic, intelligent and dedicated career diplomat named Cecil Spring Rice to St. Petersburg as its second secretary. He had sharpened his eyes, ears and wits in Washington, Berlin, Cairo, Constantinople, Tokyo and Teheran, learning the languages and traditions, assiduously infiltrating circles of power in each capital. Seventeen years earlier, in 1886, Roosevelt and Spring Rice happened to travel to Europe on the same liner. Spring Rice sought out Roosevelt and found him "one of the most amusing men I ever met." Their quick minds, wide interests, good sense and high morals bound them together. Three weeks after arriving in London, Roosevelt asked his new friend to be best man for his wedding at St. George's Church in London's Hanover Square to Edith Kermit Carow. "He knew no one in London," Spring Rice explained to his family. Roosevelt told his family, "He had me married in bright orange gloves." From that day on, Spring Rice wrote long letters, mixing gossip with precise accounts of local affairs from his various posts, sprinkling in praise of Roosevelt: "As high, noble, pure, devoted a character as it is possible to find in this world". . ."I wish England had a man like you. . ." "It is a real pleasure to see a real man in the proper place for him." During his years in Washington, the Roosevelts, the Cabot Lodges, John Hay, "Uncle Henry" Adams, the Whitelaw Reids, the Whitneys and many others had opened their doors to him. Because protocol and common sense prevented a diplomat from writing secret reports to the head of another government, Spring Rice addressed his White House letters to Mrs. Roosevelt, knowing she would hand them to the President and he would pass them to Hay. The President replied directly.

The two men agreed Britain and the United States should try to work in harmony in foreign affairs. Roosevelt told Spring Rice he considered any weakening of the British empire would be "a disaster to the civilized world and to the progress of mankind." But Roosevelt could not accept Spring Rice's conviction, developed during his years in Berlin, that the Kaiser and Germany were preparing for eventual war with Britain and were trying to isolate Britain from the continent.

Soon after arriving in St. Petersburg, Spring Rice hardened his warning against Germany, reporting that the Kaiser was encouraging the Czar to go to war with Japan and assuring him that Russia would win an easy victory. The Czar would emerge as emperor of the Pacific and the Kaiser as emperor of the Atlantic. At the end of the year, Spring Rice reported Japan was considering going to war with Russia. Early in the new year, Japan formally demanded that Russia yield some rights in Manchuria. The Czar did not reply, assuming Japan was bluffing, Spring Rice told the President. In February, the Japanese navy blockaded Port Arthur, home base of Russia's far eastern fleet, and invaded Korea. The Czar, surprised and irate, declared America and Britain had encouraged the Japanese to attack and he was determined that the two countries "must be punished." Spring Rice said he did not see how Russia could invade America but it had "a succulent British morsel" at hand in India and the Persian Gulf.

"The papers abuse Americans like anything," he wrote to the President from St. Petersburg. "Soon you will be hated here as much as the English. No, that is an exaggeration. But I never see a paper without seeing something against the President." He said the Russian foreign minister put out a story that the President's family were German Jews named Rosenfeld. None of this apparently was being reported by Ambassador McCormick. "I knew the Russians disliked the Americans but I did not know they singled out me," Roosevelt wrote to the Briton. The President said Hay found Spring Rice's reports "convincing." "He knows his trade better than any of them," Hay commented. Soon Spring Rice reported Russia intended to close China trade to America and Britain.

Sensing that the White House was beginning to share his own dissatisfaction with McCormick, Spring Rice told the President, "Your ambassador here is a very nice man. He is very fond of this country, which is a good thing for an ambassador to be, and like most diplomats he is slave of the smile of royalty."

During the late winter and early spring, Japan sent its entire new army of 270,000 men into Korea and Manchuria while its navy maintained the blockade of Port Arthur and sank any Russian warships which ventured out. Russia sent 30,000 men monthly over the Siberian railroad to reinforce its Far Eastern force of 80,000 men. Both armies maneuvered. By late spring, Japan had lost 23,000 and Russia 19,000, but the losses were edited out of reports to the citizens. In both nations the war was popular and expectations of quick victory high.

Spring Rice repeatedly stressed a growing German influence in St. Petersburg and noted that Britain might have to send its fleet to the Far East, leaving its homeland open for invasion by Germany. Roosevelt did not share his alarm. By summer Roosevelt was considering how he might intervene between Russia and Japan to prevent the spread of the war. He told Spring Rice the Japanese minister in Washington had spoken to him about the possibility of an international arrangement over Manchuria. Spring Rice encouraged the President's eagerness to interfere by reporting that Russia, with German support, was planning complete control of China; that a victorious Russia might recruit Mongol soldiers to fight in Europe; that Germany was planning to cease buying American grain. In the autumn, as Russian families learned of casualties, Spring Rice saw the possibility of a palace revolution.

Spring Rice hacked at McCormick's credibility.

"Mrs. McCormick," he wrote, "had some evenings at home and asked the Russians whom she knew. Only two came, a lady and a man, of all of her acquaintances. The rest of the company were foreign dips. The same thing happened to our ambassadress. She was boycotted with determination and success. This is a curious contrast to American manners. It seems to me to be silly to treat the McCormicks in this way because they have been particularly friendly to the Russians—indeed, some of us thought too friendly. Certainly McCormick sympathized more with the Russians than with Japanese and did all he could to influence public feeling in America in favor of the Russians. I was talking the other day to a painted lady who owns the house now occupied by the McCormicks. She said she had written to him asking him to give up the house and was much hurt at McCormick's refusal. It appears also that McCormick once wrote a letter to 'My Dear Grand Duke' which was thought an unheard-of atrocity. Also that he pressed the Emperor's hand with too much effusion on one occasion. The fact is that the feeling against the English and Americans in court circles is about as bitter as can be and any excuse is good enough. . . . The absurd thing is that a word from the Emperor could make the whole of society polite but this word is never spoken. Unfortunately, a diplomat is rather prone to accept any snub from princes and emperors and I think both the American and English embassies were somewhat undignified in making any attempt at all to be civil to people who certainly don't mean to be civil. This will interest you from the social view. It is rather odd."

In December of 1904, Spring Rice wrote a gossipy letter to Mrs. Roosevelt relating that the Russian government had organized a raid on the American chancery to steal the cipher and already had photographed the American diplomatic letter book. "The organizer of this game is an army officer who drinks champagne with the chancery servant," he related. "In contrast," he said, "the British caught an intruder in its embassy and half-killed him before kicking him out in the snow."

He taunted Roosevelt: "If you were English, you might well say that the American government has a very big voice and a very little stick."

The next day Spring Rice wrote at length directly to the President reporting that the Russians were about to offer peace to Japan in an effort to eliminate American and British influence from the Far East. He said Russia had the approval of both Germany and France and added that Russia was planning to interrupt the $20-million-a-year sale of American cotton to Japan.

"I wish," he ended, "you had a really good man here. Our man is a very good man. Strong and independent."

The letter shattered Roosevelt's last shred of confidence in McCormick. Two days after Christmas the President wrote a your-eyes-only letter to Spring Rice saying he had decided "largely because of what you set forth" to replace McCormick with a close friend, George Meyer. "I told Meyer that an Englishman—I didn't mention your name—would speak to him and tell him he had been in communication with me and by my request was to keep in touch with him. You can show him this letter."

Events moved quickly. McCormick wrote his resignation, saying he would happily serve his president and country in any task the President wished. Roosevelt responded gently and appointed him ambassador to Paris. Port Arthur fell to Japan after a year's siege; the Japanese clobbered the Russian army at Mukden and annihilated the Russian Baltic fleet on its arrival in the Far East. Roosevelt sent his new ambassador to talk with the Czar and tell him that both Russia and Japan should leave Manchuria, Russia should hand back half of Sakhalin and Japan drop its demand for compensation. The Czar agreed in writing, thinking, Spring Rice reported, that the Japanese would refuse. But Roosevelt convinced the Japanese that continuing the war would cost more than the indemnity they demanded of Russia. They agreed to peace. The Czar then protested he had been tricked, but the two warring governments signed for peace at Portsmouth, New Hampshire. In time, Roosevelt was given the Nobel Peace Prize. In 1912, Britain sent Spring Rice to Washington as ambassador. His long friendship with Roosevelt was now a complication, as was his enmity toward Germany. He advised the British government to keep a low profile in America and let Germany itself destroy the sympathy of its supporters there.

For the McCormicks, Paris was a much more pleasant post than St. Petersburg, but McCormick was discontented. The fun had gone from diplomacy. He had failed in Russia, apart from persuading the Czar's government to honor passports issued to American Jews. Kate needed support and turned to Bert—her long unwanted second son—writing to him to come to Paris for a long, long visit. As though conscious her son lacked any reason to please her, she added a crass sweetener—she would give him $20,000.

6. Servant of the People
1905—1910

The Chicago River, which made Chicago the best harbor at the
southern end of Lake Michigan and gave such impetus to the
early growth of the city, was blocking development of the new
prime residential area along the lake to the north. Twenty-five-
year-old Bert, now Alderman McCormick, was appointed to a
committee with prominent architects Ernest Graham and Jarvis
Hunt to consider how best to overcome the barrier. Mayor
Dunne proposed digging a tunnel, but because of the thick soft
mud the tunnel would have to be about six blocks long, although
the river itself was only 250 feet wide. Hunt had a better idea—
widen Michigan Avenue into a boulevard and double deck the
approaches to the river and the bridge. Bert favored the proposal. It met his promise to Gold Coast voters. From the council
chamber, Bert wrote to his mother.

"Our plan for widening Michigan Avenue has been approved
by the council," he said. "Twenty-five thousand dollars has been
appropriated to begin work. I hope that, upon your return from
Paris, you will find a boulevard not inferior in natural beauty to
the Champs Elysees."

The Mayor's board of improvements rejected the proposal and
Hunt's innovative, bold plan was filed away but it lodged firmly
in Bert's mind, awaiting the appropriate time to emerge and
ripen into a project enhancing the city and giving The Tribune a
new home worthy of the "World's Greatest Newspaper."

Bert came up against William Hale Thompson, Big Bill. The
Republicans had put Thompson on the council two years ahead
of Bert, but in Thompson's first term he had supported—he fell
for, in Bert's eyes—a Democratic proposal to redraw district
boundaries. Too late did Thompson discover the Democrats had
taken away so many of his Republicans that he lost his seat. Bert
considered Thompson not very smart but did respect him as an

effective public speaker and recognized gains made possible by his willingness to spend his own money. The most powerful Republican in Illinois, William Lorimer, adopted Thompson as a protege and placed him on Chicago's Cook County Board.

Thompson and Bert were delegates to the 1904 state Republican convention. The delegates were divided fiercely for or against Charles S. Deneen as gubernatorial nominee. Bert supported Deneen; Lorimer led the opposition with Thompson as his whip. Day after day, the delegates shouted and whispered, threatened and bribed. On the 22nd day—no convention had struggled so long—Deneen won and went on to win the governorship. The long contest, often bitter, between McCormick and Thompson had begun.

* * * * *

Joe joined the Democrats and Mayor Dunne rewarded the convert by appointing him Commissioner of Public Works. Joe barely settled behind his new desk before he ordered his father-in-law into court for illegal use of streets to load and unload Marshall Field Company wagons. Giving equal treatment to his own family, he tried to collect more taxes from newspapers. The Mayor shouted betrayal and fired Joe. Joe wrote an open letter announcing that capitalism had had its day, although conceding that a few capitalists were good men and might earn their way into heaven. Public acquisition of street cars and all other public utilities, he said, would go only a fourth of the necessary way. To bring social justice, laws which had been written to maintain capitalists must go; the United States must adopt welfare measures introduced into Germany by Bismarck; if such ideas made Joe Patterson a socialist, Joe said, he was a socialist.

* * * * *

Cissy was no quitter. A journey to Vienna promised better days ahead, but at the Sacher Hotel the Count awakened her in the middle of one night and demanded $11,000 to pay his night's gambling losses. She gave it to him. They returned to the castle. She became pregnant and unwell. The Count was often away, even for the birth. A midwife presided. Cissy named the girl Felicia. The Count welcomed the child. Now, certainly, the parents would open their purse to him. They did not. One night Cissy broke open the absent Count's desk and found a diary listing his assignations. That did it. Two years was enough.

* * * * *

During one of his frequent confrontations in the Democrat-controlled council, Bert was handed a note from his sponsor Busse asking him to come to the Republican party headquarters. Bert sent word he was too busy. Soon in came Busse, Roy O. Best and James Reddick, power wielders in the party. They drew Bert aside and made a proposition that flabbergasted and flattered him.

During the ten years since Judge Prendergast had left the Sanitary District meetings, Chicago politicians, Democrats and Republicans, had taken turns using the canal project to entrench themselves, awarding contracts in return for generous contributions to the party, giving jobs in return for marshaling voters on election day. Citizens shouted "Graft! Corruption!" but Chicago politicians refused to end the looting and to clean up the administration. So the state legislators did the job, rewriting the District's constitution to give power to one man, the president, presumably honest and capable even though elected.

The Republican party bosses told Bert, just 25, they wanted to present him as the party's candidate for the District presidency. Why did the bosses select him? In two years, he had become recognized by interested voters of both parties as honest, earnest, intelligent, independent-minded. Mayor Dunne could not openly support Bert but he could ease the Democratic effort against him. Blind Republican committeemen may have thought that Bert, recognizing his inexperience, would rely on old hands for guidance and things would go on as usual but behind a shining pure facade. Calculating committeemen knew the party's long list of debts to The Tribune and considered the election would please the paper and reinforce its support in this and future elections. Editor Robert Patterson had a special reason to favor the selection. The assignment permanently could remove from The Tribune one of the Medill grandsons, albeit the least troublesome. But there was something more subtle. In selecting Bert, the party was presenting voters with the disciple of two men—Editor Medill and Judge Prendergast—who had been so effective in creating the Sanitary District and organizing the project. The good that the two allies had done had not died with them, nor had their power. Bert said he would accept the nomination. Two days later he wrote to his parents in Paris.

"Dear People," he began. He said he had just received his mother's letter asking him to come to Paris for a long, long stay and he much appreciated the offer of $20,000. Had the letter not been delayed in the mail and had it reached him two days earlier, before he accepted the nomination for the Sanitary District position, he would have come to Paris. Now, he said, duty demanded he stay in Chicago. He would continue his law studies at Northwestern University and work hard at the Sanitary District. If all went well, in five years he should be established as one of the leading political figures in Chicago and Illinois and a member of the Illinois bar. He ended: "Your loving son, Rutherford."

Bert campaigned diligently, promising to provide an honest, efficient administration free of political bribery, collusion and theft, the right words for the times. How the bosses must have glowed. Their boy was sure a crackerjack. Why, he spoke all those lines as though he really meant them. The Republicans swept the election.

*   *   *   *   *

R. R. McCormick assumed the presidential chair at the Sanitary District offices on December 5, 1905, called the staff to attention, decreed the board must meet promptly at 2 o'clock every Wednesday, handed out a long list of precise rules and announced that merit, not political pull, will prevail. He hired auditors. He signed contracts. When a trustee told him about a provision requiring that all work costing more than $500 be put out for 60-day bids, McCormick said the District's financial plight did not permit such delays and continued to sign. He dictated a stream of notices. A clerk said he lacked stamps to mail them; buy the stamps from the emergency fund, Bert said. We have no emergency fund, the clerk replied; Bert set up the fund. Finding the offices too small, he rented the entire 15th floor of a building just being completed by the American Trust and committed the Board to rent of $1,000 a month to be paid in gold coin. He thought builders of lift bridges across the canal were charging too much for patent rights. Draw our own designs, he told engineers. He demanded the city of Chicago pay instantly $14,000 long overdue to the District. He told department heads they must make more detailed reports. In 12 months 375 reports came in, more than treble the number under the old Board.

The President followed his own decrees. The former President had made four reports to the Board in a year. McCormick sent in 62 during his first 12 months. Before awarding contracts, he read the fine print, walked over the site with engineers and had his officers check details minutely. As a result, payments overran contract prices by only 1.9 per cent. McCormick suspected that in the past contractors frequently had gathered in secret, allocated jobs among their number and rigged bids so the trustees had to give the contracts to the chosen men and pay a price which would yield generous sums for the party manipulators. McCormick's two years on the city council had tipped him where to look.

True to his now established habit of wanting to see things for himself but not squander money hiring cars at $100 a day, he had the District buy an automobile for $4,000. One day he stepped into a small boat to survey the waterway. The boatman cranked the heavy engine. It responded only after expenditure of considerable time and sweat. McCormick noted the boat also had a small motor to drive an electricity generator. It started easily. Why not, McCormick asked the boatman, gear the small engine into the big one, start the little one and let it crank the big one? The boatman talked to the machine shop, found the idea practical and linked the engines. That, the Colonel said later, was the beginning of self-starters which, in time, became standard on cars, trucks and many kinds of vehicles and stationary engines. He did not patent the invention. "I did not have good business sense," he reflected.

* * * * *

In Robert McCormick was emerging the inventiveness, initiative and self-confidence that, a century earlier, helped his great grandfather and namesake to create a comfortable, productive plantation in the wilderness of western Virginia. Four days' ride from Richmond, Walnut Grove demanded self-reliance. Two grist mills ground McCormick grain. Two sawmills sawed lumber. Close-grained walnut was crafted into cabinets and tables. At two forges, slaves hammered iron into nails, hinges, straps, axles. The efficient bellows and crane were of McCormick design and manufacture. Men tanned hides and cobbled shoes. Women spun wool, wove cloth, sewed clothing, made lye from wood ash and turned that into soap. They rendered fat and dipped candles, dried fruit, cured hams. At Walnut Grove everyone was busy from dawn until starlight and then the master settled himself under an adjustable candle holder with his books on astronomy and a glass of Walnut Grove distilled libation. The mistress, Mary Ann Hall, a planter's daughter, embroidered and their three sons and two daughters studied their five school books, Murray's reader, Webster's speller, Dilworth's arithmetic, the shorter catechism and the Bible. Mary Ann was ambitious for her children. "You must get ahead," she told them.

The words slid off William but rooted deeply in Cyrus. When old enough to wield a hammer, he joined his father in the workshops tinkering with a machine that could cut grain and allow McCormick to extend his fields without adding to his slaves. In 1816, the father hitched two horses to his contraption of whirling blades. It was quite a spectacle, sending some stalks flying and crushing others, creating a shambles. Neighbors laughed and McCormick hauled the machine back to the workshop and closed the doors. Fifteen years passed before Cyrus, at 22, displayed an improved machine and cut six acres of grain in one afternoon, a task that would have required the sickles of 24 men. Neighbors gathered at Steele's tavern. None asked Cyrus to make a machine, but the McCormick inventiveness was reinforced with McCormick determination and the world was never the same. The Colonel later said he derived his "general instinct for machinery" entirely from the McCormicks. The Medills, he added, "didn't know a fence from a lawn mower."

*   *   *   *   *

The quality of determination, so powerful in both the Medills and the McCormicks, equipped Bert to face the most explosive task facing the new Sanitary District president—the sorting out of incompetent District employees who had been hired as a reward for services to the Democratic party. One day McCormick saw a young foreman tell a loitering appointee to get busy. The man snapped back something like "get lost." The foreman shot out a clenched fist and knocked down the man. McCormick hurried to the foreman, complimented him and marked him for promotion, but a few days later the foreman resigned. "What's this for?" McCormick asked. "I'm a Democrat, you're a Republican," the man said. "I'm quitting before you fire me." "Go back to work," McCormick said. In time Foreman Edward J. Kelly became one of Chicago's most memorable mayors. He and the Colonel worked together with mutual respect. When, many years later, Kelly was being investigated for possible income tax evasion, McCormick invited him to lunch at the Chicago Club and, before Chicago's business elite, silently and effectively demonstrated his personal regard for Kelly.

McCormick ordered departments to favor union labor but instructed his 12-man police force to oust any "walking delegates" trying to enroll employees. The police were told also to shut any illegal drinking saloons catering to workmen living in contractor dormitories for $3 or $4 a week, room and board. The police took the order as authority to burn down the establishments and they did. On the kind side, the police rescued a woman and baby from a shack floating down the canal. Almost every month they pulled a body or two from the water.

Any enterprise, McCormick said, is only as efficient as its department heads and foremen. He sought new graduates from engineering colleges and built a staff of men from his own college Yale, Northwestern, Chicago, Illinois, Michigan, Wisconsin, Washington, Lewis Institute, Boston School of Technology and even his old rival Harvard.

Now and then, McCormick lost a good man to private enterprise. He raised pay scales to provide bonuses for key men. "A good man," he said, "may for some time be stimulated and inspired to noble efforts by the hope of future rewards, but a failure to realize the hope is likely to cause corresponding inattention to the District business." "Discontent," he said another day, "can only breed carelessness and slovenliness."

McCormick, still in his final year of law school, asked the District law department for its files on all outstanding cases. The files more than filled a table. He went through them and learned that all important suits were being handled by outside lawyers. He ordered District lawyers to do all District legal work. The annual legal costs were cut from $158,312.94 to $37,486.99. So efficiently did the reorganized staff operate that damage suits demanding $220,000 were settled for $8,487. A jury gave a landowner $750 for flood damage and awarded his lawyers $7,500. "Don't pay the lawyers," McCormick ordered, explaining publicly so all of his future brother lawyers could hear that such an award "opens the door to unscrupulous lawyers and makes them feel assured that with the help of a friendly judge, they will be well paid from District funds." The District appealed, arguing that the case was so trivial the landowner need not have employed three "eminent lawyers" and that, even for men of such standing and qualifications, $7,500 was too much. The appeal judge agreed with the second plea and cut the award to $4,000, but as to whether a person going to court should be content with a bread-and-butter lawyer, the judge did not say. A judge who hopes for reelection can go only so far in taking rich cake from his profession.

The District paid the $4,000 but McCormick, dissatisfied, asked the state legislature to pass laws limiting legal costs to 10 percent of the damage award and to relieve the District of its obligation to pay legal costs of persons claiming damage. A state Senator killed the bill during the committee stage, saying some farmers living along the canal were so poor they could not afford to hire a lawyer in a just effort to recover damages from the rich, powerful Board. McCormick replied that nine tenths of the cases in the Senator's district were brought by "one great corporation." The legislators preferred to ignore the fact, but the contest between McCormick and Samuel Insull, creator of the "great corporation," had begun.

McCormick said Insull's "great corporation" had gone to court asking for flood damage, it said, to certain lands near the canal, while in another suit it demanded a tenfold jump in price of land condemned by the District stating the new uses for the land made possible by the coming new electric power had magnified the land value. "They want everything both ways," McCormick said.

Work on diversion canals and foundations for the power house had begun in 1903. The assistant engineer, George Wisner, reported to McCormick that the major contractor, Joseph Duffy, was behind schedule and some work had not been done properly. Banks were slipping; concrete walls were crumbling; steam shovels were idle; rail lines were so wobbly that trains jumped the tracks. Duffy must be replaced. Writing a new contract would be almost impossible, because no one could even guess how much work must be redone. No one could say how many workmen were incompetent political pals. District records do not explain but it seems highly probable that Duffy had been given the contract as part of the long-functioning conspiracy among contractors and politicians.

McCormick had a personal dilemma. Everything he had

learned from his grandfather, his parents, their friends and his teachers prejudiced him against government and for private enterprise, but here was a case in which private enterprise had failed. McCormick set aside the teaching, cancelled, instantly, right now, the contract with Duffy, seized all of his equipment, fired all of the Duffy employees and recommended the Board finish the job itself. One trustee suggested that before the work be resumed by the Board, District engineers should be asked to find out how much needed to be done and the probable cost. McCormick said the delay would cost $40,000 a week. The trustee withdrew the proposal.

The Board handed Duffy an ultimatum stating that if the cost of completing the job were less than the sum which would have been paid to Duffy, the District would keep the savings but if, as seemed probable with so much work having to be redone, the cost would be more, Duffy would pay, and if he did not pay, the trustees would sell enough of his equipment to reimburse the District. Lo and behold, Duffy signed. The record does not identify the arguments made to him, but someone must have said something such as: We know what went on down at the party headquarters, dividing up the work and the excess profits. If you don't sign, we'll spill it all and that will finish your political friends.

There were Democratic howls of pain and Republican moans of amazement that a declared conservative should behave in such a manner. McCormick stated his position: "I am in hearty accord with the principle that public corporations ought not do things which can be better and more economically done by private corporations and individuals. But it frequently occurs that bidders combine to obtain extortionate prices, and contractors may not be able to carry out the project. Wicked combinations should not be able to mulct our treasury. In such cases, the Sanitary District should be able to hire direct labor. This right should be used as a defensive weapon only, not as the pretext for wandering into the wild and unfruitful field of unreasoning radicalism."

On another day he confessed, again in public, that "the trustees acted more radically than any radical politician had dared suggest and found themselves conducting matters in a way almost socialistic."

"The action," he added, "was taken not as political propaganda but of necessity to preserve the public interest."

Another day he said, "Students of municipal affairs differ on whether public work is better done by contract or by day labor.

91

The advocates of each juggle figures and misrepresent facts. If the contractors can do the work better, will they do so? Not unless they must. Contractors are not free of failings of the human race and naturally take as much as they can. The responsibility for efficient, cheap public work rests upon public officials. They have tried to accomplish the goal by competitive bidding. But combinations, legal or otherwise, control all public bidding. Competition can be brought only by the municipality and this competition can be effective only if the municipality is equipped to do the work itself."

Another time he said, "While it is comparatively easy to find the solution to a problem of municipal engineering, it is difficult to carry out any plan for the greatest public advantage in the face of obstacles thrown in the way by the class of citizens who make a practice of living off the public."

All this from a man just turned 25.

Assistant Engineer Wisner, given command, brought work back onto schedule despite a massive cloudburst at the peak of the spring thaw. The costs did exceed the original contract price, and the trustees billed Duffy. He refused to pay, went to court and lost.

*　*　*　*　*

Cissy's marriage problems pursued Ambassador McCormick to Paris. Cissy had served two tumultuous years with the Count and then one cold winter night when, she recalled, hungry wolves hunted tasty prey in the Polish forests, she persuaded friendly servants in the castle to bring horses and sleigh and take her and her baby out of Poland to Germany.

She went on by train to Paris, the Count following. Let's try again, he proposed; take a villa in Pau, I'll join you there. Cissy did go to Pau, the Count did come but the story was the same—gambling, women and drink. One night she mocked him for blatantly seducing his dinner partner. He complained that her parents had refused to pay his gambling losses. Give me money now, he shouted. She laughed. He beat her to the floor, and walked away. She packed, took the child and moved to London. She handed the child to a governess and established herself at the Savoy Hotel. London society absorbed her. One day when the governess was airing Felicia in a park, a car with three men stopped nearby. While two men engaged the governess, the third, the Count, grabbed Felicia and carried her into the car. The three drove off. There is another version: The Count came to London and told the governess Cissy wanted her to bring the child to Paris and the woman did so without asking Cissy. Whichever account is true, the Count later sent word that Felicia was in an Austrian convent and Cissy had lost all rights to the daughter by leaving him and his castle.

To Cissy, the Count's deed was blatant kidnapping. Did the Count love his daughter? Of course not. Did he want Cissy to return to him? Rubbish. What did he want? The answer was clear: money. The purpose of kidnapping is ransom!

Cissy's father, in Europe to rest and recuperate, sought intermediaries. The granddaughter of General Grant was married to a Russian prince. Could she help? She said, sorry, no. Cissy appealed to Kate. Could she help? Kate returned to St. Petersburg with Cissy and arranged a meeting with the Dowager Empress. Cissy told her story. The Empress sympathized with Cissy and said she would have the Count arrested and put in prison and kept there until he gave up the child. Kate and Cissy returned to Paris. Nothing happened.

Aside from Cissy, Ambassador McCormick found diplomatic peace in Paris. The United States and France were friends and admirers. Cartoonists drew robed matronly figures of Columbia and La Belle France in affectionate embrace. Only a dispute between American insurance companies and the French bureaucracy caused harsh words and the Ambassador produced a mutually satisfactory compromise. The diplomatic corps, most suave in Europe, and the embassy staff spoke of McCormick's "unfailing kindnesses, considerate courtesy and manly dependability." As he and Kate packed in 1907 to go home, the American Club gathered 80 notables for a farewell banquet on Washington's birthday. The club president, William S. Dalliba, commented that in the Ambassador "the heart of the boy is still the heart of the man, warm, generous, unspoiled by contact with the world."

The Ambassador, in a carefully considered address, reported that conditions in nations and among nations had shown "tremendous improvement" since he was assigned to London 18 years earlier. He repeated advice of his father-in-law, Joseph Medill, that common sense should be applied to all matters. "Every interest," he said, "demands an end of prejudice, nation against nation, Gentile against Jew, black against white, capital against labor." There is unrest in the world, he conceded, but unrest is necessary to bring changes. He praised the Czar for doing his best to bring constitutional changes in Russia, but he saw a possibility that "persons crying against oppression might themselves, on gaining power, become oppressors." He praised the Czar also for his part in the creation of the Hague Tribunal, to which nations now would bring their disputes. McCormick advanced a position, then becoming popular, that commerce and finance had become so interwoven in the world that "one can scarcely conceive of a war between two great powers," and the "growing voice of the people," as expressed in newspapers, was "deepening understanding and providing a check on governments and rulers." He reported Japan had "proven itself to be a first class power able to use arms if necessary to gain its will."

"As peace becomes universal," he mused, "soldiers and sailors will have to be content with their new role of world policeman. Poets will praise no longer the heroes of war but the heroes of peace."

"All this will happen," he ended, "unless I am too optimistic."

It was quite a speech. The Paris edition of the New York Herald thought it merited two-thirds of its front page. The French government awarded him its Grand Cross Legion of Merit which he on retirement could wear beside the Order of the Rising Sun given him by the Mikado for tending the Emperor's business in St. Petersburg during the war between Russia and Japan.

As he and Kate sailed for home, the Ambassador promised, "I'll be back, often."

The two years in Paris had danced past, although Kate later claimed the diplomatic labor had "undermined" her husband's health.

*　*　*　*　*

Robert Todd Lincoln, who introduced Robert Sanderson McCormick into the diplomatic service, had introduced Insull to Chicago, drawing him from Thomas Edison's headquarters at Menlo Park, New Jersey. Lincoln had a glimpse of the almost limitless potential of electricity and the great profits which awaited any group which could combine the many small companies providing steam-generated electricity in neighborhood plants. Insull, by purchase and merger, acquired many companies and killed off holdouts by offering power at rates cut more deeply than the small company could meet. The giant raised rates in its other areas to offset temporary losses. By 1907, only four or five small Chicago power companies remained outside the Insull monopoly and they no longer were a threat. The Sanitary District was another matter. Its plant could produce electricity from water power at a third of the cost of Insull's steam plants. Here was indeed a rich prize if Insull could get the District's power. Equally, here was a serious rival if the District did not cooperate.

Once more McCormick's years of teaching about the merits of private enterprise collided with his duty as trustee of a $60 million project paid for by the people out of taxes and maintained by the people out of taxes for the health and betterment of all Chicago people.

The situation, McCormick said, was a repeat on a larger scale of the quandary he had faced as alderman over city streetcars. There he had taken the middle road, leaving ownership and operation in private hands while giving the city the right to fix the fare and to receive part of the profits. A similar compromise might be possible with power, but McCormick shared a popular turn-of-century dislike for trusts, heightened by President Theodore Roosevelt's exhortations. McCormick's aldermanic experience had not built faith in the city council to keep its hands off power revenue.

McCormick summoned the Board to consider how the power should be sold, to whom it should be sold, and at what prices. The District, he told the trustees, is a unique municipal corporation and should make its power available to other municipal corporations for their own use at cost. If the District had power surplus to the needs of the municipalities, it should sell the surplus either to private users for as much as it could get or to municipalities at cost and let them sell it to private users for as much as they could get. He said he preferred the first course. The trustees agreed.

The decision became a direct challenge to Insull. The city of Chicago was using about 200,000 horsepower of electricity, the suburbs another 20,000. The District would produce, at the start, about 17,000 horsepower but, fully developed, could put out 80,000 horsepower. It would be, thus, a major provider of power for some time. The municipalities used electricity almost entirely for street lighting and wanted power only at night. A water power plant is most economic if it works at full capacity constantly. Electricity cannot be stored. To keep its turbines run-

95

ning in daytime, the District would have to find private users who needed power by day. McCormick ordered an aggressive sales campaign, aimed at the heart of Insull's market.

The Board engineers and accountants reported the total cost of the District's electricity, including interest, depreciation and other indirect charges, would be $14.97 a horsepower a year. McCormick recommended the District sell power to municipalities for their own use for $1.25 per horsepower per month, barely above cost, if they would take power 24 hours a day, or $2.20 if they could use power only during the dark hours. The suburb of Oak Park was first to accept. Other suburbs soon subscribed. The city of Chicago offered to buy power for street lighting for 46 cents a horsepower. Insull also offered to take power at a rate less than cost. McCormick discarded both offers with one word: "Paltry."

McCormick warned the Board that Insull might use the tactic he had found so effective against stubborn producers and offer municipalities power at a rate below the District's cost price on the presumption that all suburbs would sign with him, forcing the District, unable to gain customers, to concede to him. The threat did not materialize. Insull's accountant must have told him that his losses would be too large and continue too long to be paid out of profits earned elsewhere unless general rates, currently a little below those in other cities, were raised sharply. Insull also learned quickly that McCormick and the other trustees could not be persuaded, in one way or another, to change their position.

So he turned to the courts and the Illinois legislature. From the courts he asked, among other things, that his utility be permitted to condemn the Board's power properties. The judges ruled that public property cannot be condemned for private purposes; condemnation works only the other way around.

To the legislature Insull proposed that the District's application to raise taxes and sell more bonds be put to the voters, assuming the voters would say no. He was wrong; they said yes. McCormick issued more bonds but did not raise taxes. Future earnings, he said, would pay off the bonds. Taxes should be the final measure, he added; they take money from the people.

McCormick carried the lobbying fight to Insull, telling the legislature that District investigations had uncovered "startling and atrocious facts of a series of carefully thought out and brilliantly executed plans which deprived the state and District of immense water power rights created by the state and District and turned the rights over to a certain body of capitalists." As an instance, he said a previous board had built a steam power plant and turned its power over to the Insull utility.

He spoke up publicly against "men who are glad to fill their pockets at the cost of the taxpayer, glad to reap what they have not sown, whose greed for gain is greater than their sense of propriety." He said one power company had "acquired not one of its possessions in an upright and straightforward manner." He said the state must try, by every means, to recover the power rights and the properties. Future boards, he said, "should be wary of disposing of rights or property which would become valuable in coming years." In all things, McCormick said, the Board "must seek the greatest good for all people."

The shortest route for a District transmission line to one suburb passed through Chicago. The District asked for a permit to erect poles along streets. The city attorney—Insull may have been leaning on him—replied that the city council could give permits only for purposes specifically cited in ordinances and no ordinance mentioned poles for District power. The District reminded citizens that Chicago had 10,000 street lights and by buying District power the city could save $30 a lamp, or $300,000 a year. The city council soon passed an ordinance letting it give the District the necessary permit for poles and before long asked to hook its lights to the District network.

Architects designing a new city hall included use of District power. McCormick said the new public library could qualify for cheap District power. Private users joined, paying on average, about twice as much as the municipalities. When the turbines began turning, the amount of power created was limited only by lines completed. At the end of the first year, the District was earning about $64,000 a month from power sales, more than half of the money coming from private users. The production cost was only $19,000. After other charges were written off, the net profit for the month was $24,000. During the year, McCormick told the council, the District saved power users about one million dollars, money that would have gone to Insull, and he predicted that as power needs increased, the savings would multiply.

The District used the profits to finance new work and to pay off bonds early. Power used in factories by day soon matched that needed for street lighting. The city of Chicago planned to scrap its extravagant steam plants, but McCormick advised:

Save the best and use them during peak periods. The city did so, enabling the District to increase the amount of power it safely could pledge to deliver.

There was another repercussion. Insull's customers began asking why he charged so much more for power than did the District. Insull had come against the most difficult competitor—a rival able to produce the product much more cheaply than he could—and in McCormick he had come against a public servant determined to keep public power profits for the people. Many times Insull must have cursed McCormick. Years ahead, after Insull's empire collapsed from upside down financing, Insull formally faced accusations of defrauding his stockholders. He blamed McCormick.

"I was not responsible," McCormick replied. "I looked upon Insull as a political corruptionist, a person who would use any means to gain support of politicians, but I never thought Insull would be dishonest with his business associates."

"People tend to forget," he added, "all the good Insull did. His companies became financial successes." Here he quoted Shakespeare: "The evil that men do lives after them; the good is oft interred with their bones," and added, "It was the reverse with Insull."

*　*　*　*　*

Joe, after his triple resignations, joined the Socialist party led by Grandfather Medill's arch enemy, "Dictator" Eugene Debs. Joe happily wrote and published leaflets condemning free enterprise, asserting "moral disease pervades every walk of life," and demanding a new deal for the little man. He wrote four plays, Keeley joining in one about newspapers called "The Fourth Estate." Three succeeded. Joe wrote a novel, "A Little Brother of the Rich," about a boy of modest means who attended Yale, sold out to the wealth and superficial values of some of his classmates, took to drink and joined in exploiting the poor. Joe poured vitriol on the rich. Of a mill owner he wrote: "On that scorching day in a mill he entered not once or twice a year, 200 children were burning out their lives in order that his palms might be softly white." Joe moved on to stockbrokers, having an actress declare to them: "Your life is useless. The world is better off without you. You add not one jot of wisdom or happiness or wealth or health or virtue to the world yet, by crooked tricks of your trade, you have filched from it ease, emolument, respect, luxury, power. Social position? To whom does society owe social position? To me, an actress, who gives society education and happiness and thought and recreation, or to you, who take everything you can swindle out of it and return sneers, corruption, evil example, depraved tastes, debased amusement?"

Joe also saw the problems of being rich: "Friends and toadies and sycophants and servants pretend to like me, but would not give two hurrahs if I were John Smith."

He defended chorus girls: "You pay a girl six or eight dollars a week to stand all day in a store and you offer the same girl $18 a week to wear tights and stand on a stage. Which is the decenter proposition, the girl working for her living or the rich loafer in the bald-headed row who comes night after night to tempt her, if he can?" Joe demolished "women of fashion": "Complete inefficiency dominates their lives. They can't sing, dance, act, paint, sew, cook, educate. They are inept, unthorough, inconsequential, rudderless, compassionless. They don't know life because they have never lived life. They are like perpetual typhoid fever patients, supported always on a rubber mattress. Helpless, hapless, hopeless, they exist for a few years, seeking to have all their living done for them by paid dependents. They delegate all of their functions in life except one, and even that they don't do very well, or very often." Joe's rich young man condemns his wife: "Do you call this marble palace home, with a woman who would bear you only one child for fear of spoiling her figure and missing the season, who tells you she married you only for your money, who considers you nothing but a combined pearl fishery and diamond mine?" Of socially busy couples, Joe wrote: "Life was so easy for them that they drifted apart after a dozen years. A world existed for each of them, so there was no reason for them to serve each other. They were not helpmates. They had one child, (Joe had three) and hired nurses, governesses, tutors, boarding schools to rear him. They had no common worries, no common sorrows, no common troubles. When the passion wore out, there was nothing left, not even companionship. They seldom saw each other except in the presence of fashionable folk. He turned to other women and she to other men, and each consented to the arrangement." Joe wrote off New Englanders as "a lot of fossils," and condemned New York City as being "mighty enough to enslave a continent and filthy enough to poison the heaven above." Joe included a minor comic character named Bertie:

"A funny man and quite harmless, wearing the very latest in neckties, socks, collars, shirts, an animated shop window. Besides wearing the latest importations in male lingerie, he goes to tailors to have his clothes made to order. He invariably wears patent leather shoes. His favorite expressions are 'Egad' and 'Bah Jove.' He must have caught them from an English society play. Still, Bertie's heart is not bad. He is probably as good as the rest of us." He sent cousin Bert a copy inscribed: "To Bert McC from J. M. P. Aug. 1908."

The Socialist party, noisy but powerless, welcomed Joe. Debs asked Joe to direct his 1908 campaign for the presidency and Joe accepted. Joe also took a crash course in farming at the University of Wisconsin and began applying the lessons at an inherited farm near Libertyville. He traded polo ponies for Percherons. "Plowing," he said, "is better than polo." Altogether, Joe was having an exhilarating time. But his mother, Nellie, was troubled by Joe's shattered career at The Tribune and her smashed dreams.

* * * * *

Medill McCormick effectively demonstrated in Cleveland that he did not meet his grandfather's goals for "journalistic taste and capacity." The Leader lost money and after three years Medill asked his mother for more cash. Kate, awakened to the probability that his presence in Cleveland was countering her plans for him at The Tribune, refused. Medill must come home. He sold the paper to his brother-in-law, Daniel Hanna, and came back to Chicago and the destiny plotted by his mother. He was 30 years old. Unwanted by Keeley and Beck in the editorial offices, Medill found a desk in the business offices. The Tribune did not aggressively seek advertising. Medill, recognizing an opportunity, hired hungry, energetic salesmen who found a rich market waiting. As Tribune revenue swelled, the directors rewarded Medill by appointing him vice president and secretary and giving him a salary of $20,000 a year, which was $5,000 more than Robert Patterson was paid after 30 dedicated years.

One year after Medill's return from Cleveland, the directors, to the dismay of Keeley and Beck, appointed him assistant editor-in-chief. His mother's plans for him seemed near realization but Ruth did not abandon her political dreaming of and laboring for her White House goal. Medill, a book addict—he bought every

Kate

volume mentioning Napoleon—took on his father's one-time assignment as literary editor, seeking short stories and novels which could be capsuled into daily rations. To help him find the rare jewel among manuscripts brought in by aspiring writers, Medill hired a Catholic doctor's 22-year-old, carefully reared daughter named Mary King. No one could foresee the effects that minor assignment was to have on journalism, The Tribune and Joe Patterson.

Robert Patterson, at 55, could find satisfaction in his newspaper career. He was one of the best known, most quoted editors in the land. Detractors could say Nellie had put him into the editor's chair but, looking back, he could see quite a few times when his wife and her raw feud with her sister brought problems and disagreeableness. Yes, as a newspaperman, Patterson could be happy with himself. But as a family man? Joy early had gone from his marriage. Only nineteenth century social mores kept Robert and Nellie from divorce. Hopes that son Joe might follow him at The Tribune had collapsed; he had a father's wishes for the happiness of his daughter. Poor, poor Cissy. It all was enough to drive a man to drink and, bottle by bottle, Father-in-law Medill's warnings about the hazard of alcohol grew faint for Robert Patterson. His judgment wavered. Kate demanded the directors fire him. He went again to Europe, to a new clinic opened by Carl Jung. Medill McCormick moved himself into Patterson's office and chair. Keeley exploded, marched from the office, packed a trunk and sailed for Japan, not saying when he would return. His instructions to Beck were simple: "Do as Medill says."

What Medill told Beck was curious: Compile a list of all important Chicago citizens owning houses used by prostitutes. He would expose the new-rich, high-talking, church-going hypocrites! Beck saw only trouble coming from such effort but directed his reporters to search property records and bring him names and addresses which he wrote in a little red book. Keeley came home as suddenly as he left. Beck showed him the red book. Lock it up, Keeley said. Keeley went into the back shop to help put the paper to bed. In strode Medill, with opera hat, cape and cane. He clasped Keeley warmly. The next day Medill followed Patterson senior to Europe and the Jung clinic. He too had ignored Grandfather Medill's warning against alcohol. His mother, trying to save his career at The Tribune, asked the directors to grant Medill a two-month leave of absence. The red book disappeared, never to surface.

102

It so happened that cousins Joe Patterson and Robert McCormick one day met on a sidewalk and Joe proposed the two of them move in on The Tribune and put Joe's father out on his return from Europe. Bert declined, saying he thought Robert Patterson deserved better after his years of hard work for The Tribune. Anyway, he added, he and Joe had no votes on the board.

* * * * *

Theodore Roosevelt's term as United States president was ending. He chose as his successor Taft, of even greater girth, his popularity enhanced by his work in the Philippines. Voters accepted the choice. Before Taft could move into the White House, Kate asked him for a new ambassadorship for her husband. She said The Tribune would look kindly on such an appointment, but brother-in-law Patterson, home from Europe, wrote an angry eight-page letter to the President-elect relating that Kate had told him if The Tribune did not support her request for an appointment, she would no longer help Cissy in her bitter struggle with the Count. Patterson said The Tribune did not support any appointment for McCormick. The man, Patterson said, is incompetent. "You may show this letter to McCormick," he ended. He sent copies to five other men of high influence in Washington, so bitter had become the family feud. Patterson's letter ended Robert Sanderson McCormick's diplomatic career. Taft did not give the former ambassador another position. The Tribune trusteeship was transferred to Kate on her demand as her husband's health deteriorated, partly because he too had not heeded father-in-law Medill's ceaseless words about the peril of alcohol.

Patterson's wife Nellie also wrote to President-elect Taft asking his help in regaining Cissy's child. Taft, without waiting for his inauguration in 1909, penned a note to the Czar saying only the Czar could return Felicia to Cissy. The Czar wrote the order but the Count was out of his reach in Austria. Six months later, business matters on the Count's estate required his presence. There the Czar's police arrested him. The Count agreed to give up the child. Cissy was told she should go to Vienna and the child would be delivered. Cousin Medill went with her and waited until in toddled little Felicia. The girl never again saw her father. Cissy proposed remaining in Europe, but Medill persuaded her that she should take Felicia home to Chicago. Cissy asked for a Chicago divorce; the Count's lawyer presented counter-petitions. The romance was dead but the marriage remained legally intact.

So ended the McCormicks' flirtation with Europe. Bert, although only a spectator, saw little cause to think kindly of Europe and its conniving, greedy, selfish, quarrelsome governments and people.

* * * * *

Medill McCormick returned to Chicago from Europe after a few months and reassumed his position at The Tribune. His health seemed improved. He brought in a Yale classmate, William H. Field, as business manager. A Vermonter, Field had risen fast on the business side of the Frank Munsey publications in New York. Medill offered him $18,000 a year, an aristocratic salary at the time. The directors said that was too much but Medill had his way and Field came. He was a bargain. He developed the aggressive advertising department Medill had started. Field studied consumer buying in the five-state Chicago territory and assembled the statistics in a booklet called "Winning a Great Market on Facts." With it, a salesman could go to a manufacturer, wholesaler or retailer and tell him how many of his products were bought in Chicago Territory and reasons given by buyers for choosing the product. He also could predict, with fair accuracy, how many more people would buy the product if they knew about it. "The Book of Facts," regularly updated, and ads placed in newspapers in other manufacturing cities, helped The Tribune bring in more national advertising than any other American publication except the Saturday Evening Post. Field could afford to order salesmen to turn down ads from disreputable firms or for trashy goods. To advertise in The Tribune became recognized as a mark of quality. Other newspapers copied the system.

* * * * *

In 1907 the Sanitary District was under attack from the city it had been set up to help, from the state of Illinois, from the federal government and even from the king of England. This massive alliance was preventing the District from starting work on two projects ordered by the legislature in 1903, a large feeder canal to connect the Calumet River with the main canal and carry waste from the heavily industrial southern suburbs and a small feeder canal from Evanston to serve the rich residential northern suburbs. Both areas were pouring their waste far out into Lake Michigan, but wind from the east carried it back into the city's water intake pipes.

The District applied to army engineers for permission to divert lake water into the Calumet River. The army men reported to Taft, then Secretary of War, that the diversion would lower the level of Lake Michigan and, consequently, of all the lakes, closing to big ships the 106 Great Lake harbors on the U.S. side on which the engineers had spent 100 million dollars. Canadian ports similarly would be affected, the flow at Niagara would be reduced and the falls either would dry up or power plants there would have to divert less water around the falls. The engineers recommended Taft not give the permit.

The army engineers relied on a report produced for the International Waterways Commission, a body created by the governments of the United States and Canada to protect interests of shippers in the Great Lakes. The study was made by Hering, the New York engineer who designed the original Chicago diversionary canal 20 years earlier. Hering commented that so much progress had been made in the design of sewage disposal plants using bacteria and chemicals that Chicago had an alternative to diverting its waste through canals into rivers flowing away from the lake.

Taft told the District he lacked power to overrule the army engineers and he must decline permission for the Calumet Canal. McCormick, the engineer and the attorney went to Washington to try to persuade Taft to change his mind. They were not admitted to his office.

McCormick and the District used a new approach. They persuaded the Illinois legislature to pass a law giving the District the authority to build the canal. The federal government said the state had no constitutional right to pass such a law; the state replied that the federal government had no constitutional right to interfere in matters pertaining to Illinois, but the Supreme Court, reasoning that the canal would affect areas beyond the borders of Illinois, ruled for the federal government. The state of Missouri, emboldened, asked federal judges to issue an injunction forcing the District to stop diverting waste through the main canal and eventually into the Mississippi River just above St. Louis, arguing that St. Louis drew its water from the river and

Chicago was imperiling the city's health. District engineers for years had claimed that by the time water diverted into the canal to carry the waste reached Joliet, 50 miles away, it was almost purified, and was totally clean at Peoria, still only half way to St. Louis. McCormick asked if the engineers were correct. He must see for himself. One afternoon he, a relative named William McCormick Blair, Engineer Wisner and Donald Ryerson, a friend, rode the train to Joliet and there borrowed a rowboat. They paddled out into the Des Plaines River, studying the water. McCormick noted with satisfaction that the oily, sooty film so prevalent closer to Chicago had vanished, as had the unpleasant smell. Green blotches did float about but Wisner assured him they were composed of organisms completing the purification.

The four floated downstream, not noting daylight was fading; nor did they worry about the sound of rushing water. As night closed in, they drifted on, looking for an easy spot to come ashore.

"It occurred to none of us," McCormick told the trustees, "that the dam of the Economy Power and Light Company had made a veritable cataract of the stream. Our first knowledge of this fact was in the capsizing of our frail vessel and the submerging of ourselves. It was the matter of only a few minutes until we passed through the rapids and not much more than a half hour before our swamped boat was brought to the shore. None of us noticed any peculiarity in the taste or smell of the water which, 40 miles upstream, would be considered poison. There was a certain uneasiness of mind during the next two weeks but none of us developed any intestinal disorder."

The testimony strengthened the District's arguments that the canal was no hazard to St. Louis. As for the practice of dumping waste into a river, how did St. Louis dispose of its waste? The city emptied its sewers into the Mississippi.

The federal judges denied Missouri's request for an injunction and ordered Missouri to pay legal costs, a little over $10,000. The District learned St. Louis had been a silent partner in the suit and had agreed to pay half of the costs. The District board, seeing an opportunity to turn a frustrated foe into an ally, sent St. Louis a check for its half of the costs and then joined with St. Louis businessmen in organizing an inland waterway conference in St. Louis to demand that the United States government not enter into any treaty with a foreign country which might interfere with American inland waterways.

The State Department did not listen. It concluded a treaty with Great Britain, acting on behalf of Canada, pledging the United States never to take more than 40,000 cubic feet of water from the Great Lakes for power purposes and not more than 10,000 for the Chicago Canal. Britain's king signed for Canada.

The District went again to the army to ask if it could reduce its flow into the Chicago River by 1,000 feet and draw that amount into the proposed Calumet feeder canal. Taft again said no.

McCormick advised the trustees that the Board must start considering alternatives to the Calumet Canal as a method of disposing of southern suburban waste. The Board set up a small pilot plant to test known methods of purification and to seek new ones while its engineers surveyed systems used by scores of inland towns, although the Board did not give up hope for the Calumet Canal. The Board engaged Hering to study the Calumet area, to report every possible method of treating waste being dumped into the lake, and to make a recommendation.

McCormick, while tramping the sand dunes along the southern curve of Lake Michigan one day in 1907 to see for himself the region to be served by the Calumet Canal, came upon a man with large, flimsy wings tied to his arms. He was running down the steep face of a dune and being wafted, now and then, a few feet into the air. McCormick introduced himself.

The winged man identified himself as Octave Chanute and explained that although most people said he was balmy he was convinced that by mastering the flow of air over curved surfaces man could fly safely. Chanute, who was an engineer, said two bicycle mechanics in Ohio, brothers named Wright, had made a flying machine and would demonstrate it in a few days to the army at Fort Myer not far from Washington. Secretary of War Taft would be there.

McCormick rode a train to the capital, invited Alice Roosevelt to lunch, told her about the amazing event and persuaded her to use her father's influence to let them attend the demonstration. She drove him to the Fort in her electric car. The wind was blowing too strongly, the brothers said, for them to bring their frail craft from a barn where it was sheltered but in late afternoon the wind died, the brothers pushed the weird contraption onto the field and started its motor. The craft bumped over the grass and then, as if by magic, it rose from the earth, circled the field and landed. Many years later, the Colonel told a radio audience that watching the flight "was the greatest thrill of my life."

107

Halfway through his five-year term as Sanitary District president, McCormick could look upon himself as well established in a political career that reasonably could take him to the governor's mansion. As an alderman he had recognized that, if a politician were to be his own master, he must have income outside politics. He did not want to rely on continued remittances from his mother nor on eventual inheritance of a portion of her Tribune shares. He would earn his own money at law. In 1908 he was admitted to the Illinois bar and, with Samuel Emory Thomason, a Yale classmate, and Stuart Shepard, formed a law partnership and opened an office in the Tribune building, within easy reach of any Tribune office needing legal advice, the only relationship he, or anyone else, foresaw for Kate's unwanted second son.

*   *   *   *   *

Approaching 30, McCormick was not yet contemplating marriage but was finding a peaceful refuge with Cousin Ed Adams and Amie. McCormick continued to maintain an apartment and the Chicago Club base but his periods in the Adams home became longer. The three had a natural affinity. They did not share the wealth and fame brought by the reaper. They could not accept the explanation that the fortune their Great Uncle Cyrus made came not so much from the invention itself as from Cyrus' diligence and acumen in mass building and selling the wondrous machine.

Neither Bert nor Ed could condemn Cyrus wholeheartedly. Bert's grandfather, William Sanderson McCormick, died before the family feud became bitter and Ed's father, Hugh Adams, on coming to Chicago with Amanda in 1859, was financed by Cyrus in expanding the grain business he had begun in Virginia. The partnership was called McCormick and Co., testifying to Cyrus' demand for domination in all things. Hugh named his first son Cyrus and in 1871 turned over to him his share in the grain partnership. Cyrus Adams soon saw the need and desire of farmers, millers and shippers to buy and sell grain for future delivery and helped develop a futures market. Cyrus brought into the firm his younger brothers, Hugh and Edward. His son, Cyrus Adams II, was born on the same date as Bert but one year later. The cousins sometimes celebrated their birthday together.

Ed's father had died in 1880, the year Bert was born. Amanda lived until Bert was 11. Friends remembered her "remarkable

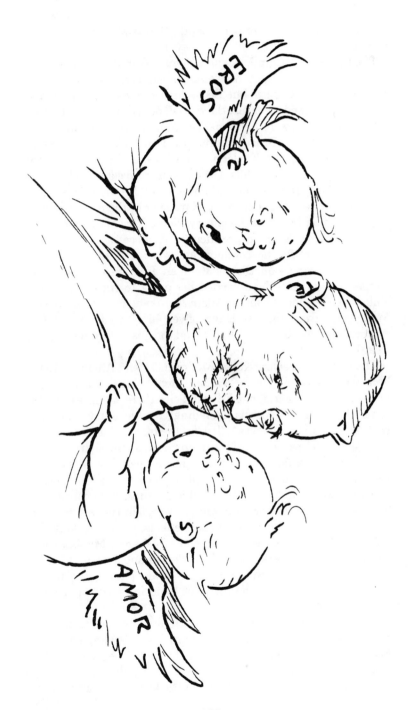

Christian character representing all that was honorable and right", and spoke of her "unselfish devotion to her family."

The Chicago McCormicks and Adamses considered themselves part of a dynasty. Some McCormicks claimed descent from an early Irish King Cormac but Bert's father traced his line to Virginia, then Ireland, then Scotland's Island of Mull. Ed's earliest Adams forebears were Scots named Adam. An early Adam soldiered with Robert Bruce. Another died on Flodden Field. Some went to the border of England and Wales, added an "s" to the name and joined the Tudors. Others went to Ireland and then to America. McCormicks and Adamses were Presbyterians, firm, strict and, if need be, belligerent. A number of them started coming to Virginia in the 18th century. Some Virginia Adamses accepted the New England presidential Adamses as relatives but could not identify the common ancestor. The most romantic Adams forebear swam the moat of an Irish earl's castle, kidnapped the daughter and carried her away to America. In Virginia, McCormicks and Adamses owned slaves. Cyrus McCormick freed the two slaves given him by his father. One Adams sent his slaves to Liberia and, on his death, divided his wealth among them.

The Civil War separated the McCormicks and Adamses. Bert's hero was his Great Uncle William Medill, killed chasing Lee's army from Gettysburg, but Ed could cite three Adamses who became Confederate generals, including General John Adams, as the record asserts, who was killed "in the terrible battle of Franklin, Tennessee, as he, on his war horse, rode through a lake of blood where his faithful men had made their last stand" and General Wirt Adams who declined a place in the Confederate cabinet and, "standing six feet in his stirrups, rode continously and fiercely through the whirlwind of war." In the last spring of the war, as flowers arose on the battlefields, an Adams lady, Sue Landon Vaughan, roused the women of Jackson, Mississippi, to garland every soldier's grave, Confederate and Union. "Decoration day" she called the tribute. As years passed, the nation, North and South, saw the merit of honoring the war dead on Sue's Decoration day.

When talking of family heroes, Bert and Ed had to listen to Amie. Her Scotch-Irish father, Bernard John Dowling Irwin, had been an army surgeon, a "fighting doctor." One night in 1861 Irwin, then a captain in the medical corps, slipped through a large war party of Indians who had attacked a small army patrol

110

GEN.
B.J.D.
IRWIN

111

in Apache Pass, Arizona. Massacre was near. The doctor reached the men and cared for the wounded until a rescue party arrived. For that act of bravery beyond the call of duty, he was awarded the earliest Congressional Medal of Honor. He was appointed chief medical officer at West Point, reorganized military medical care, attended international medical conferences and retired as a brigadier general. The army hospital at Fort Riley, Kansas, home of the 1st Division after the Second World War, is named for him.

Amie's brother, four years older than she, George Le Roy Irwin, was graduated from West Point in 1889 and became an army gunner in Cuba, the Philippines and Mexico and, by 1910, was an authority on the development and use of modern field guns and ammunition.

Amie was brought up in the army but brat she was not. She was sweet of face and character, of more than medium height, with light brown hair, a loving heart and, deep within, her father's strength and boldness. She was an excellent horsewoman and loved animals. She and Ed Adams married in 1895 when she was 23 and he 35. They had no children to bind them together. In the soaring galaxy of cousins, Ed lagged and increasingly dulled his disappointment with booze. Slowly Amie grew closer to Bert and away from Ed.

* * * * *

McCormick began weekly meetings with Chicago's mayor to unite efforts for the Calumet Canal. The city health officer, Dr. W. A. Evans, made speeches about the health hazards faced by 130,000 people living in the southern suburbs, an equal number living across the state line in Indiana and at least half a million people in Chicago who drank water from the intake most often contaminated by Calumet sewage. Dr. Evans said the reversing of the Chicago River in the past five years had decreased the number of typhoid deaths in Chicago from 175 a year per 100,000 to 15 and proved that a diversion canal does function as the Board claimed.

Hering laid out the problem, the various courses of possible action and the good and bad of each course. In the last paragraph he said he must conclude that the Calumet Canal was the most desirable solution.

The District's engineers produced the decisive fact: Unchallengeable records showed that the water level had not fallen since the Chicago Canal opened in 1900, as army engineers had predicted, but had risen. The army engineers were wrong, without question, about the effects of the original canal. They might be equally wrong about the Calumet Canal. The army engineers retreated, agreed Chicago could build the Calumet Canal and, temporarily, could divert into it 1,000 feet of the 10,000 allocated to the District by the treaty.

"Don't worry about the temporary nature of the permit; dig the canal and dig it now." McCormick ordered, and went to Europe on a personal errand. There he and Wisner, by now chief engineer, examined sewage plants in Berlin and Birmingham and the Manchester ship canal.

On his return, he told the Board that he and Wisner saw nothing in Berlin which had not been learned already at the District's own pilot disposal plant, described by McCormick as the most advanced in the nation. He ranked as second a laboratory at the Massachusetts Institute of Technology. He reported no efficient method of artificial disposal of waste had been developed in Berlin, but warned that the District must press ahead with pilot plant experiments. The 1910 census report, he predicted, would prove that the city was continuing to grow at a rate which would, by 1922, create the maximum amount of waste that the diversion canal system could carry away safely. By then, he said, the District must have alternative methods in operation and drain into the canals only effluent from the plants. In a further 30 years, he said, Chicago would have six million people and the carrying capacity of the canals for effluent would be reached, but by then, 1952, he predicted sewage treatment would have become so efficient that the citizens could safely and happily drink effluent from the plants.

A new problem arose. McCormick reported that "a few real estate speculators have walked into the controversy, each desirous that the work be done not in a way to benefit the general taxpayers but in a way to benefit his private purse. The conduct of these men has been intemperate and immoral in the extreme and can bring good to no one."

Compared to the drama over electrical power and the Calumet Canal, digging the Evanston Canal was a before-lunch-on-Monday affair. The canal was small. True, it had to pass through some of the finest residential parts of Chicago. From the start, McCormick proposed that, to disturb the residents as little as

113

possible, the District do the job itself. The District acquired equipment and hired labor. McCormick appointed Ed Kelly superintendent. Here and there someone gave trouble. One property owner said the canal could not pass through his two lots. He expected a long delay until the matter could be settled. No sir. McCormick ordered the crews to start digging at once. They finished that bit of ditch before the man was aware the work was being done. Of course the property owner could sue, McCormick said, but the most he could collect was the value of the land, which the District intended to pay anyway. The brick company dug one mile of ditch for nothing and used the clay to make bricks for the lovely homes rising in Evanston, Kenilworth, Wilmette and Lake Forest. The Evanston city council demanded that all rock and dirt be carried away. Fine. The District dumped the rock into the lake to form a breakwater to protect its intake and dumped earth behind it to form a new park.

7. Suddenly, A Career and a Wife
1910—1915

In 1909 to celebrate the 100th anniversary of the birth of Abraham Lincoln, The Tribune, normally 12 pages on weekdays and 64 on Sundays, published its biggest paper up to that time —194 pages. In those days circulation, not advertising, produced the profits. Across the top of the front page was a box stating: "The Greatest Issue of the World's Greatest Newspaper." The last three words remained on The Tribune's masthead for 68 years.

Medill McCormick saw in Robert Patterson's collapse a pure gold possibility of becoming controlling owner of The Tribune. He urged his mother to buy out her sister, but Kate said no, telling her favorite son she did not have that much money and if she did she would not put her entire worth into The Tribune. Too risky, she said. Victor Lawson, owner of Chicago's biggest circulation paper, The Daily News, and a puny morning paper, The Record-Herald, began talking with Tribune directors and minority stockholders about selling to him. Robert Patterson, seeing no place for himself on a paper owned by Lawson, asked Nellie not to sell. Bert, hearing of his mother's interest, wrote to Kate urging her not to sell, promising he would do anything to prevent a sale. To strengthen the management he proposed Keeley be made a director. The directors did give Keeley the added title and the vice presidency but no stock. The sisters were willing to share power and responsibility but not cash. Patterson came home, marginally improved in health. The crisis passed.

One day Bert, in the locker room at the Chicago Athletic Club after a workout in the boxing ring, was told by a club member he had just seen the oddest thing—an obviously intoxicated man in the steam room signing Tribune checks. Bert reported to his uncle, Patterson, who advised Bert to take a greater interest in Tribune affairs. The directors at their next meeting made him treasurer with the task of signing checks but with little other power and with no pay. He examined the books, saw no sign of auditing, asked who did that job and was told, "No one." The Tribune had no auditor! Bert moved the Sanitary District auditor, Daniel Deininger, to The Tribune to make sure everything was right. Never again was there a question about the correctness of Tribune accounts.

The comings and goings of Robert Patterson and Medill McCormick worried minority stockholders interested primarily in earnings. They looked with fright at William Randolph Hearst who for 10 years had used sensational journalism, Chicago thugs and profits from his papers in other cities to try to crush The Tribune and was not yet ready to concede defeat. Now a new peril emerged as Victor Lawson, a worthy rival for 35 years, decided to stop giving subsidies from his fine, rich evening paper, The Daily News, to his weak morning Record-Herald. He decreed Chicago had too many morning newspapers. One must go— The Tribune.

At this hour of crisis Robert Patterson could not be counted on and Medill was a dubious hope for the future. The two majority stockholders, Kate and Nellie, could be relied on only for infighting. Medill again collapsed and returned to Europe. Bert wrote to his brother, urging him to come home, promising him half his polo ponies. He doubted if Medill were benefiting from the Jung treatment and, wanting to see for himself, he wrote Jung asking him to drop in during a coming visit to America. If he does not come, McCormick told others, I'll consider him a charlatan. Jung did not come.

Medill resigned his Tribune positions. His mother agreed that he and Ruth would not return to Chicago but move to Washington, where the Hanna name was still powerful, and, as a part-time vocation, seek a political career. However Kate still did not recognize Medill's lack of journalistic fire and talent nor did she concede to Ruth's campaign to move her husband totally away from The Tribune. Arriving in Washington, Medill ignored the Hanna traditions and relationships and announced he would work for the election of the Wisconsin liberal, Robert La Follette, to the presidency.

In the spring of 1910 Bert and his uncle Robert Patterson happened to meet in Washington. Patterson said Bert should succeed him at the paper and then went to Philadelphia. Nobody today knows what took him there. Bert came home. On April

Fool's Day, The Tribune's head telephone operator, Anna Garrow, called Bert in his law office and told him that Patterson had died suddenly in Philadelphia and directors were gathering to consider a firm offer from Lawson. Patterson's death, creating a massive vacuum at the top of the Tribune structure, unnerved the directors. Lawson gave them two options: He would buy The Tribune for ten times average earnings, which had ranged from $625,000 to $824,000 a year, or he would give to the holders of the 2,000 Tribune shares ten million dollars of seven percent preferred stock in a new company which would merge The Tribune and his Record-Herald. The new company also would issue $14 million in common stock and use part of the receipts to reimburse Record-Herald stockholders. If Tribune directors refused the deal, he would cut the Record-Herald price to one cent. The Tribune could continue at two cents and lose circulation, or it could drop to one cent and lose its profits. He would wage war to the finish. To Bert, Lawson whispered a promise: Support the sale and I will back you for any elective position you may seek.

One of the larger minority stockholders, Alfred Cowles, heir of the early partner, sought out Bert, told him that if he would take over the leadership, Cowles would not sell his stock to Lawson and he thought other minority holders would follow. Bert's Aunt Nellie told him she did not like to see The Tribune pass out of the family and, looking among the grandchildren, could see only Bert, still at the Sanitary District, as the one to function for the family.

What about Nellie's own son Joe? Should he come back into The Tribune? It so happened that the Sunday editor's wife won a divorce and was awarded more alimony than the Sunday editor, Bill Handy, was willing to pay. He lagged in payments. In 1910 judges did not pass lightly over citizens who ignored court orders and, to avoid trouble, the Sunday editor fled to South America. At Bert's suggestion Joe was appointed The Tribune's Sunday editor. Joe's feeling for "the ordinary people," their likes, their goals, their fantasies, their needs, their despair, made almost everyone in Chicago a potential Tribune reader and, later in New York, led to the creation of the country's biggest circulation newspaper.

The directors rejected Lawson's offer and authorized Bert to inform the awesome publisher. Lawson said he would improve the offer and suggested that Bert carry the new proposal to his mother, aunt and Attorney Beale, all in Europe. Bert, trying to

117

calm his nerves, smoked a pack of cigarettes. He emerged from the meeting smoke filled and coughing and gave up smoking forever. Not wanting to alert others that The Tribune might be sold to Lawson, Bert announced he and District Engineer Wisner were going to Europe to inspect the new sewage disposal plants and the ship canal. The subterfuge worked. Bert met with his mother, aunt and Beale and told them the seven percent preferred stock offered by Lawson would reduce their income and offer no opportunity for capital gain whereas if the family kept the paper and if the cousins could supply good leadership, Tribune stock might decline briefly but then it would grow in value and dividends. The three decided to keep The Tribune in the family and to give Bert and Joe a chance. If the pair failed, the trustees could always sell. The three accepted his argument.

Lawson, spurned, dropped the Record-Herald price to one cent. The Tribune followed. The Tribune's new circulation manager, Max Annenberg, tried in one way or another, including thuggery, to persuade newsstand dealers to favor The Tribune and Tribune circulation rose while Record-Herald and Examiner sales fell.

Bert was in a quandary. After five years of running the Sanitary District, he was looked upon as a coming power in politics. His law partnership was promising. Now the door to command of The Tribune was waiting for him to turn the handle. Should he be a politician first and an editor second or the other way around? A voter praised McCormick for his "integrity and initiative." The Chicago Journal described him as "clear-headed and clean blooded, an immensely vigorous, practically capable young man, yet offhand in manner." The voters were to end his quandary. McCormick suspected that he and his fellow conservatives who had been behaving as socialists might not be reelected. The Chicago Democrats had regrouped; Chicago Republicans were in trouble. As for McCormick, how many voters would support someone who had been looking out for their welfare instead of being a party's faithful errand boy? The Democrats proposed Ed Kelly as their candidate but he declined to run against McCormick, saying he admired his boss and believed no one could beat him. Do people get the government they need, or the government they deserve? Is there a better way to choose men and women to run a district or a city or a state or a nation than by popping into a booth and marking a row of x's?

Just before the election McCormick delivered a farewell speech. "The District has been fearless in its advance," he said. "It has ignored pressure by interested parties. Every department has a standard of efficiency which will challenge comparison with any privately conducted business. Upon the nine trustees who hold office from December 5th will devolve the responsibility of maintaining this efficiency, or of allowing it to decrease for personal or political purposes. I am far from ignorant of the pressure brought to secure appointments for those who are unqualified or whose services are not needed, and to secure increases of salary not merited by quality of service rendered. This pressure, I am afraid, will be greater in the immediate future for the reason that newly elected Democratic county officers have turned their offices into employment bureaus for political workers. The trustees will do well to bear in mind that they will suffer in reputation and character if they act in a too-yielding spirit."

At 1:45 p.m. on December 6, 1910, McCormick called the trustees to order for the last time and yielded the chair to the newly elected Democratic president. His political career was over. In 1912 he was offered the Republican nomination as United States Congressman but declined. "By then," he said later, "I had been transported to other spheres."

*　*　*　*　*

The cousins were as different as salt and sugar. McCormick dressed carefully; Patterson put on any old thing at hand. McCormick was cool toward almost everyone; Patterson warm; McCormick thought individuals could prosper through hard work if the government stayed off their backs; Patterson thought most people needed help which could come only from government.

Different they were, yes, but must that mean conflict? Of course you will fight each other, Nellie told her son. Joe replied they would not fight because each was too selfish. He need not say that he and Bert had seen the unhappiness and unnecessary difficulties brought about by their mothers' feud.

Could a newspaper have two persons at the top? No, Grandfather Medill had said. A newspaper, he stated, must have one voice. The cousins worked out a division of labor. Joe would expand his work as Sunday editor and develop new features; Bert would conduct the business. Joe recommended the directors double Bert's pay of $5,000 a year. The news would be left to Keeley, with Joe supervising him one month and Bert the next. The

119

masthead would carry both names, McCormick as president and Patterson as chairman. Which ranked first? No one could say.

One day the cousins wrote a few lines on two pieces of paper, torn from the top of a newspaper page, promising never to disagree but, should irreconcilable differences arise, a third person would make the decision and they would abide by it. They called their declaration an "iron-bound" agreement. Each signed both slips, took one of them and locked it away. The pledge came to light only after their deaths, just as did the equally effective covenant of Cyrus and Nettie, their great uncle and aunt.

A cleavage did open between the cousins and Keeley when he asked to be made editor and publisher and the directors made him only general manager. Then he asked to bring in Theodore Roosevelt as editor at $15,000 a year but Bert and Joe spent that money buying the Katzenjammer Kids comic strip.

Lorimer, the GOP state boss, had been elected to the Senate by the cooperative Illinois legislature. Keeley suspected fraud. A reporter learned that one of the legislators, Charles White, had received $1,900 to vote for Lorimer and The Tribune printed the fact. Other legislators confessed they too had been given money. Who paid? The Tribune asked. A Chicagoan, Clarence Funk, started The Tribune on a trail that led, as Keeley suspected, to Lorimer. The Lorimer response, the Colonel later said, was to trump up a blackmail plot against Funk. But The Tribune persisted and in 1911 the United States Senate found Lorimer guilty of election fraud and took away his Senate seat. Bert was widely credited for bringing down Lorimer. Big Bill Thompson declared his new goal was to "smash Bob McCormick." "I was not frightened," the Colonel later told a radio audience. "We had rid Illinois of Lorimerism which was our public duty. If we spoiled a few political opportunities for Thompson, that was his misfortune and Illinois' gain." Thompson found a new sponsor, Fred Lundin.

The Colonel credited Keeley for the leg work that brought down Lorimer. Keeley told a congressional hearing that his control over The Tribune was absolute, but he must have realized that the coming of the cousins eliminated his chances of ever gaining command of The Tribune. He was an outsider. To rise to the top of a newspaper he would have to move from The Tribune.

* * * * *

One of the more pressing business problems was the cost of newsprint. Bert wondered if The Tribune should make its own paper. He set his mind to it. Who makes paper? Where? How? Who buys it? Who pays how much? Is the supply equal to the demand?

Some answers were easy. Wood was ground into pulp, mixed with wood chips, steamed with sulphur and limestone and sometimes with rags. The mush was spread on a long, moving copper screen. As water drained away, the soggy mat was pressed between steel rollers and driers. Presto, newsprint! American mills out-produced Canadian mills, 1.3 million tons to 400,000. Prices soared in good times when supply was short and plunged in bad times when supply was abundant. Hearst, the biggest buyer, demanded and got a $5-a-ton discount. The message was clear: The Tribune must have its own newsprint source. Where? Forests of black spruce with some balsam, best for newsprint, were fast disappearing in the United States but still ran to the horizon, untouched, in Canada. American papers had paid an import duty on Canadian newsprint but Congress had dropped that charge, although no American paper had yet taken advantage of the change.

McCormick's eyes turned north.

Now came another of those coincidences which propelled him into new projects all his life. The business manager, Field, met while fishing in Canada a short, plump, happy man named Warren Curtis, Jr., who had grown up in paper mills. His father owned a plant near Corinth, New York. The son had just completed a plant at International Falls, Minnesota, drawing water power from rapids on the river that divides Canada and the United States. He and his father had drawn plans for Hearst whenever Hearst was negotiating a new paper contract, but Hearst tucked away the plans after the supplier cut his price.

McCormick sought the son and told him The Tribune was thinking of building a mill. Would he be interested? The son talked to the father who advised, "Go with McCormick." The pair listed their requirements: Abundant cheap wood, abundant cheap electricity and fast cheap rail transportation. The younger Curtis thought a falls on the Abitibi River north of Lake Huron was promising. He and McCormick traveled 400 miles north. The arctic wind bit. "Let's go south to Niagara Falls," McCormick said. "It is warmer there," he joked.

Curtis found a 30-acre pasture at Thorold ten miles from Niagara Falls, almost within the happy sound of generators producing power to spare, especially at night. Curtis signed an option to buy normal power at $13.50 a horsepower and off-peak power at $3.37. Railroads passed nearby and adjoining the pasture was the Welland Canal, which in time would let ocean freighters pass from the St. Lawrence into the Great Lakes. Bert liked the picture; he also liked the presence of men trained to run machines properly.

Let's be bold, Curtis said.

Why depend on others for pulp? Let's bring in logs and grind them with off-peak electricity instead of water power. Let's buy 12,000-volt motors for the grinders so we can use power straight from the falls and avoid losses in transformers. Let's run the mill with steam turbines and use the exhaust steam to heat the driers. Let's, let's, let's. Great ideas all, but untried. No one in the United States knew how to build such powerful motors.

Let's do it all, McCormick said.

McCormick asked Tribune directors for a million dollars to start on the mill. They gave it to him. Curtis learned of a company in Sweden that built 12,000-volt motors. McCormick and Curtis boarded a train to Wilmington, Delaware, to buy machinery. McCormick, hearing that the president of the Ontario Power Company was berthless on the packed train, invited him to share his stateroom. The grateful president whispered that if McCormick let the power option expire, the directors would not renew it at such a low off-peak price. McCormick signed at once. Much later he credited the event to Tribune good luck but students of management can see in it the reward for taking decisive action at the right time.

All fell into place except securing a large, single source of wood. Curtis chose 300 square miles of good timberland but the Ontario government would not grant cutting rights. McCormick was disappointed but not discouraged. Canadian merchants competed sharply to dispose of wood coming off land being cleared by new settlers. Sulphite pulp could come from Sweden.

Start construction, McCormick ordered on June 5, 1911.

There were many problems. Motors burned out. Turbines failed. McCormick commuted between Chicago and Niagara Falls. As the first machine was assembled, he lived at the mill, watching, adjusting, cursing. On September 4, 1913, the first paper rolled out at half speed. McCormick went home, aware that the innovative plant would "take a lot of managing," and the demands of The Tribune would leave him "no time for public activities nor private enjoyment." Gone was the vision of moving

someday into the governor's mansion in Springfield, a loss that did not dismay. He was also content to leave to Keeley The Tribune's political clout. A small loss, he consoled himself; look at Hearst and other publishers who tried to use their papers to assume political leadership. All had failed, and at considerable cost to the papers.

* * * * *

In 1912 Kate gave Red Oaks Farm to Bert. He left it with tenants and considered selling it but reckoned that the best offer, $35,000, was $20,000 too low. The decision was wiser than he suspected.

* * * * *

Medill McCormick became a national committeeman for the new Bull Moose party created by Theodore Roosevelt after the Republicans at their 1912 convention preferred Taft to him. Four years earlier Roosevelt had chosen Taft to follow him in the White House and happily had gone off to Africa to shoot lions and elephants, assuming that Taft would continue the battle against the trusts. But Taft had defaulted and by 1912 Roosevelt accused him of joining the greedy, grasping trust barons.

The new party became sensitive to women's demand for the vote and admitted them to the convention. Roosevelt outdrew Taft six million to four million but Roosevelt had split the Republicans and eight million Democratic votes were enough to put Woodrow Wilson into the White House.

* * * * *

In 1913, on August 8, the first child was born to Ruth and Medill, ten years after their marriage. She was christened Katharine Augusta but called Katrina, a name which could have softened Kate's grip on her son but didn't. Medill, having temporarily mastered alcohol, rejoined the Republican party and aspired to a seat in Congress. He knew victory was impossible in Chicago, the city being the personal duchy of Big Bill Thompson who wanted only poverty, disgrace and perhaps death for all McCormicks.

* * * * *

To reach out to women readers, no one could match Mary

124

King, neat and young, with direct blue eyes, a quiet voice and a firm, resourceful, steady way. Her judgment already had been tested finding readable fiction for The Tribune. Promoted to the Sunday staff Mary took on winnowing usable contributions to a column called "Bright Sayings" and other tasks under the direction of Joe Patterson. One day her mother complained tartly to her that a fruitcake baked from a Tribune recipe had turned out badly, wasting four dollars she had paid for the ingredients. At the time, Mary had no control over the recipes but the scolding, she said later, "opened my newspaper conscience" and convinced her that a good newspaper must hold itself responsible for every word it prints.

Patterson and Mary King became a team, spurring on each other. Ideas bounced back and forth. "Every good idea I ever had came from Mary," Patterson said at the end of his life. Patterson appointed Mary assistant Sunday editor of The Tribune and then, in 1914, Sunday editor, a post never held by a woman on any major American newspaper, responsible for features in the daily as well as the Sunday paper. She insisted all recipes be tested, leading to creation of the Tribune kitchen. She demanded equal accuracy in articles discussing personalities, news situations, dress patterns, home furnishings, beauty treatments, diet, care of children. Tribune readers learned they could trust The Tribune. If The Tribune said a product was good, it really was good. If The Tribune advocated certain conduct, the advice was wise. Under Mary's editorship The Sunday Tribune doubled in circulation. No one admired her more than Joe Patterson.

*　　*　　*　　*　　*

Amie and Bert could talk about Europe where both had been during their young years. They knew the same cities, trains, parks, hotels. They could argue about nations rising and nations falling. They could slip into French in gentle conspiracies. Both loved horses and were proud of their horsemanship. Both loved dogs with special regard for strong, brave Alsatians. Both read books and could share their newest discoveries. Undoubtedly Bert had delighted in reporting to Amie his newest triumph over opponents at the Sanitary District and undoubtedly she had listened with comforting words when he spilled out the treacheries his opponents tried to work on him. Both were on the fringe of powerful rich families, but no place was offered by the heads of the families to the unwanted second son and the army daughter. In time Bert was staying overnight, then days, then weeks. His club rooms or his apartment must have seemed cold, lonely places for a young man who had grown up starved of love and now was tasting the calm joy of devotion and sympathy. Would it not be natural that on evenings, while sitting before a gentle, almost burned-out fire, their daily store of chat spent, each saw in the eyes of the other a desperate loneliness?

Adams' business was not flourishing and at times Bert supplied wads of a thousand dollars or more to help pay household bills. Adams drank more and more. It is probable that he knew how far the relationship between his wife and his cousin had developed and accepted it, but with souring patience. In summer the Adamses lived in a house on Deerpath in the country-like northern suburb of Lake Forest. Bert went along. Amie developed a fine stable of high spirited horses and Bert played polo. Both rode in shows at the Onwentsia Club. The wooded shore offered long trails where the couple could ride, jumping fallen trees and creeks.

Everybody loved Amie. The Hearst society editor wrote that Amie was "one of the most popular women in Chicago society, associated with every fashionable women's club on the North Shore, dashing rider in hunts, owner of blue ribbon horses and dogs. Her beauty is sensational." Her speaking voice was praised —"low, clear, beautiful."

Would it not be strange if, now and then, the possibility of marriage did not drift into their minds and their conversation? If so, the thought was for some time put aside. Adams was in good health, likely to live for many years. Divorce was just not done in good families. Affairs, yes, but divorce, no. But one day a young ward of Adams, Ruth Roberts, was with the three at dinner. A small occurrence during the main course burned into her mind. Out of the blue, she said many years later, Amie turned to her husband and said, "Edward, I want a divorce. I am going to marry Robert." Bert, Ruth said, was so startled he fainted and fell from his chair. It is possible that McCormick merely was so startled as to almost fall from his chair and passing years and much retelling intensified in the girl's mind Bert's reaction. Ruth Roberts did not remember what led up to the announcement nor what followed, but she went through life certain that McCormick had behaved in a most ungentlemanly manner toward his cousin and the entire Adams side of the family.

Adams moved out of the house. Gossip rampaged through the North Shore. No longer did Bert and Cyrus Adams II, Amanda's grandson, celebrate their birthday. Bert rented a small house in Lake Forest and shared it with another lawyer. He needed someone to tend the house and did not want a woman. Amie suggested Gottfried. He often had held her horse when she rode in the park. He was so courteous, so kind. Gottfried Hintersdorf had come to the United States after serving in the German army. He recalled almost 70 years later, when he was 107 years old, the day he first saw McCormick. It was an afternoon in 1907 and Gottfried was working for the Fields. Bert had come to call on Alice Roosevelt who was visiting Chicago. Newspapers had been bothering Alice, and Gottfried was under orders not to admit any newspaperman to the house. Bert, coming as a friend, arrived astride a new big hunter. Up the steps came man and horse, through the door, into the hallway, and there the pair waited until Gottfried announced them and Alice presented herself. Bert showed off his horse, chatted a minute, turned, rode out the door, down the steps and out of sight but never out of Gottfried's mind. It was six years later when Bert, at Amie's suggestion, sent word for Gottfried to present himself at The Tribune. Gottfried came. Bert hired him to look after the Lake Forest house and downtown apartment and do odd jobs, such as riding a pony from the farm at Wheaton, 30 miles west of Chicago, to Lake Forest, 25 miles north, to deliver the pony to a little girl as a gift from Bert. Gottfried became a faithful supporter of the Colonel so long as both did live. Gottfried married at 48. "I'll pay for the first baby," the Colonel said. He did, a year and a half later.

*　*　*　*　*

Things were not going well with the paper mill at Thorold. It was producing only half as much paper as the designers had promised. McCormick "barked and growled" from afar and, during a dismal year-end period, gave Curtis one month to get better performance. "I have stayed away," McCormick wrote, "because I fear my presence was confusing rather than stimulating. The directors have shown rare patience which has been more painful than anger because it is based entirely on confidence which, once shaken, will not readily return. The prospect of failure is revolting. It has never occurred to me before. The only alternative is success."

By spring the mill's major troubles had been overcome, assuring success, and McCormick could turn his attention to the next problem, a source of wood. Most of the wood was coming from Anticosti Island near the mouth of the St. Lawrence, where mighty waves and high tides made loading difficult and dangerous. A ship might pick up the wood or it might not. We must have our own ships, McCormick ordered. He had lawyers set up a subsidiary corporation which bought a small ship, the *Honoreva,* to bring wood to Thorold and take American coal back as far as Montreal.

Impatiently he waited for the St. Lawrence ice to break so he could get out of the gossip-fouled Chicago air and into the clean north woods. He met Curtis and a veteran woodsman, William Carter, in Quebec. The three rode to the end of the last railroad spur on the north shore of the St. Lawrence and went on by dog sled. They put up tents and early the next morning set off on snowshoes into the white wilderness. The thin frozen crust firmly supported the snowshoes but, as the sun softened the snow, shoes broke through. Progress was arduous. The men camped early. Curtis, no believer in exercise, collapsed from exhaustion. McCormick sent Carter to the railroad spur to fetch a doctor. Carter brought also a Quebec newspaper. While the doctor examined the patient, McCormick read the paper.

A small item startled him: Keeley had deserted The Tribune; he was taking over Lawson's Record-Herald and combining it with The Interocean. McCormick saw disaster. How many Tribune men had gone with Keeley? Joe Patterson was in Vera Cruz with the marines trying to stop German arms from reaching the gringo-hating rebel government in Mexico.

McCormick snowshoed to the spur, telegraphed Field to keep Beck, Annenberg and other key men, roused a switch engine driver, rode the engine to the main line and cursed the train's slowness on its 48-hour trip to Chicago. He found all vital men still on the job but, by the time things settled down and The Tribune had established its defense lines against Keeley, the north woods had thawed into a mire. The search for wood would have to wait.

Joe and his cameramen came home from Vera Cruz. They had seen little action and the films did not draw many people into the nickelodeon, although the experience later would prove useful. So would another Patterson innovation. So many sailors had asked him "What's the news from home?" that he had printed a small paper in Vera Cruz and distributed it among the men.

To fill the editorship vacated by Keeley, Bert and Joe decided to take turns monthly. Joe, a socialist, favored radical moves such as government ownership and votes for women. Bert, a conservative, opposed all government expansion. Bert tried to end the long antipathy between his mother and his aunt. He accepted, and printed, editorials composed by his mother, and when she protested about changes made in the text he agreed that her version was better than the printed one but recalled that even her father had accepted changes in his editorials.

*   *   *   *   *

As weeks passed, neighbors, friends and just plain gossips told one another that Amie and Adams were about to be reconciled, but Amie filed a petition for divorce, stating she had "reached the limit of tolerance for drunken abuse." Adams did not reply. The case came before Judge Denis E. Sullivan in the Illinois Superior Court for Cook County on March 5, 1914. Adams did not appear, nor did he send a lawyer. Amie repeated her charge of drunkenness. Her sister's husband, Dr. Arthur Small, confirmed the charge. The next day the Judge granted the divorce. In those days one year must pass before a divorce became final and the two individuals were legally free to remarry.

*   *   *   *   *

Few in Chicago noticed when on June 28, 1914, a Serb shot Emperor Francis Joseph's heir, Archduke Francis Ferdinand in Sarajevo. They began to pay some attention when Serbia and Austria went to war one month later. Germany and Russia joined the war on opposite sides on August 1, then France, then two days later Britain. Before the month was out Joe was in Europe with photographer Edwin Weigel to report the war. France denied him access to the trenches, so he crossed to Germany.

*   *   *   *   *

In September Adams asked the Chicago court to reopen the divorce case to receive new evidence indicating that McCormick and Amie had been lovers since August 5, 1909. He accused McCormick of alienating his wife's affections and asked compensation for lost love and a lost wife. Some reports put his figure at $100,000, others at $300,000. The court records are missing. Gossips craftily told one another that Adams must have been promised, or thought he had been promised, quite a bit of money by McCormick if he would give up his wife peacefully and McCormick must not have paid.

McCormick fought back in court. He asked Adams be declared an involuntary bankrupt, stating that Adams had signed a series of promissory notes totaling $38,000 and, having only $10,000 to his name, could not pay. Adams replied to the court that the notes were given on occasions over the years when Bert and Amie were lovers and that McCormick had cancelled them. Adams' reply complicated his request for rehearing of the divorce by indicating that he knew about the alleged adultery when the case was heard and thus he could not now present the information as new evidence. Abruptly, with no explanation, all charges were withdrawn.

"An affair of the heart," the Judge commented.

But gossips now told one another that Bert must have paid, and paid heavily. In later days of confrontation journalism it is surprising that no Chicago daily newspaper printed a word of the court duel, although a small sheet, the Day Book, did shout the developments in its loudest voice, boasting that it was not a member of "the publishers' trust." Papers in Milwaukee and New York City also carried the news and became prized documents passed underhand to underhand in North Shore society.

Why had Adams spoken up so viciously? Had he warned Bert he had changed his mind about granting the divorce in gentlemanly fashion? If money were the reason, why did not Bert pay? Is it possible that McCormick thought Adams would not really return to court with his exposure or, if he did, Adams' statements would be hushed up or quickly forgotten? But it is probable that McCormick would have looked upon a demand for money as blackmail and fervently declared: Not one penny for tribute; damn the torpedoes; full steam ahead. Whatever the reason, the decision and the events that evolved deeply affected Bert's plans for his personal life, altered his behavior and drove him more deeply into his shell at a time when a loving marriage could have opened a new life for him.

It is not difficult to imagine the consternation felt by Amie and Bert, both sensitive, at the way heads nodded and eyes flicked, only half surreptitiously, whenever either came into a room. The

130

heavenly Onwentsia Club must have become a hell. McCormick, a loner since early childhood, turned further away from people and, in self-protection, became more wary and aloof. Aloof! How often that label was hung on him. Aloof! Austere! Autocratic! Even imperious! Carpers saw what they wanted to see and made no effort to find a reason, to see the ache behind the steel facade, the aloneness that was easier to bear than the private jibes of false friends, jealous enemies and dubious bystanders. Bert began to comment that dogs made better friends than people.

Kate was furious. Her son must not marry Amie! Kate set about blocking the wedding. She offered Bert $50,000 on the condition that he would give up Amie and, in another Edwardian tradition, plotted a long separation. Bert, in her mind, must go away, take a long trip, find other attractions, meet other women. But what sort of trip? He had seen so much of the world that the thought of going abroad would have no more appeal than a ride on a rollercoaster. She must arrange something unique, a trip that would take him away from Amie for a long period, engage his mind, further his new newspaper career and give him added stature on his return to Chicago. It must be an adventure so exciting that no gossip could brand Kate as being a designing mother.

Kate had moved into her father's house after his death. It was a substantial structure but decidedly of second rank on the Chicago listing of social venues, far below the fake castles and palaces on the Gold Coast a half-mile to the east. The splendors of court and diplomatic life in Europe had raised Kate's expectations. Medill's house would not do. Kate's income from the Tribune enabled her to erect a structure that would rival the Potter Palmer castle and its neighbors but why shouldn't she rejoin the diplomatic and government circles she had enjoyed in Europe? Why not a house in Washington? Yes, she would go to Washington, where Nellie already was proving that a woman with money and energy could find prominence as a hostess to people who were of interest to her. Kate purchased a piece of land at 3000 Massachusetts Avenue, so far from the White House that Nellie taunted her, "You'll be murdered in your bed out there in the sticks." Kate retorted, "Better than dying of malaria in your swamp."

Of course Kate and her architect disputed. The parting came over the staircase. Kate wanted a broad, gently-stepped promenade down which she could progress regally in full view of the admiring, or envious, guests waiting below. She tore up the architect's design. Why, a boy could do better, even Rutherford. She gave the task to her son. The result was structurally sound, aesthetically pleasing and socially effective. In time it was to please wives of ambassadors who made the house their official American residence. Alas, Nellie's rival house on Du Pont Circle was considered fit for a president and was to serve briefly as a temporary White House.

The Russian ambassador in 1915, George Bakhmeteff, had been Kate's friend since the years her husband was ambassador to the Czar in St. Petersburg. His American wife was one of Kate's best friends. The Russian was popular in Washington, having learned how to survive by doing favors for important Americans. War was raging in Europe but no news, other than official communiques, was coming out of the Eastern front. Kate saw a powerful diversion for Bert. She asked the Ambassador if he could arrange for her son to go to Russia as a war correspondent. No foreign newspaperman had been given such a privilege—the Czar did not want curious, intelligent people roaming around the Eastern front seeing things not reported by official communiques, but for Mrs. McCormick the Ambassador obtained a letter from Grand Duke Nicholas, commander-in-chief of the Russian army and cousin of the Czar. The Grand Duke wrote that he "preserves the best remembrance of the late ambassador, Mr. McCormick, and consents, as a unique exception, to admit your Mr. McCormick on the field of active fighting as a distinguished foreigner personally known to the Grand Duke." Mrs. McCormick sent the Czar $1,000 to help care for injured Russian soldiers.

Bert accepted the $50,000 and prepared for a long trip abroad.

8. On the Russian Front
1915

In the last days of winter, stories about heavy losses were seeping out of Russia. Were they true? Many newspapermen considered how they might get the story. The way was open only to McCormick. The Grand Duke had, in his letter, described McCormick as a "distinguished foreigner." It was an extravagant term for a man who had been a Chicago alderman for two years, president of the Sanitary District for five and was now a poorly paid co-editor of Chicago's second ranking newspaper. McCormick needed enhancement, quickly. "A subterfuge" is the way he put it. He put his mind to it. Who could help? There's . . .and there's. . .but what could they do, really? Mayor Ed Dunne had become Governor Dunne. McCormick went to Springfield, called on the Governor and told him of his plan to go to Russia as a guest of the Grand Duke and his need to appear distinguished in the Czar's eyes. Would it be possible for the Governor to make McCormick an officer in the newly established Illinois National Guard and appoint him to the Governor's own staff? Happy to do it for an old family friend, the Governor said.

McCormick returned to Chicago a colonel. He had a uniform tailored and bought a pair of colonel's eagle insignia. In February he boarded the liner *Adriatic* in New York for England. Aboard also was Amie. On March 10, 1915, the new colonel and Amie walked into the parish registry office of fashionable St. George's Hanover Square in London. Amie's sister Ida, Mrs. Arthur Small, was with them as matron of honor. The best man was a British army officer, Major H. Maitland Kersey who, as London agent for a Canadian shipping line, had been helpful to McCormick. There Amie and Bert were married, he giving his address as the London Ritz. She was at the genteel Stafford Hotel around the corner. One year and four days had passed since the divorce decree. The Adams appeal, a potential trap, was defused quietly six weeks later. The Chicago Hearst society editor commented on the marriage: "Friends were not surprised. When they went to England on the same ship, society made up its mind that a long-planned wedding was not far off." Kate burst into a flaming rage. She rewrote her will, removing her son Robert and blaming Amie for entrapment. For the remainder of her life, Kate never opened her heart to Amie. One cruel day, Cissy told Kate: "You ruined your husband and your older son. Do you want to ruin this one also?"

Bert did not return the $50,000 to his mother. In an act that underlined the marriage as a declaration of independence from her he spent the $50,000 on two necklaces of fine pearls and gave them to his bride. Amie wore pearls from morning until night every day for the rest of her life.

Twelve Yale alumni who had been members with Rubberfoot in the Scroll and Key sent a handsome wedding gift, a three-handled silver loving cup engraved with the society emblem and their names. Among the donors was Joseph B. Thomas, Jr. He was to come again into the Colonel's life.

McCormick had yet to become concerned with how the Medill dynasty at The Tribune would be carried into the fourth generation. Had he early taken that responsibility upon himself, he would not have delayed marriage until 35 and then married a childless woman of 43. At that time his brother Medill had one child, a daughter; Cousin Joe had three children, all girls, and was unlikely to have more, such being the solid ice state of that marriage. Cousin Cissy had Felicia and was tied to the Count for who knew how long. In those days, girls could be ignored when allocating leadership. Where was Grandfather's dream of a dynasty?

* * * * *

In London the American wife of Lord Essex took McCormick to lunch with Prime Minister Herbert Asquith. She wanted her fellow American to tell Asquith about public opinion in the United States about the war. McCormick reported the "small element known as society" was strongly pro-Ally, but the bulk of the nation was inclined to be critical of all nations involved, and Americans born in Germany or of German ancestry were "naturally pro-German." The report surprised Asquith. He replied that his government's moves toward home rule in Ireland, its efforts to improve living conditions and the reduced parliamentary power of the House of Lords entitled it to American support.

McCormick came away with an admiration for Asquith, reminded of his grandfather's description of Lincoln as a "patient, comprehending politician confronted with jealousy, hate and distrust." McCormick noted that, although Asquith was said to be a heavy drinker, his consumption at lunch was modest. The Prime Minister said he would try to help McCormick to visit the British troops on the front and sent him to talk with the foreign minister, Sir Edward Grey. It was McCormick's turn to be surprised. He had looked upon a British foreign minister as a duplicate of an American secretary of state—an important politician who depended upon his second secretary, a career man, to gather information and make decisions—but he found Grey expertly informed and exercising in foreign affairs the powers of an American president. Grey said negotiations to preserve peace failed because Germany and Austria refused to consider any compromise.

Winston Churchill, first lord of the admiralty, invited McCormick to lunch, smoked cigars and drank heavily without, McCormick noted, any effect. McCormick mentioned that Churchill and his own elder brother, Medill, had been classmates at Harrow. No, Churchill said, their years differed. McCormick praised Churchill for his "master stroke" in having the British fleet mobilized the day war began. McCormick said he planned to go to France, cross through the front lines into Germany as had a Tribune cartoonist, John McCutcheon, and then continue on to Russia. Impossible, Churchill said. Later McCormick learned he could have gone from France to Switzerland and then to Germany but to progress on to Russia he would have had to go through Sweden, which was "not practical" so early in spring.

McCormick called on Lord Northcliffe, Britain's most powerful publisher, owner of The Times for the elite, of The Daily Mail for the civil servants and of The Mirror for everyone else. In the afternoon there was The Evening News with race results and the day's goriest murder trial. The most powerful man in England, people called him. Joe Patterson already had visited Northcliffe. Joe wanted to know about the tabloid Mirror, a new kind of publication which Joe thought would do well in New York City. He made such an impression on the press lord that a few days later when Joe was arrested as a spy by the German army in conquered Belgium, it was Northcliffe who arranged for his freedom. Joe's time with Northcliffe was to lead to crucial changes in the

135

lives of the cousins and give New Yorkers a bright newspaper.

McCormick, in his turn with Northcliffe, talked at length about the evils of propaganda and censorship. All warring nations imposed tight restrictions on gathering news and barred newspapermen from the front. Northcliffe said many government reports about atrocities were false and McCormick agreed, reporting Joe had found them so in Belgium. McCormick said he hoped to see for himself, with Asquith's promised help.

At a dinner party McCormick told a young English woman of his desire to visit the front. She wrote a note for him to take to the British commander in France, Sir John French, introducing McCormick and asking the Commander to help him. McCormick put the note in a pocket and forgot it.

In a cabled dispatch to The Tribune, McCormick reported: "I am entirely safe in saying that Great Britain will never make peace until utterly defeated or until Germany evacuates Belgium and pays Belgium compensation."

When no permit came from Asquith, McCormick decided to go to Paris and try from there. U-boats had stopped daylight channel traffic so McCormick and Amie crossed by night. In Paris McCormick met with the foreign minister, Theophile Delcasse, an old friend of his father. The Frenchman said America, a republic, certainly must side with France, a republic, against Germany, an empire. He did not mention the vital help France gave to our colonies during our war of independence, but somehow the deed came forward in McCormick's mind. The minister told McCormick about German atrocities but McCormick said the American public doubted the truth of such stories. The startled minister said McCormick must go to Arras and see for himself the destroyed cathedral; he would telegraph the French commander there.

A French officer advised McCormick not to wear his new uniform as an Illinois National Guard colonel during his visit to the trenches. Having brought no civilian day clothing, he combined army breeches with a waistcoat, jacket and an automobile cap, presenting, he commented, "the fine likeness of a racehorse trainer."

McCormick rode a train to Calais, was arrested for being a newspaperman in a closed area but soon was cleared to proceed to the regional French command where he was welcomed, the message from the foreign minister having arrived. The minister ordered that McCormick be escorted to Arras one hour away, be shown the German atrocities and be returned.

Early the next morning a courteous French officer and a sullen driver collected McCormick in an enormous limousine. A cold drizzle chilled the driver, unprotected in the open front seat, while the passengers were warm and dry in the enclosed rear seat. The driver drove badly. "These drivers," the officer muttered. "Just because they owned the automobile before the war, they think they own it now." McCormick laughed but the officer saw no humor. Nearing Arras, the driver said he would not proceed if the Germans were shelling the road and stopped on a ridge three miles from town. Shells were landing in town but not on the road so the car sped down the hill. Sixty. Seventy. Eighty miles an hour. McCormick remarked no shell could catch up with them but what would happen if one burst just in front of the car?

As soon as the car reached Arras, watchful Germans unsuccessfully sought it with shells, assuming such cars carried only generals and other important people. An officer took McCormick to the hospital and to the shattered city hall and cathedral. McCormick picked up a piece of broken stone and put it in his pocket, remarking that the stone buildings of French towns provided excellent protection from enemy guns and shells. The officer apologized that on the return the car could not go up the hill as fast as it came down. McCormick expressed his gratitude. Arriving safely back at headquarters, he was told that while he had been at Arras a shell had killed ten French soldiers and, just outside the town, French soldiers had used bayonets to clear Boche—the usual French term for German soldiers—from a trench.

McCormick told the general that Russians would ask him about the French 75. "Have you seen any?" the general asked. "Not one," McCormick said. "Tell that to the Russians," the general said. "That will show them how well we conceal our gun positions."

McCormick recorded that although he passed through an army of 200,000 men, he had seen only 2,000, so well were they kept out of sight of Germans. He noted that German tan uniforms blended with the mud while the French blue and gray could be plainly seen from afar.

McCormick went on to the British headquarters to ask if permission to visit British forces at the front had arrived from London. None had. He produced the note given him by the young English woman. Miracle! Field Marshal Sir John French invited

137

McCormick to dine and appointed as escorts for a thorough visit to the lines a Coldstream Guards major, Charles Grant, one of seven survivors in a company of 230, and Lord Brooke, a colonel and veteran of three wars, son of the Earl of Warwick and the Countess, known in London society, the Colonel later noted, as Babbling Brooke.

McCormick admired the Field Marshal for before the war having gone on his own back and forth across Belgium and northern France to learn about the countryside in which a war probably would be fought, for resigning as chief of staff rather than to force home rule on Ulster and for having supported his sister, a militant suffragette.

Brooke and Grant, in turn, took McCormick along the front. At an observation post, Grant stopped to instruct a newly arrived officer. Shells fell. McCormick thought all should seek shelter but the Briton continued the lesson "as though in a school room."

"I was very much afraid," McCormick recalled after the war. "I did not resist by a very large margin my desire to ask my conductor to move to a safe place. This confession is not easy to make, but is put down with the hope that other boys will be instructed in courage as I never was. I never did learn to enjoy the crash of shells nor was I overwhelmed with a desire to rush into a shower of machine gun fire. But I never again approached the point of disgracing myself on the firing line. Physical courage varies with the individual but it can be improved, like piano playing and polite conversation, and is a more desirable accomplishment for a man than either. We in America have got to teach courage and not cowardice."

McCormick left the British army "very much in its debt, uplifted by the association with men who sacrifice themselves to their country." He noted, "I had been in the company of very gallant gentlemen."

At Ypres, McCormick collected another stone and dined with the British corps commander, General Sir Douglas Haig, becoming aware of staff jealousies and noticing disapprovingly that noble officers used their title rather than their rank. Haig sent McCormick to Calais in the Field Marshal's own car. Such wonders had the young woman's letter wrought! "What was her source of power?" McCormick asked. The young woman, he was told, was "the daughter of a hundred earls."

Back in Paris, McCormick called on the Russian ambassador to

France and collected an official document permitting him to enter Russia and also a box, "big enough to use as a seat," filled, he was told, with secret signals for the British fleet to be used when the British and Russian fleets joined in the Black Sea or Bosphorus. McCormick may have surmised a joint action by Britain and Russia was planned. British troops did land at the Dardanelles, hoping to enter central Europe by the back door or, as Churchill was to say in the next war, the soft underbelly.

McCormick drew from a bank a thousand gold sovereigns to add to his English and American letters of credit. He and Amie boarded the Kaisar-i-Hind, bound for Malta on its way to Suez and India. At Gibralter, all non-Britons were kept below deck. McCormick ever after prized a photograph of a British warship he took through his cabin porthole. He also treasured the memory of a little girl who, when greeted, would reply, "No, no, my dear fellow." McCormick asked why. That, she said, was the way her older sister greeted her male friends. McCormick was amused at the embarrassment of some young army wives who had been having a happy time with young officers going to India when their husbands unexpectedly came aboard at Gibraltar.

The McCormicks traveled by freighter from Malta to Greece. At the Athena Palace Hotel in Athens, McCormick asked that the Russian ambassador's box be placed in the hotel safe but on reaching his room found the box had been carried there, the proprietor explaining he could not be responsible for "Mrs. Rockefeller McCormick's jewelry." "The story preceded me all the way to Russia," the Colonel remembered, "and whatever danger it brought from robbers, it freed us of all suspicion of secret service and spy work." In Salonika, a hotel concierge named Charley told McCormick he never should present his passport, only his calling card, thereby impressing authorities with his importance. McCormick tipped him generously; Charley sent word ahead on the concierge network; everywhere the McCormicks were well received.

A train carried the McCormicks into Serbia. Typhoid was ravaging that country and coaches were disinfected so heavily that the McCormicks retreated to a platform whenever possible. The Crown Prince of Serbia, traveling in a private car, did not invite the McCormicks to share his lunch. "Discourteous," McCormick judged. The McCormicks had brought their own basket of bread, wine, sausage and cheese. McCormick kept the basket as a souvenir.

Because of the epidemic, Bulgaria would not allow passengers from Serbia to leave the train at Sofia, but McCormick, wanting to see something of the city, slipped from the train. A policeman ordered him back and "a somewhat difficult controversy ensued." A Bulgarian doctor, summoned to interpret, recognized McCormick as a former classmate at Northwestern. "At the time Northwestern was a small school but there are those who love it," the Colonel later commented. Amie recognized in Sofia a small man with lemon-colored hair as one she had seen now and then in Salonika. He followed all the way to Russia, never speaking a word to the McCormicks, "nor causing us any annoyance." Who was he? The Colonel never learned.

In Bucharest the McCormicks were entertained by the American minister, a Chicagoan, Charles J. Vopicka, but they did not meet Rumania's Queen Marie "or her husband whose name I forget." McCormick did meet the Queen after the war when she came to America "in the impossible attempt to get money out of Coolidge; she should have waited for the New Deal."

Leaving Rumania, McCormick was insulted by a group of men who, in the diner, mocked his wife. McCormick had lunch sent to their compartment and, on arriving at the Russian border, reported the incident. The Russian officials paraded the passengers but the mockers had left the train.

Arriving in Kiev, McCormick sent a telegram to St. Petersburg asking if he should deliver the ambassador's box to Odessa, the Russian naval headquarters. Bring it to St. Petersburg, he was told. On arriving in the Russian capital, he delivered the box to the assistant minister of foreign affairs whose wife, a San Franciscan, was an old friend of Amie. McCormick never did learn for certain the contents of the box.

The next day, Foreign Minister Serghei Sazonov received Colonel McCormick of the National Guard and won his admiration by his thorough knowledge of European and American affairs, including the recent Republican victory in the Chicago mayoral election. The Minister spoke strongly of Russia's desire for trade with America, saying Russia hoped never again to come under German commercial domination. McCormick was convinced Russia would favor American businessmen but "letters or drummers with suitcases of samples and cigars would not suffice." American business, he concluded, must establish permanent agencies in Russia if it were to enter "the largest market in the world." He was fascinated by the Minister's aide, a member of the Orlov family which had been important at court since the time of Peter the Great and, McCormick remembered, had been involved in the death of the husband of Catherine the Great.

He also came away with an appointment to be received by the Czar at the palace of Tsarskoye Selo 15 miles south of the city. The "subterfuge" was producing results. The court chamberlain sent word through the American ambassador that McCormick should attire himself in white tie and tails, which the Colonel, remembering his father's ambassadorial days in Russia, had brought with him from Chicago, and travel on the one o'clock train. Security was strict on the train, the conductor moving through the cars preceded and followed by gendarmes. Other gendarmes were stationed every 100 yards along the track and saluted the train as it passed but sentries further out in the snow did not. McCormick did not think the precautions reflected any threat to the regime.

At the station, an imperial footman in red with gold eagles on his collar spotted McCormick by his tall silk hat and led him to a brougham. McCormick, with his newspaperman's interest in customs and costumes, decided the coachman turned his own hat side ways to identify his passenger as not royal. The palace gates stood open. McCormick thought the building similar to our White House but larger. Police saluted as McCormick walked up 12 steps. An official with a "headdress big as a sofa cushion" opened the door; a footman took his coat, then his hat. McCormick was aware of "several heavy beards" as he was ushered to the waiting room. Clocks showed 1:40. The appointment was set for 2 o'clock. The chamberlain had arranged things well.

McCormick studied the room. He noted a portrait of a woman he assumed to be the Czarina, a fireplace in which the fire lately had burned out, a painting of a boy king being held high by a soldier in green, another of the little king at the top of a staircase being saluted, a painting of peasants harvesting grain, a watercolor of a steamship, a map of a crooked stream, an engraving of the Czar's father given by Parisian students, a pair of double-glazed French windows each with three thermometers: the outside registered eight degrees centigrade, the one between the double windows 12 degrees and the one in the room 15 degrees; a desk with two horse hooves, one with the usual shoe, the other with a sliding joint—apparently a humane contrivance which the Czar was investigating; a table with books about Reims, hydraulic engineering and military automobiles, a large egg-shaped decoration, a Turkish carpet, dark oak paneling.

A clock struck two. The inner door opened. Through it came two men, stiff and straight as oak timbers in scarlet, with many medals. "For a moment I felt as Marco Polo must have felt in the great and strange court of China," McCormick reported. One courtier said in English, "I cannot remember the exact year your father left us." Before McCormick could admit that he too had forgotten, the aide in the sofa cushion headdress made an announcement in Russian which McCormick assumed meant the Czar is waiting. No one moved. McCormick walked through the door alone.

The Czar, standing at a far window, came forward, hand outstretched, and said, "I am very pleased to meet you, Mr. McCormick," asked about McCormick's father and said he was gratified that an American newspaperman had come to seek the truth. McCormick replied he hoped he would be permitted to go to the extreme front and found significance in a remark by the Czar that the war had come upon Russia suddenly and unexpectedly. The Czar spoke English with "less of an accent than Britain's Edward VII." McCormick reported that the Czar's eyes were "the largest I have ever seen in a living mortal"; his thinning hair was slightly gray, his complexion healthy, his beard brushed wide in Slavic style, his olive jacket garnished with just one medal but many golden loops, his trousers of dark blue with red stripes, knee boots blackened but not shined.

A pretty girl came in—the Czar's daughter, McCormick later learned—and spoke a few words in Russian, "I am very sorry I must go now," the Czar said.

McCormick's earlier experience, his mother's rehearsal of going to Buckingham Palace, had taught him that no one turns his back on royalty, so he walked backwards to the door. It opened magically; he passed through; the door closed; he turned around and walked to the vestibule where he was helped with his hat, then coat. The brougham took him to the station in time for a snack before the 3:07 train. McCormick entered the station restaurant, marked four items on the Russian language menu at random and was pleased to find them to be, when they were served, a cheese sandwich, two kinds of caviar and a bottle of kvass, "upsetting, but suitable."

Joe Patterson had taken a movie cameraman on his trip to the Western front. His films, first of their kind, had drawn capacity audiences in Chicago and New York theaters. McCormick searched St. Petersburg for a cameraman, found a Kansan, Donald Thompson, and arranged for him to come along to the front as his aide. He equipped himself with a fur coat, rubber boots and a cot and, with the photographer, rode a train to the headquarters of the Russian commander-in-chief.

There, McCormick was met by a young Oriental-looking man named Dimitri Toundoutoff, a prince and a God to his people, the Kalmuks, who for 200 years had been loyal subjects of the Czar. He was under orders to stay with McCormick throughout the visit and tend to all his needs, a task he did with efficiency, courtesy and pleasure. McCormick's first official call was on the chief of staff, General Yanouskevich, who had been a classmate of the Czar at military school. The General showed the visitor, on a map, the Russian dispositions and proposed places along the 550-mile-long front which he might like to see. For many years, the Russian told him, Germany had planted German farm families at strategic places in Poland, building their houses with thick, windowless walls facing Russia and linking them by underground telephone to provide an "instant defense system" for Germany.

McCormick found at the field headquarters a dozen trains parked on sidings fanning out into the woods, providing offices and billets for the staff. There he was received by the Grand Duke Nicholas, commander-in-chief, 58 and six feet six, even taller than himself, McCormick noted, spare, blue eyes blazing from a thin face, a neatly trimmed beard below a steely mouth. He wore a dagger on his belt. His handshake had the firmness of a young athlete. He asked McCormick about the morale of the English and French armies. He introduced his brother, Grand Duke Peter, who, without rank, served as companion to the Commander. Later McCormick saw the brother sitting in the shade of a tree beside the headquarters train. The Commander came out of his car. The sun had moved onto his chair. Instantly the brother got up, ran to the chair and carried it into the shade. McCormick found the small act a sign of brotherly devotion.

"Jealousy," he commented, "is a microbe that knows no station. History and the experience of all of us tell the rarity of such spirit as I saw revealed."

McCormick was given a position ahead of all other colonels at the headquarters "as a compliment to America." His rank as colonel in the Illinois National Guard impressed the Russians excessively. Was not the Czar himself a colonel of the Guards? And of all Russian army units, was not the Guard foremost, its officers automatically advancing one rank when assigned to regular troops? The Guard supplied half of all high officers. Finns and Balts also held more high places than their numbers in the empire deserved.

A young aide, Dimitri Pavlovich, did not salute as McCormick was introduced. He was a lieutenant but also a grand duke. His uncle, the Commander-in-chief, reprimanded the young officer. "It did not lend to intimacy," the Colonel recalled.

The headquarters followed a formal routine. Officers assembled for lunch at 12:30 and dinner at 6:30, remaining standing until the Commander arrived. He kissed the chaplain's hand and shook hands with all officers he had not seen that day. The headquarters served the high officers red wine despite the wartime ban on sale of alcoholic drinks. Lieutenants were given wine bottles filled with milk. At his first lunch, McCormick poured Narzan water into his half-filled glass of claret until the Commander spoke loudly in French: "That you are doing is not good." A vision of his strict schoolmaster barking a reprimand popped into McCormick's head, but this was not a reprimand; the Commander merely was warning him that claret and Narzan water did not mix. After the meal, no officer departed before the Commander, who did not leave until all had finished eating. Tea was offered at breakfast, again at 5 p.m. and at 10 p.m.

Only once did McCormick see the Commander angry. Then he was fierce. He told McCormick, "I have a particular incident for you," and related that a 17-year-old Russian nurse was in a hospital with syphilis and peritonitis after being raped by an entire German raiding party. "Tell that to the world," the Commander ordered.

The Colonel found optimism about the war still high and faith in the invincibility of "the Russian steamroller" unshaken. In the first weeks of war the previous autumn, one Russian army of 200,000 men, led by Cossack cavalry, had rampaged into East Prussia, sending the Prussian landlords scurrying from their horizon-to-horizon estates to safety in Berlin. A second army of equal size was rolling northwest in a classic pincers movement to join the northern force on the east bank of the Vistula River, cutting off the rich provinces of East Prussia. The united force was to cross the river near Danzig and open a route to Berlin 150 miles away.

Austria, seeking quick territorial gains, had sent the best of its million soldiers northward toward Warsaw, hoping to wrest eastern Poland from a century of Russian rule, but the force was shattered by a third Russian army. The Austrians retreated into their homeland, abandoning the "invincible" fortress of Pyrzemysl and the provincial capital of Lemberg, and letting the Russian commander sleep in Francis Joseph's bed in the governor's palace. Cossacks romped after the Austrians into the Carpathian mountains. One more push and the Russians would break through into the Danube valley, Vienna would be within their grasp and, as promised by the Czar, Austria would be out of the war by Christmas. The Russian successes raised fears in Berlin and hopes in Paris. The Kaiser and his high command had rated France as an easier enemy than Russia and, seeking to deal with it quickly so Germany could concentrate its forces against the real enemy of Russia, had dispatched a million men through Belgium, bypassing the strong French defenses on the French-German border, and speeding down the straight military roads built by Napoleon to within 50 miles of Paris. The French government, seeing salvation only if the Russians could draw off German troops, appealed to the Russians to strike more fiercely at Germany instead of Austria. In an act of generosity rare among allies in wartime, the Czar ordered the Commander-in-chief to withdraw half of the forces so successfully pursuing the Austrians and turn them northwest against Germany even though, by then, German artillery and machine guns were slaughtering Cossack horsemen attacking with sabers and foot soldiers attacking with bayonets.

The Russian pincers, instead of closing on East Prussia, was being chewed up. German and Russian bodies by the thousands were ground into the shell-churned mud. The Kaiser, harassed by the nightmarish vision of Cossacks dashing along the streets hacking apart Berliners unable to escape, ordered that new troops marked for the final drive on Paris be sent east and also withdrew thousands of men from the dash to Paris. The shifts and counter shifts helped cost Russia a quick victory over Austria and Germany a quick victory over France.

All armies dug trenches and settled down for the winter, waiting for more men, more guns, more supplies. In five months the Czar had lost a million men, dead, wounded or captured — one fourth of its trained army. But from villages throughout the empire the first of another 11 million men were answering the call of the Czar and Mother Russia. For Siberian recruits to

reach the front meant a six to eight-week crawl on the single-track railroad, but by spring the Russian steamroller was ready again to roll. Ominously, the Russians were running out of weapons and ammunition. The command had planned for only a short war and brought limited supplies from England and France. Now the Baltic and Black Sea ports were blockaded and Russia's own few factories could make rifles and shells by the thousands instead of the millions which would be needed. Some artillery crews were sent to the front with only enough shells to fire one barrage and could expect to receive no more. The Commander-in-chief almost daily wrote telegrams and letters to the minister of war, General Vladimir Sukhomlinov, but the Minister, for many years a bitter rival of the Commander, did nothing.

Of these troubles, the headquarters officers told McCormick nothing. They seemed unworried he would learn the terrible truth for himself and sent him with his princely guide and Photographer Thompson by train to Warsaw and the battlefields, a privilege given to no other reporter.

McCormick expected Warsaw to be empty. No. Its streets bustled by day; at night the Moscow ballet performed in the opera house, and men filled dining clubs while their wives went from salon to salon playing bridge. McCormick thought the women were shirking until, visiting hospitals the next day, he met again last night's bridge players, now tending the wounded. "When I saw a woman sitting at the bedside of a dying Mongolian youth expending a passion of tenderness to save that strange life, I realized I had come upon something that was worth traveling 10,000 miles to see," McCormick recorded. He urged American Red Cross officers to come to Warsaw to see how Poles had created hospitals overnight. Their need was great; 30,000 wounded Russians had been carried in from one battlefield. McCormick met a wounded Pole who had worked in a Chicago steel mill. "Chicago will welcome you back," McCormick said. The soldier replied he never could go back and pulled away his sheet to reveal two short stumps. "Over his face came an expression which I would not describe if I could," McCormick wrote. McCormick found most harrowing the soldiers blinded by gas. He was told he could photograph an eyeless victim. The man would not know. "Nothing could have made me do it," McCormick said. "It is enough that his expression is seared upon my memory forever."

The headquarters asked him to photograph an earless soldier

named Ignatoff Panatsuk. His German captors, he said, had snipped off his ears with scissors trying to make him reveal Russian positions.

The command supplied McCormick with a brake-less car and a very small driver with a madness for traveling fast. The driver took him more than 500 miles to various fronts with just one accident—the car knocked over a carriage with two officers who surprisingly spoke not one angry word.

The command's chief aviator, a rich young Russian who had learned to fly as a hobby, asked McCormick if many young rich Americans flew. McCormick replied no. "Why?" the aviator asked. "Because it is considered too dangerous," McCormick answered.

One day while McCormick was in a front line trench, a Russian soldier unknowingly exposed himself to a German sniper. One shot killed him. McCormick raised a periscope to study the German lines 50 yards away. A sharpshooter's bullet smashed the glass. Thompson shoved his camera above the trench and quickly ground out a few feet of film. McCormick wished he had a recorder to take home the sound of the bullets splattering around the camera. He also must have wished for some protection to his head.

A captain invited McCormick to lunch and led him to a dugout at the end of a cross trench. There a feast awaited—caviar, sardines, radishes, cold meat, canned lobster, cake and tea—choice of weak or strong, sweet or plain. A soldier played the accordion while two others danced, one pretending to be a woman. All that, after 50 days of front-line war. McCormick mused: "Poor, patient Ivan, putting on a show for a visitor from America."

Back at regimental headquarters that night the band played "My Country 'Tis of Thee." The officers all stood. McCormick tried to speak his thanks but his feelings demanded "vigorous use of the handkerchief." He went to sleep "wishing for companions such as these in event that, in event that —"

Back at command headquarters, McCormick attended the trial of a soldier exposed as an Austrian who had enlisted under false identity. The army prosecutor said the man must be a spy; what other reason could he have for joining the Russian army and fighting against his own county? The judges found the evidence inconclusive and decreed no execution but did send the Austrian to a prison camp.

McCormick attended a church service for 4,000 soldiers lined up in an orchard. The Grand Duke sat astride a horse. As two priests sang the service, the soldiers moved their lips in unison.

During a night battle a Russian searchlight, called a "projector," caught a German soldier moving alone in open country. McCormick waited for the unfortunate man to be shot down but no Russian fired and the man was allowed to return to a trench. McCormick asked the commander why fire was withheld. The commander replied, "What would be gained by killing the poor man?" The incident led McCormick to note a strange psychology in the Russian army. "Their tradition is founded upon an ability to undergo a greater butchery than the enemy," he commented, "and yet they would not take a life clearly forfeited. I do not believe any other nationality would have allowed the enemy to escape."

One night as McCormick drove back from a front, a deer bounded through a woods thick with hungry infantrymen. Fresh meat! But no one fired. Russian soldiers were trained to fire only when ordered. The deer bounded on.

The Czar came to Lemberg to congratulate the troops. His retinue commandeered all cars, so McCormick's trio rode a troop train. McCormick saw soldiers pass cigarettes to Austrian prisoners and hand sugar to children waiting beside the tracks, even to two girls who, hand in hand, sang a pretty song not knowing it was the enemy anthem. At night the station floor was solid with sleeping refugees. Thompson started to take a flash picture but the station master stopped him, wishing sleepers not to be disturbed.

In the morning the Prince found a car and the three started for Lemberg. The car broke down. An imperial car stopped and officers offered a lift. McCormick never had seen such a luxurious vehicle, with two armchairs and a collapsible top. In Lemberg, McCormick came upon the chief of staff shopping for a gift for his wife. In the evening, McCormick went to a cabaret to hear a singer with an American accent. He found no lack of liquor.

McCormick followed the Russian advance into the Carpathian mountains, where so many Austrians surrendered that the Russians detached only one man to guard each 100 prisoners. McCormick was told about an officer being sharply reprimanded because he arrived with ten more prisoners than he had been given at the start. McCormick watched the Czar present medals to Cossacks who had repulsed a Prussian force four times their size. He saw Russian steam bath wagons, to counter lice and typhus, stationed about every five miles, and traveling kitchens with great caldrons of ever-simmering stew ladled out to anyone, civilian or soldier.

McCormick watched Russian infantrymen scramble up a steep hill pursuing Austrians hurriedly dug in along the crest. The Russians were paying a high price. McCormick asked the commander why he did not use his artillery to demolish the Austrian positions before sending in the infantry. "Shells are in short supply; men are not," the officer replied. On following days McCormick saw Russian infantry being sent into attack without rifles. The soldiers were expected to arm themselves during the day with rifles of fallen comrades.

A Cossack battery gave a party for the visitor from afar. Each horseman rode his mount through a tight maze and across ditches and picked up with the point of his saber a bag of straw representing an enemy soldier. Two men riding one horse picked up a comrade. A rider stood on a galloping animal and somersaulted. A much-decorated sergeant repeated all these feats with a saber in his mouth. As a final test, the riders tied the stirrups beneath the horses and, holding on with their legs, lowered themselves and snatched handkerchiefs lying on the ground. As reward and encouragement their colonel had knotted five rubles in each handkerchief. No rider used spurs. Each Cossack tended his own horse. The dinner featured newly-caught fish and caviar. A chorus of 20 sang folk fables. The Cossack colonel invited McCormick to dance but McCormick declined and watched his host, the Cossack colonel, well past 65, dance young lieutenants off their feet. McCormick, in recording his visit, said Cossacks are sometimes described as untrained guerrillas. The truth, McCormick corrected, is that their tradition as frontiersmen and their long hereditary military organization and training from childhood make the Cossacks "a body of soldiers such as exists nowhere else in the world." The Cossacks were cruel. If a groom displeased, the rider might slash out with his sword, perhaps slicing off an ear. Americans, the Colonel sometimes said much later, never would understand the Russians.

The early days of war had created a belief that large howitzers had made fortresses worthless. On the western front, Liege fell in ten days, Namur in two, Maugeuge in 14. On the eastern front, the retreating Austrian army left 120,000 in the fortress at Pyrzemysl. The advancing Russians swept around it, cut off supplies and brought about the surrender.

But the Russians still were holding their fortress of Ossowetz after three months of heavy German attack. Why? McCormick asked to see for himself. The fort, built in 1888 and rebuilt in 1910, stood on a ridge in a 40-mile-wide marsh. McCormick arrived before the early morning bombardment began. The commander, a Balt named Miller, told him that before the first German attack, the Germans sent an envoy to offer the commander half a million rubles and a home in Germany if he would surrender the fort. If he refused, the envoy said, the Germans would begin in 48 hours the heaviest bombardment ever mounted. Miller answered by shooting the envoy as a spy. The Germans rained 250,000 shells on the fort and sent infantry in waves. The fort stood.

A modern fortress, the commander explained, is not a place to save a soldier from contact with the enemy but to make a small defending force equal to a larger attacking force. The defense must fight not in the fortress but outside it although within reach of the fort's guns. When troops retreat behind the walls, he said, all is lost. Then the enemy can concentrate its attack. In truth, he said, infantry in the trenches are better off than men within the fort. The infantry must face rifle bullets, grenades and bayonets, but the men in the fort must withstand the crash of heavy shells. In the fort or out, the commander went on, there is no substitute for training. No untrained soldiers, he said, can be expected to stop a bayonet attack nor stand up to a bombardment.

To gain entrance to the fortress, McCormick pledged not to reveal any military secrets. He wrote no description of Ossowetz but he did compile directions for building a perfect fortress. Forts, he said, should be built on main lines of communication—railroads, highways and rivers. The most easily defended position is a wooded ridge behind a stream running through a marsh. Mud and woods are a defender's best natural aids. The modern fortress is not one heavy concrete or stone building but a series of connected earth embankments, each enclosing an area up to one square mile. The embankment, about 40 feet high, should be topped with a 10-foot concrete wall painted green. Outside the embankment is a spike-filled moat; inside is a sunken road for vehicles and a railroad to distribute supplies quickly and safely along the entire length. The interior should, for camouflage, be planted with evergreen trees which do not lose their leaves in winter. Scattered through the woods are five times as many gun-pits as the fortress has guns, allowing guns to be moved frequently. During attack or siege a few guns are placed in concrete bunkers and bigger bunkers are provided as refuge for reserve troops during shelling. During gas attack, the bunkers are sealed and the men breathe oxygen from bottles. Outside each fort is a maze of trenches and barbed wire entanglements. There the defenders fight.

McCormick summed up: "It is taken as a matter generally admitted that in the event of war if any military power should obtain command of the sea, it would be impossible for the United States to hold our coastal states. Our object would be to hold the enemy away from the center of our nation during the years it would take to organize a sufficient force to retake the lost provinces." To help save the heartland McCormick proposed that America build forts at Albany, Buffalo, Pittsburgh, Atlanta, Vicksburg, Houston and in passes of the Sierra Nevadas and Rocky Mountains.

McCormick returned to St. Petersburg and went on to Moscow. He found the old section squalid but the modern part resembling Paris. He wondered why the Russians had not melted down the many French cannon captured from Napoleon which decorated Red Square outside the Kremlin and concluded the Russians are not factory minded. He attended the ballet twice. One prima ballerina was oversize and a poor dancer but the crowd applauded her loudly. McCormick was puzzled. Why the ovation? "She's a mistress of the Czar," a Russian explained. McCormick met the chief of ordnance and told him that he had seen motor vehicles in bad condition. The chief offered to make him a general and commander of the motor corps but friends warned McCormick that if he accepted the position many Russians who had welcomed him would become jealous and plot against him. He declined. He wondered at the power of the mad monk Rasputin. The Colonel reckoned that the monk's message—a person must sin before he can be forgiven—would find a welcome audience and helped explain the dissolute behavior of court women, including, gossip said, the Czarina herself.

So back to St. Petersburg to say goodbye. The governor-general's wife, a princess, told him that she, the governor-general and their two children were in Germany at a hot springs taking the cure when the war began. German police arrested the Russians' servants and ordered the governor-general put under room arrest. The princess called her cousin, daughter-in-law of the

Kaiser, who, incensed at police treatment of a relative, even though an enemy, said she would speak to the Kaiser and come immediately in her carriage to set things right. A half hour later, the royal daughter-in-law telephoned, most distraught. She reported the Kaiser said her Russian relatives must stay under arrest. The family escaped on their own to Denmark and sailed across the Baltic and home. One of the sons tried to poison Rasputin and, failing that, shot the monk and threw his body in the River Neva, only to have the ice bring it ashore. The body was buried at Tsarskoye Selo and daily the Czarina paused there to pray.

Saying goodbye to the Commander-in-chief, McCormick asked if he could come again the next year. Certainly, the Commander-in-chief said, adding, "or the year after." The comment convinced McCormick he was correct in surmising that the world was only at the beginning of a long war. Despite defeats while McCormick was in Moscow, Russian commanders spoke of eventual victory. McCormick left Russia with no suspicion that the Russian army would lose ten million men, killed, wounded or captured, and rebel, that the Czar and his family would be murdered. An army band, ordered to salute McCormick with the American national anthem, played "A Hot Time in the Old Town Tonight."

At the Ritz Hotel the Colonel noticed a "grande cocotte" dining variously with a grand duke, a general, an admiral and a bishop, all apparently, McCormick noted, seeking a sin from which to repent. On his departure from the hotel she was in the line of employees waiting to be tipped. McCormick told her, "We have not met." She replied, "No, you are on your honeymoon, but the next time you come. . ."

The Commander-in-chief gave him a letter to carry to Marshal Joffre. The governor-general gave him a permit authorizing him to quit Russia without his baggage being opened and the British ambassador appointed McCormick a king's messenger to ease him through British borders.

In Helsinki he admired the handsome new railroad station and became a lifetime supporter of its architect, an original-minded Finn, Eliel Saarinen. A decade later, McCormick was to admire a radical design entered by Saarinen for Tribune Tower but, "as with first things," there was a "defect" and another design was chosen. Saarinen went on to "profit from his originality" and to build structures that McCormick thought handsome.

A train carried the Colonel and Amie northward through Finland, into Lapland, across the top of the Gulf of Bothnia, home of Lapps and reindeer, and slowly south through Swedish forests, stopping at meal time for complicated smorgasbord at restaurants in the habit of the early American western trains and Harvey houses.

The American minister to Sweden, Chicagoan Ira Nelson Morris, had, on his appointment, asked McCormick to have The Tribune please cease referring to him as a pig butcher. He explained he had sold all of his stock in the Morris Meat Packing House and had become director of the Art Institute, the Opera and the First National Bank. McCormick had so instructed Managing Editor Beck and the story was so written, but the copy editor composed a headline: "Pork Packer Appointed Minister." Regardless, the Minister met the McCormicks at the station and took them to his ministerial palace for a week until the Colonel's sinus ailment cleared. McCormick saw the royal palace and Stockholm's "pink seals"—Swedes swimming naked. He was amazed how quickly he accepted the custom as natural. Sweden was neutral and, while he was there, gave asylum to a French army deserter who had escaped from prison and stowed away to Sweden. McCormick admired hotels which had glassed over their courtyards, providing year-round gardens. He rated Stockholm the most beautiful city he ever had seen but later explained that, at the time, 1915, Chicago had not yet beautified its lakefront.

In the Norwegian capital, then called Christiania, now Oslo, a friend took him to see King Haakon, chosen to preside over the newly established monarchy at the insistence of his father-in-law, Britain's King Edward VII who, the Colonel wrote, had told Norwegians that the creation of a republic would be "very unfortunate." McCormick also met the Arctic explorer, Fridtjof Nansen, who had built a ship which rose as ice closed in. He had planned to drift across the North Pole, but the current carried him away from it. Nansen and one other set off on foot. He did not reach the Pole but he wrote a book which, McCormick remembered, made him rich. McCormick sought out another Arctic explorer, Roald Amundsen, who later was first to reach the South Pole. McCormick then syndicated Amundsen's account. The Norwegians succeeded where the British explorer, Captain Robert Scott, perished because, McCormick reasoned, the Norwegians traveled with dog sleds, killed the dogs one by one, and ate the flesh and fed it also to remaining dogs. The British used ponies and had to carry fodder. As a result, men and beasts starved and froze. Three years later Amundsen came to the front in France to see McCormick but was stopped at division head-quarters. To go further, he was told, would be "too dangerous." The ruling amused the bold Amundsen.

The McCormicks crossed the North Sea from Bergen to Brit-ain, sighting one periscope. As king's messenger, McCormick left the ship before the British. "An extreme pleasure," the Colonel commented later.

In London he lunched again with Prime Minister Asquith, For-eign Minister Grey and other cabinet members. The Foreign Minister said he saw no solution to the Serbian problem, which had set off the war, because Bulgaria wanted land west of the Bosphorus which Britain had promised to the Russians. McCormick called on Lord Kitchener and found him a shell, his mind wandering, retained as field marshal because of his reputa-tion and because his staff had learned they could govern in his name. Later the government, "to get rid of him," McCormick said, sent him to Russia, a mine or torpedo sank his ship and the no-longer-wanted hero drowned. McCormick called on old school-mates—the war already was taking its toll—and on that Chicago friend from his youth, beautiful Hazel Martyn, by then Lady Lavery. In Paris he delivered Russian Commander-in-chief Grand Duke Nicholas' letter to Marshal Joffre at his headquar-ters at Compiegne where later the armistice was signed.

The McCormicks came home on a Canadian Pacific liner via Montreal. On the way, the wife of an English merchant captain confided to him and to the ship's captain that she had seen a tor-pedo churn past the liner. During the voyage McCormick dictated his first book, "With the Russian Army." It had a moral: America's situation in 1915 was similar to that of Britain a year earlier when Germany invaded Belgium, forcing unpre-pared Britain to go to war to protect its own independence. The British liberals, in power for seven years, had been so busy reor-ganizing taxes and dealing with Irish rebels and Welsh non-con-formists that they had neglected the army, but they had main-tained the fleet, giving Britain an advantage the United States did not have. British government parsimony, like American gov-ernment parsimony, had provided for a poorly equipped army of only 150,000 but, unlike the American Congress, Britain had kept the units intact and not distributed them around the country as "pie" for congressmen. McCormick said Britain, as the United States, found false security in its water barrier. The heroic

Kitchener had asked for a million volunteers, but government propaganda about false victories led British people to think the war was being won without their joining the forces, and let workmen retain their peacetime methods to limit production. When Lord Northcliffe used his Times to reveal blunders, the government prosecuted him and people burned his papers. A judge supported the publisher. Only the British, McCormick complimented, have the non-political protection of an independent court. David Lloyd George assumed the unpopular task of changing British opinion but, until the nation could produce, train and equip an army of the size needed, Britain would continue to send men to unnecessary death in France. Let America note: Britain survived its lack of foresight because of its navy. In 1915 American had no such protection.

"At least three naval powers can wipe us off the seas," McCormick said.

He phrased his book "not as a wise man should with an eye to sales, but to serve my country. When the great debouch comes to us, a million men must fall while we learn lessons we could have so easily learned in peace. If my book serves to minimize the crime of unpreparedness, what matter be a few kopecks?" Repeating an act of his mother, he sent the Czar $1,000 to help care for wounded Russian soldiers. He also sent a copy of his book to the Czar. Years later American travelers told him his book still lay on the desk where the Czar had placed it.

McCormick combined with another author in writing a doomsday novel, "1917," in which German forces invade the United States and reach the Mississippi River before being stopped. The book urged the government to build a big navy, a course being advocated by schoolmate Franklin Roosevelt, navy undersecretary. In every phase of life McCormick said Americans must learn courage.

The nightmare of so many soldiers shot through the forehead while peering over the top of the trench haunted McCormick. He had noted that every infantryman carried a small spade—the army called it an entrenching tool. If the handle were detachable and if the spade were curved a little more so that it matched a man's forehead, then a cotton webbing belt could be passed through a slot at each side of the spade, enabling the soldier to wear the spade upside down, protecting the forehead. No army took up the suggestion, opting instead for steel helmets, but the United States government gave McCormick a patent, his first.

Thirty more, mostly concerned with improving printing presses, were to follow from that inventive McCormick mind.

By the time McCormick reached home, the Germans had turned loose their massed guns. On one 15-mile front, 700,000 shells fell in 24 hours on 16,000 Russian soldiers. In the morning, only 600 Russians survived. The Czar marched up 40,000 more. The guns churned up earth and flesh until only 6,000 men could move. They ran, many dropping their rifles. For two more years the Russians sent men against guns. Then soldiers and their families rebelled against the slaughter. The Czar abdicated, handing the jeweled crown to a cousin, who within a few hours rejected it, and the power fell to a provisional government which proved to be more provisional than governmental. The new leaders asked for peace and gave up a 200-mile-wide strip of Russia. Anarchy spread through the land. Out of the turmoil came Joseph Stalin, who lashed the Russian people back into obedience with a fierceness unknown since the days of Ivan the Terrible.

* * * * *

The Colonel last saw Grand Duke Nicholas on the Riviera, at Cap d'Antibes. The Russian needed money. The Duchess asked the Colonel if he could help sell her jewels. The Colonel did sell a large yellow diamond, gift from the Sultan of Turkey, but could find no buyer for a pink diamond big as a man's thumbnail valued at a half million dollars.

9. A Cold Wilderness — A Hot Border
1915—1916

The first snows of 1915 were sweeping down from the Arctic into Canada's north woods. Since spring Carter had been scouting the always green forests along the north shore of the broad St. Lawrence. For a while he thought the Trinity River area might be acceptable. The trees were there, the waterfalls for power were there, but Carter decided the river was too shallow to carry logs from the winter storage areas deep in the interior to the coast. He moved on to Rocky River, appropriately named for the rounded crags which rise hippo-like from the water. A small falls less than a mile inland could provide power and beyond two miles of rapids the river widened to form natural log-holding areas. On September 5 Carter sent word to McCormick he had found the right place. Carter had proved himself a diligent scout, an expert woodsman, but McCormick wanted to see for himself the condition of the river and the richness of the timberlands. He had learned that some woodsmen composed detailed reports, almost tree by tree, while sitting safely and snugly in camp and letting their imagination fight its way through the wilderness. Paper was selling for $140 a ton—four times the pre-war cost—and the prospect was for even higher prices. The war was increasing newspaper sales and demand for paper was starting to outrun supply. Action was needed urgently.

McCormick and Amy—he had dropped the French spelling of Amie—packed their warmest Russian clothes and met Carter and Mrs. Carter in Quebec. The four clambered onto the Anticosti Island mail boat, the *Savoy*, a majestic name for a tub with only two cabins and eight berths. Carter brought tents, supplies and a woodsman, Arthur Parent, to set up and tend the camp. The good ship *Savoy* dropped the five on the Rocky River shore October 8.

The wilderness was unchanged since the French explorer

159

Jacques Cartier first passed that way more than 350 years earlier and, shuddering, called it "the land God gave Cain." The only human habitation was an Indian log hut a mile along the shore. Carter had arranged with an Indian trapper who lived there, named Tibasse, to join the party. Parent set up the tents. The *Savoy* tooted and churned back into the St. Lawrence and plowed down the river. Until she returned, the five were alone. There was no way out, no way to send a message.

Early the next morning McCormick, Carter and Tibasse set off, carrying supplies and a canoe of birch bark over thin ribs of white cedar across three miles of rough rock to bypass the rapids and falls, then paddled for two days up the river and through a chain of lakes. A small hill a few miles from a large lake offered a view of the forests. On the shore was an Indian cabin. "Drop me here," McCormick said. "You go on to the point at the other end of the lake (some 10 miles distant) and I will hike up the hill and meet you there late this afternoon." McCormick set a course in a big arc which would take him deep into the woods and bring him back to the lake near the far point. He noted the compass reading and wrote it in a small notebook. He counted his strides. On each change of direction he recorded the number of strides and the new course. He studied the trees and liked what he saw. In early afternoon, as he was arching back toward the lake, snow fell, first lightly, next heavily, then so heavily that it pulled a white curtain tightly around him and covered his footprints before he could take a half dozen steps. McCormick knew if he continued in the arc, he would reach the lake. But then which way should he turn, left or right? If he chose wrongly. . .

There was just one route to take—back the way he had come. It was longer but he knew the way; he needed only to reverse his route, setting each compass course 180 degrees opposite, again counting the strides. At times the wilderness seemed strange; he thought he had strayed and was tempted to use his intuition and change the course. But no, he must follow his book. He strode on encouraged whenever he came to a path he had chopped through a thicket in the morning. Just before dark he came to the lake and the cabin. A dozen Indians sheltering there took him in and shared the evening meal. From that night on McCormick looked upon that dinner as the best he ever ate, although he did not ever learn the menu. In the morning the Indians rowed him to the camp Carter had established at the point. Carter had been awake all night, peering into the snow, shouting, piling wood on the fire,

160

patrolling the lake shore. He feared McCormick was lost in the woods.

Years later the Colonel warned people never to go into the woods alone. The best number, he said, is three. When lost and differing on which course to take, the three can vote. If one turns an ankle, the other two can carry HER out. Bring a dog only for company, the Colonel advised. A dog is content to be with its master and will stay with him or go with him but never lead him. On its own a dog has extraordinary homing ability. The Colonel told of a dog that was given by its owner at Rocky River to a woodsman and taken 40 miles up the St. Lawrence and then 30 miles by canoe and foot into the woods. When the new master was killed in a river accident, the dog found its way back to its previous master.

McCormick, Carter and Tibasse continued their patrol until McCormick saw for himself that Carter's estimates of the timberlands were correct. The two paddled downstream and portaged around the falls to the base camp. The sight alarmed them. One tent was a charred smudge in the new snow. What had happened? One wife, hoping to drive the chill from her bones, had fed extra logs into the tin stove, overheating it. The canvas smoked, then erupted. The woman fled to the other tent. Was she Mrs. McCormick or Mrs. Carter? The Colonel never did say.

The good ship *Savoy* returned. McCormick, Amy and Mrs. Carter boarded her but Carter decided to stay in the camp all winter and, with the help of the Indians and farmer-woodsmen from the south shore, prepare logs needed to build a pier in the spring. Ptarmigan and fish would dominate his diet. Indians could pluck a fish from the river and lakes, a deft feat McCormick never saw a white man perform. Nor could any Canadian or American ever take him, as did Tibasse, in a canoe through rapids without dumping him in the roiling icy water. McCormick liked everything about Rocky River except its name. "What ship captain," he asked Carter, "will come happily into a port with such a name? Call it Shelter Bay." For many years sailors looking at any good map saw a haven called Shelter Bay but should they go there, the rocky mounds still waited to smash an ignorant ship.

The expedition gave McCormick a deep appreciation for Indians and their ways. He thought the practice of allowing boys to leave their mothers only after they could handle a trap line demonstrated how customs can be an incentive to education. Tibasse became McCormick's favorite woods companion. The most courteous of men, he pulled branches aside for McCormick, gave him a strong hand over slippery rocks, pointed out where to put the next boot while crossing a bog. Sometimes McCormick thought Tibasse was a little too helpful. One day while coming home from a 14 mile hike McCormick thought he would teach the Indian a thing or two about moving quickly through the woods. His long legs let him cover in two strides the same ground for which the smaller Indian needed three. McCormick set off at a five-mile-an-hour clip. He heard Tibasse break into a dog trot to keep up. "With a feeling something less than Christian," McCormick maintained the pace. He perspired. His heart pumped. His lungs smarted. But he strode on. The pair came to a fork. McCormick stopped at the entrance to the path that would take him back to his camp. Tibasse skimmed past, shouting a "bon soir, monsieur," and trotted on along the route to his cabin. As soon as Tibasse disappeared around the bend, McCormick slumped onto a log and there he remained for some time, letting the exhaustion drain away. McCormick found the experience "good for reducing my ego."

McCormick obtained from Quebec Province a lease on 312 square miles of timberland and bought timber rights which had been gained earlier by another pioneer, Mossom Martin Boyd, who had died before he could start development. From the *Savoy's* captain, McCormick heard terror stories about 30-foot waves that roll from Spain across the Atlantic and up the St. Lawrence. He asked wharf builders how the curse could be overcome. No one knew.

McCormick planned to return to Russia in the spring of 1916 to resume his war reporting on the Eastern front but he delayed the trip to supervise the addition of a third paper-making machine at the Thorold mill. The war was adding problems. American coal could no longer be shipped to Canada, river steamers were being drafted for war service, rail cars had become scarce, the price of logs had tripled and the Canadian government was considering the diversion of Thorold paper from The Tribune to Canadian newspapers. American entry into the war steadily was becoming more probable and down on the Mexican border a band of outlaws headed by Pancho Villa was raiding the American frontier. The Tribune told President Wilson he should talk less and do more. McCormick, as co-editor, could not himself ignore the advice.

On the night of March 8, 1916, Francesco Villa, known as Pancho, and his band of Mexican outlaws crossed into New Mexico, entered the town of Columbus, set several buildings alight and killed 16 Americans. A nation slowly becoming aware that the war in Europe might involve the United States sharply awoke to the frightening fact that its own borders were not secure. The next day President Wilson dispatched 15,000 soldiers to the border to capture Villa, telling the world, "We are going down to Mexico to serve mankind. We don't want to fight Mexicans. We want to serve Mexicans."

The command was given to John J. Pershing, a fighter of American Indians and Philippine Moro tribesmen. McCormick noted that President Theodore Roosevelt had jumped Pershing from captain to brigadier general in 1905 after the soldier's marriage to Helen Warren, daughter of Senator Francis E. Warren, member of the Senate Military Affairs Committee and chairman of the Senate Claims Committee.

Villa, a bandit and cattle thief, had joined in a revolt against the Mexican government in 1910. He was captured by Mexican General Victoriano Huerta but escaped to Texas. Huerta declared himself president, Villa returned to Mexico and, with his guerrillas, helped two generals, Venustiano Carranza and Alvaro Obregon, drive Huerta from the country. Carranza assumed the presidency and, to Villa's amazement, classified Villa as not a helpful ally but a rebel and ordered Obregon to bring him in. Villa hid in the northern mountains, striking out both north and south of the border. The Wilson administration recognized the Carranza government and assumed that the Mexican army would cooperate with the American soldiers in capturing Villa. But no, Carranza said American troops crossing the border would be met with gunfire.

The Tribune dispatched a fast-talking reporter, Floyd Gibbons, who found little action with Pershing's men, crossed into Mexico, located Villa, sent home an interview and remained with Villa.

On coming home from Russia, McCormick could have resigned his commission in the Illinois National Guard but instead he signed on with the 1st Illinois Cavalry, a National Guard unit. He was elected major. Joe Patterson enlisted as a private in Battery C of the 1st Illinois Artillery. Bert was continuing a proud tradition. In Scotland an early McCormick had fought so valiantly defending the neighboring clan, the Maclaines of Lochbuie, that he had been given the privilege of wearing the Mac-

laine tartan and been promised that any McCormick always would find food and drink waiting at the Maclaine table. In Londonderry, another McCormick helped break the siege and then battled so fiercely on the River Boyne he gained the royal soubriquet "Without Fear" and the right to flaunt as the family crest a mailed fist grasping a spear. During the American Revolutionary War, one McCormick was killed by English settlers loyal to King George. Another was captured by the British army, escaped, returned to the battlefield, lost a leg, hobbled home to find his farm confiscated and received from the new federal government lands beyond the mountains. A third McCormick was with Washington for Cornwallis' surrender at Yorktown.

The commander of the 1st Illinois Cavalry was a McCormick colleague from city hall days, Alderman Milton J. Foreman. He had become fat, lame and deaf and his sight was failing, but he was an efficient organizer and administrator and a strict disciplinarian. His adjutant, Frank Schwengel, had been an officer in the German army and declared, on joining the Guard, that if America entered the European war he would not fight for England against his native country. But when the time came, he fought well for his adopted land.

Officers provided their own horses, uniforms and weapons. McCormick chose a revolver. A pistol could be fired more quickly in close combat but a revolver was more accurate at distance and —the deciding factor—it would not fire accidentally if the rider fell, as might the always cocked pistol.

To raise money for horses for the enlisted men the regiment gave riding lessons. McCormick was surprised at how few men could ride but pleased that they quickly learned under the tutelage of Captain George Van Horn Moseley. He was a regular officer from nearby Evanston who was assigned by the army to conduct drills one night a week and during the two-week summer camp.

Pershing's regular soldiers chased Villa back and forth across the border but could not catch him. "It's all a farce," McCormick said. Early in June McCormick, on horseback, led a preparedness parade along Chicago's Michigan Avenue that drew 130,000 marchers. A week later Republicans met in Chicago for their national convention. The Illinois delegation, including McCormick, was pledged to back an Illinois senator, Lawrence Sherman, for the presidency, but on the third ballot the Senator released his 66 votes to Charles Evans Hughes, who as governor of New York had reduced fraud and waste, leading to his appointment to the Supreme Court. The Senator, grateful for McCormick's help, advanced his brother Medill as congressman-at-large. The brother declined, saying the position was worthless as a step toward the presidency. But Bert, being helpful to his brother as well as to himself, reminded him that William Henry Harrison had gone to Washington as a congressman, advanced to the Senate and then to the White House. Medill McCormick consented and was elected, removing himself from the family competition for The Tribune inheritance at least temporarily while Bert was playing soldier.

Young men were slow to volunteer for National Guard service on the Mexican border. The Tribune told its employees that if they volunteered it would continue to pay their wages and would hold jobs open for their return. Other employers gave less support to the Guard. The Tribune opened a public fund to reimburse volunteers from such companies. A Ford Motor Company executive was quoted as saying any Ford employee in Detroit who volunteered would lose his job. The next day, Clifford Raymond, The Tribune's chief editorial writer, showed McCormick an editorial he had just composed condemning Henry Ford. McCormick skimmed it, handed it back and said, "Run it." The editorial was headed, "Flivver Patriotism." It stated: "If Henry Ford allows this rule to stand, he will reveal himself not merely as an ignorant idealist but as an anarchistic enemy of the nation which protects his wealth. The proper place for such a deluded human being is a region where no government exists except as he furnishes. . . Any place in Mexico should be a good location for Ford factories."

Ford had been conducting a one-man effort to stop the war in Europe, sending a small ship to Europe to carry the message of peace and to convince European leaders, at war for months, that war is murder and that reason and common sense demanded the restoration of peace. Ford was a hero to millions of Americans who looked upon him as a farm boy who had made good and produced a car that would bring motoring within their income, transforming their lives. Most of those millions opposed war and wanted America to stay out of the newest European fighting. Among these was McCormick. He and Ford differed only on how to remain neutral. McCormick thought America would be left alone only if it were prepared to fight. Ford opposed any increase in the army or navy.

The day after the editorial was printed, Ford stated that his employees would not lose their jobs on joining the Guard, but he did not say his officer had been misquoted in The Tribune. It is possible that Tribune publicity changed Ford's mind and policy. The Tribune printed Ford's denial. Much later McCormick said had Ford asked for a retraction, it would have "met a hearty response." Instead, McCormick recalled, Ford's lawyer, Alfred Lucking, "thought he could make a great reputation and persuaded Ford to sue for a million dollars."

McCormick had no glimpse that the casual order, "Run it," would start him and The Tribune on a long course which would establish in the United States Supreme Court the broad scope of press freedom stated in the First Amendment to the Constitution of the United States and deprive lawmakers of the ability to legislate for themselves a refuge from a vigilant press but also— and this would have appalled him—would open the press, magazines, books and theater to unchecked pornography.

That day the Colonel had something more imminent on his mind—how he could get machine guns for the cavalrymen he was soon to take to the border. He had learned on the Western front that the machine gun was the most effective weapon for controlling no-man's-land between the trenches. The German and British armies used their adaptations of a gun with a water-cooled barrel and a bullet belt invented by American-born Hiram Maxim 30 years earlier. The French adapted a gun with a heavy air-cooled barrel and a 25-bullet clip invented in 1873 by another American, Benjamin Hotchkiss. Colt sold European armies its own version of the Maxim gun. During the Civil War the Union army used in the battle of Petersburg a rapid-firing gun with rotating barrels invented by a Chicago doctor, Richard Gatling, but abandoned it because of overheating. The American army revived it for the Cuban campaign. In 1903 the army bought 283 Colt Maxim guns, but by 1916 it had not yet assigned the weapon to a combat unit. In confrontations with Villa's guerrillas Pershing's regulars, armed with carbines, paid dearly when they met rapid fire from the Mexicans' American-made machine guns. President Wilson, alarmed by Mexican government threats to go to war unless Pershing's "punitive expedition" into Mexico was withdrawn, ordered all 150,000 National Guardsmen to the border to reinforce the regulars.

Major McCormick was unable to draw any machine guns from the Ordnance department. He condemned the department for

being as backward as it had been in 1861 when it gave Great Uncle Willie a sword instead of a pistol. Unwilling to send his men to meet the death he had seen in Europe to be the fate of men and horses when confronted with machine guns, McCormick asked Chicago banker Charles Dawes, later vice president of the United States, to beg money from Chicago businessmen and buy machine guns for McCormick's cavalrymen who, McCormick assumed, must fight on foot if they were to survive and win. Dawes obtained the money easily, but when placing orders learned that all American machine gun makers had committed their entire production to their European customers. He did manage to buy six machine guns.

McCormick took his battalion south by train. His houseman, Hintersdorf, went along as a civilian. Hearst's Examiner reported: "McCormick has rushed off to the fighting front. He is a man of enormous physique, both tall and broad. He is as fearless as a tiger." At Austin, McCormick halted the train long enough for the men to wash off the dust and cinders of the hot trip. Nearing San Antonio, he received a message that a Villa band was preparing to attack the train. McCormick collected all rifle bullets and reapportioned them among his best marksmen, telling the others they would have to fight with sabers. No attack came.

At Brownsville the battalion set up its tents, Hintersdorf as a civilian merited no billet, so McCormick took him into his own tent.

McCormick found waiting for him only a few polo ponies and some tired milk horses, no maps, no traveling kitchen. To learn the terrain he bought an old Baedeker travel guide. He paid a smith $750 to build a mobile kitchen similar to those he had seen in Russia. When the machine guns arrived, Brigadier General Frank Parker commandeered them and gave them to regular soldiers guarding river crossings. For the first time the United States army used American machine guns in combat. A generation later the Colonel, replying to a critic, wrote that he had introduced the machine gun into the American army. The recipient published the letter and the Colonel's political foes exploded into hoots of derision. The Colonel did not amplify.

The Mexicans, impressed by the activity on the American side, stayed beyond the river. One day McCormick nominated himself to ride alone along the bank, hoping to entice Mexicans into charging into his concealed waiting troops or at least expose their positions. Hintersdorf followed. "Go back," McCormick ordered. Hintersdorf continued. His words stayed forever in McCormick's mind: "Ver der machor goes, I goes."

One Mexican rode out. He fired a rifle, but his aim was bad. McCormick slid off his horse and, standing behind it and levelling his pistol on the saddle, fired. The Mexican dropped into the tall grass and was not seen again. "That was no war," the German-trained cavalryman Hintersdorf recalled 66 years later with a back still straight as a sword at the age of 107.

Among the Illinois volunteers on the border was Ed Prendergast, youngest son of the Judge and neighbor adjoining Red Oaks Farm. Ed had flunked out of Harvard but remained at Cambridge for the companionship. Then, for more companionship, he joined the Guard. Awash with the Irish leprechaun spirit, Ed appeared one morning before a ceremonial inspection, saluted his commanding officer, protested with great dignity that the army had supplied him only with a hatband and a pair of shoes and, to prove his words, flung open a long raincoat. He was wearing only shoes and hatband. For some such prank he was engaged one day shoveling manure when the trustee for the Prendergast sons and daughters, Ed Dunne—now governor—drove past. The Governor, also a true Irish imp, invited Ed to a dinner being given in the Governor's honor that evening. Ed came. The Governor took him by the arm, led him to the top table and seated him on his right. The officers reshuffled themselves.

As the prospect of war on the border faded, guardsmen settled down to training and recreation. McCormick sent his cavalrymen against infantrymen in every known form of attack and was convinced further the machine gun had ended the usefulness of the horse except to move guns and carry messages.

McCormick rented a large house with a beautiful rose garden and tall date trees. Amy came, bringing a maid and an Alsatian. The army supplied a cook. Hintersdorf devoted himself to the Colonel's horses. Officers took up polo. Hintersdorf told McCormick that he must grip the horse more tightly but McCormick did not change his upright style. Hintersdorf decided McCormick's long thin legs were too weak for polo. One day a fallen horse trapped McCormick. Hintersdorf freed him and told him, "You should not do this." McCormick conceded that because Hintersdorf was six years his senior, he would respect his advice. "About horses only," he added. Despite Hintersdorf's advice, polo continued to be McCormick's favorite sport for many years, bringing pleasure, yes, but also pain.

Officers were eager to hear of his experiences in the British and French trenches and with the Russian army on the eastern front. He won the pistol competition and placed near the top in the rifle shoot. Pershing was well aware of McCormick's presence.

In Chicago a paper shortage was developing. McCormick obtained leave to go to New York. Finding no paper available there, he asked a broker to call a San Francisco supplier. Forgetting the three-hour time difference between the east and west coasts, the broker awoke the supplier before dawn. The supplier might have guessed The Tribune was in deep need but the broker apologized so expertly for getting the supplier out of bed that the supplier agreed to sell. The price was high, but on arriving at his office the supplier found other buyers waiting and willing to pay more. While in New York McCormick visited Presidential Nominee Hughes who was confident he would win in November.

Back in Texas McCormick became a confidant of the commander, General Frederick Funston. The General told him that in June the Secret Service had intercepted a telegram from Mexican President Carranza ordering General Obregon to cross into San Antonio with a force that would outnumber the Americans ten to one. That's why, the General said, Wilson had rushed the Guard south. Funston said he later asked permission to make a deep raid into Mexico to cut the railroad line but Wilson ordered him to cross the river and dig in on the Mexican side. That Funston refused to do. Fight with his back to the river? Never, said the veteran of Indian wars, Cuba and the Philippines. McCormick gave a poor rating to the President as a war strategist, a rating he later extended to Franklin D. Roosevelt.

One day McCormick's Alsatian tangled with a bulldog owned by a Pershing aide but the dogs were parted before Pershing was disturbed. Another day the men went swimming in the Gulf of Mexico. Shark had been reported, so the men swam with sabers, "looking like ancient Greeks." Heat and sun disabled the northern guardsmen. Dust, talc and women's face powder could not save tender skins from burning and the quartermaster offered no aid. McCormick fumed at the inefficient supply corps. A trooper and future playwright, Charlie MacArthur, tucked into his memory a remark by Pershing describing the Illinois cavalry as "Colonel Foreman's dog and pony show."

In October the 1st Illinois Cavalry was sent home via Houston where a captain was killed in a race riot. At New Orleans their train was put on a siding until McCormick sent a roughly worded telegram to the president of the railroad. "I suppose it was unmilitary but it got action," the Colonel recalled. The troops passed the home-going time playing poker. McCormick limited the ante to 10 cents. A regular army sergeant instructor pulled in pot after pot until McCormick took him out of the game with "my simple boys."

The performance of American soldiers and guardsmen had been appalling. McCormick, called before the Senate Military Affairs Committee, testified that the United States must introduce compulsory military training. He later mused that the Kaiser and his strategists could have been justified, when seeking excuses for their 1918 defeat, if they had insisted that the Mexican border fiasco had been arranged deliberately by the American government to deceive the German government into believing that it had nothing to fear from the United States army and thus could sink American ships with impunity.

*　　*　　*　　*　　*

On the 25th of August that year, 1916, a son was born to Ruth and Medill McCormick, the first great grandson of Joseph Medill. The parents christened him Joseph Medill McCormick but, refraining from emphasizing a succession, called him John.

*　　*　　*　　*　　*

Medill's campaign for election to the Congress was complicated by his having supported Theodore Roosevelt for the presidency in 1912. Ruth recognized that many Republicans damned Roosevelt for splitting the party and losing that election. By 1916 she had steered her husband back into the Republican mainstream supporting Hughes. Chicago's Republican boss Big Bill Thompson opposed Medill, but Medill and Ruth reckoned that the war in Europe, with Germany and Austria fighting Britain, France and Russia, was widening differences between Thompson's German and Irish voters in Chicago and the downstate "old Americans."

Hughes had no answer to Democrats urging the reelection of President Woodrow Wilson because "he kept us out of the war." Roosevelt predicted America would be drawn into the war and at once should build up its army and navy. Robert McCormick and

Joe Patterson preached the Roosevelt gospel in The Tribune and Medill McCormick from electioneering platforms.

Southerners arrived home in time for the election, but some Northerners were still on the way on voting day. The South and West favored Wilson; the North and East wanted Hughes. The Tribune accused Wilson of being "a little sluggish in deeds." The popular vote added up to 9,129,606 for Wilson and 8,538,221 for Hughes. The electoral college divided 277 to 254. Had the Northern troop trains been deliberately delayed? McCormick never could find the answer, but the experience increased his growing suspicion that governments connive to maintain themselves in office.

*　　*　　*　　*　　*

Illinois voters liked Medill McCormick's demand for a bigger army and navy and sent him to Congress. There at last he found contentment. He enjoyed the capital, and Ruth was at home with the politicians. Congressman McCormick worked for legislation to strengthen the military forces, finding an ally in Theodore Roosevelt's fifth cousin Franklin, assistant secretary of the navy and husband of Theodore's niece Eleanor. Medill's easy ways won friends and his wide knowledge of European governments and his ability with European languages earned respect. Medill wrote to his mother: "America is not a republic but an oligarchy of people who work together by day and dine together by night. They run the country. The President is no match for them. I'd love being an oligarch. It is a proud life, and an easy one." Everyone was happy, except Kate and Big Bill Thompson.

10. Into the Trenches

1917—1918

On April 2, 1917, President Wilson asked Congress to declare war on Germany. On the fourth the Senate voted for war, 82-6, and on the sixth the House of Representatives followed 373-59.

The next morning McCormick and Patterson, showing the promptness displayed by Great Uncle Willie 56 years earlier, placed a full-page notice in The Tribune inviting volunteers to come to the Tribune office between 9:30 a.m. and 6 p.m. to join either Major McCormick in the 1st Illinois Cavalry or Patterson, now a captain, in the 1st Illinois Artillery.

Before nightfall 135 men signed up and were sworn in. The notice ran for the remainder of the week but drew only another 110, a disappointingly weak response that truly reflected the reluctance of Chicago's German and Irish communities to fight for England and France. One afternoon recruiting officers went to the Cubs' park during a ball game. Sixteen thousand men were there—"All able bodied," The Tribune commented—but not one joined the colors. The Tribune noted bitterly that on that same day 1,236 men applied for marriage licenses, an insulator against the draft.

"We are going to do our bit!" The Tribune declared defiantly. The Tribune accused Mayor Thompson and his machine of not supporting the war effort. As an instance, The Tribune said the city did not put up war posters sent from Washington. Thompson claimed libel and set the damages to him personally at half a million dollars. The Tribune continued its campaign. Thompson added two more personal libel suits and raised his estimate of damage to himself to $1,350,000.

The President appointed Pershing to command the American Expeditionary Force in France, bypassing General Leonard Wood, former chief of staff. Wilson wrote off as too old a possible commander, General J. Franklin Bell, known as Ding-dong,

McCormick noted, to distinguish him from another General Bell call Ting-a-ling.

Before a month passed, France's Marshal Joffre came to Washington and told a meeting of army officers and congressmen the United States must send a division to France immediately to prevent a collapse of French morale and must institute a draft to produce the million men needed in coming months. Joffre spoke in French and no officer produced a translation, but Medill McCormick, the new congressman, was present and he, fluent in French, "gave the message to the nation," his brother later reported with pride. Associated Press publishers, in a rare political action, voted almost unanimously to back a draft. Joffre came on to Chicago. There Robert McCormick was so affected upon hearing him speak that on returning to The Tribune office, he dictated a letter to General Pershing offering "my services in any capacity." By morning he "repented of the sentimentalism" and realized that he, as an officer in the Illinois National Guard, could be sent anywhere with his unit. He told his secretary not to mail the letter, but the letter was already on its way, unsigned. Pershing's chief of staff, Major James G. Harbord, replied the General was requesting that McCormick be mustered into regular army service and report to Pershing's headquarters in France. Years later the Colonel looked back on the unintended mailing of the letter as fortunate, explaining his poor eyes and a football-injured knee might have kept him out of action.

Not wanting to appear at Pershing's headquarters in Paris with glasses, McCormick bought a monocle. He would have preferred the French lorgnette, "a most practical French contrivance," but decided American prejudice would not let any American use the device. He purchased, too, a strong cane.

McCormick had been swept along in the sharp reversal of national public opinion inspired by Joffre. The French Marshal, the Colonel later wrote, "exercised the greatest influence over our people and upon our destiny. He captured public opinion, and the people imposed his recommendations upon Congress. His appearance was so venerable, his manner of statement of fact so devoid of artifice, and revealing a condition so appalling that the nation realized it had entered a fight which threatened its very existence. The American people forged a cohesion of purpose such as never existed and which was to last throughout the war."

Pershing surveyed the 77,000 man regular army for troops which could be sent to Europe quickly. The largest American units were regiments of about 5,000 men. In Europe troops were being moved by 25,000-man divisions. Pershing ordered the creation of the 1st Expeditionary Division and into it placed four infantry regiments, the 16th, 18th, 26th, and 28th; three artillery regiments, the 5th, oldest unit in the army formed by Alexander Hamilton a few months before the Declaration of Independence, 6th and 7th and various supporting units. He ordered the units to assemble in New York City.

In mid-May, infantrymen left their camps in Texas and Arizona. Outside Hoboken, New Jersey, their trains were halted on a siding. After nightfall the troops marched through the dark streets to the docks and quietly boarded transport ships which sneaked into the harbor and there drifted at anchor. The army did not want spies to tip Berlin that the first American troops were on the way. On June 14th a convoy of 12 ships sailed, divided into three groups. The fastest sailed first, the slowest last, each flotilla escorted by a cruiser and four destroyers. British-based destroyers took over in mid-ocean.

General Pershing had assembled a staff of 182 under secret orders to report to Governors Island on May 28th. Officers were told they would sail immediately for France but enlisted men were told they were being assigned to recruiting duty. All were told to say nothing and to wear civilian clothes but some officers arrived in uniform and had marked their baggage "With the American Expeditionary Force, care of General Pershing." They were allowed to board two tugs, the *Thomas Patton* and the *Bailey*, which carried them to the British Cunard passsenger liner, *Baltic*, already loaded with its civilian passengers and waiting in the harbor. Strong winds roughened the water. Pershing won the hearts of the enlisted men by ordering officers to carry their own baggage up the ladders. The ship's British captain, who had had one ship sunk under him, ordered the disobedient uniformed officers to strip, explaining that the presence of just one uniformed man on a ship was used by the Germans as justification for sinking the ship. Officers and men continued to disobey army rules and regulations. Still civilian at heart, they looked on a camouflage order as equal to keep-off-the-grass signs in a park, on being absent without leave as playing hooky from school, on desertion as quitting a job. "They did not realize that in war lives are at stake," the Colonel commented later.

Dorothy Gish, silent movie actress, was among the passengers and gave nightly concerts. Pershing ordered crash courses in

French, with varied success. On June 8, 1917, the liner *Baltic* arrived at Liverpool. Waiting were the British commander, Sir John French, American Ambassador Walter Page, the Welsh Fusiliers' honor guard with band and goat mascot and a train including, for Pershing, the royal coach. In London, the General and his officers were taken to the Savoy Hotel and the enlisted men to the Tower of London. During four days in the British capital, Pershing went to Buckingham Palace to hear King George V say: "I have long dreamed of the two English-speaking nations fighting side by side. Now that dream has been realized." On arrival in Paris Pershing saluted the tomb of Lafayette and said, "Lafayette, we are here."

The nation began converting from peace to war. Within a month, Congress passed the draft law to enroll 10 million men, starting in September, and ordered the state National Guard into federal service. Illinois guardsmen assembled in Springfield.

Major McCormick knew he was leaving The Tribune with a serious shortage of paper brought about by increased circulation of newspapers generally, by a halt in the delivery of pulp from Sweden, by a governmental freeze on construction of new mills in America and Canada and by a shortage of rail cars and ships. He had anticipated the shortage. The Thorold mill was starting to make pulp to replace that from Sweden and installing a new paper-making machine which would increase capacity by about a third to 45,000 tons a year. The *S. S. Honoreva*, which carried wood into Thorold, had been requisitioned for war service in the English Channel but the compensation fully covered her cost with enough left over to buy another ship, the *S. S. Toiler*. On his way to New York McCormick, in uniform, detoured through Canada to inspect the new ship. She was a seaworthy craft but dirty and worn. Clean her up, he said; scrap all the furnishings and buy new; put in showers. Tribune crews, he said, live in comfort.

Amy resolved to help with the war effort and crossed to France with the Colonel. On the last evening aboard ship, McCormick told his dinner companion, the beautiful wife of the manager of the French Line, that he did not fear being killed in battle and he would not be taken prisoner, but he worried about being injured and left to die in no-man's-land between the Allied and German trenches. The woman was dying slowly of cancer and, understanding McCormick's feeling, gave him two capsules of morphine she was saving for herself against the day when the pain became unbearable. McCormick sewed them into the lapel of his army blouse. Not long after arriving in France, McCormick heard that the woman died and her husband killed himself.

*   *   *   *   *

The first troop ships arrived at St. Nazaire, in northwest France, on June 26th. German prisoners had begun work on a rough camp three miles outside the town. American trucks had been loaded on the slower ships, still at sea, so for several days the Americans marched each morning with full pack to the camp and at night, again with full pack, back to the ships to sleep. Daily the men marched to build fitness and to train for the foot-war to come. Although the weather was warm, officers, stressing neatness, required that all blouses be buttoned. On the second day a St. Nazaire girl told authorities an American soldier tried to rape her. He said she had made eyes at him and he tried to kiss her, but a court martial jailed him for 50 years. News of the rough punishment swept through the Division and was repeated to later arrivals. Throughout the year and a half in France no other division had a better record of conduct. "A battalion could pass through an orchard and eat not one apple," states the official record.

The French government organized a parade in Paris on the Fourth of July. The second battalion of the 16th Infantry won the privilege of representing the U. S. Army. The men were drowned in French cheers and offers of hospitality. The very next day the battalion was loaded into a French troop train made up of 40-et-8 cars designed for 40 men and eight horses and taken to the Gondrecourt area 125 miles east of Paris. The French government chose the site, McCormick was told, because it was relatively quiet but also because it was far from the British sector, thus thwarting Britain's designs to integrate Americans into its force. Also the site far from the sea would prevent an American flight from France should disaster strike.

At Gondrecourt, French troops moved out of billets in houses, barns and stables to make room for the Americans. Each unit, on arriving, received French commanders, instructors and equipment. By September, all of the Division's infantrymen had reached France safely. Only one transport had been challenged by a U-boat, resulting, the official history reported uninformatively, "in a lively action."

179

A Tribune copyreader, Joseph Pierson, earlier suggested to McCormick that The Tribune print a special edition in Paris to keep American troops in touch with home. During the brief expedition by marines in Vera Cruz, Joe Patterson had noted how troops missed news from home and printed a sheet. McCormick sent Pierson to Paris. Pierson rented rooms above Maxim's Restaurant, checked in with the French government censor on Rue de Grenelle and hired time in a Montmartre printing plant. The first edition was ready when the first soldiers arrived. When McCormick reported to the American headquarters, General Pershing showed him a copy of the Paris Tribune and told him it would help morale. The daily paper, intended as a wartime service only, was to continue for 17 years.

*   *   *   *   *

McCormick and Amy set up house in a Paris hotel. Pershing assigned McCormick to the intelligence section and, partly because of his fluency in French, added the special duty of liaison with the French government.

The General's first order to him was a challenge: Find out how many divisions the French have at the front. McCormick put the question to congenial French officers and received friendly chat but no statistics. He put his mind to the problem. In his 1920 memoirs he wrote that the subterfuge he used to secure the information must remain a military secret but 35 years later he told all in a radio broadcast. He said he learned which officer held the roster and in which desk drawer it was kept. He arranged a fracas in the hall outside the officer's room. After the officer hurried from his room to see what was going on, in popped McCormick and out of the drawer came the record. McCormick copied the list, restored the book and slipped out. Pershing was grateful. After the war, McCormick framed the list and hung it on a wall of his office at The Tribune.

A few nights later the McCormicks were dinner guests of the American embassy counselor, Robert Woods Bliss. An English general, whom the McCormicks found charming, told McCormick the British staff considered American soldiers "every bit as good as British colonial troops," but this war, the general went on bluntly, is not a colonial war and America would be wise to place its army under British command. McCormick rebutted the charming general strongly. Why did the general make such a proposition to McCormick? Obviously, the Colonel explained long later, the Englishman wanted McCormick to push the idea, assuming that the son of an ambassador would adopt the state department manner and "subordinate ourselves to the English." The next morning McCormick told Pershing of the encounter. Pershing's face, McCormick saw, turned fiery red.

"You acted exactly right, McCormick," the General said, "as I would have expected you to do."

From the day Pershing arrived in Paris, the French and British courted him assiduously, bestowing extravagant praise, the Colonel said. McCormick marveled that the General's head was not turned and that he continued determined to have an independent American command.

French intelligence officers, becoming cooperative, told McCormick that in a secret alliance Britain had pledged itself to fight on the continent in return for full access to French military intelligence, that Belgian vacillation had prevented the French and British from sending troops into Belgium to protect its border with Germany and consequently the Germans drove through Belgium and straight south for Paris, avoiding the prepared defenses in the east. The Allies accused Germany of violating rules of war by crossing through neutral Belgium but McCormick thought the Germans were justified in putting into use a strategy long advanced by both sides. The French told McCormick that Britain, France and Russia had agreed to divide the Turkish empire, Britain gaining Persia, Palestine and Alexandretta; France gaining Syria, and Russia gaining Armenia and Constantinople. The Bulgars learned of the deal, the officers said, and joined the war on Germany's side. The arrangement later had to be modified to bring Greece and Italy into the war. The Germans, the French said, had tried to entice Italy into the war by promising it part of southeastern France and Morocco. Italy remained neutral, allowing France to shift its troops from the Italian border to face Germany. The intelligence officers, talking much about Russia, were interested in McCormick's own experiences there. The Czar had been deposed in May and Marshal Kornilov was trying to keep the Russian army from disintegrating. The Allied governments threw their backing to the socialist leader Kerensky. Attaches in St. Petersburg predicted the country would fall into anarchy.

The French told McCormick that a German mission working through the Vatican had proposed peace, with Germany removing its troops from France but paying no damages, France recovering Alsace-Lorraine captured by Germany in 1870, Germany recovering its colonies and gaining new areas some place in the world. "When I told this to Pershing," the Colonel recalled 35 years later, "he was terribly disturbed that peace might come before he could have his war."

One day a French army intelligence officer told McCormick the French army had intercepted and decoded a radio message from Spain to Germany listing all American ships in the French harbor of LeHavre. McCormick tested the report on the American naval attache, who said he had not heard it, nor, McCormick learned, had the French navy. Before long a French woman was arrested in LeHavre as a spy and accused of passing the list. She said she would never, never betray France, but she had no feeling of responsibility toward Americans. The French executed her.

"Catching spies is essential," the Colonel reminisced, "but being responsible for their execution is not pleasant."

The French saw spies in many places. With each defeat, someone tried to blame a traitor, a man often in high places. McCormick noted abundant evidence to justify such rumors. A half-Dutch, half-Javanese dancer, Mata Hari, was executed by a firing squad as a spy for the Germans. McCormick thought the story told to the public did not seem true and questioned French and British staff officers. They whispered to him that Mata Hari had been the mistress of a prominent French political figure, Louis Jean Malvy, who, with a colleague, Joseph Caillaux, one time premier of France, secretly was negotiating with Germans about the possibility of an agreement for peace and using Mata Hari to carry messages to Germans in Madrid. Malvy, McCormick was told, promised her that if she did not confess and would not testify at the trial, she would be found innocent. She agreed and remained silent. However, the court found her guilty and sentenced her to death. Malvy then promised that if she would continue her silence, the execution would be a hoax; the riflemen would fire blanks and she, giving one of her masterful performances as an actress, would collapse, be placed in a coffin and taken to the cemetery where waiting accomplices would open the coffin and provide a car and driver to take her safely to Spain. But the bullets were real and, compounding the politicians' duplicity, the authorities wrote her name in history as a spy.

Another intermediary, a Spaniard named Miguel Almereyda, also arrested, died in his cell while awaiting trial. The authorities

ALLIED INTRIGUE

PERSHING'S
PROBLEM—

announced he had been arrested as a smuggler of opium and had killed himself with an overdose of the drug he had smuggled into prison. The state buried the body but relatives, exercising their right, had the body dug up and hired medical examiners who found no trace of opium in the body but did see signs of suffocation. The authorities changed their report and said that the man had hanged himself with his suspenders. "Bosh," an English peer, Lord Esher, told McCormick. Hang himself? Why, the highest hook in the room was on the bedhead 30 inches from the floor; they would have you believe he hanged himself lying down; he was strangled, confound it, so that he could not talk. The scandal brought down the government. Malvy and Caillaux were tried but, McCormick noted, "being men of great political influence, got off with a small prison sentence and exile." The dramas deepened the Colonel's already low opinion of French politicians inherited from his father's time as ambassador. He carried the opinion through his life.

As summer wore on, the staff watched for effects of American efforts to cut off supplies reaching Germany through Scandinavia and Switzerland. The Scandinavians, having to choose between Germany and the Allies, decided they needed Allied help more than German supplies, but the Swiss said: If you stop sending food from America, we will open our borders to German troops and you will have a new front to defend. The United States gave in to the Swiss. So did the French, even supplying scarce rail freight cars to haul the American food across France to Switzerland. Watching the manipulations, McCormick's trust of foreign friendships weakened.

Theodore Roosevelt, eager for action, asked for command of a division in France and General Wood offered his services, McCormick noted, but Pershing rejected the two men responsible for his meteoric promotion a decade earlier. Why? Staff officers told McCormick, he said, that Pershing didn't want to be overshadowed and McCormick agreed. He agreed also that Pershing's refusal was "an act of base ingratitude."

Censorship troubled McCormick. The American staff had followed the French, British and German lead in decreeing tight control of war news. The stated object was to prevent valuable information from reaching the enemy, but McCormick saw how censorship was being used to cover up errors and to present defeats as victories. Newly arrived American war correspondents went to St. Nazaire to welcome troops. Denied official information, some reporters took up positions on the docks and counted troops as they left the ships. However, reporters were unable to distinguish between troops previously counted and troops disembarking for the first time. Some newspapermen, noting that British soldiers were called affectionately Tommies, dubbed the Americans "Sammies." McCormick was pleased that the name did not stick.

Problems arising from poor quality of officers and shortage of supplies led Pershing to wish censorship could be reduced. He wanted Americans to learn that poorly made shoes, though properly designed by a doctor, wore out with one day's marching. He wanted politically appointed, inept officers sent home. He wanted Americans to know of the precarious balance between the Allied and German armies, that the Germans currently were winning all along the line and that, with the collapse of Russia, German troops would be moved from the Eastern front.

Censorship prevented the British public from knowing American troops were slow in arriving because, McCormick said, Britain would not divert ships still assigned to empire trade. Censorship prevented the French public from knowing of the bitter struggle being waged in the French Chamber of Deputies against President Raymond Poincare, but despite censorship the French people were learning from soldiers home on leave or discharged because of wounds that battles claimed to be victories had been serious defeats. They were losing faith in their army and in their government. In Russia censorship had contributed to the Czar's loss of his crown and, later, of his life.

Why had Germany ordered its U-boats to attack ships without warning, thereby bringing America into the war? The staff debated the question. McCormick argued that Germany had hoped its U-boats would starve Britain but American neutrality had allowed supplies to reach Britain. To make the blockade effective, the Germans reasoned, the U-boats must sink the American ships even though such action might bring America into the war. McCormick argued that the German command had decided Germany had little to fear from the American army, reckoning that the United States had only 77,000 soldiers, the army's efforts against Mexico had been a fiasco, America lacked enthusiasm for war, America could not assemble, equip and train an army of dangerous size in less than two years and by then the war would be won. McCormick surmised the German command decided it could ignore America as a serious combat force and tighten the blockade, a miscalculation of an enormity matched only by the Japanese decision to attack Pearl Harbor 24 years later.

The first American troops arrived, McCormick reported, with only the clothes on their backs. And what clothes! The world's worst uniform, riding breeches and rolled leggings which forever unrolled. A soldier must carry many things but, to save a few cents, the quartermaster had reduced the size of pockets. The quartermaster? Better off without that agency, McCormick snorted. Negro engineer corps troops wore dark blue uniforms made for Union soldiers half a century earlier.

As for the Ordnance bureau, it still was experimenting with machine gun design. Its own weapon did not reach France until the war was over. Joffre had brought to America details of the design of the French 75mm cannon but Ordnance shunned that also, saying again it was designing its own artillery. The 1st Division went into battle in the spring of 1918 with French guns.

Planes. Tanks. Poisoned gas. Radios. Telephones. Flame throwers. For all these the Americans had to draw on France. Pershing sent for Dawes, an old friend from Pershing's Nebraska days and provider of the six machine guns for McCormick's Mexican border patrol, and put Dawes in charge of purchasing.

The headquarters had adopted formal English army social customs. One British tradition demanded that no one smoke until all had toasted the King. Dawes lighted a cigar as soon as he sat down at his first formal dinner. He asked his dinner partner her name. Lady Anne Rutledge, she said. "Call me Charlie, Anne," Dawes said. "Dawes completely wrecked the British ascendency," McCormick remembered. "He was the dominating influence on inter-army relations the rest of the war."

Colonel Billy Mitchell of the Signal Corps, one of the American army's first fliers, taught McCormick how to fly. McCormick, in return, wrote regulations for the aviation branch Mitchell was establishing.

Automobiles were scarce. McCormick asked a friend in England to buy a car and ship it to France where another friend passed it through customs. McCormick lent the car to Charlie MacArthur, who drove it through a shelling and into a confrontation with a truck.

McCormick was impressed by the way the regular officers had kept well abreast of military developments, even if they had to buy books themselves. Almost everything they had learned at

West Point was outmoded by the three years of war. They had been taught to live in the open, but in France troops sought shelter in thick-walled stone barns, stables and houses. Junior officers had increased responsibility. Constant communications were essential. The weather was different—mild but wet, producing abundant mud. The light was different, causing difficulty in estimating distances to targets.

Combat officers ridiculed headquarters. They called its officers "the general stuff" and quipped that Britain's Tommies were correct in telling one another that a German soldier was given 10 marks for killing a British lieutenant but jailed for 100 days for killing a British general.

As the summer wore on, the French became big brothers to the Americans. The British had the ships and controlled the seas but the French provided the supplies, the roads, the railroads and the battlefields. In each American unit French officers and non-coms still acted as instructors.

In July McCormick's old National Guard outfit, transformed from cavalry into artillery, arrived in France as part of the 1st Expeditionary Division. McCormick asked to join it, although he had learned that Pershing did not intend to put any American force into combat until the following spring.

"So much," McCormick commented, "for people who said America could field a million men before sundown."

McCormick, appointed deputy battalion commander, reported to headquarters in Valdahon near Dijon in the Burgundy wine country 150 miles southeast of Paris. The commander was the same George Van Horn Moseley, now a colonel, who had been instructor to the National Guard. McCormick was assigned to a billet with three French instructors and, with cannon still lacking, submerged himself in French manuals, translating those he considered vital for the troops. He was surprised to find no courses for officers above the grade of captain and nothing on tactics. "We will take care of all that," the French told him. During a visit by Pershing, McCormick told the General about the gaps. Pershing assured him American officers would assume command as soon as they became competent.

*　*　*　*　*

A Chicago court finally gave Cissy the divorce she had requested nine years earlier. Felicia was 11. As revolution neared in

Russia, the Count fled to France. The Bolsheviks confiscated his estates. He found refuge in a Riviera hotel until old family friends took him into their home in Austria. He did not marry again nor did he and Cissy ever meet again. However, in the middle of one night in 1925, their daughter Felicia said, Cissy saw him in his cavalry uniform leaning over the foot of her bed. He was smiling kindly, just as he had when they first met at the ball in Vienna. A few days later Cissy received a notice that the Count had died on the night of her vision and had been buried in his cavalry uniform.

* * * * *

By the autumn of 1917, the Western front had settled into a war of attrition. For 400 miles, from the Swiss border to the English Channel, the Germans shifted their troops back and forth, trying to mass enough men and guns in one area to break through the trenches of the French on the east and the British on the west. The German commander, drawing on long cynical experience with military alliances, expected the junction of the British and French troops would be the weakest, and there the Germans most frequently struck. The British and French generals moved their men up and down the line, matching German buildups, sometimes reinforcing the other's line and always seeking a weak German sector. Early into the war each side believed victory would come to the side which marshaled the bigger number of men. The Germans had lost six million soldiers, dead or wounded, and the British and French together had lost even more. Both sides were giving rifles to boys barely out of grade school and to veterans of wars a generation earlier. The collapse of the Czar's regime and the surrender of the Russian armies enabled Germany to transfer a million men from the Eastern front to France. The British and French looked to Americans for rescue from the looming defeat.

The war was being waged desperately also in factories making ever more shells, more and bigger guns—a shell from Big Bertha could reach Paris—more rifles and machine guns, bullets by the million. Britain spent the accumulated wealth of empire to buy American supplies. Factories were pouring into hollow shells a highly caustic liquid which burst into a mist and burned flesh, melted eyes, ate lungs and lay unseen in trenches and gun pits and even nature's own shaded hollows, one more challenge to courage. The French said soldiers must not flee from gas; they must stand and endure, nostrils clamped shut, sucking in air through a mouthpiece clenched between the teeth. When the menace had cleared, they carefully must clean their guns and rifles and pray that the quartermaster soon would bring clothing free of man's diabolic contamination.

To peer behind enemy lines, the armies filled big cloth sausages with hydrogen gas and let them rise a few feet on tethers, dangling wicker baskets in which artillery officers with field glasses counted enemy reserves and compared the count with that of previous days. By 1917 fragile flying machines made of slats, cloth and wire darted across the front and along supply roads, searching for troops on the move. The pilots, in leather coats and helmets to ward off the wind, discovered they could set the balloons alight and, first with pistols, then machine guns, were challenging enemy pilots to a duel in the sky.

Some American officers resented the French instructors who drove home each lesson with exercises conducted, over and over, on earlier battlefields or on dummy fronts created to demonstrate specific tactics. The poor student, the French warned, would pay with his life. Few instructors knew English but conveyed their message with gestures and demonstrations. After the victory McCormick could not recall the failure of any American officer who "accepted the grim lessons of war which had been learned by the French."

The first lesson: How to maneuver. Get up. Pack up. Line up. Get moving. An order to move could be expected every three or four days for the duration of the war. For infantrymen, the lesson demanded more stamina than brains. Artillery men had to learn how to overcome unwilling horses, heavy guns and thick, cloying, slimy mud. Gunnery commanders had to read maps and follow the compass or the stars. At an intersection the commander chose one road; McCormick, his deputy, the other. They took the commander's route and reached their destination. "It's my Indian blood," the commander said. But McCormick mused the commander must have traveled the road before. At the end of the day the men had to find a place to sleep. Men at the head of the column might find a snug barn; men at the tail might make do with a bush.

Next lesson: How to dig in. To survive the first hours, dive into a shell hole, scoop out with a small spade, the entrenching tool, the slope facing the enemy to get better protection from bullets

189

and shells coming in at a low angle. Then, as daylight fades, start digging a trench, eight feet deep, wide enough for two men to pass, zig-zagging sharply to confine to a small area the carnage of shrapnel from a burst shell. The trench must be at an angle to the enemy's front or, better, in a curve so, should an enemy gunner find the correct range to one end of the trench, he must reset his sights each time he moves the barrel to walk the shells along the trench. If the trench were in chalk or clay, the soldier added to his life expectancy by carving a little cave near the base of the forward wall. There he would be safe from any shell except one that burst directly in front of him. The men dug trenches in rows, sometimes 50 feet apart, other times 300 feet or more, and connected the rows with cross trenches. Laterals to the rear led to the latrines. Forward laterals into no-man's-land ended in circular pits four or five feet broad, homes for machine gun crews who filled sacks with dirt and built a parapet, a foot or so high, leaving only a peekhole for the gun muzzle. A centrally placed lateral led to the platoon or company command dug out, six feet square or less—the smaller the safer—and roofed with 18 inches of dirt held up by iron posts intended to support barbed wire entanglements and any pieces of wood at hand. A cautious commander sometimes dug into the floor a grave-like pit and there he slept. At night he hung a blanket over the entrance to contain light from the candle by which he wrote reports, listed casualties, corrected maps to show the day's developments and re-read letters from home. The commander might have a phone, with a crank to ring the colonel, and a pigeon or two to carry emergency messages wrapped to its leg if the phone line had been broken, not a rare occurrence. The commander ordered his men to scatter thinly along the trenches, no man closer than the next zag, reducing the fatal toll of a shell to one soldier. Order or no, soldiers clustered; companionship was the only pleasure of civilization which could be brought into the trenches. In long-fought-over battlefields, the opposing trench systems were five or ten miles wide. The narrow strip of no-man's-land shifted back and forth as the armies went through the deadly dance, now advancing, now retreating.

When the Division's artillery arrived, the French taught battery commanders how to position the guns. The 75s must be close enough to the trenches to drop shells on all enemy trenches in front of their section. Learn to fire four or five shells a minute, the French advised. Eager Americans organized a team which, by eliminating waste motions, could fire 10 shells a minute, sometimes 12. Stop it, the French shouted; you are overheating the barrel and twisting it out of shape; you won't be able to hit anything. The bigger 105s were placed farther back yet close enough to hit the enemy supply areas—this was essential—and the big German guns which harassed the Allied rear. Within these restrictions, the commander chose advantages offered by the terrain, preferably a woods or the reverse side of a hill. Each gun had its own pit, big enough to let the gun swing to cover the entire section assigned to it. Small caves in the pit's forward wall held shells and offered temporary refuge for the gunners from incoming shells. Horses which brought the guns quickly were sent to the rear. The gunners learned to listen to the enemy guns and to tell by the whistle which shells could be dangerous to them and should send them scrambling into the caves. The gunners also learned how quickly the enemy gunners could reload and thus time their own reloading with some safety. The gun pits were connected by telephone and radio but the army relied fundamentally on the written message carried by a runner. Each side tried to eavesdrop on the other's radio, tap the enemy telephone lines and capture runners. The Americans developed slang into an impromptu code. The French showed the American gunners which trees to cut to provide a field of fire and taught them how to hang camouflage nets over the guns and place boughs along the pit rim to reduce the sharp shadows easily seen from enemy balloons or planes.

The infantrymen in the trenches and the gunners in their pits were self sufficient from dawn to dusk. The injured must wait until dark for comrades or first aid crews to carry them, sometimes a half mile or more, to the nearest aid station or ambulance. During darkness replacements and reinforcements arrived as did supplies, carried through the mud. The kitchen, tucked into a woods, could not light its stoves by day; the first wisp of smoke seeping up through the trees brought enemy shells. At sometime during the night runners set off with hot meals and hot water for the men in the forward lines, choosing a different time and route each night. It was a rare night when all runners delivered their food and returned safely.

The high command ordered the 1st Division to prepare for two assignments: to gain information about the enemy by raiding his trenches and bringing back reports or prisoners, a nightly occurrence along the front, and to join in general offensives to drive the enemy out of a salient he had made into the Allied lines or to push a wedge-shaped Allied salient into the German lines from which reinforcements could spread out behind the line and destroy enemy supplies and headquarters.

The raids were the more dangerous. The men had to cross no-man's-land twice, out and back. Being few in number, perhaps only six, maybe as many as 200, they faced concentrated fire.

Each raid was carefully planned, aimed at a small stretch in which suspicious activity had been seen. The raid begins two or three hours after dark, with the guns roaming for an hour up and down the enemy trenches opposite; then for an hour laying a barrage around the target area, isolating it and preventing enemy troops from moving in or out, then spreading their shelling widely. Now machine guns and automatic rifles send a horizontal rain of thousands of .50 calibre bullets across no-man's-land, skimming over the target trenches and keeping enemy heads down. The raiders make sure bayonets are firmly fixed to the rifle barrel. The raid commander counts the minutes, the seconds. The commander signals, "Come on!" Over the top! Three simple words that filled cemeteries in four countries. The raiders scramble up ladders leaning against the forward wall, officers going first, pistols pulled. The engineers are one step behind, carrying the bangalore torpedoes—long metal tubes filled with explosives which, thrown like a javelin, blow paths through the tangled barbed wire. Noncoms run among the private soldiers, all bent double, shifting from side to side to prevent a sharp-shooter from drawing a bead on him. But there is no dodging of the bullets from the enemy machine guns and automatic rifles. When a soldier is hit, no comrade can stop to help him. The fallen man is left to crawl, if able, into a shellhole. No soldier turns back. Get the Boche! The drilled-in order commands each soldier. Get there fast, the soldiers' sense of survival adds. The first raiders reach the trench. They pause on the rim only long enough to empty rifles into any Boche still firing. They leap and slide into the trench. They thrust bayonets into Boche crouching there. The officers empty their pistols, pull their trench knives and stab out. The commander seeks the command post and grabs any pieces of paper he finds. The commander chooses two, four, eight, 10 Boche—whatever quota of prisoners he had been given. No mercy is shown; the raiders do not want to leave behind any Boche who might rise and shoot them through the back as they run for home. Civilians who never have been in close combat may consider such conduct a return to barbarism. War is indeed the ultimate in barbarism and fine men and women who have experienced the perils of battle and shared the risk of death instinctively demand retaliation for loss of a comrade. In France in 1917 and 1918 all troops so behaved. Indeed, it has been so since the beginning of war.

Now out of the trench. A half-dozen mèn help the commander herd the prisoners, placing a barbed wire noose around the neck of the recalcitrant. Already first aid men are darting from shell hole to shell hole, picking up or dragging injured men who still breathe, leaving the dead. The homegoing is more hazardous than the attack. By now the enemy's artillery has found the range and is dropping shells on the battleground. If 100 men went out, only 80 may come back, maybe fewer. Sometimes not one. And what was the gain? Perhaps the prisoners revealed they were part of a regiment newly arrived in the lines, or perhaps a scrap of paper told of reinforcements on the way or of orders to shift down the line—dearly bought words which let the headquarters move two or three pins on its map and cogitate on what the field marshal might be up to. Much later the Colonel reflected that commanders on both sides "exhausted the complete category of errors."

Late in the night, if a lull settles over the battlefield, each side sends out soldiers to recover the dead. If shells and bullets continue, the dead are carried only to the nearest shell hole and covered with a few shovels of dirt. In the next barrage the spewed-up dirt might well contain bits of a comrade's bones and flesh. "The stench of a decomposed human body," a sergeant, Arthur Empey, recalled, "is hard to describe. It produces nausea and causes vomiting, then a weakening. You go limp. Your spirits fail. You are seized by a hopeless helplessness, a mad desire to escape. There is a sharp prickling in the nostrils. You want to sneeze but cannot. The stench makes you hate war and wonder why such things are countenanced by civilization. But after moving on and filling your lungs with pure air, you forget it and once again want to be up and at the enemy."

The second tactic taught by the French to the 1st Division concerned conduct of a general offensive by thousands of men, even tens of thousands. Three or four hours before dawn the guns begin firing on the enemy front lines and the immediate rear, each battery having specific targets. The guns move back and forth in concert, concentrating bursts, hoping to destroy enemy guns, to weaken the front-line defense troops and to prevent the enemy from moving up reserves. Dawn brings the jump-off time. The guns now drop shells into no-man's-land, just ahead of the Allied line, seeking enemy machine guns and automatic rifle posts and blowing gaps in the enemy entanglements. Then over the top! The barrage moves forward 100 yards every two, three or four minutes, the timing depending upon how fast the commanders think the troops can advance. The first wave captures the first enemy line of trenches and halts. The second wave passes through and occupies the second trench line, the third wave the third trench. The fourth wave spreads out to the enemy rear, overpowering the smaller guns and, if the attack is a complete success, capturing the bigger guns farther back. Now the guns shift to remote enemy guns capable of reaching the newly captured lines and to roads the enemy may use to mount a counter-attack.

General Pershing, from his first day in France, planned to build an American organization which could drive east, on a line level with Paris, to Metz, the main German supply area. Knock that out, he argued, and the Germans would have to surrender. He hoped his troops would advance miles in a day instead of yards, that foxholes would be sufficient cover and be used only during pauses for regrouping. But all that had to wait for men and weapons.

General Pershing came often to Gondrecourt. The men of the 1st liked him and he liked the 1st. Marshals Foch and Petain came also, stared grimly at the unbloodied American officers and strode off.

The autumn was cold and wet. McCormick developed a lung fever. Doctors ordered him to the south of France to recover but the next day, October 14th, the 1st Division was commanded to send detachments to fill gaps in the thinly held French lines between Luneville and Nancy in Lorraine. McCormick tore up the doctor's orders and moved out with the artillery. A French priest gave him wine and brandy and prescribed McCormick drink the wine with meals and the brandy before going to sleep. During an afternoon on the march his guns were held up to let an infantry regiment pass. McCormick lay down. He soon was deeply asleep.

A brigadier general came by, bent over him, stalked away and reported McCormick for being asleep and smelling of alcohol while on duty. It was the brigadier, McCormick noted later with some satisfaction, who was sent home, a failure.

As the men approached the trenches, the Divison commander, Maj. Gen. Robert Lee Bullard, in high piping voice, addressed them: "There are two things I don't want to hear about," he said. "I don't want to hear anything about enemy atrocities. Such talk only encourages the enemy. If they commit atrocities, we will do likewise. And I don't want to hear anything about no-man's-land. All land is American land up to the the enemy wire and that will be ours when General Pershing gives the order."

At 6:05 a.m. on October 23, Battery C, 6th Field Artillery, fired the first American shot of the war, a 75mm high-explosive shell. Sergeant Alex L. Arch pulled the lanyard. The target was a German battery a mile and a half away.

The Germans gradually became aware of movement in the area. At 3 a.m. on the morning of November 3rd, a heavy German barrage fell upon the Americans. The guns then fired a box around a 14-man platoon of the 16th Infantry in an outpost. Out of the night came German soldiers. They shot two Americans, slit the throat of a third, ordered the other 11 to drop their rifles and come with them back to the German lines. The 11 went. In the morning the Americans buried the first American dead. Engineers put up a small cross with the words: "Here lie the first soldiers of the United States to fall on the fields of France for justice and liberty." Never again did the 1st Division lose so many men as prisoners in a single raid. When the fighting ceased one year and eight days later, only 98 of the more than 50,000 who had served with the 1st Division—"Expeditionary" disappeared from the name—had surrendered to the enemy. On November 20th, the detachments were withdrawn. In its first six weeks on the line the Division lost 36 dead, 36 wounded and 11 captured.

Late in November rumors seeped through the trenches that the British had produced a new weapon, an armored juggernaut that moved not on wheels but on the endless tracks which enabled a machine to pull multiple plows through the thick heavy soil of the American Midwest. The monster surged across craters and trenches and waddled relentlessly onto machine gun pits, crushing weapons and men. The monster broke barbed wire as though it were cotton thread; its thick steel sides shed enemy bullets. The British had shaped the parts in isolated workshops and assembled them in a most secret place where workmen were pledged to silence. To disguise the monster's real purpose, blueprints identified it as a carrier designed to bring water to empire troops fighting in the desert of Mesopotamia, later Iraq. Supervi-

195

sors spoke of it as "the water tank" or, if in a hurry, as "the tank." Later, after the world adopted the term, the Colonel quibbled that the vehicle, being tracked, should be called a tractor.

The British introduced the secret weapon in an attack on Cambrai. The tanks moved so far so fast that they found themselves almost isolated, vulnerable to German forces still intact and closing in on the flanks. The tanks retreated and ended the day behind their starting positions. The lesson was clear: tanks are a spearhead for infantry, not a replacement for foot soldiers.

Britain announced the Cambrai attack as an important victory. McCormick happened to be at British headquarters that day and learned the facts. He went to the American command to report the near disaster. Again censorship prevented the truth from becoming known. A shame, the Colonel reminisced after the war, arguing that had the British people known of the failure, Britain would have made shipping available to bring Americans to Europe more quickly. The British command, McCormick said, thought they could win without American help. "The sporting instinct," McCormick mused.

The 1st Division assembled again in the Gondrecourt area, dispersing its 26,000 men over a stretch of French farming country 15 or 20 miles from east to west and from north to south. Most officers were placed in farmhouses, enlisted men in barns and stables. Everyone, soldier and civilian, was cold. France had lost almost all of its coal mines to the Germans or to the battlefields. Wood was closely rationed. The Americans saw in the markets bundles of faggots—branches and twigs pruned from trees and vines—and bought them by the armload, paying whatever price was asked, until they learned that farmwives now had nothing for their cooking stoves and the command ordered men to use only fuel issued to them. Fortunate was the officer quartered with a family that spared a down quilt. More fortunate were those who gained a pass to Paris and used the few hours there to buy an English Burberry lined raincoat.

The country people did their best to welcome the soldiers, and the French government gave each man two Christmas presents, a steel helmet and, for non-danger hours, an overseas cap which could be folded and tucked into the belt. The Americans happily discarded the worse-than-useless campaign felt hat with four big dimples in the crown and a wide brim which crumbled in the lightest rain.

Just before Christmas, Amy's father, General Irwin, the earliest Congressional Medal of Honor recipient, died at 87. He was buried at West Point.

* * * * *

During that winter, Americans arrived faster than supplies. By January men were being excused from training because their only pair of boots had come apart. In mid-January, the entire Division was shifted 15 miles for a week of mock warfare. The men walked. So many horses had starved that only the most essential supplies could be moved on wagons. The gunners pretended to have guns. Icy rain drenched all. The earth froze. Trenches of a 1916 battlefield provided the only shelter. Pershing said he would come for the last day but was delayed. At midnight orders went out to repeat the last day of mock war, solely for the General.

* * * * *

After the engineers hammered together large wooden sheds in a meadow, out of the gray winter sky darted the first American fliers, led by a French-American, Maj. Raoul Lufbery. He had shot down 17 German planes and balloons as a member of the Lafayette Escadrille, that band of 180 romantic Americans who had flown for the French before America entered the war. Fifty-one had been killed in action. He delighted the ground soldiers by completely rolling over—a barrel roll, the maneuver was called—his Nieuport-28 before circling and, taking his course from a cloth bag flying atop a pole, landed into the wind. Later came the bigger, slower observation planes, English Sopwiths and French Salmsons. The American pilots and the observers—artillerymen who on volunteering for the exciting duty had happily found their pay raised 25 percent to $190 a month—had been trained by the French near Tours.

The Germans had been the first to lift the war into the sky. No longer were commanders content to perch atop hills as had Napoleon a century earlier to see the enemy approach. For a better view, the German command drafted dirigibles, but soon developed mini-dirigibles, without engines, tethered on cables two or three miles behind the line, out of range of enemy machine guns. The Allies imitated. By early 1918 sausage balloons floated along the front lines from the Channel to Switzerland. On a clear day infantrymen could look up from their trenches and see four or five balloons. The observers could see everything happening along the front, but the information most vital to the command —what was happening behind the front—remained unknown. Daring Frenchmen began darting across the front in fragile flying machines, little more than winged canvas bathtubs big enough for two small men. The plane had two engines and needed both to lift it up from the pasture and whisk it over the battlefield at the astounding speed of 100 kilometers an hour—60 miles. The pilot was indeed "going like sixty," the ultimate desire of the motor-minded generation of young men. The French knew the plane as the Caudron G-Quatre. Americans Americanized the name to Jaycat. The pilot took orders from the observer who was also the navigator. Because no compass would function in those early airplanes, the observer found his way out and back with aid of a map, keeping one eye on the sky for enemy planes, the other on the ground for urgent messages conveyed by panels laid on the ground. He also had to locate enemy positions and tap out his sightings in Morse code on the radio transmitter. Plane vibrations made use of field glasses difficult. Sometimes after completing the spy mission, pilot and observer detoured on the way home to shoot at the nearest enemy balloon. A bullet could explode the hydrogen and set alight the cloth which slowly settled to earth, a fiery shroud of black and gold enveloping the observer in his wicker basket. By 1918, the French and Germans had developed a parachute and the observer could jump from a doomed balloon, hoping the chute would land him safely away from the flaming wreck. But no parachute could carry a flier away from a doomed plane.

To counter observation planes, both sides developed small, fast, nippy one-man pursuit planes, with one or two firmly-fixed British Vickers machine guns firing through the propellor. The pilot, aiming his plane, attacked the victim from behind. For defense, observers were issued two obsolete British Lewis machine guns, each with a drum of 100 bullets. The observer had to hold his fire until the attacker was almost on him or he would be out of bullets at the critical moment. The favorite French pursuit plane, the Nieuport-28, was being replaced by the faster Spad, made by the Society Pour l'Aviation et Ses Derives, and the Germans introduced a new Dutch-designed Fokker with three stubby wings that could rise almost vertically. A young observer, Lt. Theodore Boyd, remembered 65 years later the foreboding that seized him whenever a Fokker came at him, guns flashing, and he swung his machine guns to their utmost arc but could not bring them to bear on the enemy. Careful observers loaded their own drums, discarding any misshapen bullet that might jam his weapon.

The command, wanting eyes more perceptive than those in a human head, gave each observer a camera, a bulky contraption bolted over a hole in the plywood floor, its lens pointing straight downward. Properly operated, the camera produced 12 overlapping photographs which, fitted together, gave the command a picture of a long stretch of road, trench system or supply dump. The task proved deadly. For eight or ten minutes the pilot must fly straight and level over the target area at 120 miles an hour, the plane's maximum, disregarding anti-aircraft shells, machine gun bullets and nearby Fokkers. The observer, hunched over the camera, stopwatch in one hand, camera trigger in the other, had no eyes to detect incoming Fokkers, no hands to swing the machine gun. Anti-aircraft batteries fired in unison to create a larger killing area around the plane but gunners needed several shots to get the correct range and direction. If bursts closed in, a good pilot pointed his plane's nose straight up and cut the engine. The plane slipped onto its side and fell, twisting like a leaf in a wind. Lieutenant Boyd and many other observers thought when first exposed to this maneuver that surely the pilot had been killed or the engine shattered. With death seconds away the pilot switched on the engine, brought the plane level, darted away in a new direction and was gone before the gunners could reset their sights. Some pilots thought they could fly under anti-aircraft gun bursts but learned that a more deadly peril waited them: machine guns, with tracer bullets interspersed in the belt. Pilots flew higher and higher, 4,000 feet, 8,000, 12,000, finally 16,000 where lack of oxygen made heads as light as could two bottles of champagne. Many observers rode to earth behind a dead pilot and many more pilots came home with a corpse in the second seat. A French observer named Chappuis, seeing his pilot shot in the head, climbed onto the wing, pulled himself to the forward seat, pushed the dead pilot aside, slid in and brought the plane home. In mortality lists observers outranked pilots, and both gave up life more often than pursuit pilots. Yet, to the ire of observers, it was the pursuit pilots, the German Red Baron, the American Eddie Rickenbacker, the French Georges Guynemer, who became national heroes. The press recorded their kills with the enthusiasm given to sports teams and rarely mentioned that most of their victims were men in the vulnerable observer planes and balloons.

The observer crews were promised they would be escorted by pursuit planes on missions deep into the enemy territory but rarely did escorts arrive, so observers learned to provide their own guards, sending out three or four planes to ring the plane taking the photographs. Their combined firepower earned the respect of German pursuit pilots.

All fliers learned to identify planes long before the red, white, and blue circle or iron cross was visible. While a plane was only a dot in the sky, fliers could distinguish friend from foe by the color of the shells bursting around it. If the puff were black, the gunners were German; if white, Allies, a helpful distinction never intended by the munitions makers.

West Point majors commanded the 1st Division's air squadrons. One, Lewis Brereton, lived to command the 10th Air Force in the China-Burma theater in the next war. Another, Joseph McNarney, ended his career as Chief of the Joint Chiefs of Staff. Ralph Royce was General MacArthur's air commander in the Philippines and George Kenney, a lieutenant at Gondrecourt, commanded MacArthur's 5th Air Force in the Southwest Pacific. Lieutenant Boyd, a reserve officer, became a medical researcher at Loyola University and directed the successful search for vaccines against polio.

* * * * *

The Americans tried to make Christmas festive. They joined village folk in parties. With so many young Frenchmen dead, mothers were eager for daughters to meet eligible Americans, especially officers. Soldiers picked envoys to go to Paris to buy presents for children and food for the parents. Men competed in prettying up billets and posts. Gunners polished brass shell casings as vases for sprigs of evergreens. Men discovered unknown artistic talents and painted pictures to hang on walls. Kitchen

200

crews lined paths with stones and, here and there, transplanted bushes to improve and landscape. The mayor of Gondrecourt, M. Jacquinot, sent his official thanks.

"Never," the Mayor wrote, "have such bonds been obtained between two nations. It is, indeed, a feast of two great families and a foretaste of the victory to which the high spirit of the American army will contribute."

On January 5, 1918, staff inspectors pronounced the 1st Division ready for combat on its own, four months ahead of schedule but nine months after the United States declaration of war. The staff ordered the Division to move 60 miles north to the Ansauville sector and take over a five-mile front from the 1st Moroccan Division, one of the most famous combat units in the French army. The French Foreign Legion formed one of its regiments.

The Americans could expect an unpleasant reception. The Moroccans had just completed a heavy raid, killing and capturing with much vigor and no mercy. Retaliation was expected. The Division set off on January 15th. The winter had been very cold for France, with snow and ice. Each man carried a full pack of two blankets, half a pup tent, a change of shoes and underwear, helmet, two gas masks—one British, one French—rifle and full ammunition ration. Sleet soaked the long overcoats. Horses slipped and fell on the icy roads. On hills, men helped push the guns, the supply wagons, the kitchen.

Since coming to France, the Americans had heard French soldiers and civilians note how slowly men and weapons were arriving from across the Atlantic and declare that the United States was "not taking the war seriously" and would not do so until a division was decimated. As the 1st marched to battle, Floyd Gibbons, Tribune war correspondent who had lived through the sinking of the *Laconia* off Ireland, overheard men repeat the French comments, ask one another if the French were correct and then wonder if the Division were being sent forward as a sacrifice.

"I found perfect willingness to meet the unknown," Gibbons wrote, "a willingness to march on, feeling that if the loss of their lives would help bring a greater prosecution of the war by our country, they would not have died in vain. If death awaited, these men were marching toward it with a song. It takes a hard march to test the morale of soldiers. When feet are road sore, when legs ache from endless pounding, when pack straps cut, when the tin hat weights down like a crown of thorns, keep your ears open for a jest and, if you hear it, you will know you march with men."

That first day the Division walked 25 miles. At night each outfit found its own billet. The men were tired, wet, cold and hungry. How welcome was a pile of straw in a stone barn, especially to the young officers fresh from camps in America sent to the regiment to watch, learn and help whenever possible. Some evenings McCormick organized song contests.

One weary, wet night an order arrived from headquarters that a patrol must be sent out. The peril would be small but the discomfort considerable. McCormick looked toward a cluster of 20 lieutenants just arrived from home. All eyes turned away except one pair. "You," McCormick said, "take the patrol." He asked the young man's name. "Lieutenant Schmon, sir!" the young man replied and went out into the storm. McCormick was impressed. Before long McCormick made Arthur Schmon his adjutant, beginning a working comradeship that was to continue for the remainder of their lives.

McCormick soon noted that Schmon was very much in love. His fiancee, Celeste Reynolds, wrote poems and sent them in her letters. "Schmon thought the poetry wonderful," McCormick remembered. "I allowed him to read it to me and of course did not criticize it." One night the battalion officers found a billet in a French farm home still presided over by the attractive young wife. During the evening bombs fell nearby. The wife came into the room and said, "Pardon me, sirs, but I am frightened by the bombs. I wish to go to the cellars. May Lieutenant Schmon accompany me?"

"Certainly not," McCormick said. Looking around the room, he pointed to the oldest man in the group, a doctor. "This gentlemen," McCormick said, "will escort you." Of the unromantic doctor the hostess had no need. She flounced out alone.

A runner from general headquarters brought an envelope covered with stamps and a series of forwarding instructions. "It must be important," the runner said. McCormick opened it, read the message, laughed and handed it around. The letter, from the Yale Alumni association, urged its members to support the war by contributing to a fund to buy cigarettes for the Expeditionary Force.

One morning the commander of the 6th Artillery asked McCormick if his lighter guns could go ahead of McCormick's heavier and slower 155s. McCormick saw the military logic. He also knew that the earlier arrivals got the best billets. McCormick let military logic rule, but somehow buckets of water were spilled on the entry road the 6th's guns would have to use. The lead gun slipped into a ditch, blocking the road. Recovering it would take some time. McCormick's 155s went first.

Arriving at the front, each unit took over from a similar French force. On February 5th, although the last unit would not be in place for another eight days, the commander, Major General Bullard, known kindly by his men as Sitting Bull, notified all units:

"There are no orders which require us to wait for the enemy to fire on us before we fire on him. Do not wait for him to fire first. Be active over no-man's-land. Do not leave control of it to the enemy. Front-line commanders will immediately locate and report all places where there is a favorable opportunity for strong ambushes and for raids on the enemy's lines and advance posts."

McCormick rated the balloon as the ideal location for a daytime artillery command post. There the artillery officer could see for himself promising targets and guide guns to them. He could learn which of his guns were efficient. Telephone lines tied to the anchoring ropes kept the commander in constant touch with his guns.

Unknown to the Yanks, the German high command had limited the operations in the sector to holding the line and keeping watch for an Allied buildup until German troops could be brought from the Eastern front to join regrouped and resupplied divisions for a massive assault in spring. The Germans hoped this assault would shatter the Allied line, open the way to Paris and end the most costly of all wars.

The Division planned its first large raid for the dawn of March 4th. Planes, now American, photographed the German lines, enabling engineers to build a replica in the rear beyond the reach of German guns. There the assault units rehearsed their assignments time and again.

On February 26th 100 gas shells dropped on American batteries, sending the crews scurrying and making the guns temporarily useless. A large German raiding party, the men bent double under the weight of round metal drums strapped on their backs, wobbled across no-man's-land. Each carried a long wand. As they approached the first machine gun posts, the wands spit tongues of flame. The Americans, never having seen flamethrowers, abandoned the trench and ran back into the woods. The Germans sacked the trenches and withdrew without prisoners. The Americans returned to the trench. The Division command wondered if the Germans found documents that might tip them off about the coming attack but decided against postponing or altering the March 4th exercise. On the eve of the attack, the assault troops walked quietly through the darkness along the trenches. Engineers brought bangalore torpedoes. Someone had erred. The torpedoes were so long that they could not be carried through the sharply zig-zag trench network. The command delayed the attack for a week. Then, at dawn, the men went over the top, the torpedoes opened the wire, the men ran on. Not one shot came from the German lines. The Americans entered the first trench. It was vacant. The second. Vacant. The third and last. Vacant. Where had the Germans gone?

Ten days later Germans who had been quietly massing before the British sector to the west opened the spring offensive, catching the British off-guard and using mustard gas for the first time. The British wavered. Disaster was near. The French quickly marched an army group behind the lines and helped the British stop the advance. The frightened British government ordered every imperial ship to steam to America and bring to France the long-waiting troops.

In two months the 1st had lost 143 dead and 403 wounded. Just three men had been captured. The Division had anticipated heavier casualties in the first combat assignment, but the lack of experience made the Division's losses three times those of the veteran French divisions on each flank. The Germans, McCormick noted, were teaching the Americans that the rules of war must be obeyed.

Eleven months after the declaration of war only four American divisions, the 1st, 2nd, 26th and 42nd, had arrived in France. Now they came in a flood, but Pershing realized that he would not have enough time to give the new troops experience in quiet areas. They would have to be taken from ships direct to the trenches. Would the men stand up before a concentrated German drive? If they collapsed, the Germans could sweep in behind the British and French, the war would be lost and America's young men would be herded into German prison camps. Pershing considered only briefly whether he should stop the transports. McCormick applauded his boldness.

On April 1st the 26th Division began relieving the 1st. To speed the exchange, the 1st gave its 155s to the newcomers and, singing, marched to the rail line where the first of 40 troop trains, each with 50 40-men-and-eight-horse cars, were waiting to carry them 100 miles west to Gisors, due north of Paris, for rest, re-equipping and training before going to the Montdidier front. Some officers, including McCormick, detoured through Paris to see wives or "the city, but not long enough to soften up."

Spring brought sweet blossoms to a beautiful soft rich Gisors farmland as yet untouched by war. The French farms and villages welcomed the Americans to their homes with hospitality that grew out of the French appreciation for Americans helping to save their country. The thunder of guns to the north was a continuous reminder of how close were death and disaster. After two weeks commanders reported bodies fit and morale high.

On April 17th the 1st Division again was ordered to the front. To save exhausted, scarce horses, all wagoners walked. Officers cut their packs from 150 pounds to 20 pounds. For three nights the men found comfortable, friendly billets. On the fourth they were in the front lines, wedging themselves between a French division and a colonial division which moved aside. German artillery had been so active that the French had not dug proper trenches.

The American front was zigged through wheat fields and woods on a slope south of Cantigny, a village of 20 or 30 stone farmhouses sheltering around a Catholic church and a chateau. The Germans had captured the village in March. Twice the French had driven out the Germans but each time the Germans had returned. The German aggressiveness led the command to believe Cantigny would be the main jump-off point for the next drive on Paris expected in late May.

The French corps commander, General Duport, told the Americans: "I welcome the troops of the noble American nation, and salute your flags, come to unfold themselves upon the soil of France."

On the night of April 24th the 18th Infantry took over two miles of the front from the French. The 5th Artillery was assigned an area near Rocquencourt. The French sent two artillery battalions, planes and balloons for observers and scores of heavy howitzers, antique but considered useful in smashing the web of connected cellars known to be under the chateau.

Opposite were two German divisions and more than 90 artillery batteries. German guns ranged along roads and paths and shattered buildings that might offer refuge to the Americans. The prime target was the American guns. One barrage destroyed all four guns of a 7th Artillery battery. Gas shells drenched ravines with mustard gas, denying the Americans a limited topographic advantage.

McCormick spread his guns across a road and darted from battery to battery, dropping into a shell hole on one side of the road, waiting until the next group of shells landed, then dashing to a hole across the road. One day while McCormick bounded from hole to hole on his way to the regimental command in the cellars of a smashed chateau, a general came along in a car and offered McCormick a lift. McCormick said no, thanks; he preferred his hole-to-hole approach. The general said the car was safer, that it passed through the danger zone more quickly. Each was satisfied he was right, and each continued to progress in his chosen manner. One happy day a group of coal miners arrived as replacements. They dug trenches as could no engineers. A blast from a bursting shell flattened McCormick as he neared a battery. Schmon ran to him and helped him to the pit. Another blast picked up a gunner and wrapped him, stomach first, around a tree 50 feet away. The gunner recovered his wind and went back to a gun. A messenger and his motorcycle disintegrated when hit by a high velocity shell called a whizbang. Another burst flung a horse high into a tree. The carcass hung there for weeks, slowly rotting. Future playwright Charlie MacArthur, seeking refuge from an incoming shell while walking behind the lines, dived into a pit that seemingly offered sanctuary. It was an abandoned latrine. MacArthur comforted himself with the assessment that, from that moment on, things could only improve.

Late one night McCormick heard German mortars fire on the flank. He reported to headquarters that the Germans were starting an attack. The officer on duty said guns merely were firing at a patrol. McCormick phoned a veteran observer in a forward trench who confirmed that an attack was beginning. McCormick ordered his guns to fire. The attackers retreated, leaving dead and wounded. A soldier scurried out to harry the retreat, came upon two wounded Germans, killed one and brought back the other as a prisoner. In the morning a colonel accused McCormick of violating an order. "I did violate an order," McCormick replied, "but I had to do so because the Division officer was misinformed." McCormick was ordered to appear before the brigade commander, General Summerall, the smasher of the Peking gates. The entire staff was present. As a wary McCormick entered, the General said, "Thank heaven somebody in the brigade knows when to disobey an order."

"I almost cried," the Colonel remembered.

Fliers, both American and French, became more active at the Division front. After one flight Lieutenant Boyd reported German aircraft battery well within reach of French guns. "Yes, we know," the French intelligence officer said. "Then why don't you shell it?" the American asked. "It's this way," the Frenchman said. "We have a similar battery just within our lines. The Germans know it is there. They could wipe us out and we could wipe out them. So long as we don't fire at them, they don't fire at us. That's the way it is. Of course, if they start a push or if we go on the offensive, both batteries will be among the first to disappear."

To Americans on the ground, planes were a curiosity. One day a gun crew ran from its position concealed in a woods to look up at a German plane circling low overhead. Within minutes German shells shattered the woods and guns. In retaliation gunners and infantrymen, unable to tell flier friend from foe, fired at all planes coming into range. Allied fliers complained they were losing more planes to American guns than to the enemy. The command ordered machine gunners to fire only at planes which wore the iron cross and decreed court martial for shooting at a friend. One day a plane clearly marked with the Allied red, white and blue circle flew low along the 1st Division front. As it reached a newly dug trench, it loosed a puff of black smoke and continued to lay a thin cloud all along the trench. The men were puzzled. The fool was showing the Germans the location of the trench! The plane turned sharply and darted across no-man's-land. The amazed Americans watched it land behind the German lines. The Boche had tricked the green Yanks by using false marking! At dusk the young lieutenant in command of the trench moved his men to the rear and at midnight German guns demolished the now-vacant trench. To teach the gunners and infantrymen to differentiate between enemy and Allied planes, the command marched squad and platoon leaders to the nearest airfield where they could see Allied planes for themselves, close up.

McCormick yearned for the arrival of American planes assigned to the regiment. The planes were fast—135 miles an hour —but their Liberty motors were prone to catch fire and pilots already were talking of the craft as flying coffins. McCormick promised himself that when his plane arrived, he would paint his regiment's markings on it so his men would know he was up there in the sky and take heart from his boldness. Soon after the United States entered the war, the American Aircraft Production board had declared that within a year 10,000 American pilots would be flying American planes over the front. The forecast soon was doubled. By April of 1918 the first American plane was yet to appear on the front. By Armistice day the United States had spent $868 million and drawn 170,000 men into the air service, but only 682 planes were in action. The Americans had shot down 848 German planes and balloons at a cost of 289 American planes.

A battery reported by telephone that a French officer had arrived to inspect the position. "Arrest him," McCormick ordered. McCormick reported to French headquarters and was told that no envoy had been sent. A French officer came and collected the visitor. The French shot him as a spy at dusk.

Water trickled along the trenches. Sometimes a man scooped a short stretch dry, built a little dam at each end to hold back the water, lay down in the drained bit and, in a minute, was solidly asleep, men passing along the trench carefully stepping over him, disturbing neither man nor dam nor his dreams.

A young lieutenant, Jeremiah Evarts, commanded a platoon of the 18th Infantry holding a section directly in front of Cantigny. Twenty years later he remembered an endless afternoon of cold rain and shrapnel, when death was as close as the next shell. "A 155 ripped out the end of the next bay," he wrote. "I knew three men were there. I met Sergeant James and we went along together. The air reeked of high explosive. Two men seemed so peaceful that one could lift off their helmets and almost believe they were asleep. The third was wounded beyond all hope, as he told us over and over while we tried to bind his wounds. Finally we only talked to him and gave him water and watched him die under the evil sky. We left the three there and no one ever again so much as paused in the bay. The bombardment continued with great intensity. When I returned to my hole I found to my disgust it had been demolished by a 155. I poked around and found my Luger pistol but I had no great desire to stay in that bay any longer. I met James and we went to his hole. The ground thumped and shook and the air suffocated. James and I had reached the stage where we could only look at one another in the eye and give each other what passed for a smile.

"Gradually we became almost rigid with expectancy as the 155s moved up and down the trench. Each second was becoming an hour. We smoked incessantly as the odds narrowed. We reached for cigarettes. I had the matches for the two of us in a safety box. I struck one on the box but the head broke off. I took out another match and saw to my horror it was one of two. Again the head broke off. I took the last match and looked at James and noticed that he was regarding the match with as much interest as I. I shouted, 'For God's sake, James, take it. I'll bet you a hundred francs you won't light it.' 'I'll take the bet,' James said, and he took the match and the box and, as he did so, a 155 landed in the traverse of our bay. James struck the match the opposite from the way I had tried and it lit. There was a fierce noise of another very close 155. The bay shuddered and heaved. James kept the match burning. We looked at each other in the eye and lit our cigarettes. We crawled out. The 155 had struck eight feet away. We grinned and crawled back into the hole. I handed him the francs. Somehow we both knew that eight feet was as close as we would come to cashing in that afternoon. The spell was broken and we started to talk again."

Three nights in a row food runners did not reach an isolated platoon. Emergency rations had been eaten long ago. A sergeant borrowed his lieutenant's field glasses, walked through a forward traverse to an unmanned machine gun post and studied the stretch of no-man's-land. He put down the glasses, crawled out of the pit, squirmed through the wire 50 yards or so. He reached his objective, the corpses of two French colonials killed two weeks earlier. The sergeant searched the mounds of rotting flesh, found what he was after, squirmed back through the wire to the machine gun pit. He ambled along to Lieutenant Evarts.

"May I see you, sir, in your post?" the sergeant asked. The lieutenant led the way. "Pull the blanket, sir," the sergeant said. The puzzled lieutenant did so. The sergeant took from his pocket two four-ounce cans of bully beef. "I knew the Moroccans would have rations," he said. "Here's one for you and one for me."

Such, Evarts remembered, are the spoils of war.

By late May the Americans had 386 guns in position before Cantigny. They could draw on French guns on the flanks. Both Allies and Germans had overcome their ammunition shortages. The American batteries at Cantigny rarely fired fewer than 15,000 shells in 24 hours. In one three-day period they dropped 600 tons of exploding metal on the Germans and the enemy replied in kind. One concentration of 15,000 shells, including hundreds carrying gas, so shattered the 18th Infantry that the entire

210

force had to be withdrawn after dark. As men ran to the rear, they stripped off their gas-soaked clothing. The quartermaster had no replacements. French neighbors did.

As May advanced, the 1st, working all night, completed a trench system which could bring the assault troops to the jump-off positions before Cantigny. Some 200,000 shells—more than two million pounds—were carried in for the batteries.

Almost every night, a small band raided a German trench seeking prisoners and information. Sergeant Empey recalled the first time he went over the top:

"A line of shells lighted up no-man's-land. The din was terrific and the ground shook. We gathered at the foot of the ladders of death, as we all called them, and veritably. I felt sick and weak. Sharp whistle blasts rang along the trench. How I got up that ladder I never knew. The 10 feet to our wire was agony. White patches on the ground, guiding us through a gap in the wire, seemed to float past to the rear as though I were on a treadmill. I knew I was running but could feel no motion below the waist. I got into no-man's-land. A soldier on my right turned and looked in my direction, put his hand to his mouth and yelled. Then he coughed and pitched forward and lay still. His body seemed to float in the rear. Passing bullets cracked and little spurts of mud rose. Ricochets whined and shells burst all around. The crossing of no-man's-land remains a blank. The German wire, smashed up by our shelling, came into view and was carried to the rear as if on a tide. A trench about four feet wide loomed in front of me. Queer forms looking like mud turtles were scrambling up the wall. One slipped and rolled back into the trench. I leaped the trench. The man on my left seemed to pause in mid air and then pitch down head first into the trench. I laughed out loud in my delirium. In front of me emerged a giant form with a rifle that seemed 10 feet long and bristling with seven bayonets. I tried to remember my bayonet drill. I closed my eyes and lunged at the form. My rifle was torn from me. I must have gotten the German, for he dropped. About 20 feet to my left a fine specimen of Prussian manhood clutched his rifle barrel with both hands and swung the butt around and around. Three soldiers engaged him, ducking the swinging butt until the wood smacked one just below the right temple and crushed the head as though it were an egg shell. A convulsive shudder ran through his body as he pitched forward. One of the others got behind the Prussian. Suddenly, about four inches of American bayonet protruded from the front of the Prussian's throat. I will never forget his look of astonishment. Then something hit me in the left shoulder and my left side went numb. It felt as if a hot poker, not a cold bayonet, were being driven into me. I fell backward but was not unconscious. Then something hit me on the head. I never found out what it was. A light flashed and I knew no more. When I opened my eyes, the moon was shining and I was on a stretcher being carried to a first aid station behind our lines. In six weeks I rejoined my company at the front."

Soldiers saved their sanity by playing little games. Future playwright MacArthur organized a few comrades, all privates, into a special force, gave each the rank of "Most Excellent One" and demanded that members, on encountering one another, acknowledge the rank by bowing twice from the waist, a considerable improvement over the sloppy hand salute given to officers.

General Pershing came to tell the men their victory would mark a turn in the war. He did not tell them that the direction of attack was being changed and the laboriously dug trench system would be only partly available in the approach. Nor did he tell them they would halt their advance after passing through Cantigny and would set up defense lines in the fields just beyond, leaving the German guns intact. Nor did he tell them that the flanking French guns would be withdrawn by nightfall. Nor did he tell them that 36 German divisions were within rescue call to the north. Nor did he tell them that German Field Marshal Ludendorff had given firm command that wherever the Americans first attacked, they must be smashed.

The 1st Division's operations officer, George C. Marshall, then a lieutenant colonel who was to become chief of staff in World War II, wrote in his memoirs published 38 years later that the operation was planned with the expectation that the German reaction would be fierce but the tenuous stage of the war demanded the Division pay the price.

Unit commanders gathered to hear details of the attack. May 28th was designated as J-day, assault day. The Americans, accustomed to receiving the official word quietly, sat mute until they heard the French speak up. Then they too proposed modifications, citing reasons based on their local knowledge or experience. The 28th Infantry was chosen to lead the assault on a one-mile front.

Two nights before J-day, a young lieutenant, Oliver "Judd" Kendall, an engineer helping to prepare outposts from which to launch the first wave, reported hearing "strange noises" in no-man's-land, indicating some kind of German activity there. He asked for a volunteer and together the two climbed over the parapet and crawled through the shell holes and barbed wire. Nearing the source of the noise, the lieutenant told the soldier to wait for him while he went ahead alone. After some time, the volunteer crawled back to the outpost alone. The commander assumed Kendall had been killed or captured and reported him as missing in action. Late that night, a strong German raiding party darted across the battlefield, ordered to overcome an American outpost and gain captives to learn if German suspicions about an American buildup were justified. The American guns, alerted by the lieutenant's report of "strange noises," dropped a shield of shells ahead of the American trench. The Germans retreated, harried by the guns. A platoon of the 28th Infantry pursued the Germans. The Huns reached their own trench but, with shells dropping around them and the Yanks only a few steps away, they abandoned that ditch and retreated to a stronger secondary line. The Americans captured an officer lingering in the trench. Command ordered the platoon to hold the trench and sent forward engineers to improve it, shortening the distance to be crossed on J-day.

The German captive, taken to headquarters, said that earlier in the night an American engineer lieutenant had been captured. The Yank was asked how long he had been in the line, what other troops were there, had any reinforcements arrived. He remained silent, the officer said, so the Yank was shot as a spy. Marshall did not wholly accept the story and worried that either from the lieutenant or from the thwarted raiders the German command had been tipped off about J-day.

On the 27th, French tanks and flamethrowers arrived. Ambulance companies set up advance receiving stations.

The night was clear.

An added torment was an outbreak of Spanish influenza, striking first the older officers. During the final assembly, flu struck down 38-year-old McCormick. On the eve of the assault he tottered from battery to battery, observation post to observation post. At one post he found a new lieutenant had established himself and his three men in a position which, when dawn came, would be in full view of the German observers. Furthermore, none had his gas mask. McCormick spoke his mind. He returned to his command post. The raging fever overcame him. When next he opened his eyes, a nurse was bending over him. "How did you get to the front?" he asked.

* * * * *

At 4:45 a.m. all guns fired ranging shots. The Germans fired back. One burst killed or wounded 33 men grouped to go over the top. At 5:45 every gun began rapid fire—the 220, 240 and 280 howitzers, the old trench mortars, the 155s and 75s of American and French batteries, the machine guns.

At 6:45 the guns began moving their shots forward 100 yards every two minutes.

Men of the 28th gathered in threes and scrambled up the ladders. Over the top they went, running, bent over, in three lines abreast. French tanks clattered ahead with the men, crushing enemy machine gun outposts. A war correspondent from Collier's ran with the first wave.

The first wave found the forward German trench and its outposts only lightly held. The Yanks disposed of the Germans and ran on and in 35 minutes the first Americans were in Cantigny.

Tanks crawled through the rubble of battered buildings. Flame throwers squirted liquid fire into cellar openings. Germans came out, hands up. The war correspondent, hiding behind a building to watch a tank smash into the adjoining house, heard a noise behind him. He turned. Twenty Germans stood there, all with hands up, shouting "Kamerad." The startled reporter, armed only with a pencil, motioned for the men to lift their hands even higher. They complied and froze in the position of accepted surrender until an infantry patrol came along. By breakfast time, had there been breakfast, the Americans had taken 520 prisoners. The prisoners said they had just arrived from the Russian front and were relieving the previous defenders. The attack, they said, was a complete surprise. Lieutenant Kendall had kept his silence.

The infantry moved into the grain fields beyond Cantigny. Engineers began to link shell holes into a skimpy trench line. Machine gunners set up their guns in shell holes and were ready when at 7:30 and again at 9 o'clock small German forces ran toward them. The machine guns stopped both attacks. By noon, reserve German artillery had been brought forward to fire on Cantigny. Americans now began to pay heavily. At 5:30 p.m. several hundred Germans attacked. The Allied artillery stopped them before they came within reach of American rifles and machine guns. A few minutes later a much larger force appeared out of the woods and advanced in three waves behind a rolling barrage. The machine gunners and riflemen, though only partly dug in, stopped the first wave. Artillery shattered the second and third. Cantigny was firmly in American hands.

German shells broke the newly laid telephone wire leading to Division headquarters safe in a wine cellar. A pigeon arrived in the early evening carrying a message that a unit had lost many men and needed help. Two soldiers in shock tottered in and mumbled they were the only survivors of their companies. The news from corps headquarters was more frightening. The Germans suddenly had struck at dawn 20 miles to the east, had broken through the French line and were advancing fast toward Chateau Thierry on the road to Paris. Some French guns were dispatched from Cantigny without having fired a shot. Others left as soon as the village was taken. By evening all French guns were gone, leaving the Division's own guns heavily outmatched.

Holding Cantigny was proving, as expected, more difficult than the taking. During the night the brigade sent reinforcements. The engineers and the infantry became one in the urgent need to dig and hold the line north of Cantigny. Runners laid new phone lines to the headquarters. At dawn French aviators saw two new attack forces. American guns stopped them. During the afternoon the fliers saw a larger force starting an advance. This time the Germans reached American outposts but were stopped there by the machine guns. To the west, another attack overcame the American outposts. Surviving infantry men climbed out of the new shallow trenches and ran back to the pre-J-day positions. There they stood fast.

By late afternoon telephoned reports reaching Division headquarters indicated the German pressure was lessening. But at five minutes to six a second pigeon arrived with the same message of disaster: "Heavy losses. Need help." Marshall stared at the slip of tissue paper. He read it aloud, over and over. The message carried no date, only the time, 6 p.m. Six o'clock! But the bird arrived at 5:55. The message must have been sent the previous day. The pigeon must have wandered about for 24 hours. Later, when it was all over, a captain explained that he had sent a pigeon during the first German counter attack but the bird, a male, mistakenly had been caged with a female and when released with its message had circled and then returned to the female and refused to leave, so the commander sent a second bird which promptly proceeded with its military business. The first bird dallied a day before setting off on its mission. Its military career probably ended abruptly in a stew pot.

On May 30th the Germans made a final attempt, advancing in two strong waves. Both failed, leaving many dead. The 28th Infantry was relieved. In three days the 1st Division had lost 199 dead, 652 injured, 200 gassed. Sixteen men were missing. The Division commander told the men: "Your losses were very large and the strain upon you very great, but you won." Pershing sent his congratulations: "The engagement, though relatively small, marks a distinct step forward in American participation in the war." Marshal Petain added his praise: "The 28th Regiment, inspired by a magnificent offensive spirit, rushed forward in irresistable dash to attack a strongly fortified village. It reached all its objectives and held the conquered ground in spite of repeated counter attacks." The army weekly newspaper, The Stars and Stripes, made the capture its main story.

On June 1st the French quick-marched one of the flanking divisions to follow their artillery in helping to stop the German advance toward Chateau Thierry. Pershing rushed forward Americans newly arrived from home. The 1st Division took over the French sector at Cantigny. With its extended front so thinly held, the Americans needed to detect as quickly as possible any concentration of opposition. Nightly raids went out to get prisoners. A raid on June 8th produced captured documents telling plans for a heavy assault the following morning. The opening German bombardment, right on schedule, was heavily loaded with mustard gas. American batteries were freed to fire at will. German aviators, trying to blind the gunners, attacked balloons. The German bombardment continued for a week. Then the pressure eased. The Germans gave up trying to smash the Americans at Cantigny.

In his 1976 memoirs, General Marshall summed up: "Little has been heard of this action. The enemy's rush on Chateau Thierry and the dramatic entrance of our troops at that psychological moment naturally attracted the undivided attention of the public in America. The price paid at Cantigny was a heavy one. It demonstrated conclusively the fighting qualities and fortitude of the American soldier. It was not the ordeal of personal combat that proved the greatest strain in that war. It was the endurance for days at a time of artillery bombardments that proved the fortitude of the troops. To be struck by these hideous impersonal agents without the power personally to strike back was the lot of the American soldier at Cantigny. Never again did he have to undergo such heavy shelling. The heights of Cantigny were of no strategic importance. The issue was a moral one. This was our first offensive, ordered primarily for its effect on the morale of the French and British armies. For the 1st Division to lose its first objective was unthinkable. It would have had a most depressing effect on our army and those of the allies. For similar reasons, the Germans were determined to demonstrate to the world that the American soldier was of poorer stuff than the German. Our losses were justified many times over by the victory's far-reaching considerations. The little village of Cantigny marks a circle in American history. Quitting Europe to escape oppression and loss of personal liberty, the early settlers laid foundations for a government based on equality, personal liberty and justice. Their descendants returned to Europe and on May 28, 1918, launched their first attack on the forces of autocracy to secure these principles for the peoples of the Old World."

Marshall had seen none of the assault. Two days before the attack, Marshall's horse fell and rolled on him. The doctor diagnosed a broken left ankle, bound it and confined Marshall to the headquarters wine cellar, foot propped up on a chair.

* * * * *

Men stretched out in the sun to let nature ease chilled bones and tired muscles. The 1st Field Artillery headquarters began printing a daily mimeographed newspaper. Its most popular feature was cartoons submitted by the men, drawn crudely but reflecting acutely the experiences and feelings of the men in the trenches. Supply trucks trundled, unofficially, to beleaguered Rheims where wine growers parted with champagne for 20 cents a bottle rather than let it fall into German hands. On July 4th, one year after the march down the Champs Elysees, the headquarters organized a horse show in a woods out of sight of German balloons. French, American and British artillery and supply corps groomed their best horses, oiled harnesses, polished brass. A French general judged the entries. Gunners competed for the best laid-out battery. Winners received passes to Paris with a truck ride there and back. The 18th Infantry and a French battalion marched in review. Sharp on noon 155s fired 48 salvos, each directed at a suspected German position. As night fell, the

217

American 75s for the first time fired gas—6,000 shells, French-made. The 16th Infantry sent out a small raiding party and brought back three prisoners.

On July 5th the high command ordered the 1st Division to Beauvais for rest and rehabilitation. In 72 days at Cantigny the Division lost 1,022 dead, 3,897 wounded, 16 missing or captured —one soldier in seven.

Then came Soissons. Pershing's long-planned fast offensive was finally in action. The 1st Division advanced four miles in three days, capturing 7,500 prisoners and driving the Germans across the Marne River. The enemy burned supplies he could not take and villages which might be useful to the Americans. Cost to the Division: 1,714 dead, 5,492 wounded, 76 missing, 35 captured.

Then St. Mihiel. The Division received its first American tanks, 49 of them. The crews offered to drive the tanks into a river were it not fordable and form a bridge, giving up their lives to let the troops cross over the submerged vehicles, but engineers damned the outlet of the lake feeding the river, reducing the water flow. The sacrifice was not necessary, but in the battle beyond the river every tank was destroyed. Advance: nine miles. Cost: 93 dead, 441 injured, 10 missing.

Then the Argonne Forest, the trees already stripped by shells. One awful morning one battalion lost 240 of its 841 men. In nine days the Division advanced four and a half miles. Cost: 1,594 dead, 5,834 wounded, 59 missing, 33 captured. Three hundred fifty artillery horses were killed.

General Pershing wrote a general order: "The Commander-in-chief has noted in this division a special pride of service and a high state of morale never broken by hardship or battle."

The citation proved to be unique, never given to another division.

Then nine days to receive 8,000 replacements, some drafted only in July, and new equipment.

Then the breakthrough, farewell to trenches, and the race to Sedan. Fight, march, fight, march, fight, march, without pause from 4:30 p.m. on November 5th until midnight, November 7th. The advance: 46 miles. The cost: 74 dead, 413 wounded, 15 captured, four missing.

* * * * *

In the thick of the American offensive through Verdun and Alsace was the 57th Field Artillery, commanded by Amy's brother George, by now a brigadier general.

At 5:45 a.m. on November 11th the Division radio stuttered out a message from Marshal Foch directing that all fighting must cease at 11 a.m. and no troops were to advance after that hour. Popular war histories state that the message brought a tremendous outpouring of joy among the soldiers. Not so with the men of the 1st Division. To them the unexpected message was incredulous. No more fighting? How could it be true? No, there was a mistake. It was merely a pause. The men were hungry, cold, tired. They wanted food, warmth, sleep. Did the message mean they could light fires? Yes. Eagerly men chopped wood and soon were toasting themselves before leaping flames. They rediscovered the caveman's delight over his conquest of cold. As days passed and guns remained silent, the men began to ask: When do we go home? Germany, they were told, merely had surrendered, peace had not yet come, Germany must be occupied. In six days, the 1st was back on its feet, walking to Germany. In Luxembourg they slept in beds, real beds, with sheets. They crossed into Germany November 22nd. The citizens were sullen as the 1st commandeered the best houses for the night. Everyone was on guard. One month after the armistice the men of the 1st walked into their destination, Coblenz. They had walked 200 miles. They settled in hotels. Other divisions were given orders to go home, but the 1st was given the honor—so the orders said—of being the last to go home.

*　*　*　*　*

The 1st finally came home on September 12, 1919, and marched up 5th Avenue in a victory parade with General Pershing at the head. The parade took four and a half hours to pass the receiving stand, but the men who marched to the cheers were fewer than the 24,775 left behind in cemeteries and hospitals. Of the 50,000 men serving in the 1st, only two killed themselves, a flier after being court martialed for a love affair with a married woman, and a corporal who broke under the strain of battle.

*　*　*　*　*

Before the Division came home, its commander, General Summerall, wrote to Mrs. F. A. Kendall, the widowed mother of the engineer lieutenant who disappeared on his self-assigned search of the battlefield two nights before the Cantigny operation. The

General told her that a graves registration unit had found an unmarked grave just beyond Cantigny and had identified the body as that of her son. Lieutenant Kendall's remains were reburied in an American military cemetery near St. Quentin in France. Two decades later Veterans of Foreign Wars formed a post at Naperville, Illinois, 25 miles west of Chicago. The lieutenant's father had been mayor and superintendent of schools there. The veterans named the post for the engineer. They called him, "Our Nathan Hale."

*　*　*　*　*

"How did you get to the front?"

The nurse said she had not come to the front. McCormick, she told him, had been carried, in semi-coma, out of the front lines at Cantigny and brought to the receiving station. He must be quiet and sleep. When the fever breaks, he would be moved to a hospital in the south of France. McCormick asked he be sent instead to a hospital in Paris. Amy was there. She was working with the Red Cross Duryea Relief Fund, which helped 40,000 crippled French soldiers. The nurse advanced his case and doctors rewrote the orders.

In Paris McCormick slept for 48 hours. He awoke to hear the nurses talking about the continued German advance on the Chateau Thierry road toward Paris. McCormick dressed, walked out of the hospital, got his car and a driver and had himself driven to the headquarters at Chateau Thierry. He offered to do anything helpful but the doctor suggested he go back to the hospital. There two ward mates, young lieutenants, impressed him. One had been left for dead on the battlefield after a German bullet had struck him in the face. Later someone heard him groan and rescued him. In the hospital, doctors found the bullet had gone around his head between skin and skull without serious damage. "German pistols are too weak," McCormick commented.

The other had broken an ankle. "How?" McCormick asked.

"Kicking a wounded German in the head," the lieutenant replied cheerily.

Three weeks after the assault on Cantigny McCormick was promoted to lieutenant colonel and assigned, at his request, to the 122nd Field Artillery. McCormick drafted instructions for the regiment to observe when it enters the line. The voice of experience and common sense speaks through the 26 printed pages.

For officers going into battle, he made these points:

Enforcement of regulations is imperative. Vehicles must be neatly packed. Columns never shall halt in a village. Each wagon must have a machine gun ready to fight off attack by an airplane. Attach extra horses before entering a muddy lane, not after a wagon is stuck. Drivers must walk half of the time to spare the horses. Officers must learn to find their way by the stars. Camouflage is vital. Use telephones only for official messages. Don't waste food.

In July McCormick and other older officers with combat experience were ordered home to train new regiments and bring them to Europe. McCormick, preferring to remain with the artillery, drove to Paris and asked to see General Pershing. An aide refused to take him in even though the aide had been a classmate at Yale. A Big Bertha shell burst nearby. When the General came from his office to see the damage, McCormick approached him and asked if the order could be altered, explaining he had been offered command of a regiment and, if he could accept, he would waive the advancement to colonel such an assignment normally carried. He argued that his experience was in combat, not training.

"No," Pershing said. "Go home. Organize a regiment. Bring it to Europe. You will then have a brigade and a general's star." Pershing added that the heavy fighting was over for the year. He said the big push would come in the spring of 1919.

Before leaving France, McCormick drove to the headquarters of the 42nd Division and sought out his cousin Joe, an artillery captain. Lacking helmet and gas mask, McCormick borrowed those of Brigadier General Douglas MacArthur. Later McCormick mused that had he known how famous MacArthur would become, he would have asked to keep the helmet. The chateau was agog with chatter. Bert and Joe, seeking a quiet place to talk, walked through a French window and sat on a strawpile. Later the Colonel found amusement in talking about "the manure heap on which The News was born." On that barnyard pile, be it fresh or ripe, Patterson said he thought a paper such as London's Mirror would go well in New York City. It would be half newspaper and half magazine, half pictures, one fourth features and one fourth news told briefly in terms they thought any shop girl or cab driver could understand. The sentences would be short; the language, though proper, enriched with street slang and humor. The paper would be half-sized so it could be read on subways and commuter trains. McCormick liked the proposition. It was new; it was risky; it had promise, and, best of all, it would divert Patterson's attention away from The Tribune and probably remove him from Chicago altogether, leaving The Tribune to the Colonel alone. McCormick agreed with Joe that The Tribune would invade New York as soon as the war was over.

That evening McCormick stopped for the night at a small hotel filled, he recalled later, with "drunken French officers and dissolute French women." He had his driver dine with him and then sleep in his room, "to keep him from any bad influences," McCormick recalled.

In August on the way to Chicago to assume command of the 61st Field Artillery he paused in Washington. A State Department officer told him the war would be over in a few weeks. McCormick was startled. Pershing had told him the big push would not come until spring. Why the widely different assessments? The diplomat did not say. The Allies had made heavy gains in the past two weeks, but also, McCormick considered, the American Secret Service may have gained information about deterioration in Germany unknown to the high command in Paris.

McCormick, reaching Chicago, telephoned families of Chicago men in his regiment to tell them about their sons and husbands. He took command of the new regiment at Fort Sheridan, outside Chicago, and moved it to Camp Jackson, North Carolina. On September 5th he was appointed colonel of artillery. In October the army ordered the regiment overseas but did not provide a ship. On November 11th the war ended. McCormick was discharged the last day of the year and remained a colonel in the reserves for another 10 years. The Colonel sent Pershing a check for 106,902.87 francs, the profits from The Tribune's Paris edition, to be used for the good of the troops "as you deem wise."

General Pershing awarded the Colonel the Distinguished Service Medal for "exceptionally meritorious and distinguished service, rare leadership and organizing ability, unusual executive ability, sound tactical judgment, ceaseless energy."

* * * * *

As the war came to an end, Big Bill Thompson thought the time had come for him to move politically from the local to the national stage. He resigned as mayor to seek the Republican nomination for senator, also sought by Medill McCormick. The campaign was bitter. Medill believed farmers and small town communities downstate still outnumbered the Irish and Germans of Chicago and further, that Thompson's mutterings about Britain and France and his reluctant support of the war had cost him support of Chicagoans without Irish and German heritage. He was right. Medill won the primary and the November election. Thompson hastily recovered the mayor's chair and vowed revenge on all McCormicks.

* * * * *

McCormick came out of the war with deep convictions which were to govern his political philosophy and managerial strategy in building the Chicago Tribune into a newspaper empire and giving it a voice heard throughout the nation and around the world:

On International Affairs: Governments behave in a manner more base than any decent individual would dare do. War is the ultimate crime against humanity.

On Government: Government is inherently inefficient and corrupt. Popular institutions give a nation strength. A powerful military organization is a threat to popular government. Morale is as important to a nation's fighting ability as the artillery.

On Pacifists: Their sins fill many graves. (American dead in Europe numbered 126,000.)

On a Free Press: Censorship is a crime against the nation. Governments use it to hide defeats and errors. Censorship prevents people from correcting errors. Censorship destroys morale.

On Individual Development: Commanders are not born; they are made by training and experience. No man ever completely masters any profession. No education is ever complete. A commander must see and experience conditions for himself. No man can do more than successfully meet an emergency.

* * * * *

McCormick came home to Chicago a colonel. To his last day he was the complete colonel. The rank became part of his name. People might ask who is Robert McCormick, but they knew The Colonel.

He had not wasted those long hours in the dugouts. Like many other soldiers, he turned his mind to the glorious time when the

223

war would be won and he could get on with life. For the Colonel, the future was full of promise and opportunity, although beset with problems. He was eager to get back to the St. Lawrence and see if that wilderness could be put to work producing paper for The Tribune. He had to work out with Joe the starting of the new kind of newspaper in New York. He had to look into the marvels of radio and try to determine if radio could be a helpful tool to The Tribune, or would it be a dangerous rival? The demands of Henry Ford and Mayor Big Bill Thompson for millions of dollars for claimed libel hung over The Tribune and no one knew where that situation would lead. The Tribune was outgrowing its plant and offices. Where should he build? In Chicago's Loop or outside it? What advances had been made in presses? How could he get more color in the paper? Should he close the Paris edition or use it to provide an American voice and service to Americans touring Europe? He and Amy had to find a home away from gossiping tongues of the North Shore. Oh yes, he'd like to find some place where he could play polo with experts.

McCormick wrote to Joe saying he was determined "to have a great life and an adventurous one." Looking ahead on New Year's Day of 1919, the Colonel could not be sure of a great life, but he could be certain of one rich with adventure. He had come home with deep loyalty to the 1st Division but without forming any tight bonds that war can forge among men. He was more than ever a solitary man, walking alone.

11. Forty, Not a Minute to Waste
1919—1922

Amy and the Colonel seldom had been at Red Oaks Farm since their marriage. After almost a quarter century of little care, the house was nearly derelict, the fields unproductive, the barns rundown, the equipment out of date. The Colonel sent Deininger, now Tribune auditor, to see what could be done to make the farm profitable.

Deininger camped in a tent, reorganized the farm and raised pigs to help pay taxes. As winter eased, Amy and the Colonel came to the farm now and then to ride. Here was room for any number of horses and a polo field. But live at Red Oaks? Make the farm their home? Hardly. The North Shore was their habitat. Amy's house there was comfortable; its stables could shelter more than enough horses. The Onwentsia club well served the wealthy, socially minded community. But whenever Amy or the Colonel entered the club house or rode from the stables they could not escape the watchful eyes, the whispered asides. The return of the soldier and the Red Cross worker to the North Shore relighted the still smoldering gossip about Amy's divorce and the runaway marriage. The Colonel concentrated his mind on tackling the adventurous challenges he had set for himself.

* * * * *

Only six weeks after coming home, the Colonel, without waiting for Joe Patterson to return from Europe, told Tribune directors about Joe's desire to start a new kind of newspaper in New York City and his own agreement. He asked the directors to provide the money, $20,000 at a time, in return for promissory notes that would be repaid as soon as the new paper produced profits, probably in three or four years, or earlier on demand from the directors. The directors agreed. Money was no problem,

225

Tribune earnings having multiplied during the war. For Joe, there now could be no second thoughts.

A month later, with Patterson still absent, the Colonel gained from the directors authority to send William Field to New York immediately to search for a paper which could be bought at a fair price or, failing that, to find an evening paper that would make its plant available to the new morning paper. Field had just asked to resign. Since being brought into The Tribune as a business manager by Medill McCormick a decade earlier and evolving advertising into a science, he had taken on added responsibilities from Medill McCormick and Robert Patterson when their health broke and later from the Colonel and Joe Patterson when they went to war. By the end of 1918 Field was directing the day-to-day operations of The Tribune and the Thorold mill. He had moved into Joe's office, placing on the wall a sign: "This is Joe Patterson's office. He is fighting in France. I am sitting in his chair for a while until he comes home." The sign accurately expressed his acceptance that Patterson and the Colonel would recover their powers. He welcomed the prospect of a rest but was not pleased by the thought of returning to a subordinate position. Owning no stock and with no expectation of acquiring any, he realized he would be forever an employee, not sharing in Tribune profits. To stay at the top, he must start anew somewhere else. Thus, his request to resign.

The Colonel's proposal that Field go to New York turned a deteriorating outlook into one of limitless opportunity. Field accepted and took the next train to New York. He learned no newspaper, good or bad, could be bought for a price he considered reasonable, but the evening Mail, which Joseph Pulitzer had made into a great paper, was deteriorating under his eldest son. "From being a paper devoted to the interests of the people," the Colonel said, "the son, a Harvard graduate, tried to make it into an aristocratic highbrow paper and left the popular field open to us." The son welcomed an opportunity to keep the plant at work after running off the last of the Mail editions and, for $166.67 a month extra, cleared out the fifth floor of the 14-story building for the new editorial and business staff.

The addition of a second newspaper required an increased supply of paper. On the last day of 1918, wearing his uniform the final time, the Colonel wrote to Schmon, the eager young officer who had not hesitated to take his squad out into the winter night and who had served McCormick so well as adjutant. Schmon, now a captain, was on occupation duties with the 1st Division in Germany.

"I leave the service today," the Colonel wrote. "Is it forever or will we be out again soon? If you can get mustered out by the middle of April, I will have a position open with very fine prospects but very likely not one to appeal to a retired soldier. We have a property on the north shore of the Gulf of St. Lawrence that needs a manager. The work will be entirely new to you but I have no reason to doubt you can learn that as well as you learned artillery. The opportunities are very great; the difficulties also far from inconsiderable. If you should happen to want this, please write me at once."

Schmon replied he was interested but did not know when the army would let him go. He wondered if his English literature studies at Princeton equipped him for the task broached by the Colonel.

* * * * *

Also, the Tribune's 18-story 1.2 million dollar building was only 18 years old but the basement could hold no more presses and the increasing traffic in the Loop was impeding the delivery of the heavy paper rolls and the distribution of four million Tribunes each week. The Colonel considered joining the newspaper trek to the western limits of the Loop to be near the new railroad stations which, through the night, sent trains deep into Chicagoland with the early editions. As an alderman 16 years earlier, the Colonel had been a member of the committee that recommended widening North Michigan Avenue and building a double-decked bridge across the Chicago River. The city at last had undertaken the task. The Colonel acquired a piece of land adjoining the north bank of the river, an area reeking from soap factories, barge and rail freight yards and other malodorous enterprises. Trustees approved building a printing plant there. Offices would follow.

* * * * *

And the lawsuits!

During the war, lawyers for both Ford and Thompson had delayed going into court to ask juries to give Ford a million dollars, Thompson $1,350,000 and the city of Chicago 10 million. Now

227

briefs were ready. The Ford Company had converted its factories to war work and had become a major advertiser. Perhaps The Tribune should seek its friendship. But the Colonel instructed Tribune lawyers not to settle with Ford and to fight Thompson in every possible way. Forget Thompson's wartime posturing before the Irish and Germans; go after him for fraud; tell the people of Chicago how much money his bad administration was costing the people.

*   *   *   *   *

And communications!

How often in the trenches on the Western front had Major McCormick, later Lieutenant Colonel McCormick, artillery battalion commander, sworn at the French army's field telephones. Something—a bursting shell, a supply wagon, an ambulance, a runner taking a shortcut—frequently broke the wire. The commander had to send a runner or go himself to find the break, darting from shell hole to shell hole if the enemy's guns were active.

The first law of gunnery was unchallenged: To be effective, artillery must have instant and constant communications. Alexander Graham Bell had invented the telephone 40 years earlier and by 1915 there were more than 10 million telephones in America. By 1917 the French had developed an efficient field telephone. The problem was the wire, the damned wire. Miles and miles of it ran across every battlefield in a crazy web.

Sixteen years earlier Marconi had sent dot-dash-dot messages without a wire, and electrical wizards began developing a voice telephone that needed no wire. In 1915 Western Electric experimenters talked between Washington and Hawaii, 5,000 miles apart, and between Washington and the Eiffel Tower in Paris, not quite so far, but the equipment was bulky. By 1917 the French had developed low-power radio telephones that were mobile but hardly portable and not weatherproof and thus effective only for use in corps and division headquarters snug in chateaux, schools or wine cellars. In 1918 the United States army opened a powerful station at Bordeaux to carry messages between General Pershing's headquarters in France and the War Department in Washington. McCormick's endless curiosity must have led him on duty calls to higher echelons to seek detailed explanations of the wireless wonder.

AUTHOR—

229

Think of it! What a help wireless telegraphy would be in moving dispatches from Tribune foreign correspondents, quickly and cheaply! No more of that five dollars a word paid to bring from Hong Kong the barest details of Dewey's sinking the Spanish Far Eastern fleet in Manila harbor. No more government officials claiming priority and shoving news dispatches back into the box of copy waiting to be sent. The Colonel arranged with the army to transmit Tribune foreign news from the Bordeaux station at a cost 30 percent less than the Marconi cable and four to six hours more quickly. A receiver at The Tribune, using the call letters 9ZN, picked out of the air the dispatches from Bordeaux. After a few months of peace, the army, clearing out of Europe, sold the station to the French government, which made an exchange arrangement with Radio Corporation of America, closing the circuit to The Tribune.

The Colonel asked Tribune engineers to look into the possibility of establishing a private wireless news circuit from Europe to America and asked other newspapers with foreign news sources if they would be interested in joining the project. The response was sufficient for the Colonel to help found the News Traffic Board and build a receiving station at Halifax, Nova Scotia, to bring in news from England, France and Italy.

Were there wider uses for the wireless telephone? If voices and music could be sent to everyone with proper receiving equipment over a wide area, a new world of entertainment and instruction would be at hand.

* * * * *

On April 16, 1919, the Colonel's father, Ambassador Robert Sanderson McCormick, died of pneumonia in a nursing home in Hinsdale, the western suburb of Chicago where he had been treated as an alcoholic. Kate made a suite in the Paris Ritz her home and began wandering around Europe, sometimes in a private railroad car. Now and then Larry Rue or Henry Wales or another Tribune foreign correspondent helped her back to the Ritz. Joseph Medill's preaching of temperance had slipped past her, too.

* * * * *

The Ford case came to trial in May and lasted 98 days. Ford's lawyers asked that the hearing be moved out of Chicago. A neutral site was found in Mount Clemens, a farm community in southeastern Michigan. McCormick admitted on the stand that he had approved the editorial but added that his mind at the time was dominated by a lack of machine guns for his cavalry troops. One reason for the lack, he said, was Mr. Ford. "Objection," Ford lawyers said. "Sustained," the judge said. Tribune lawyers said Ford's international stand grew out of muddled thinking arising from ignorance about world affairs. They pointed out that The Tribune consistently praised Ford for looking after the welfare of his employees.

The dispute centered around the term "anarchistic." To McCormick since his boyhood days, when labor riots blamed on "anarchists" kept him locked in the house, "anarchist" had been a political epithet matched in evil by "communist" and "dictator." Tribune lawyers questioned Ford about his knowledge of past events. His ignorance was quickly apparent. Defending himself Ford said, "History is more or less bunk. We want to live in the present and the only history that is worth a tinker's dam is the history we make today."

The comment went into American folklore shortened to "History is bunk." His lawyers reminded the jurors that although Ford early thought he could stop the war, his factories later produced weapons. A Ford advertising man, quizzed about damage done to Ford's image by Tribune criticism, said The Tribune was one of the most influential newspapers in the country; it certainly did sell Ford cars. The Tribune reproduced the comment in paid advertisements coast to coast. In the end the Michigan farmer jurors found The Tribune guilty and awarded Ford six cents damages and six cents for costs. McCormick did not pay, "hoping to force Ford to sue for collection in an Illinois court where all expected to go through all the pyrotechnics again." Ford did not appeal the 12-cent judgment. The Colonel had spent $300,000 for lawyers, Ford probably more. No one ever denied that the Ford executive had made the statement which set off the whole episode. Of the 78 Ford employees who volunteered for the border campaign, most got their jobs back. Was the publicity a factor? Who can say? The Ford trial had been legal acrobatics, a contest between two rich men with large staffs of eager lawyers.

The Ford Motor Company and The Tribune, both fast-growing, practical business enterprises, needed each other. "I came to know and esteem Henry Ford, previously known largely for his political peculiarities and his peace ship," McCormick said. After a dozen years Ford, a daily reader of the adventures of Little Orphan Annie, sent a note to The Tribune saying, "Please do all you can to help Annie recover Sandy." On July 30, 1941, the birthday for both men—McCormick was 61 and Ford was 78—McCormick wrote to Ford: "It occurs to me on this our birthday to write and say I regret the editorial we published about you so many years ago. I only wonder why the idea never occurred to me before. It was a product of war psychology which is bringing out so many familiar expressions today. I am not planning to publish this myself but you are perfectly welcome to use it in any way you wish." Later Ford and McCormick met in Chicago in Ford's private railroad car. McCormick reported: "We agreed the whole thing was a mistake, that we should never have let our lawyers get us into it."

*   *   *   *   *

Ruth Hanna McCormick formed the first GOP women's national committee with herself as chairman. She bought two papers in Rockford, Illinois, the Morning Star and the Register-Republican, to spread the news about her husband's good work in the Senate. Medill McCormick was helping to create the Bureau of the Budget to check on government spending, writing laws to reduce the miseries of children working long hours at low pay, voting against American entry into the League of Nations. In the Senate Medill's voice was strong, his information vast, his advice sound. Good looking, rich, kind, erudite, religious—the worn pages of his Bible testify to much use—full of grace, he was welcome at every dining table. He and Ruth bought a 2,400-acre Illinois farm near Middle Creek for use during vacations and developed a prize herd.

*   *   *   *   *

Red Oaks Farm offered a haven, an island where Amy, 47, and the Colonel, 39, together could build a little new world of their own. The Colonel sent crews to help Deininger and to renew the electrical, plumbing and heating services. Amy and the Colonel filled the stables with horses and built homes for families to tend the animals, work the fields, help in the house. The Colonel opened vistas through the woods, planted a half-mile-long avenue of elms and tried to persuade the county to line with trees the road to Winfield railroad station a mile distant. Just before prohibition sent federal agents with sledgehammers through the nation's warehouses, the Colonel stocked the basement with so much scotch that, according to servant tales, untouched cases remained when that unhappy experiment ended 14 years later.

The Colonel renamed the farm "Cantigny" in remembrance of the 1st Division's first battle and its first victory. He pronounced the name Can-teen-ny, accenting the second syllable, avoiding both the American Can-tig-ny and the French Cahn-tee-nyee, accenting all syllables equally.

In June, the Colonel invited Chicago-area veterans of the 1st Division to a reunion at Cantigny. About 200 rode a special interurban train to Winfield Road and marched the final mile to Cantigny where an ox roasted over a pit of coals. The men played baseball, pitched horseshoes and quoits, ran wheelbarrow races, shot arrows, boxed, slapped backs, sang war songs and told war stories, feasted, drank lemonade and coffee and then marched back to the station and the waiting train.

*　*　*　*　*

Patterson came home and assumed direction of The News but remained in Chicago, leaving Field to recruit a staff. Field chose as managing editor Arthur Clarke, a New York native who had worked briefly for The Tribune in London reporting the Boer War and then in Chicago as city editor. Clarke had left The Tribune to restore ailing papers for Hearst and came back to The Tribune as city editor. He chose as his assistant another Hearst man, Merton Burke, who during the war as International News Service correspondent in Italy so impressed King Victor Emmanuel's chamberlain that the King asked Burke to take over Italy's public relations. He declined. As features editor Field chose Sumner Blossom, a veteran of the Associated Press and of Hearst, just released from the navy, and for photo editor and artist, long time New York newspaper art editor and horse fancier Edward Miner.

The four, working in a room at The Tribune's advertising office at 251 Park Avenue, began assembling articles, comics and cartoons borrowed from The Tribune, news from the United Press wire, photos from Underwood and Underwood. A worn leather couch served as a layout table. At the end of May the editorial staff, enlarged to nine, produced its first 16-page paper. The Mail ran off a few copies which satisfied no one. The staff looked for new material, reassigned pages, decided that one photograph fancied up by an artist must dominate the front page with, over it, a short headline in thick black letters telling of the main story inside. Everyone agreed a second mockup had lost its homemade appearance but salesmen who showed it to potential advertisers brought back not one ad. Rejigging resumed. By the last week in June reporters were bringing in snappy stories and adopting a breezy style, editors were taking the mud out of features and composing teasing headlines but photographers still froze their subjects into wooden Indians and had much to learn before the paper could live up to its name, The Illustrated Daily News, and to its trademark, a winged camera. On the night of June 25, 1919, Field told the pressmen, "Let her roll." The handsome golden haired Prince of Wales, soon to visit New York and pinup boy for New York shop and office girls, rode a horse across the front page and, in an oval inset, boldly lit a cigarette. A murder trial was the main story. Overnight the Mail's press printed 150,000 copies. Trucks and wagons operated jointly by New York newspapers delivered the strange-looking sheet to Manhattan newsstands. The other papers saw no threat in the funny-looking paper, telling one another it soon would disappear. Curious New Yorkers cleared the stands in a few hours but by the third day, curiosity satisfied, sales dropped below 100,000, then below 50,000, then below 30,000. One dreadful day in August only 11,000 copies were sold. Annenberg, The Tribune's energetic circulation director loaned to help establish the new paper, said, "Boss, we're licked. We might as well pick up our marbles and go back to Chicago," and went. Field gave Annenberg's task to a young man, Ed Sullivan, who had built the wartime Paris edition from 6,000 to 150,000 and was willing to bet his reputation that The News would pass 100,000 by the end of the year. Field shared Sullivan's optimism. Hearing The Herald refused to take delivery of a giant press which could turn out 200,000 copies a night, Field bought it and stored it.

Patterson long had argued that a paper must be talked about if it were to succeed. Everyone loves contests and everyone likes to look at pretty girls, so the first issue announced that The News would find the most beautiful girl in New York and give her $10,000. From photographs sent by families and friends, movie master D. W. Griffith and Broadway producer George M. Cohan

chose a girl working in a corset factory. A cosmetic maker hired her for $100 a week—then a queen's allowance—and sent her around the country. Her mother warned her not to marry, explaining, "People will say he married you for your fortune." She ignored the advice, married secretly and was abandoned within a year. By then The News had chosen New York's most beautiful child.

Patterson didn't like the paper's name. "The Illustrated Daily News" is too big a mouthful, he said. He snipped it to The New York News but, told that already was copyrighted, settled simply for The News. The winged camera remained. Patterson had not given up his conviction that people like to look at pictures.

In September the circulation was back up to 30,000 and climbing by 10,000 a month. In December The News announced the paper would print each day the first four lines of a limerick and give $100 to the reader supplying a fifth line which The News best liked. New Yorkers found a new fad. Subway riders swapped limericks. Hostesses enlivened dinners by asking guests to complete the jingles. The presses ran long into the night. By December 31 the circulation was barely short of Sullivan's promised 100,000.

Arthur Brisbane, Hearst's big man, invited Field to dinner and offered to take over The News from McCormick and Patterson "for a nominal consideration." Field reported the offer. The cousins wondered if Brisbane were speaking for Hearst or for himself and decided to wait and see. Brisbane did not raise the subject again and five years passed before Hearst brought out his own New York tabloid.

Other publishers, becoming aware that the upstart was a serious rival, encouraged wagon and truck drivers to forget to drop bundles of The News at busy street stands. McCormick and Patterson, no believers in sharing an enterprise with rivals, authorized Field to develop his own delivery services. He bought 42 horse wagons and 18 trucks. Similarly, problems arose in the shared plant. Before The News was a year old, Field looked around for a building to accommodate the stored press and the rapidly growing staff. He settled for a 41-year lease on a five-story structure, about 40 years old, at 23-25 Park Place, off Broadway and almost next door to the Woolworth Building, tallest in the world. Remodeling and installing equipment took 11 months and cost $200,000.

In September of 1920, 15 months after its birth, The News earned its first profit. It had borrowed from The Tribune just under one million dollars. Advertisements were coming in. The paper added pages. Some nights the presses of the evening Telegram were drafted and ran off wagon loads of The News. Color comics were brought from Chicago. Two weeks after moving into the remodeled Park Place quarters, The News added a Sunday edition, with a press run of a quarter of a million.

Movies were becoming popular. During visits to New York Patterson passed many afternoons in the new film palaces, noting which films were popular and which were not. He thought his readers would like to know more about films than advertisements told them. The assignment went to Paul Gallico, a young reporter who was most disrespectful about movies featuring Marion Davies, thereby further alienating her sponsor, William Randolph Hearst. Gallico moved on to sports and fame.

Pictures were a problem from the start. The west coast was three days distant by the fastest train and Europe a week by the fastest liner, whereas news came instantly by wire and radio. Matching pictures and news was a challenge. The art department developed a system for sending pictures by wire. The photographer squared off the picture, numbering the vertical lines and lettering the horizontal ones. He telegraphed a description of the picture and the coordinates of the main features. In New York an artist charted the coordinates, connected the dots to reproduce the outline of the figures and then filled in the picture, augmenting the description with his own knowledge and imagination, sometimes producing a scene much more spectacular than the photograph. Walking around New York Patterson saw pictures everywhere and hired photographers with imagination and initiative. One snapped a mother duck leading her family across a busy street while a happy cop held back cars. Another caught Ruth Snyder sizzling in the electric chair in Sing Sing. Both photographs became classics.

Patterson wanted The News to be part of the lives of its reading newsstands he noted that women were heavy buyers. He must reach out to them. just as he had on The Tribune. He asked Mary King to repeat for The News her success with The Tribune in obtaining good attractive fiction. She must find a short story for each Sunday and novels which could be serialized in the daily paper. Mary accepted, without giving up her Tribune position as Sunday editor.

237

Mary King drew on the most popular writers, E. Phillips Oppenheim, Sax Rohmer, Booth Tarkington, John Galsworthy, Fannie Hurst, Earle Stanley Gardner, F. Scott Fitzgerald, Zane Grey. She persuaded Winston Churchill to condense six classic novels and to write his autobiography, for which Mary paid him $6,000. One day she told Patterson she wished someone could condense Tolstoy's two-volume masterpiece, "War and Peace," into 5,000 words. "Impossible," Patterson replied. Mary asked Churchill; he did the chop job. Mary became a power in the literary world. Only the Saturday Evening Post bought more fiction. She paid well but Patterson recovered most or all of the expense by selling reprint rights to more than 60 newspapers.

The wide variation in styles and subjects of Mary's authors testify to her own catholic tastes in literature, although Mary said her favorite stories were built around love and family life. She claimed she had no taboos, but her heroes and heroines were pure in heart and tongue and were guided by high principle. No mother ever betrayed a daughter in a Mary story; all improper words instantly were edited out. Mary returned promptly and firmly any story she considered propaganda or derogatory of any group. Patterson labeled her stories "Blue Ribbon Fiction."

The newspaper magic that brought together Joseph Patterson and Mary King in the editorial offices developed into a happy comradeship and then into love. Patterson's marriage to Alice Higinbotham early had become bankrupt. For years Patterson had gone home at night to the Chicago Lake Shore apartment and entered only the small library off the hall which, with addition of a bathroom, had become his quarters. Patterson had asked many times for a divorce. His wife refused until many years had passed. Mary moved to New York to become woman's editor of The News. She and Patterson had a son, Jimmy.

12. Getting To Know The Wilderness
1919—1922

M IcCormick was eager to start harvesting wood in the Rocky
Riv er area but it was July, 1919, before he was free to go to the
St. Lawrence. He had not heard from Schmon since January. The
Col onel telephoned Schmon's fiancee, Celeste Reynolds, in Newark , New Jersey, to ask if Schmon were still in the army. She told
hin ı Schmon had arrived in Newark the previous day on a 15-day
lea ve before being discharged. By nightfall Schmon arranged to
joi n the Colonel in Quebec and go with him to the North Shore
an d see what the offered job involved. At Quebec Curtis was
wa ıting with a retired submarine chaser christened by the Colo-
ne l the *S. S. Mareuilendole* for the French chateau where he and
Pa ıtterson had decided to start The News.

Long ago the forest, lakes and rivers north of the St. Lawrence
w ere shared by Indians who had come up from the south and Es-
ki mos who had come down from the north. Who arrived first no
or ıe knows. The Indians won the territory, killing off enough Es-
ki .mos to drive out the survivors. The Indians learned to survive
th ıe long winters when, for months, the temperature seldom rose
al bove zero and frequently was minus 20 or lower, the wind blew
c(onstantly, snow fell almost every day until it was as deep as two
n ıen. The flesh of creatures thriving in the woods and under the
i(;e provided the Indians with food and the skins gave them cloth-
iı ıg. The skins drew explorers. For a few shiny beads an Indian
p ıarted with a beaver pelt worth a month's labor in Normandy or
F 3rittany. Before long French entrepreneurs built a log cabin at
t he mouth of the Saguenay River and word spread through the
ν νoods that bright treasure, the like of which no Indian ever had
ε ;een, could be had for the choosing; the Indian need only to bring
ε ı few pelts. Priests followed. In France word spread that land
ι reaching from horizon to horizon could be had for the asking.
: Men and women who saw only continued toil and poverty, sick-

239

ness and early death for themselves and their children in their unfair world bound together their few belongings and joined adventurers crossing the stormy ocean to the new world.

The North Shore provided few anchorages. If a ship's captain did pause in an estuary, settlers sent ashore in a small boat came back in a few hours saying the land could not produce grass for their cow nor grain for their bread. The South Shore was kindlier. It did not offer the rich loam of Normandy but the soil could produce grain, and the land would be owned by them, not by a landlord. They settled along that shore and labored to build a New France, telling themselves each year that next year would be better. The next year was a little better but even the strongest, most diligent family could not draw from the harsh land enough to meet their expectations. Young men left home in October or November, paddled 20 miles across the St. Lawrence and disappeared on snowshoes into the woods. They did not come home until May or June.

How did they survive? What did they wear? What did they eat? How did they sleep? How did they move about? The Colonel was more than curious when he asked the questions. On his first voyage down the St. Lawrence in 1914 searching for trees which could be made at a profit into paper for The Tribune, he had seen the unbroken forests along the North Shore. At the time St. Lawrence trees were being harvested in any quantity only on the island of Anticosti at the top of the Gulf. He learned on arrival there that the operation survived only because the island's rich owner paid losses from earnings as chocolate king of France. McCormick tramped the Anticosti woods to help the seigneur, Henri Menier, kill the deer that were destroying young trees. The tramp told him why the Anticosti project was a loser: the island's streams were too small to carry the logs to the sea so that task was done the expensive way, by men and horses. Had the island bigger streams, the operation would have been profitable. Moving slowly back up the St. Lawrence, McCormick saw tremendous rivers spilling out of the forests on the North Shore. Here and there he saw a stump carved into the rough likeness of a man's face and topped with a bit of cloth. Manitou, the Indians called their God guarding paths leading into the woods. Fur trappers must have used those paths. Trappers learned how to live in the winter wilderness. So could woodsmen!

No man could have better North Woods mentors than the Colonel had in Napoleon Comeau, Arthur Parent and Paul Provencher. Comeau had been born when furs were a way of life and he was already a legend when McCormick began entering the woods. Parent and Provencher had gone into the woods as boys. Provencher became one of McCormick's woodland-cruising companions and his favorite storyteller. "Provencher," the Colonel said, "has forgotten more about the woods than I can ever learn." He encouraged Provencher to write about life in the woods and arranged for publication of the book "so his knowledge will be available to everyone entering the woods, to save themselves hardship and trouble and also to save their lives."

Provencher said he hoped his accounts of trappers and explorers "might fire newcomers with the courage and endurance" of the pioneers. The earliest woodsmen, he told the Colonel, survived by learning the ways of Indians and adapting them, adding a few bits of European magic, most importantly the compass, the hatchet and a crooked knife made from a file. Some trappers carried a gun although many preferred the Indian's bow. It weighed less, it never failed to fire and arrows could be replenished along the way. Do not doubt the power of the bow. One night Provencher killed a 300-pound bear at 40 paces. It staggered 100 feet before its blood ran out. He could produce a witness and certificate to prove the story.

For trappers the vital garment was a loose, belted cloak reaching just below the knees, made from a furred animal, worn with the fur inside. Deerskin leggings reaching from above the knees to the ankle were held in place by strings tied to a belt worn around the waist next to the skin. The leggings overlapped moccasins made of deerskin, caribou or moose. Deerskin was softer; moose and caribou were more durable. The only underwear was the Indian's breechcloth, kin of the bikini. On the head a woolen cap, preferably red.

By the Colonel's time the leggings had yielded to thick trousers gathered at the ankle, the cloak to a parka reaching below the knees and gathered at the wrists by strong elastic. Moccasins had become thick boots with wide toes. The woodsmen had added thick stockings—sometimes worn double—a flannel shirt, woolen sweater, a peaked cap, mittens—not gloves—and at least one layer of woolen underwear. The Colonel, with that inner twinkle, said he liked to wear an extra layer of underwear so during the night someone else first became chilly, awakened and threw another log on the fire while he slept snugly on.

The early trapper went into the woods on snowshoes, carrying at least 200 pounds in a backpack hung low from a forehead strap. If the load were heavier, up to 450 pounds, a second strap crossed the chest or harnessed each shoulder. Provencher once saw a half-breed named Henry Pitlegan carry 600 pounds of flour a quarter of a mile. If the trapper were carrying many trading goods, he built a toboggan. He chose a tall straight tree, birch or tamarack, felled it, cut out a section ten and a half feet long, split it down the middle and then split one plank from each half. He trimmed one edge straight and curved the other edge outwards until the plank was about five inches wide at each end and about six inches wide a third of the way along. Then came the patient part, holding one end of each plank in steam from a kettle boiling over a fire or wrapping it with rags soaked in boiling water until the wood was pliable and the tip could be bent backward until it almost touched the plank. There it was bound with a thong and allowed to dry. The two planks were bound together with cross pieces. The job took about a week. The trapper pulled the toboggan with a forehead strap, the toboggan following in his tracks. A toboggan was most useful in the early winter months when the snow was soft. In March and April the snow was hard; the trapper then abandoned the toboggan and built a sled with two runners. He could push it at a merry clip over frozen rivers and lakes as he hurried home, the sled high with pelts. Somewhere along the shore he recovered a canoe he had left there the previous autumn, tied it on the sled, bottom down, and secured the pelts in it. If the ice gave way, he kicked off his snowshoes, hopped into the canoe, now floating, cut loose the now submerged sled, wriggled the canoe onto the ice, recovered the sled, regained the shore, built a fire, dried out and continued homeward.

Or he could remain in the woods until the ice broke, paddle along the lakes and down rivers, carrying canoe and pelts around rapids. Few trappers could run rapids which the Indians traveled safely. The secret, the Colonel learned, was that the white man sat on a bench while the Indian knelt on the canoe floor, feet and toes pressed backward against the floor. The Colonel demonstrated the kneeling position at the Tribune Book Section's Christmas party, but to Children's Book Editor Polly Goodwin he explained he could not long remain in that position. Few white men can; they have not, when young, stretched foot muscles as had the Indian. By kneeling the Indian lowered the center of gravity and added stability to the unstable craft. The taller and heavier the man, the more unstable was the canoe. Trappers were small men, rarely over five feet six inches. Indians were even smaller, many under five feet.

Trappers were tempted to run rapids to avoid carrying the canoe and cargo. A canoe 18 feet long weighed about 60 pounds but after a few weeks in the water doubled its weight. A canoe could carry 600 pounds with expert handling. Otherwise 200 pounds was a safe maximum.

A long-time trapper often lightened his labor by harnessing dogs to the sled. Provencher preferred one dog, trained to follow in his tracks, but most Indians liked two, permitting the man to hop on for a free ride now and then. A 15-pound dog could pull 50 pounds, a 50-pounder could pull 150 pounds but he often dropped through the snow. A strong woodsman and dog could cover five miles in an hour. The most useful snowshoes were 45 inches long and 21 inches wide. If a snowshoe broke, a woodsman moved along on a carefully chosen and trimmed balsam bough.

A trapper often traveled a hundred or more miles before he began laying traps. On the move he was content to travel until nine or 10 o'clock at night, halt on the sheltered side of a large tree or steep rock that protected him from the wind, clear away with a snowshoe the loose surface snow making a fire pit, chop wood, lay logs in the pit, then twigs and shavings and finally a bit of precious charred cotton cloth cradled on birch bark or decayed wood, strike steel against flint, catch the spark on the cotton and tenderly waft up a flame.

As the fire grew, he put snow in a kettle along with a chunk of frozen meat from a bird or animal killed the previous day or two or spiked the meat on a spit. Lynx is tasty, like rabbit. Beaver tail, broiled until it is blistered, has its advocates. As dinner cooked he scooped a narrow trench, just wide enough and long enough to accommodate his body. He ate, he lay in the trench and swept snow over his body. In the morning he was on his way as soon as he awoke, hours before daylight.

On reaching his hunting grounds he spent two hours or more preparing a home for the next few days. He again chose a large tree or a stone face, dug a hole in the snow six feet by eight feet and five feet deep and half filled it with balsam boughs. He stripped a dozen branches and shoved the sticks into the snow in a half circle on the windward side of the pit and tied to them a thin tightly woven cotton sheet. He piled branches on the outside of the sheet and covered them with snow. At the opposite end of the pit, he closely piled together several logs as base for the fire.

As the flames rose high and the heat reflected from the sheet, the trapper took off all of his clothes and dried them and himself of the day's perspiration. Going to sleep wet was an invitation to pneumonia and death. He might make some tea from leaves he had gathered during the summer from the tamarack, cook a bit of salt pork and mix into its fat some flour and water, put the dough into a kettle and set it beside the fire. While waiting for the meat to cook and bread to bake, he carefully examined his coat, his leggings, his moccasins. If he found a tear, he cursed, took from a pouch a sinew he had cut some time earlier from the back of a caribou. As it dried, the ends had hardened into sharp points, providing a ready-threaded needle. The sinew was a hundred times stronger than the best thread and it would not rot.

His garments repaired, the trapper dressed and feasted, then lay on the balsam and wrapped himself in a blanket he had woven loosely from strips of skins from 100 rabbits. It was warmer and lighter than Europe's finest woolen blanket but tore easily. It could not be washed but who in the woods ever washed anything? He lit his pipe and soon was dreaming, awake or asleep, of the luxuries he would lavish upon his proud family from the fortune that awaited him in the beautiful, generous, kind, white wilderness.

*   *   *   *   *

Little had happened on Rocky River since McCormick and Amy were there in 1915. The 1918 summer influenza epidemic, which took a greater toll in America than the war, had attacked Curtis' small crew. Curtis prescribed Epsom salts and scotch and every man recovered. The new name, Shelter Bay, had not altered the granite mounds which rose from the river mouth, waiting to tear apart an unwary ship. When the tide was out and the river flow was low, the bay was too shallow to admit a cargo ship. Curtis had selected an island a half mile from shore as the best site for a wharf and had begun assembling logs there. He discussed with various engineers how a wharf might be built. None had produced an acceptable plan. The wharf had to withstand the mammoth waves which roll across the Atlantic from Spain and concentrate their power as they sweep up the St. Lawrence. No piles could be driven into the granite river bed. The Colonel proposed that Curtis buy a ship hulk, sink it next to the island and use it as the foundation for a wharf. Curtis found such a hulk, the *Wiley M. Egan*, bought her for $2,000, filled her with worn grindstones at Thorold and towed her down the St. Lawrence to Shelter Bay. In July Curtis was ready to sink her. The Colonel said he would come down to watch and bring Schmon.

Curtis placed dynamite deep in the hulk, next to the keel. As McCormick, Curtis and Schmon watched, the blast tore a large hole in the hulk. Water flooded in. Slowly the hulk sank. Grindstones held her upright as she settled firmly on the bottom. McCormick led the cheers. In the morning the crew could start adding timber for the wharf. McCormick, Curtis and Schmon had a celebration dinner. Curtis talked about plans for a mill to grind logs coming down the Rocky River into pulp which could be shipped to Thorold. The shipping cost would be less than that for wood.

Schmon was intrigued by Shelter Bay. The management job did indeed offer unlimited opportunities and, as the Colonel also had written, its problems were truly far from inconsiderable. He must talk to Celeste. He wondered if she would be happy in the wilderness. You may both live in Montreal in the winter, the Colonel said. Schmon said he would sleep on it. During the night a sudden storm crashed waves against the hulk. Fists of water thrust through the dynamited hole and tore at the blast-shattered timbers, wrenching them free, one by one. The waves rolled the grindstones along the riverbed. By the morning the hulk was worthless.

Cheer up, the Colonel said, the idea is sound, the flaw was in the way we carried it out. We should not have dynamited the hulk. We should have left her intact and filled her with stone blasted from the island until she sank. Try again that way. Curtis did. The second hulk provided a firm base for a wharf. It still does.

McCormick returned to Chicago. Schmon went to Celeste and told her he would like to try the job. It had challenge and prospects. Shelter Bay was a primitive place just now but would be a lot more comfortable next year. Could they put off the wedding until then? No, Arthur, no, Celeste said. She had put off the wedding for two years because of the war but she would have no further postponement. So they married, went to Shelter Bay and turned a log hut into a happy honeymoon cottage. In October, just before the river froze, she returned to Newark. He promised to build a proper house during the winter. It even might have electricity but he did not see how he could eliminate the outside privy just yet. He would ask her advice in everything. He did ask, but the questions departed by dogsled, and when her replies came two months later each task had been done. During the fall the wharf was finished. Schmon started clearing the woods for a settlement.

The next summer the Colonel came often to Shelter Bay. He wanted to be certain how much wood could be harvested in the Rocky River basin. With Tibasse and Arthur Parent he paddled up the river and along the quiet lakes seeking places where logs could be chained together to form a boom and hold back the logs being brought down the river. One day the 12-foot-long logs jammed. The Colonel walked out on the boom to see how the jam could be blasted open. Parent followed. With a crack the boom broke. The jammed logs whirled through the gap. The two men ran along the loose boom for the shore. The Frenchman paused. "After you, sir," he said. "Run," the Colonel shouted, adding a curse that was necessary, the Colonel later explained, to "overcome the Frenchman's sense of propriety." The men were lucky. Their half of the boom swung toward shore. The other half swung into the rapids. Had the men been on that, they would have been tumbled to death amidst the logs whirling in the foaming white water.

The Colonel, when traveling the woods with an Indian, took along a squaw to do the cooking. That's women's work, the Indians said. It probably never occurred to the Colonel that he cook. Two bits of Indian high cuisine must have amused the Colonel while not tempting him to incorporate them into his menu; he was a meat-and-potatoes man. Indian men swore that the paw was the tastiest part of a bear, but all properly reared squaws tactfully shunned it, leaving it to the men. From very early girls were told, by fathers and brothers no doubt, that any woman who bit into a bear's paw would have cold feet for the rest of her life. Provencher said the most prized Indian delicacy was made by mixing the blood of a newly killed caribou with the contents of its stomach and hanging the mess in a pot near a fire for several days until it fermented. What does it taste like? Provencher could not say; he always declined a helping, not wanting to deprive his host.

During the summer a small mill was built on the wharf island to cut into four foot lengths and debark logs which had been collected into rafts at the river mouth and towed to the island. Each boat brought supplies for the winter. In the late autumn Schmon brought from the South Shore 1,500 men eager to supplement their farm incomes, just as had their grandfathers in the fur days, by winter work in the woods. Some hired on piece rates brought their families. Most brought horses to drag logs out of the woods to the river or lakes. The lucky horses were hoisted from the boat anchored offshore onto barges and taken to land. The unlucky ones, pushed overboard, swam ashore.

The early crews established winter camps in the woods. The central structure was a small log cabin with, running across one side, two six-foot-wide shelves, one above the other. On these, covered with balsam branches, the men slept, clothed and unwashed. Muzzle loaders, the men called bunks.

The cook was expected to produce cereal, fried potatoes, cold pork or beef, pancakes, a liver paste called creton, pie, coffee, tea and milk before dawn, supply each man with a lunch to take into the woods and have ready on their return soup, meat pie, potatoes, vegetable salad, cold pork, creton, pie and drink. Alcohol was banned. Men's bodies demanded sugar. The cooks expected to divide a pie among three or four men but at some camps men said they would not work unless each was given a whole pie at each meal. They got whole pies.

One midwinter day a cook came upon a loaf of bread that had been left out of doors. Curious, he put the frozen loaf into the oven. Soon the room smelled sweetly of new bread. The cook removed the loaf. He broke it open. It felt like new bread. He bit into it. It tasted like new bread. Soon the cook was baking enough bread for a month or more, storing it out of doors and bringing in only enough for each meal. Some loggers, wanting fresh bread for lunch in the woods, set off in the morning with a frozen loaf under the parka. At noon the hard-working, heat-generating woodsmen opened the jacket and—voila—warm, fresh bread. The miracle of rejuvenated bread remained a secret of the forest. Many years passed before big city bakers offered frozen bread, and housewives, by turning an oven switch, filled the house with the glorious aroma that once pervaded homes on baking day.

The men's appetite was mild compared to that of the horses. Hay and oats outweighed all other supplies. One day the Colonel sent a note asking why the horses were not fed alfalfa as were his horses at Cantigny. The answer: Alfalfa does not grow along the St. Lawrence; to import it would cost more than hay and oats. "That ends alfalfa," the Colonel replied. After the first snow only potatoes, butter and other fresh foods were carried in on dog sleds. A pound of butter delivered in the woods, Schmon once noted, cost almost as much as a pound of gold. Woodsmen, paid according to the amount of wood cut and stacked, left the camp by six o'clock and often did not return until nine or 10 at night, working more than half of the time by lantern light. A doctor and a priest hiked from camp to camp. Twice a month the mail came through on dog sled from Bersimis more than 100 miles away.

During the second summer, 1921, brown skies in the north announced that a fire was sweeping through the forest 100 miles inland, beyond Tribune lands. When the sky cleared, Schmon set off with Tibasse and others into the unexplored burned-over territory. They found 450 square miles of charred trees. Such timber can be made into pulp if cut within a few years. On Schmon's advice the Colonel bought from the Quebec government the right to harvest it at a charge far below the royalty he paid on trees from living woods nearer the coasts. During the next summer timber camps were moved into the flame-mangled woods and supplies were carried there for more than 5,000 men and 200 women and children. Just as ice was forming in the late autumn the Colonel's speedboat carrying the priest, the doctor, a newly wed couple and six others was sheared open by sheet ice. The skipper jammed blankets into the split hull but the boat filled quickly with water. Passengers scrambled onto the ice but it broke under them. All drowned. The next day only a glove on the ice marked the tragedy. Schmon sent a crew in a heavy boat to break the ice and, with grappling hooks, to recover the bodies.

During the winter men cut the charred trees, covering themselves with soot. Horses dragged the logs to the lakes. Schmon planned to marshal log rafts in the spring and tow them along the lakes to the river. In early spring the Colonel noticed ice was breaking up on the Chicago River and cabled Schmon to inspect all booms and make sure they were firm and ready to hold the logs that soon would come. A few days later he urged Schmon to scatter bark chips on the ice and hasten the thaw; the dark wood would draw more heat from the sun than could the reflecting ice. After the thaw Schmon happily reported the wind was blowing the logs along the lakes and no tow would be needed.

McCormick expected Shelter Bay to be a company camp, used only by men working each season. But just as Celeste would not be separated from Schmon, other wives chose to join their husbands in the wilderness. Husbands built log shacks until the

248

Colonel provided cut lumber. A missionary built a Catholic church. McCormick had Schmon build a school and a small hospital. He sent an engineer experienced in building hydroelectric plants who, after walking about, proclaimed the Rocky River too turbulent to be tamed and chose as site for a hydroplant a small nearby stream which fell over a precipice into the St. Lawrence. The plant was built but in the winter, when its power was most needed, the stream became dry, the turbine sat idle and Celeste sat in the lamplight. So much for outside expert advice, the Colonel said. Any woodsman could have told the visiting expert that all North Shore rivers run a torrent in summer when the snow melts but become a trickle in the frozen winters. The Colonel told Schmon to dam the Rocky River and force it to give power and light to the pioneer community.

Celeste asked a carpenter from the South Shore to wall off one corner of a room in her house. He was puzzled. The space was too small for a bed, too big for a closet. What was it? It's a washroom, Celeste said. The word rippled through the settlement: Captain Schmon is building a washroom! What is a washroom? People found many reasons to call on Celeste and look at the work being done. One day crates arrived with strange white things. In time all was finished. Celeste invited everyone in town to an open house. She offered food and drink. But the complete turnout of the town was produced by curiosity over the mystery of the new room. One by one the guests entered the little room, closed the door, pulled a chain dangling over a strange white porcelain stool and jumped back as a torrent of water flooded into the stool. We must have one, each wife told her husband. There was no peace in any Shelter Bay home until the husband provided a washroom.

The log cabins harbored rats. Schmon offered a bounty of five cents a tail. Small girls lined up, presented fists full of tails and collected the money. Schmon threw the tails out the window. In a very few minutes girls were reappearing. Schmon continued to pay until he recognized an unusual crooked tail. The girls then confessed they had organized a round robin, gathering tails from the ground outside the window and presenting them anew. Schmon delivered a lecture about honesty being the best policy, and paid.

One day the wharf woodpile suddenly collapsed, trapping by his foot a young man loading logs into a ship. At any minute the remaining logs might come crashing down, but a young nurse cradled the boy's head and dripped whiskey into his mouth while a doctor sawed off the foot.

A fire broke out not far inland. The men ran to fight it. A strong wind blew the flames toward the town. Schmon ordered everyone to evacuate homes within two hours. Women and children grabbed the belongings which seemed most precious and carried them to the wharf. By then the flames had driven the men back into the town. Everyone gathered in the church. As they knelt there, thunder crashed, and 30 seconds later heavy rain drummed on the roof. Shelter Bay was saved.

Harvey Smith, Shelter Bay's social historian, recorded that the summers passed swiftly. In the long twilight, men played baseball, each department presenting its team. The champions led the entire town to Clarke City for the North Shore title game. Victory was vital. It so happened that a young man brought to Shelter Bay for a summer maintenance job was Buffalo high school's star pitcher. Clarke City, of course, charged Shelter Bay with infringing the amateurs-only rule but Schmon insisted the young man had been hired solely because of his expertise with a broom. The sweeper went on to pitch for the Chicago Cubs.

Wildlife thrived in the woods and waters. Boys became expert at snaring birds and hooking salmon and brook trout. One day the Colonel, crossing the estuary, saw swimming beside his canoe a fish so big he thought it would overturn the craft. Along the shore golden eagles gorged on dead fish until they could not fly. Everyone learned to respect the horned owl. One day as Tibasse carried home a dead fox, an owl wanting the fox struck the Indian from behind with enough force to knock him flat. Another owl attacked a boy wearing a muskrat cap and a third landed on a curly-haired cook tending an open fire and dug in its talons so firmly that the cook dislodged it only by bending over the flames until the owl roasted. Boys learned that a skunk lifted from the ground on a long pole lost its ability to spray the evil smelling fluid nature had given it for self-defense.

One day the Colonel saw a deer across a small lake. He estimated the distance by noting the relative size of trees on the near and far sides of the lake—the artilleryman's tactic. He lay down, braced the rifle on a log and fired. He saw the bullet hit the water. The Colonel continued his hike. When he arrived on the other side of the lake there lay the deer, dead, hit by the bullet that bounced. "That was the only time I killed an animal beyond point-blank range," the Colonel reported.

One wonderful summer Canada introduced air mail. At Shelter Bay, which had no landing strip, the pilot aimed his mail bags at the church steeple. One day a bag landed in a wagon; the horses bolted and did not stop until they reached the river. The post office marked a drop zone with red flags in an outlying field. A pilot mistook another set of flags warning against imminent blasting. The erupting debris buried the mail. In Clarke City the target was the mill chimney. One excellent pilot dropped a bag into the stack. The mill shut down its furnace for two days and let the chimney cool so a man could lower himself and recover the mail, charred but readable.

Historian Smith records the departure of the last boat as the saddest moment of the year. Some young wives climbed the hill behind the settlement and cried as the boat vanished. For young mothers with husbands working in the woods the winter was most difficult. The tiny cabins became prisons. In late April the church bells rang out the news that the first ship was nearing the harbor. Everyone ran to the wharf.

Celeste Schmon often recalled that her first years at Shelter Bay were the happiest of her life. She was a woman of many interests and deep inner resources, and every day she knew her husband would come home charged with enthusiasm over the day's developments. Both knew they were involved in great adventure.

*   *   *   *   *

On March 7, 1921, the third child was born to Ruth Hanna and Senator Medill McCormick. She was christened Ruth Elizabeth for her mother and an aunt who frequently visited the parents. As in many households in which mother and daughter share a name, the parents spoke to her and of her as Baby. When the child began to talk, they asked her what she wanted to be called. "Bazy," the girl replied in her child's mispronounciation of "Baby." Bazy she became and Bazy she remained. Of Joseph Medill's seven great grandchildren, Bazy was to be the one selected to carry the dynasty into the fourth generation.

13. Solid Advances
1921—1926

In 1921 Westinghouse Electric, an early entry into wireless sound communication already being spoken of as radio, built a broadcasting station in Chicago with the call letters KYW. The Tribune provided news headlines, sports summaries and market results to the 10,000 Chicagoans owning receivers. No one sought advertisers. Costs were paid by Westinghouse, which hoped to sell radio sets, and The Tribune, which hoped to earn readers. The Colonel had a radio delivered to his mother.

"I don't think you will want to keep this," he said, "but you cannot help being thrilled at the little box that picks sound out of the air."

Many other newspaper owners saw radio as a deadly competitor for readers and advertisers, but the Colonel saw radio as an auxiliary to The Tribune. He believed that anyone who heard a summary or a blow-by-blow account of an event would want to read The Tribune's report. From the start he laid down a basic law: "American radio belongs to the American people. We consider our station a sacred trust."

By 1924 Chicago had 100,000 radios. Zenith, a major radio manufacturer, built a powerful station at the Edgewater Beach Hotel. Its first experimental broadcast was heard 8,000 miles away in Australia, making it probably the first trans-Pacific voice broadcast. The Tribune transferred its reports to the Zenith station, but within weeks Zenith and the hotel clashed strongly over the station's operation. The Tribune leased a station being operated by the Board of Trade in a handball court on the top floor of the Drake Hotel. The Colonel proposed changing the call letters from WDAP to WGN, for World's Greatest Newspaper. Learning those letters had been assigned to a freighter operating on the Great Lakes, the Colonel purchased them from the ship's owner, Carl D. Bradley. After two years, The Tribune bought the station's complete equipment for $16,000.

The Colonel decreed WGN should serve the public, but what, precisely, did that mean? WGN took listeners to both national political conventions and let voters hear everything the candidates and their supporters said in Madison Square Garden. On election night WGN carried the results almost vote by vote as John W. Davis and Franklin Roosevelt lost to Calvin Coolidge and Charles G. Dawes. WGN went to Indianapolis for the 500-mile auto race and for seven hours the roar of the high-powered cars dinned into listeners' ears. WGN carried World Series baseball games and moved into Big Ten stadia to report football games play by play. Announcer Quin Ryan's eyewitness account of barelegged fullback No. 77 in the October 18 Illinois-Michigan game was part of Red Grange's start as the early superstar. WGN reported Golden Gloves amateur boxing, a Tribune promotion, and the Arts Ball. It put a commentator under a blanket in Chicago theaters to pick up performances of "The Mikado," "Pinafore" and "The Miracle." It put microphones in the courtroom at Dayton, Tennessee, to relay, word by word, the histrionic rivalry between Clarence Darrow and William Jennings Bryan over whether a Tennessee teacher, John Scopes, violated the law by telling students that the world and everything in it was not created in six days and that man's ancestor was a monkey. At the opening of one session Ryan reported Bryan had just taken his place and remarked: "His bald pate looks like a sunrise over Key West." Bryan heard, turned and laughed. Scopes was found guilty and fined $100. WGN's phone bill was $1,000 a day. On Christmas, Bill Day read Charles Dickens' "Christmas Carol," every word of it, a two-hour treat. WGN gave lessons in French, German, Spanish and English; printed study material to augment the classes was obtainable from The Tribune on request. WGN gave piano lessons to 4,000 listeners and explained the rules and tactics of auction bridge, a popular new pastime. People who loved good books talked about the majesty of literature. An announcer read Tribune comics each morning. The Colonel thought Little Orphan Annie deserved more than mere reading so Annie's adventures soon were expanded into daily episodes, thus opening the door, alas, for soap operas. WGN went to the circus, to band concerts, to Orchestra Hall and the Symphony. Washington bureau chief Arthur Sears Henning reported the news of the capital. WGN went to the Kentucky Derby and to horse shows. Announcers and reporters went down on the farm

to talk to rural folk about their successes and their problems. WGN carried speeches from the World Eucharistic Congress. The big international debate in the mid-twenties concerned the World Court. Should the United States join? WGN arranged a four-hour debate spread over two nights. Senators Thomas Walsh and Irvine Lenroot advocated joining; Henrik Shipstead and William Borah opposed. At the end, the announcer asked listeners to snip a ballot from that morning's Tribune and record their opinion. Eighty-six percent said don't join—The Tribune's position. The Senate ignored the ballot and voted American membership. The World Court erected a costly building in The Hague but achieved little else. WGN spent $10,000 reporting the 1928 conventions. In New York The News supplied a contract station with news every hour on the hour—Joe Patterson's idea.

Everything went out on the air live with one exception. WGN thought its listeners, especially those of Italian descent, should hear Benito Mussolini, then starting to make a big noise in Italy. The radio telephone did not reach to Rome, so WGN recorded one of his speeches on a phonograph record, brought the record to Chicago by ship and train and played it over the air. Floyd Gibbons, who lost an eye in the trenches, told war stories in a manner so breathless the listeners would swear he had just run all the way from the battlefield to Paris. A good-hearted duo being paid a lavish $75 a show, Sam 'n' Henry, in time became national pets as Amos 'n' Andy.

Of course there was music. The Drake Hotel provided the music of its dance orchestras and dinner artists but at the beginning the Colonel told WGN to hire its own musicians full time— five the first year, 10 the next, then 20, finally 75 who from their own membership could present a symphony, an opera, a light opera, seven kinds of bands and early morning military marches to get the body moving. McCormick asked that opera music be well known and be sung in English and that all other music be tuneful.

One day in 1926 WGN engineers displayed a box with a round, glass screen, about three inches across, on which pictures moved. A technical breakthrough! But much work must be done before television would work its wonders for better and worse.

* * * * *

WGN's first transmitter on the roof of the Drake operated on

1,000 watts, one kilowatt. Listeners outside Chicago complained reception was often poor and sometimes non-existent. After one year WGN asked the Department of Commerce for permission to raise its power to 5,000 watts. Herbert Hoover was secretary of commerce and thought radio stations should grow but not at the cost of interfering with city life. His department suggested WGN buy one of the stations then surrounding the city. Near Elgin, 50 miles from the city, were two stations, WTAS of 2,500 watts and WCEE of 1,000. WGN bought the stations and land for $400,000. Equipment included four microphones, one microphone stand, 30 chairs and some drapes. WGN asked Westinghouse to build a transmitter for the new site which could operate at 25,000 watts. The company said the task would take a year. The Colonel couldn't wait. He told WGN to build its own transmitter. A legal hassle developed over patent rights but within six months the new transmitter was sending the WGN signal at 10,000 watts from a 700-foot long antenna strung between two 250-foot towers. In 1930 WGN asked for permission to expand to 50,000 watts. Permission came in 1935 and soon a 750-foot vertical antenna, the tallest structure in the Midwest, carried WGN programs through Illinois, east to Indiana, Ohio, Michigan, north to Wisconsin, west to Iowa, southwest to Missouri.

In the early days of radio, government regulation was based on a skimpy law voted by Congress in 1912. The Department of Commerce issued permits for stations but could not enforce allocations of wavelengths. In 1926 a Chicago station began broadcasting on a channel so close to the one assigned to The Tribune that its words and music merged with those of WGN. The Colonel asked for a court injunction to prevent the station from infringing. Circuit Court Judge Francis Wilson ordered a temporary halt until the legal arguments of both stations could be heard. The other station, WGES, claimed, in effect, that no one has a right to any radio waves, that the air is open to all. WGN's lawyer, Louis Caldwell, argued that such freedom would lead to chaos. The judge agreed and decreed that priority in time gave superiority in rights, just as with water rights on rivers. In other words first come first served. WGN was first to use 720 kilocycles and thus had the right to its use. The judge made the injunction permanent. The ruling changed radio. The courts now had legal precedent on which to base all future cases arising from arguments over use of radio waves. The Colonel had not intended to provide a beacon for all broadcasters but, as a pioneer feeling his way, he was first to realize the need for courts to establish a rule to govern all.

The case made evident the need for further government regulation of radio. The Colonel, although by principle an advocate of free enterprise and a fierce opponent of expansion of governmental power, made Caldwell available in Washington to congressmen and the advisers drafting the law which set up the Federal Radio Commission, later the Federal Communications Commission. Caldwell then served the commission until it completed procedures for an orderly sharing of the air for the benefit of all.

* * * * *

On June 22, 1922, The Tribune was 75 years old. The Colonel celebrated the birthday by announcing a $100,000 world competition for the drawings of an office building which would be "the most beautiful in the world, a fitting home for the world's greatest newspaper, an inspiration to its 3,100 employees and a model for a generation of newspaper publishers."

The bridge across the Chicago River and the approaches had been completed and nondescript Pine Street had been widened into North Michigan Avenue. William Wrigley had acquired a tract just north of the bridge and was raising a wedding cake structure in white tile topped with a clock tower, all paid for by citizens chewing gum. Tribune ships from the Thorold mill were unloading paper into a warehouse adjoining the new printing plant. Pushed onto trolleys, the paper rolls were drawn by gravity down a slightly sloped tunnel, part of the city's ash removal system, into the pressroom deep below ground. Trucks and wagons loaded newspapers on the lower street level and dashed to the rail stations unimpeded by surface traffic. The Colonel predicted soap factories and other obnoxious neighbors would move elsewhere, making room for fine shops, offices, hotels and apartments.

Chicago architects, with Louis Sullivan as their leader, had turned to tall buildings after the 1871 fire to meet the growing demand within the Loop where space was restricted by the encircling elevated train tracks. Eighteen stories was for years the limit; to go taller would require walls uneconomically thick. Then cheap steel developed by Bessemer opened the way to the sky. Other new inventions—the elevator, the electric light and the telephone—eliminated the isolation of upper floors. One problem remained: A tall building acted as a chimney, drawing in air so powerfully that a person wishing to enter might not be able to open the door. The solution was a revolving door.

While Sullivan and his colleagues had developed interesting new shapes and facades, Chicago's 1893 World's Fair had revived the classical forms of Greece and Rome. The Fair, Sullivan complained, would hold up architecture for half a century! It did. The next generation of public and private builders demanded every important structure be long and flat, faced with pillars and topped with domes. Sullivan almost starved. His most radical disciple, Frank Lloyd Wright, was ignored in America but praised in Germany.

The Colonel wanted a tower. To make the building profitable, he had no alternative. The competition asked for a building filling the 100-foot 11½-inch frontage and, to meet city zoning laws, rising not more than 260 feet, although a set-back tower could rise another 146 feet. The structure would be tall for Chicago but far short of the 777-foot world's tallest building erected by F.W. Woolworth in New York City eight years earlier. The contest rules inferred a classical design. The cost was unlimited.

Six architects, including Andrew Rebori who had married Judge Prendergast's daughter Nannie, Jarvis Hunt, a member of the mayor's 1904-1905 committee, and Daniel W. Burnham, the city planner whose father had turned the lake front into a park, were invited to enter. The winning design would be chosen by the Colonel, Patterson, Managing Editor Beck, Tribune building superintendent Holmes Onderdonk and one architect, Alfred Granger, president of the American Institute of Architects, aided by six advisers. The deadline was November 1st but architects living "in distant parts" were given an extra month.

Two hundred four designs arrived by the November 1st deadline. On November 23rd the judges selected 12 designs they considered most promising and McCormick told Rebori he had won. Two days before the final deadline a packet arrived from Eliel Saarinen in Helsinki, creator of the Finnish railroad station the Colonel had admired on his way home from Russia seven years earlier. The committee reviewed all designs, by now 254 from 23 countries, and announced on December 3rd they had chosen a design by Raymond Hood, a little known 50-year-old New York architect trained at the Massachusetts Institute of Technology and the Ecole des Beaux Arts in Paris who, for the competition, had joined with a more established New York architect, John

259

Mead Howells. The judges said they were "struck by the colossal beauty" of Saarinen's design but the interior was impractical and therefore they gave it only second place. Hood had flanked his peak with buttresses, integrating it into the broader lower section. Saarinen achieved equal integrity with a series of stepbacks and unbroken central vertical lines.

Sullivan had welcomed the competition. "The craving for beauty set forth by The Tribune," he wrote, "is imbued with that high romance which is the essence of all great works of man, who is born to hope and to achieve." After seeing Hood's design, inspired by the Gothic cathedral in Rouen, Sullivan moaned that Hood had set American architecture back another half century. He and many other architects preferred Saarinen's design. "It is a voice," Sullivan wrote, "resonant and rich, rising amidst the wealth and joy of life. In its single clarity to concentrated intention, there is revealed the logic of a new order, a logic to living things. Rising from the earth in suspiration, it ascends in beauty, lofty and secret, until its lovely crest seems at one with the sky."

Most of the designs were classical, piling layers of pillars atop one another. Many capped the tower with a dome or spire but original thinkers proposed a globe, a clock, an eagle, a knight in armor fighting for the right. One architect, going back to ancient Egypt, designed a vast, windowed obelisk. Another eliminated all windows. One turned a sharpened pencil on end and drew that. Walter Gropius, gaining prestige in his native Germany, proposed an austere rectangle relieved by hard, sharp balconies. A series of narrow rectangles piled on end came into reality a half century later when Sears gave Chicago the tallest building.

Three Tribune artists topped their designs with a figure of a seated man. Gaar Williams' man was reading The Tribune, Frank King drew Uncle Walt, hero of his comic strip Gasoline Alley, while Carey Orr placed a clothespin over his man's nose to protect himself from the soap factory fragrances. All designers were required to draw one human figure to denote the scale of the building. Orr placed his citizen in the middle of Michigan Avenue, gazing raptly upward, unaware that, in a wink, he would be flattened by a speeding car.

Hood borrowed money, bought a new coat and came to Chicago to collect the first-prize check and to convince the Colonel he was capable of directing the construction of the tower. The building was completed in 25 months. Hood faced the 32-story, 473-foot structure with limestone, many pieces heavily carved,

walled the corridors with marble, made doors of solid mahogany, oak or bronze. Whether it is the world's most beautiful office building is debatable, but it was the most expensive. No one had spent $8.5 million on an office building of this size. The architect designed for the Colonel and Captain Patterson matching offices on the 24th floor, carefully paneled, each with a Gothic fireplace. The Colonel's fireplace would not draw. The building superintendent lost much sleep and spent a lot of money creating an efficient draft. One morning he proudly presented the Colonel with an enthusiastic fire. The Colonel let the fire die and no one ever again saw a fire there. The Colonel had medallions of Yale's Scroll and Key and of the 1st Division placed on the ceiling. As an afterthought the Colonel had a door cut into his secretary's adjoining room. To avoid spoiling the geometric effect of the paneling the door was merged into the woodwork and the usual knob was replaced by a kickplate in the baseboard which simplified the exit of the Colonel or anyone else whose hands were filled with papers.

The door became a toy. The Colonel was amused when first-time visitors turned to leave and saw no door. If he wanted to tease or torment, he let the visitor search the room. If he felt gentle, he pressed a button under his desk and the door swung open. No visitor's reaction amused him more than that of WGN librarian Marion Schroeder. On leaving after her first visit she said, "Colonel, I know I came in through a door somewhere. I can't walk through a wall. I'm not Jesus Christ, you know." Amy bought in Paris a handsome oversized desk of carved Italian and French marble. The Colonel added the chair from which he at 25 had presided over the Sanitary District, Grandfather Medill's roll top desk and framed letters from Abraham Lincoln.

In the exterior wall the Colonel inserted stones from historic buildings and places, including the one he had picked up at the battered cathedral in Arras. In the courtyard he later placed a replica of Yale's statue of 21-year-old Nathan "I only regret that I have but one life to lose for my country" Hale.

In time North Michigan Avenue became the Magnificent Mile, the best street in Chicago, with the Colonel's and Wrigley's towers as the gateway.

* * * * *

Medill McCormick's break from The Tribune and into politics

did not halt his mother's efforts to direct his life. Do this, she would say, do that, do the other thing, and with Medill in Washington she could tell him directly. Medill tried to hush the demanding words with booze. One summer Ruth sought to extricate Medill from his mother's torments and from alcohol by organizing a horseback camping trip for just the two of them in California's High Sierras. A galloping horseman interrupted their peace with a telegram from Washington stating that Kate was ill and dying. The dutiful son and daughter-in-law hurried down the mountains, rode the fastest train to Washington and found Kate in ideal heath, troubled only by her son's being out of her sight. "My grandmother favored my father over Uncle Bert all the way," Bazy summarized after years of reflection. "She ruined them both. I don't know which one came out the worse, probably my father, a wretchedly unhappy man."

In 1924 Medill McCormick sought a second Senate term. By then Big Bill Thompson had used the slackening animosity toward Germany to infiltrate his machine downstate. Thompson beat McCormick in the primary but lost the election to a Democrat. The Nation commented that Senator McCormick, a middle-of-the-road Republican, had been beaten because of the support given him by The Tribune and the Colonel. Ten weeks later, Medill McCormick bled to death in his apartment at the Hamilton Hotel in Washington. He was 47. The Colonel suspected suicide. The Nation eulogized: "He had a broad vision, a keen, quick understanding of popular currents, a far-reaching perception of the faults of our system of government. He illuminated problems in a manner worthy of the best tradition of world statesmanship. To find a man in Washington who knew Europe and the Europeans' languages as thoroughly is rare. At times he seemed to be the most important senator in foreign affairs. He was a devoted American who chose a life of public service in preference to one of ease. Here was no Palm Beach dweller, no intellectual idler. Some people thought him eccentric because he had a way of disappearing to the end of the earth and turning up unexpectedly, in odd garb perhaps, but loaded with facts gained first hand. He was likable and lovable. His defeat cut him to the quick because of the consciousness he had worked too hard to deserve such a loss. Like most other men in public life, he had to sustain vicious and untruthful personal attacks." The New York World added: "There remains in this country no other public figure with quite the same activity or appeal."

Friends sent stones from many states for a mausoleum built by his wife in a cornfield near Middle Creek in Illinois. Over the years the isolated tomb attracted graffiti and beer cans. The Colonel suggested the body be moved to Cantigny but the two daughters did not approve. Instead Bazy bought a lot in the Middle Creek cemetery and the body was moved there. The empty tomb, strongly built to endure to eternity, was abandoned to weeds.

*　*　*　*　*

Ruth forged ahead politically, became the first woman member of the party's national committee and in 1928 was elected congresswoman-at-large. In 1932 she married Albert G. Simms, a congressman from New Mexico, moved her political base from Illinois to New Mexico, feuded with President Franklin Roosevelt, helped Thomas Dewey win the 1944 Republican nomination and died six weeks after Dewey's defeat.

*　*　*　*　*

By 1924 the News' Park Place plant basement in New York could hold no more presses. An auxiliary plant was built in Brooklyn; a color plant followed. To occupy presses in the daytime The News started an afternoon edition. That was a mistake. McCormick and Patterson killed it after eight months. In 1926 the daily circulation passed a million, the Sunday a million and a quarter. Park Place was a throbbing ant heap.

Patterson asked award-winning Architect Raymond Hood to design a new home for The News, an upended cigar box 40 stories high cased at Patterson's command in white brick, running from 42nd Street to 41st along Second Avenue. In Hood's circular art-deco lobby Patterson placed a great globe, constantly changing weather charts and highway signs giving distances and directions to other major cities of the world. Over the entrance is carved the last half of Lincoln's remark, "God must have loved the common people. He made so many of them." The walls of an office set apart for the Colonel were covered with a harsh, sharp, mural picturing the history of printing, gaudy enough to deter the conservative Colonel from coming often to New York.

Patterson moved to New York, rented an apartment and furnished it from bargain basements. Fearful of being trapped by fire he placed his bed next to the elevator gate. He bought a car for $850. Most afternoons he went to the movies, sometimes eating an Eskimo Pie, sometimes defying managers of the classy new movie palaces by going in shirt sleeves. He never gave parties and rarely went to a party. At The News he moved around contentedly, stopping to talk to editors and reporters.

* * * * *

The Colonel hoped Cantigny would be financially self-supporting. By 1924 it still was losing money. "My lot," he said, "has been that of several million deflated farmers. With labor so high and prices falling, I have been universally unsuccessful. I hired a high class farm manager but the result was the same. I am licked and going out of the farming business. Next summer I propose to move back to Lake Forest. I have not decided whether to rent the farm or run it in the most economical manner, possibly hoping to benefit from the increased value of suburban real estate."

But North Shore gossip rolled on. Old friends continued to snub Amy. One day a gentleman came upon Amy and Maryland Hooper lunching at the Saddle and Cycle Club. He spoke to Mrs. Hooper but not to Amy and afterwards he told Mrs. Hooper's husband, "I don't think your wife is keeping good company." Kate's enmity against Amy was not softened by the passing years. One day a gentleman who had known the family for many years asked: "Why are you so hard on Amy? You are behaving as though you want to take a horse whip to her." Kate did not change her ways.

In 1925 members of North Shore society, seeking to restore relations, arranged a party for Amy and the Colonel to celebrate the tenth anniversary of their wedding. Something unpleasant happened. No one today knows the details but the day before the party Amy telephoned to say she and the Colonel could not come. She said she had discovered she had a golfing date. The party went on without them. Away slipped an opportunity for the Colonel and Amy to break out of their isolation.

The Colonel and Amy turned their full attention to making Cantigny the center of their personal lives. The Colonel packed insulation into the walls and sealed the windows and doors against arctic winds. Amy organized a staff of a cook, assistant cook, upstairs maid, downstairs maid, butler, valet and chauffeur, all living at Cantigny and expected to be available whenever needed, any hour, every day, no set vacations nor days off although they might be free during the long periods the Colonel and Amy were out of town. The Colonel enlarged the stable to house his and Amy's hunters and his dozen polo ponies. The Colonel persuaded his cousin, Chauncey McCormick, like himself a grandson of William McCormick, and Chauncey's wife, Marion Deering, to buy 1,000 adjoining acres. The two men changed the name of the road between their estates from Mack Road to Maramy Road to honor their wives, but the county persisted in using the old name.

The Colonel and Amy joined Chicago Golf Club a few minutes away, the summer fun center for wealthy, energetic families who looked upon the North Shore as too sedate. One night three golfers debated which city in the world was the most wicked. "Shanghai," said one. "No, Port Said," said the second. The third asked, "Has either of you ever had a weekend at Chicago Golf?"

By 1924 summer homes with wide vistas ringed the golf course. There were dances every Saturday night, occasional polo games on grounds carelessly dropped into the middle of the golf course. Young people lazed away the summers beside the swimming pool or lackadaisically lobbed balls across tennis nets. Par for the 6,387-yard course was 73 but for the first three years the lowest score was 77. Bobby Jones played as a member of the Walker Cup team.

The Colonel was not satisfied with the polo field and less satisfied with golf. He was among the most generous tippers, and high school boys, including football's first superstar Harold "Red" Grange, competed to be his caddy. The Colonel was a poor player; his drives went almost anywhere; his putting was equally wild. One day, playing in a foursome for so much a hole, he eventually arrived on a green long after the others. Without asking how the score stood he paid the afternoon wager and walked off. The Colonel did not take lightly to the role of a poor golfer. "You could always tell where the Colonel was," Red Grange recalled. "The air was blue." The Colonel resigned from the club. A committee called on him to ask his reasons and to say that the club would do just about anything to lure him back to membership. The Colonel told them he did not explain his reasons for anything to anyone, but it was evident that the Colonel did not enjoy participating in a sport in which he did not do well. For the club's social life he had no use at all.

At Cantigny the Colonel smoothed a large meadow into a private polo field and enlisted acquaintances to join in energetic, though hardly expert, competitions. A handsome six-foot-two Carolina-born West Point cavalry officer, Capt. Maxwell Corpening, came from Fort Sill, Oklahoma, where Amy's brother, a fellow officer, told him about Cantigny polo. The Captain, an excellent horseman, had won first place in a Madison Square Garden riding show. The Colonel signed on the Captain as a member of his team, persuaded him to resign from the army and move to Chicago to work for him at The Tribune, play polo, ride in the Cantigny hunts and organize a riding club downtown and a socially-elite Chicago Black Horse troop and band. The Colonel gave him stock in his new bank, The Lake Shore National, and made him a director of the bank. The Captain filled in for the Colonel at functions which the Colonel thought he must not ignore but wished not to attend. The Captain had married while a riding instructor at West Point but the marriage had broken up and a son was growing up in a series of military academies. Women found the Captain most attractive. He was an enthusiastic, witty storyteller. The Colonel and Amy enjoyed his company and Cantigny's door was always open to him and a room ready. A magazine described Corpening as "one of those versatile men who handle details in business hours, play polo, converse charmingly, invariably make themselves useful." One day the Colonel asked Corpening why the farm's two black swans had no offspring. Corpening investigated and reported both were males. For years Corpening was almost like a son to the Colonel and there was loose speculation that the Colonel was grooming him to take over The Tribune, a prospect that did not please career men sweating their way up the ladder. One evening the foreign editor received a long account from Corpening in the Philippines, thought it sounded famililar, checked the Encyclopedia Britannica and found the account there. He showed both to City Editor Ed Lee. "A least the son of a bitch can read," Lee said. Corpening continued his world search for news, Lee reasoning the Colonel "was happy to have Corpening out of his hair for awhile."

One summer the Colonel took Corpening on a camping hike in the Canadian wilderness. The Indian guides brought along an attractive young Indian woman as cook. Corpening flirted with her. "Take care," the Colonel told Corpening. "She's probably the wife or sister or daughter of one of the guides. They won't like what you are doing." Corpening ignored the advice. The Indians smoldered, then flared up, packed their belongings and strode off, leaving the Colonel and Corpening to fend for themselves and find their own way back to base. "Damndest man you ever saw," the Colonel recalled years later, more with admiration than disgust.

Among the Chicago Golf set welcome at Cantigny were the Richardsons, the Nicholsons, the Spencers, the Crawfords, the Caldwells. A Nicholson girl aspiring to the stage met at the Todd School in Woodstock, 50 miles northwest of Chicago, another aspiring actor, Orson Welles. The couple married and went to New York. The marriage did not last. A Spencer boy married a Richardson girl. That marriage did not last. Another Spencer married a Baltimore girl, Wallis Warfield. In time King Edward VIII chose to marry Wallis, then twice divorced, rather than accept the crown of Great Britain. As Prince of Wales, the reluctant Edward had been an honored guest at a party at the Saddle and Cycle Club. He devoted the evening to a young wife. The husband came upon the wife and the Prince on a porch sofa. The Prince, members still remembered after 50 years, tried to drink away his embarrassment and had to be carried from the club, giving a vigilant Tribune photographer an unusual picture, which The Tribune did not print.

Marjorie Caldwell, a beautiful divorcee, and her teenage daughter Tiggie lived in a Cantigny guest house. Tiggie had a crush on Max Corpening who had a crush on her mother. One stormy evening at Cantigny Mrs. Caldwell and Corpening erupted in a bitter argument and she strode out coatless into the biting rain and ran through the avenue of trees toward the guest house a mile away. Amy told Corpening he must hurry after her in his car and take her home. He balked. Amy insisted. He yielded, but by the time he caught up with Mrs. Caldwell she was almost home, soaked and chilled. Pneumonia seized her and she died. In her will she entrusted Tiggie's finances to Corpening. He invested the inheritance badly and soon it was gone. His fatal spat with Mrs. Caldwell and financial errors disrupted relations with the McCormicks for a while but his charm and usefulness in small things reopened Cantigny doors to him.

Soon the bereft Tiggie went to England and married an Englishman. The marriage ended and Tiggie came home. Some years later Corpening searched for Tiggie, found her running a beauty salon on the west coast and asked her to come to Chicago to meet with a lawyer. She came.The lawyer handed her money equal to her lost inheritance, plus interest. By then, Corpening had dropped out of the Cantigny inner circle, rejoining the army during the Second World War as an intelligence officer. His only son was killed on an air force training flight. After the war Corpening married an attractive blonde, moved to Lake Geneva and used the ballooned bank stock to develop industrial sites in Aurora.

A welcome figure who came dancing year after year into Cantigny was Ed Prendergast, as gentle and free and frivolous as the Irish mist with not a care nor a responsibility in sight. The $100,000 inherited from his father let him do as he pleased, go where whim took him. By 1929 much of the inheritance was gone. The stock market crash took the rest. Still Ed saw no need to earn money. The Colonel gave him a check each month. One day the Colonel told Howard Wood, who wrote the checks, to deduct ten cents from the $100 because Ed had taken a razor blade without asking. Prendergast protested to Wood but the decision stood. Was the Colonel making a joke, or was he warning Prendergast not to take liberties?

To Amy, Ed was a tonic, humorous, gentle, thoughtful. At bridge, he was good enough to pair with Cuthbertson. One winter Prendergast traveled to Florida with Amy, Maryland Hooper and a White Russian refugee, Vera Ivanchenko. A visitor coming upon the foursome asked Ed, "Which is Mrs. Prendergast?" "None, thank God," Prendergast declared firmly. The three women laughed but Mrs. Hooper never forgot the words.

Vera's account of her life at St. Petersburg fascinated the Colonel, reminding him of his father's ambassadorship there and his time with the Grand Duke and the Russian army two years before the army's collapse in 1917. One bright cold winter night when as a teenager she went with other girls to skate on a lake outside the capital, incipient revolutionaries killed the grooms and rode off with the horses. The girls walked home. Eleven miles, Vera said. Entering her home she came upon a servant shot dead just inside the door. Soon her family, along with other courtiers, sought safety from the red revolutionaries on the shore of the Black Sea, long a popular resort for the court. There she married Dimitri Ivanchenko, owner of wide estates. As the revolution swept into the Crimea, Vera and her husband fled to Constantinople. "We walked all the way," she said. The pair came to Chicago. Vera sold dresses at Marshall Field's. Her husband, unable to accept the loss of his wealth and position, killed himself.

The Colonel's closest companions at Cantigny were his cousin Chauncey and Ed Hurley, the neighbor to the east, whose father had sat in Wilson's war cabinet. Often on a Saturday morning the Colonel rode his favorite horse to the Hurley home and Chauncey rode in from the south. At the Hurley bar the trio ruminated over the affairs of the world. Chauncey's wife opposed his drinking before noon. One morning the Colonel placed on the bar a small hollow porcelain swan which he had filled with cloves. Now Chauncey could return home without telltale breath.

The Colonel and Chauncey erected jumps in their fields and woods and organized, as co-masters, the DuPage Hunt and Riding Club. Other neighbors joined, opening their lands to the hunt and making possible a ride of 10 miles without leaving the property of club members. Amy purchased and remodeled a farmhouse at the junction of the two estates as a clubhouse and built kennels for a pack of English fox hounds. Patiently Amy was pushing out the wall around her husband and peopling their private world with entertaining, undemanding, understanding human beings.

*　*　*　*　*

One cold day a servant at the North Shore estate of one of the Colonel's cousins, Fowler McCormick, watched a small plane fly low over Lake Michigan, dip and slide into the choppy water. The servant telephoned the Coast Guard. When rescuers reached the flier, he was only partly conscious and was blue with cold. They pulled him into the boat, took him to the Coast Guard station, placed him in a bathtub and turned on the cold water. He shivered himself awake. "Only a fish could live so long in that cold water," a rescuer told him. A reporter asked, "What's his name?" "We call him Fish," a rescuer replied. The flier went through his adventurous life known as Fish. His real name was Bert Hassell. He first had flown on June 12, 1914, and was to come into the life of the Colonel and guide him into a great adventure.

14. A Matter of Principle—and of Millions
1921—1926

With the Ford case disposed of comfortably, McCormick and The Tribune could concentrate on Big Bill Thompson. As the war receded from people's minds, The Tribune's charge that Thompson had favored Germany lost its emotional power, but Thompson's animosity for The Tribune and McCormick did not dim nor did the disapproval he received in return. Thompson demonstrated in post-war elections his popularity had survived and he was likely to be around for some time. Emboldened by the 12-cent award given Ford, The Tribune focused its attention on Thompson's performance as mayor and that of his officers. The Tribune declared that Chicago, after six years of Thompson rule, was "bankrupt, broke, in sad financial condition, and so improperly and corruptly administered that its streets are not properly cleaned and its laws not efficiently enforced."

Should Thompson bring new libel suits? He talked with the city's chief lawyer, Samuel Ettelson, who, as a former lawyer for Samuel Insull, was eager to even scores with McCormick but saw little chance of success in Thompson's adding more personal libel charges and demanding more money for claimed damages. To defend a charge of being pro-German was one matter; to defend a charge of graft and maladministration was another. Who knew what evidence The Tribune held in its files? Could Thompson rely on having a friendly judge? The lawyer decided Thompson was likely to lose more from a new libel charge than he could gain.

Ettelson chose a more promising course. The real victim of The Tribune's attack, he said, was not Thompson but the city. The Tribune was damaging Chicago's reputation. Who will lend money to a bankrupt city?

Ettelson went to court on behalf the City of Chicago, stating that The Tribune, while "impugning the Mayor's integrity," had ruined the city's credit and thus hurt its ability to borrow money. He put the city's loss at $10 million. Never before had a libel case sought such a large sum. More important, never before in the United States had a government organization claimed libel.

Ettelson placed McCormick and The Tribune in double jeopardy. Courts are always unpredictable and many Chicago judges had no kind smiles for The Tribune, which for years had claimed too many judges were tools of crooked political organizations. If such a judge presided over the case and helped a jury find The Tribune guilty and assessed damages in the millions, The Tribune could be ruined financially.

The second jeopardy was more unthinkable. A guilty verdict henceforth would make every newspaper think hard before criticizing any public official. "Freedom of the press would disappear," McCormick said, "and it would be followed quickly by freedom of speech."

McCormick determined The Tribune must fight to the finish, regardless of cost. Just as Thompson had brought the people into his defense, The Tribune now brought the people into its attack. The Tribune went to court on behalf of Chicago taxpayers and asked that Thompson and five of his aides return to the city $1,065,000 that the Tribune asserted they had received illegally. The accusation centered on construction of the double-decked bridge across the Chicago River. To let ships pass, the bridge parted in the middle and rose from each bank like trunk-to-trunk circus elephants rearing on their hind legs. The design was complicated and the city had employed a brigade of consultants. An army engineer told McCormick that many of these experts were efficient only in producing votes. The Tribune filed a second suit asking the return to the city of $1.7 million paid for poor technical advice. Now Thompson was in mortal danger. An unfavorable award would ruin him financially and open a procedure to collect millions more paid by the city on false statements during his years in office.

The Tribune charges unquestionably had damaged Thompson and his machine. There was no doubt that the charges had hurt the city's credit. There was no doubt, in the Colonel's mind, that the charges were true. But these aspects were peripheral. The central issue was simple and sharp: Could a government body sue for libel? McCormick surrounded himself with lawyers, law books, court histories. He put together the story of mankind's long struggle against despots. To McCormick, Augustus Caesar ruined the Roman Empire when he gagged citizens so fiercely that a Roman's harsh comments about the Emperor could cost him his life. Through the centuries Britons with their parliament had gained freedoms little known on the continent.

McCormick was proud and grateful that Americans, from the establishment of the first colony in Virginia, had tried to limit the power of their governors. King James' charter promised the settlers "shall have and enjoy all the liberties, franchises and immunities as if they abided within the realm of England." The first of the state constitutions, that of Virginia, stated: "The freedom of the press is one of the bulwarks of liberty and can never be restrained by despotic governments." The Massachusetts constitution went further, declaring: "Liberty of the press is essential to the security of freedom in the state. It ought not therefore be restricted in this commonwealth." Thomas Jefferson, in writing the constitution, was more general: "We hold these truths to be self evident, that all men are created equal and that they are endowed by their creator with certain inalienable rights, that among these are life, liberty and the pursuit of happiness, and that to secure these rights governments are instituted among men, deriving their just powers from the consent of the governed."

The gaps in the subsequently adopted constitution became evident as its framers noted a tendency of administrations to curb criticism. The remedy came in the Bill of Rights. The First Amendment declares: "Congress shall make no law restricting an establishment of religion, prohibiting the free exercise thereof, or abridging the freedom of speech, or of the press, or the right of people peaceably to assemble and to petition the government for a redress of grievances."

George Mason wrote the demands that government keep its hands off speech and press. Jefferson added protection of religion. McCormick, a Presbyterian by inheritance but a rare churchgoer, thought the colonists were fortunate in having come from so many different communities. As a consequence, no religious group could dominate and all could join in the fight for a common cause—freedom from rule by Britain.

The freedoms were little challenged while George Washington was president. Pressures increased for John Adams. Alexander Hamilton, leader of the Federalist Party, maneuvered against Adams while Jefferson, leader of the Democratic-Republicans and Adams' vice president, found many flaws in the President.

The Federalists sought protection by adopting King George III's sedition laws. Adams, a contentious, opinionated man, enforced them vigorously, jailing and fining critics. The introduction of despotic ways into American government aroused voters to turn out Adams. The Federalist Party died, Jefferson became president and remitted fines and commuted sentences. The sedition laws were erased, never to reappear.

McCormick's legal brief listed three incidents during the Civil War in which the Northern military gagged newspapers. Twice Lincoln overruled the military. In the South, McCormick's brief stated: "The Confederate legislature met in secret and kept the Southern press under tight control. The contrasting methods in North and South were as important in bringing about the ensuing victory for the North as the actions of armies in the field."

In October of 1921 the city's case against The Tribune came to trial in the Superior Court of Cook County. Thompson's lawyers, unable to find an American precedent for a government's accusation of libel, cited a case in Britain successfully brought by the Manchester Ship Canal. The choice was unfortunate. On his 1910 visit to Manchester to study the canal's construction and operation, McCormick had inquired into its legal status. "The canal organization," he said, "was more of a private enterprise than a government agency. British law once had permitted government bodies to sue for libel but that right has long ago been repealed." Thompson's legal base crumbled.

Judge Harry M. Fisher ruled for The Tribune, stating that the press has a duty to criticize government in war or peace. He saw in the city's suit aspects of rulers who seek power "with lustful passion." The Judge declared that if Thompson's arguments were established "public officials would have in their power one of the most effective instruments with which to intimidate the press and to silence their enemies. It is a weapon held over the head of every one who dares to print or speak unfavorably of the men in power." He said newspapers could do harm by unjustified attacks on public officials but such harm was limited, whereas the good that came from justified criticism was limitless. "A paper which indulges in falsehoods," the Judge said, "suffers the loss of confidence from which alone comes its power, its prestige and its reward."

The city appealed. After almost a year, the Illinois Supreme Court unanimously upheld Judge Fisher. Chief Justice Floyd Thompson ruled: "History teaches that human liberty cannot be

"BIG BILL" THOMPSON

CHICAGO MAYOR'S WAR WITH ENGLAND

secured unless there is freedom to express grievances. . .Prosecution for libel on government is unknown to American courts. . . The people have a right to discuss their government without fear of being called to account for their expression of opinion . . .(anyone seeking) to persuade others to violate law or to overthrow by force or other unlawful means may be punished, but all other utterances of publications against the goverment must be considered privileged against civil and criminal prosecution."

Thompson's personal libel suit came to court in May of 1922. Thompson admitted that he had worked against conscription and sending American troops to Europe. He confessed he had not distributed war posters asking Americans to subscribe to war loans and to support the Red Cross. The case was going badly for the Mayor. Two jurors became ill. The Tribune offered to continue with a jury of ten but Thompson's lawyers asked for a retrial and the case died.

The Tribune, riding high, accused Thompson's patronage chief, Fred Lundin, of obtaining abnormally high prices for land sold to the school board. Lundin left town. Thompson was advised by his lawyers he could not be directly implicated in Lundin's activities, but Thompson withdrew from the mayoral election.

The Tribune's suit seeking repayment of consultant fees reached court in June of 1926. The hearings continued for two years. Testimony of more than a hundred witnesses filled 11,000 pages, supported by 3,000 exhibits. At the end Judge Hugo Friend ordered Thompson, Cook County Treasurer George Harding and Improvements Board Chairman Michael Faherty to repay $2,245,604. "They've ruined me," Thompson cried. The trio appealed. The Supreme Court reversed the lower court, ruling that the three men personally received none of the money and that the consultants had a legal right to make contributions to the party organization. "Truth crushed to earth rises again," Thompson exulted. He continued his verbal battle against The Tribune but did not oppose Medill's widow, Ruth Hanna McCormick, for a congressional seat. Appendicitis killed Thompson in 1944. Almost two million dollars in currency and negotiables were found in his safe.

The Ford and Thompson suits established the Colonel and The Tribune as champions of freedom of the press. The American Newpaper Publishers Association named the Colonel chairman of its committee on press freedom. But the decisive struggle still lay ahead.

15. Diversions to Disaster
1924—1929

The polo center of the United States in the 1920's was a small winter resort in the pine woods of South Carolina where the Savannah River tumbles from the uplands to the broad coastal plain. The resort was Aiken, named for the president of a little band of entrepreneurs who in 1834 built America's first long distance—136-mile—railroad.

The railroad engineer laying out the right of way was in love with the daughter of a plantation owner who decreed that unless the railroad came near his place, giving him cheap, easy transportation for his cotton to Charleston, there would be no wedding. The engineer realigned the road, married the daughter and stayed to lay out a beautiful town with 15 miles of broad parkways.

Three times a week the chugging steam locomotive *Good Friend* puffed at 15 miles an hour into Aiken with two open wagons, helped up the last steep incline by a cable winched onto a big wooden drum by a steam engine at the top of the hill. The amazing *Good Friend* achieved between dawn and dusk a traveling feat that by boat took 20 days of paddling upstream and four days drifting downstream.

Aiken's town was the second settlement on the bluff above the river. Two centuries earlier an Irish adventurer named Galphin established a post there, selling trinkets, cloth, guns and whiskey to the Indians and collecting their furs—thousands of pelts in a good season. The Revolutionary War interrupted the trade and turned the Indians against the traders and settlers. The postwar rush of settlers into the uplands and the spread of railroads ended the need for the post. People moved on. Fire and weather erased the buildings.

Two centuries before Galphin, Hernando de Soto and his dwindling band of armor-plated Spanish soldiers, weary and ill from plodding through the Florida and Georgia swamps, came onto the clean, dry uplands, welcomed by a cluster of Indians who had built a good life for themselves on fish and game. The Savannah River yielded oysters in such abundance that the Indians had pearls by the bushel. "Help yourself," the Indian princess told the departing guests. They did, by the bagful, until De Soto told the men to put most of them back. The long walk, he said, had only begun and the pearls quickly would become a burden and would be discarded as soon as the men found the object of their search—gold.

* * * * *

Slowly the oaks grew along Aiken's parkways, forming a cool delightful passageway for townspeople and, increasingly, long-term visitors with weak lungs. About 1870 a wealthy New Orleans politician and member of Congress, George Eustis, sent his daughter, Louise, called Lulie by her friends, to Aiken hoping the air and the peace would rebuild her fragile, feverish body. Aiken worked its wonders and Lulie grew into a beautiful, vital young woman, eager to move about in the world. She was introduced into Long Island society and met a rich sportsman, Thomas Hitchcock. They married. Hitchcock had become a devotee of polo, foxhunts and steeplechases while at Oxford University in England and he intended to make horses his life, moving with the seasons between England and Long Island. Lulie told him about Aiken and led him there. Riding through the pine woods alive with quail, he noted how the sandy soil cushioned the horses' hooves. Why, he marveled, Aiken was perfect for horses, for breeding, for training, for riding, and the winter sun and air would be perfect for riders.

Hitchcock bought a house and urged their Long Island friends to join them for the winters. One of the first to come was William Whitney. The Hitchcocks and Whitneys bought 8,000 acres of woods and laid out a polo field, a race track and many miles of horse trails. Foxes were few but if a groom were sent ahead dragging a scented bag the hunt could be certain of an exciting and different ride every day, with fences raised or lowered according to the ability of the day's riders.

Hitchcock considered Aiken something of his personal club. New residents came at Hitchcock's invitation or with his approval. Streets were kept sanded for the comfort of the horses.

Almost all property rentals and sales were handled by a remarkable Aiken woman, Eulalie Salley. One day Hitchcock telephoned to her saying he could not find in his social register the names of a couple who, he heard, were buying a house. "You know how particular I am about who is in the Aiken colony," Hitchcock said. Mrs. Salley replied, "Mr. Hitchcock, your register must be wrong. These are lovely people. I know you will like them." Hitchcock invited them to lunch. He did like them and the couple were permitted to buy a house.

In the 1920s and 1930s a riding companion, quail-shooting mate or golfing partner—the course was the fifth oldest in the country— might be a Harriman, an Astor, a Vanderbilt. The Vanderbilts bought the courthouse as their country home. Dinner partners might be Winston Churchill or Prince Bernadotte or the Prince of Wales. Will Rogers might recount his day's anecdote; Grace Moore might be persuaded to sing. Fred Astaire might dance a tricky step or two. Chicagoan Tommy Leiter gave a party almost every Sunday. One day he told his guests he would collect them and did so on the Aiken fire engine, with siren screaming and bells ringing. One Christmas someone pushed Santa Claus into a swimming pool, breaking Santa's leg. An Aiken wife thought so tenderly of the rabbits that she planted 50 acres of carrots just for them. Franklin D. Roosevelt crept in, most quietly, to renew a long standing friendship with Lucy Mercer, formerly Eleanor Roosevelt's social secretary. Evalyn Walsh McLean was a very visible hostess. One day Eulalie Salley arranged a meeting at her home between Mrs. McLean and a detective named Gaston Means. The Charles Lindbergh baby had just been kidnapped in New Jersey. Mrs. McLean was a friend of the Lindberghs. Means told her he knew where the child was being held and said he could arrange for his safe return if Mrs. McLean would give him $150,000 and promise to keep the child hidden for three weeks to give the kidnappers time to escape. Mrs. McLean wrote a check, brought in carpenters to build a nursery so soundproof that no childish cry would seep out, hired a nurse and, with her, set off for Mexico where Means said the child would be handed over. As a precaution, she told a friend she would send a telegram every hour and if the messages stopped coming, he should notify the authorities immediately. Alas, it was a hoax.

Mrs. Hitchcock, the first woman at Aiken who dared ride astride, taught Aiken sons and daughters to be expert riders. To keep her sons in warm, healthful winter air, she started a preparatory school for boys. Pianist Josef Hofmann's wife, who had been married to Hitchcock's brother, started a school for girls. Among the students were Tiggie Caldwell and Katrina McCormick, Ruth and Medill McCormick's daughter. Every night during the season a sleeping car left New York for Aiken. During peak weeks six or eight private railroad cars were parked on the Aiken siding. During a good season, the railroad might bring in 50 or 60 horse cars. Within Aiken, Mrs. Salley distributed the newcomers according to a carefully worked out Hitchcock-approved zoning arrangement.

Almost every Sunday, Tuesday, and Thursday would produce a polo game, the teams made up casually from players present, willing, able and ready to play. Hitchcock and his son both were rated as 10-goal men, the epitome. Often the teams would include world-class players from Britain, France, India or the Argentine. Hitchcock played on America's first international team and his son was a member of all internationals from 1921 to 1939.

Colonel McCormick, a four-goal man, began going to Aiken in 1923 or 1924. He and Amy rented a house, loaded into a rail car near Cantigny his 12 polo ponies—all big beasts to carry his six-foot-four, 210 pounds of bone and muscle—and her hunters. Amy always went to the siding to make sure all was well with the horses. A Cantigny groom rode with the horses in a car hooked to an express train to Atlanta and then diverted back to Aiken. Other Cantigny staff followed.

After three winters the Colonel bought through Mrs. Salley a 26-acre estate owned by Marshall Field on Whiskey Road, the best street in the best part of town, once a trail favored by wagoners carting whiskey from the river to the upland settlements and plantations. Field had called the estate Whitehall, the name of the London palace where Charles I was beheaded on a scaffold outside the banquet room. The Field house had burned to the ground. The Colonel commissioned an architect, Willis Irvin, from Augusta across the river in Georgia from Aiken, to build a winter home. It must be southern colonial in style, have 11-foot ceilings and outside doors on all four sides as escape routes from fire. Amy set about furnishing it with antiques, some now at Cantigny. Irvin rehabilitated the Field stables. The Colonel laid out practice jumps in the woods.

One night a groom saw a magnificent bird dog wandering about the Whitehall woods, obviously lost. Anticipating a rich reward,

the groom shut the dog into an empty horse box. During the night the dog barked, awakening the Colonel, a light sleeper. He telephoned the stables. "Do you have a dog there?" he asked. "Yes, Colonel." "Turn him loose." The groom fetched a meaty bone and gave it to the dog, quieting it, but in time the dog again barked, again awakening the Colonel who again was on the telephone. "Did you turn the dog loose?" "Yes, Colonel." "Well, turn him loose again."

Once again, as at Ludgrove and Groton, the Colonel was an outsider. Eastern winter residents did not heartily welcome the newcomers from Chicago and were not won over by their building the biggest and finest house in the community.

In 1927 Mrs. McCormick bought for $3,500 a beautiful hunter named Bacchus II owned by Hitchcock. The deal was made through Hitchcock's agent. The next day a McCormick house guest rode the horse in a hunt. On Saturday the horse went lame. Mrs. McCormick told the agent the horse was faulty and asked Hitchcock to take back the horse and refund her money. The agent said the rider had injured the horse by poor horsemanship. A Hitchcock horse was no good? Amy's guest was a poor rider? No greater insults could be spoken. Mrs. McCormick stopped payment on the check. The agent sued for collection. The trial, delayed for a year, centered on whether the sale included a guarantee. The agent said he had made no such commitment but Mrs. McCormick said the sale of any horse for $3,500 implied a warranty. Her lawyer asked how much Hitchcock had paid for the horse, intending to prove his price to her was excessive, but the judge ruled the question was immaterial and ordered Mrs. McCormick to honor the check. Amy, no quitter and perhaps pushed by the Colonel, appealed. The Georgia Supreme Court ruled unanimously that the decision was correct. By then the case had divided the Aiken residents. Easterners, the large majority, sided with Hitchcock. A few Midwesterners risked their own futures in Aiken by saying Amy had been cheated. The Aiken social reporter, Emily Bull, wrote that the Easterners "gave the McCormicks the Aiken frost." The McCormicks, Ms. Bull added, "lost all hope of entree into the tight ring of Aiken society." The McCormick Scotch-Irish stubbornness, so helpful in business, completed the ruin of Aiken for the Colonel and cost him and Amy one more chance to emerge from their solitary fortress.

The next winter the Colonel sent his horses and a new horseman, Eddie Edwards, to the King Cole Hotel at Miami Beach, which offered polo for guests. But Amy sent her horses to Aiken, and after a few weeks the Colonel, disgusted with Miami's third-rate polo, returned to Aiken. He and Hitchcock met by choice only on the polo field. The Colonel preferred to play goal, an unpopular position, and his energy and aggressiveness made him a valued member of any team and outweighed personal feelings. On chance encounters away from the field the Colonel and Hitchcock barely nodded. The Hitchcock clan did not invite the McCormicks to dinners and parties and refused invitations to Whitehall. Now and then Amy had one, two or three house guests from Chicago. Maryland Hooper came one winter. Amy sometimes gave afternoon parties for Midwesterners, but the Colonel rarely joined in the chat. A Buffalo banker, Seymour Knox, and two Canadians became his best Aiken friends. Knox recalled he, the Colonel and one or two others would sit before a fire at Whitehall and talk about the nation, the world and the people in power. Whenever they disagreed or were uncertain about a fact or wanted the news, the Colonel picked up a phone with a direct line to The Tribune and asked someone there to look it up and call back.

Scotch, the Colonel's favored evening drink, was more readily obtainable at Aiken than in Chicago. At home-going time one spring quite a few contraband cases were loaded into the horse car and covered with twice as much hay as the horses would need on the trip. At each stop Edwards worried that a rail inspector would shift the hay but none did. To railroads in those days horses traveling to and from Aiken were privileged passengers.

One day in or about 1931 the Colonel, riding with Knox, said he didn't see how the United States could get out of the terrible depression, and he might not be able to return to Aiken.

*　*　*　*　*

In the last years of the 19th century English engineers had built an experimental press to reproduce pictures quickly and sharply on paper of somewhat better quality than newsprint but less costly than the coated paper needed for picture magazine presses. Ink was spread on the raised surface of type or pictures and transferred to the paper. In the new English process the letters and images were cut into copper plates, ink was spread over the entire plate and scraped off; ink remaining in the grooves was

283

transferred to the paper. The printing was sharp, the detail precise. All was done in sepia tones, more lifelike than black and white. The process was called rotogravure. By 1912 German engineers had developed the English prototype into a fast, practical press. McCormick ordered a large press to produce full-sized pages solid with pictures and a smaller one to print tabloid pages. Both were delivered on one of the last ships to sail before the war. Whistle-raising pictures of actresses, society queens and bathing beauties soon decorated college domitories and factories. The pin-up was born. So popular were the roto sections that McCormick, unable to get another press from Germany, had Tribune engineers make a reproduction.

After the war the Colonel asked Tribune Engineer Otto Wolf if he could adapt one of the presses or build a new one to print pictures in four colors. The theory was simple: The press would have four sets of rollers, each adding one color. In practice there were problems: The ink must be dried before the paper passed over the next roller; the paper must be perfectly positioned so each printing is made precisely on top of the earlier one. Wolf made a small prototype press in a year and presented the Colonel with a color picture of a girl with an armful of roses. The Colonel was delighted. Now, he said, build a real press. The task took two years. Fitted into an older rotogravure press, it produced color on four pages.

The Colonel's mind raced ahead. "Could you build a press," he asked, "to turn out 64 tabloid pages, all in color?"

"Of course," the engineer said.

Now Patterson's mind raced ahead. With a press like that, the Tribune-News organization could produce a new kind of publication devoted to news pictures. Neither the Saturday Evening Post nor Collier's could match its speed in getting pictures to readers, nor could they meet the lower costs brought by the new press.

The Colonel and Patterson yielded to temptation. They ordered the press and a new mill near Niagara Falls to make the new kind of paper needed by the press. They ordered Schmon to have his woodsmen start cutting birch and poplar, useless for usual newsprint but vital for the new mill. They ordered the transportation manager to convince the railroads that the new publication should be classified as a newspaper and thereby qualify for quick coast-to-coast delivery in the baggage cars of fast, prompt express passenger trains.

By the late winter of 1924 the press was almost assembled. The designers promised it would function. The mill was making paper but having trouble finding the right mix of various kinds of wood pulp and chips. Birch and poplar logs were being delivered to the mill although quite a few sank while being floated out of the forests. However, optimism ruled, and just as everyone had assumed there would be problems, everyone now assumed all problems would be overcome.

On March 24, 1924, the Colonel and Patterson announced that three weeks hence the world's greatest color press would begin printing the world's first weekly news picture paper. They offered $25,000 for a name.

Right on time the press rolled but after a few thousand copies, the plates smudged. Then the driers didn't dry. Then the images misprinted; a girl might wear her ruby necklace on her chin. Then the paper broke. Pressmen sweated and fiddled and cursed and cursed and cursed. Dealers were telegraphed that delivery might be late. How true! Belatedly the press printed the promised 750,000 copies, buyers quickly cleaned the stands and engineers promised the bugs would be beaten before the next press day. But they weren't. . .by the next, nor the next, nor the next.

The second issue had a name—Liberty—a happy reminder for whiskey drinkers who accused the nation of taking away their liberty to drink. That issue also proclaimed itself to be a "weekly periodical for everyone." The deadly word was "periodical." According to railroad regulations, periodicals traveled on freight trains. With one printed word, Liberty lost its time advantage over other magazines. A worse failing was the sloppy printing job. No press adjustment could make the pictures come off clean. After seven weeks, the Colonel and Patterson arranged with a commercial house to do the printing on regular picture presses using costly coated paper. Liberty became early in life just another magazine, perhaps just one more second-rate magazine. The Colonel sent Annenberg to New York to try to work on Liberty the magic he had produced in building Tribune circulation. His aggressive approach hardened prospective advertisers who already had decided Liberty could not deliver the quality readers they felt their products needed. The new press was downgraded to help turn out roto picture sections for The Tribune and The News. The new mill, its market gone, was converted to turning out roto paper.

For seven years Liberty fought for life, its losses absorbed by

The Tribune and The News. In time, its circulation passed two and a half million, second only to that of The Saturday Evening Post, but Liberty could not draw enough advertising, and in 1931 the Colonel and Patterson sold it to Bernarr Macfadden, taking in part return a Detroit newspaper. They pulled out of Detroit after 16 costly months.

"We should have waited with Liberty until we had solved the problems," the Colonel reflected. "The product was completely unacceptable."

16. Stage 2
1925—1930

In the mid twenties networks were developing. McCormick, from the first broadcast, decreed that WGN must be independent. It must choose its programs, its artists, its speakers. American Telephone and Telegraph produced in 1926 top quality programs for its station in New York, WEAF. From it WGN chose concerts by Walter Damrosch and his orchestra, the Atwater Kent Hour, the Ipana Troubadours, the Eveready Hour. When RCA bought WEAF and formed the National Broadcasting Company, WGN did not join the network but arranged to carry 10 percent of its programs. The network programs had sponsors. WGN did not delete the sponsors' ads but continued to pay all costs of its own programs. The arrangement with NBC was not happy. WGN was no happier with CBS. McCormick suggested WGN and other independent stations share their best programs. WOR Newark, WXYZ Detroit and WLW Cincinnati joined WGN and from the foursome grew Mutual Network, a cooperative enterprise and in time the biggest network in the world with 550 stations.

The Colonel, keenly thrilled by developments in communications, eulogized 1927 radio "which can be heard practically all day and all night without cost, showing that the owner of a radio set is many times better off than Caesar or Queen Victoria or Commodore Vanderbilt." Broadcasting was costing The Tribune a quarter of a million dollars a year.

During the 1920s all Chicago radio stations, encouraged by a national poll of 3,700,632 radio owners, went off the air every Monday at 7 p.m. to clear the airwaves for radio hobbyists who sat all evening twiddling dials and trying to bring in stations from afar. In the morning a fan could boast he got Chile—his window was open—and his friend could respond, that's nothing, he got Greece on his radio—his wife spilled the fried eggs. In 1927

287

business prevailed, Monday night was no longer silent and WGN went commercial. Listeners complained about the interruptions for ads, but complaints ceased when advertisers bought entire shows and camouflaged the ads.

In 1928 at the Colonel's suggestion, WGN Engineer Carl Meyers installed receivers in several Chicago police cars. Police headquarters telephoned urgent messages to WGN which interrupted its programs to relay the calls to the cars. The experiment, which cost the Tribune $40,000, proved so helpful that the police department soon had its own station. Other cities followed.

*　*　*　*　*

Looking ahead 10 years and more, the Colonel saw a need for more timber than could be cut from the Rocky River basin. Quebec Province laws demanded one tree out of five be left standing. Conservation laws, the Colonel snorted, are made by ladies at tea parties. The Colonel questioned woodsmen about forests beyond the Tribune limits. They could tell him only that the forests were there but how many of the trees could be used for paper no one could say.

The Canadian government decided it no longer needed seaplanes built during the war. The Colonel bought three and hired a pilot. With his new toys, the Colonel could learn more about distant woods in a morning than Provencher and all his woodsmen could learn in a winter. The pilot wrote his own flying regulations. Over water he flew at 10 feet. If the engine stalled—no, when the engine stalled—he could land with little risk. Over land he flew at 5,000 feet, high enough to be within gliding range of a lake or river. The Colonel accepted the rules. One day the engine did stall just after the plane rose from the estuary. The pilot put it down on the water. A few repairs, and the Colonel was aloft, without a word of complaint.

Returning from a survey of the burned area beyond the Tribune limits, the Colonel flew westward 100 miles and came upon the headwaters of the Manicouagan and the Outardes Rivers. He followed their courses, which run parallel three or four miles apart, south to the St. Lawrence. Along each river, in easy logging distance, he saw vast spreads of usable trees. He determined to annex the territory. He learned that much of the land never had been leased. Woodsmen who had started up the two rivers had been turned back by the rough rapids and boulder-strewn

falls which, they decided, would prevent the passage of logs. The Colonel made his own survey, decided the rivers were usable and asked Quebec Province for a lease. The government scheduled an auction. The Colonel, in Europe, bid by cable and won the lease but had to promise to build a power plant and pulp mill on the North Shore before the end of 1930. The Colonel sent a Tribune cameraman, Lyman Atwell, to take detailed photographs from the air of the mouth of the Outardes and fit them together into a map. From it and ground reports, the Colonel and Schmon selected a site for the powerhouse and an 850-foot-long dam to hold back enough of the summer flood water to keep turbines running all winter and to catch logs coming down the river, but the survey revealed no flat area big enough for the pulp mill nor a site for a wharf on a deep water channel.

From the air the hourglass-shaped estuary of the neighboring Manicouagan three miles away looked ideal. A boom across the narrow waist would make the upper basin perfect for holding logs. The pulp mill, town and wharf all could be built on the flat waist. Ships could move safely through the lower basin and tie up at the mill, shielded by the fjord-like granite wall on both sides. Alas, close study by rowboat and on foot shattered the dream. The flat land that formed the waist was deep, shifting sand. No mill could be built there. Sand also filled the lower basin almost to the low tide mark. Could a channel be dredged, the Colonel asked. Yes, was the reply, but the tides would require constant and costly dredging. We'll look elsewhere, the Colonel said.

Time and again the searchers passed by with hardly a glance at a triangular inlet about a mile wide and three quarters of a mile deep eight miles east of the Manicouagan. Everyone knew it was clogged with sand and therefore useless. No one had bothered to give it a name. But just outside the eastern wall of the inlet, Schmon found a deep water channel reaching up to the shore. A wharf could be built there. The Colonel and Schmon, tramping the forest behind the inlet, found a swamp and beyond that a flat granite shelf on which the mill could be built. The settlement could rise from the dried swamp. A power line could bring electricity from the powerhouse on the Outardes 12 miles away. How could the logs be brought from the Outardes and Manicouagan? By flume, Schmon said. A short rail line would carry pulp from the mill to the wharf. "Let's get to work," the Colonel said. "Start with the dam."

The year was 1925. During the winter a pioneer crew ham-

mered together a half-dozen tarpaper shacks beside the inlet and
began clearing land for a road to the Manicouagan and for a
power line onward to the Outardes dam site. One day a cleaning
crew came upon an unexpected treasure, a bed of gravel, rare on
the North Shore. They also found a cutlass someone had lost centuries earlier.

On the Outardes sand woodsmen perched a wharf big enough
to receive the shallowest of barges. Schmon ordered supplies and
hired men. The next summer supply boats anchored off shore and
transferred men and cargo to the barges for ferrying ashore. Engineers blasted a right of way for a railroad to carry cement from
the wharf to the dam site and a channel to divert water around
the dam. Indians came from afar to marvel at the fountains of
shattered rock that erupted with each clap of thunder.

The Colonel was delighted with the progress. Oh, there were
problems, but none serious enough to make impossible the 1930
completion date.

*   *   *   *   *

But in the late 1920s the Colonel was increasingly worried by
the American economy. The price of paper had slid from $130 a
ton during the post-war shortages of 1922 to $70 as new mills
added their streams of paper. However, demand was still rising.
The Tribune and The News were using a third more paper than
Thorold could produce. The Colonel authorized two more machines there. After the early post-war slump the United States
and Canada were enjoying unprecedented prosperity. The fast-
rising stock market made investors feel rich.

But. . .but. . . The Tribune, since early days, paid for new
plants from profits, past or expected. The Colonel preached the
wisdom of having money in the bank. The Outardes-Manicoua-
gan project would need millions. No one knew how many. The
Thorold mill still owed $2 million to The Tribune and a few fa-
vored executives. The mill paid eight percent interest but some
executives sold to the Colonel their half million in stock and used
the proceeds to earn higher rates in the money market. In earlier
days the Colonel, certain that problems could be overcome, happily plunged into ventures. But he was learning the cost of impatience.

In August of 1927 the Colonel called a halt. Stop everything, he
told Schmon, except work on the Outardes dam. That will be

291

completed. He also told Curtis to cancel orders for the two new machines at Thorold.

"We will think again," he said and then questioned Schmon and Curtis.

McCormick: Could a North Shore mill produce paper for less than Thorold?

Schmon: Yes, by five dollars a ton.

Curtis: But we already have a mill at Thorold. Expansion would require much less capital than building from scratch on the North Shore.

McCormick: Could we ship paper all year to New York from the North Shore?

Captain Henry Louis St. James de Beauvais (After a winter on ice breakers in the lower St. Lawrence): No. Not during the four coldest months.

Schmon: But during the other eight months sea delivery to New York would be cheaper than rail delivery from Thorold. The competitive route might encourage railroads to cut rates.

McCormick: Could we cut cost by shipping paper from Thorold to Chicago via the Welland Canal around Niagara Falls when the Canal is deepened?

Curtis: Yes, if we had a boat three times bigger than our 1,000 tonners.

McCormick: Could we store pulp at the North Shore?

Schmon: Yes.

Curtis: But pulp deteriorates quickly.

McCormick: Could we store paper in boats?

Curtis (After a winter's trial): Yes.

"We will all put our minds to it," the Colonel said. "Meanwhile do all you can to cut costs and increase efficiency and production."

McCormick did not ask his superintendents their thoughts about the world economy. Late in 1928 he wrote to his mother: "President Coolidge showed considerable sense in not having himself reelected. This crazy stock market must come to an end some day and after that I imagine it will be a long slide downhill. The fact is that all business is getting harder and harder and labor troubles are threatening in many directions. I think Hoover can look forward to quite a disagreeable time in the White House."

On the Outardes the river plunged playfully over the spillway and splashed down the face of the dam. Indians pondered the curious instincts or religion that led white men to labor so long to produce just one more waterfall.

*   *   *   *   *

From late September until the ground froze in December, the weekend at Cantigny was built around the hunt. The two or three members invited for the weekend arrived on Friday afternoon. The butler took the suitcases and the maid unpacked while the guests chatted with Amy. The Colonel arrived in time to change into his pink hunting coat before dinner with champagne and lots of light talk in which the Colonel joined, drawing out the guests, never making a speech. Amy and the guests moved on to the sitting room and the Colonel vanished with the first edition of The Tribune and then went to bed with a book and scotch. The maid awakened everyone at seven. A help-yourself breakfast, laid out on the 18th century English sideboard in the dining room, was ready by 7:30. Soon after eight all walked to the stables, where grooms had readied the horses. Amy assigned mounts to the guests, made sure the girths were tight, bits correct; then she was given a leg up onto her side saddle, pulling herself with a firm grip on a hank of mane and lowering herself gently into the saddle. To Amy it was important that members be dressed impeccably, in tightly tailored coats with scarlet and gold facings— the colors of the 1st Division which soldiers saw as red and yellow—and hard hats molded individually to the skull. It was doubly important that members ride correctly. Photos of the Colonel when young on ranches in Montana and Texas, in the Culebra Cut of the Panama Canal, on the Mexican border chasing Pancho Villa, show him looking seldom in unison with the horse, legs thrust forward, back straight and stiff, head upright. The Colonel, needing a large mount, favored long-backed English hunters. One day he overheard a visitor make a snide remark about an outsize horse. The Colonel, saying nothing, mounted the horse, rode it pellmell at a tall fence, cleared it, turned, jumped the fence coming back, repeated the circuit twice, dismounted and strode off.

When all riders were ready, the house party hacked along the avenue of elms to the place chosen for the hunt to meet. Already Edwards or some other Cantigny horseman had ridden a course chosen to fit the capabilities of the day's riders, dragging a gunnysack, known as laying the drag, with scrapings from the pens at a fox fur farm oozing from the sack. Now and then he lifted the sack and carried it a short distance to simulate a clever fox's attempt to throw off the hounds by running along the top rail of a fence or in a creek or jumping into a tree.

Riders arrived from all directions, several riding for an hour or more from their homes. Riders solemnly and silently greeted one another with a wave of the whip or a touch of the cap. From Amy's kennels on Maramy Road came Chauncey McCormick's huntsman, Cox, with the hounds. Edwards and Jensen as hunt whips on the flanks were containing the hounds with flicks of the long whips. Ann Bryant was a popular member.

About nine o'clock Amy, now joint master with Chauncey, gave the signal to Cox. There was a blast on his horn, the hounds moved off behind Cox and Amy, followed by the staff and field. The field master gave the hounds a good start, then set off with the followers, maintaining the gap between staff and field and woe to any follower who passed him! A hound picked up the scent. So did others. All set off. "Gone away!" the huntsman shouted and blew the call on his horn. The followers divided. The field pursued the hounds over fences, through woods and fields.

The "vultures," also called the "hilltoppers," took an easier, slower course giving them long periods atop a rise to watch the hunt. In a half hour the hounds were breathing hard. If Edwards had laid the course properly, the hounds had reached a place where he had lifted the drag. The hounds, checked, milled around, seeking the scent and providing rest for hounds, horses and riders. Then off again. Sometime after 11 o'clock, the scent trail ended, the huntsman blew the horn signaling the final check and calling in the hounds; then he set off for the kennels, the hounds eager to be home. Sometimes the Colonel joined the riders, all walking slowly to let their steaming horses cool. At the house the riders handed their mounts to grooms. The vultures already had gathered. Drinks awaited.

The Colonel disappeared to return in a half hour or so spotless and cool in a fresh pink coat. The cook had laid out a stout hunt breakfast: eggs cooked many ways, bacon, sausages, ham, kidney pie, chipped beef, muffins, rolls, pastries. Riders, high with the thrill of the ride, laughed over the day's spills, the runaway horses, the lost hounds, an interruption by a rabbit or deer. And gossip. Gossip about hunt members present or absent. Gossip about neighbors. Gossip about friends and enemies. By mid-afternoon members drifted out, collected their mounts and headed for home. Houseguests soaked in tubs, walked in the woods, chatted with horses in the stables, dozed, dressed for dinner, the women in long gowns, the men in tuxedos except the Colonel, for whom the pink hunting coat was formal dress at Cantigny. A few other guests might arrive for drinks and dinner.

On Sunday morning while the Colonel surrounded himself with newspapers, guests slept late, inspected the horses, perhaps went for an easy ride, listened to birds in the woods, flirted—oh how they flirted—took the dogs for a walk, sat on the porch or joined the Colonel, silently, to read the papers. Lunch and home.

*　*　*　*　*

For downtown activities and for shelter during the winter when wind and snow isolated Cantigny or during periods when he was needed at Tribune Tower from early morning until late evening, the Colonel and Amy used their house on Astor street, two blocks inland from the lake front and its Gold Coast mansions. Astor street homes are solid but small and narrow, one or two rooms wide, three or four stories tall, each house with its tiny front lawn and a more generous walled garden in the rear. The houses stood tightly shoulder to shoulder. A resident leaning from a side window could touch a hand offered from a neighbor's window. On sunny mornings the Colonel often sat in his bathroom window, happily shaving with his straight edge razor, oblivious to amused neighbors. A double row of trees gave the street a country air.

*　*　*　*　*

The Colonel regretted giving a day and night to the railroad to carry him between Chicago and Aiken. Charles Lindbergh had flown the Atlantic and adventurous young pilots were hop-skip-and-jumping from town to town, coast to coast, carrying the United States mail. Civic boosters hardened meadows to accommodate planes, the federal government erected beacons every 10 miles, and towns painted their names on the railroad station roof to serve their vanity and help lost airmen learn their whereabouts. Bold businessmen were buying planes capable of carrying three or four passengers and offering to fly citizens from city to city—on schedule, they said—but the Colonel was not one to fit his life into any schedule; he would say when and where the

295

plane flew. Into the breach came the Sikorsky workshop in New York, producing a craft of the future but also one that met the realities of the day. Its body was of metal, not wood and cloth, and shaped like a boat so the plane could land on rivers and lakes. To settle in a meadow the pilot lowered wheels. Two 150 horsepower Pratt and Whitney Wasp radial air-cooled motors pulled it through the sky at speeds, Sikorsky claimed, up to 125 miles an hour but 100 was more probable. If one engine quit, the other could keep the plane aloft until a haven came into sight. The plane was big enough to carry six persons including a pilot and a mechanic and 338 gallons of gasoline, sufficient to let it fly the 800 miles to Aiken with just one stop for more fuel.

The Colonel bought a Sikorsky in 1929. He ignored dictionaries by spelling amphibian with an "o"—thus, amphibion. Dropping into London Cockney he called the craft the *'Untin' Bowler*. On its nose he had painted the rounded black hat made by a London hatter named Bowler which, when strengthened, was worn by horse riders to prevent serious injury when they were tossed onto the head.

A Sikorsky pilot, Boris Sergievsky, delivered the plane, boldly flying a beeline over the western Pennsylvania mountains to Cleveland. He intended to refuel there, but heavy rain clouds covered the area. The pilot flew around and around looking for the airfield until one motor quit for lack of fuel, forcing him to settle in Lake Erie. Otherwise the trip to Chicago was uneventful.

The Colonel called his plane an "air yacht." A Tribune writer predicted "air cruising" would become as popular a diversion as motoring and boating.

The Colonel hired a pilot, Robert Gast, a 32-year-old Kentuckian, veteran of 12 years in the air including a year with the Royal Flying Corps seeking submarines off Ireland. By 1929 he was a federal aviation inspector and therefore very conscious of safety. The co-pilot, Parker Cramer, called Shorty and described as "small in stature but strong in courage, a crackerjack flying man," had first flown gliders in 1911. In 1928 he had joined Fish Hassell, the flier pulled from the lake, in a daring enterprise. Fish was convinced that as planes became capable of flying longer distances they would ignore existing surface routes and follow lines made by pulling a string taut across a globe. Planes flying to Europe from middle America would go not to New York, that terrible place, but head northeast across Canada and Labrador, then east to Greenland, Iceland, the Faroes, to Oslo, Stockholm, Copenhagen and Berlin.

To prove his proposition he persuaded citizens of his home town, Rockford, 50 miles west of Chicago, to buy a Stimson Detroiter, the biggest and best of the current passenger planes, and replace the four passenger seats with gasoline tanks. With Shorty beside him Fish flew the *Greater Rockford* up Lake Michigan and along the narrow gauge railroad through the Canadian wilderness to Churchill on Hudson Bay, the end of the line, refueled, slept and then flew straight east to the Greenland coast. Should they turn north or south to reach the Canadian weather and radio station run by Professor W.H. Hobbs of the University of Michigan? A landing field had been built there to supply the professor and his helpers. Over Labrador the *Greater Rockford's* compass had misbehaved and Hassell merely guessed when he turned south. Too late he realized he was wrong and turned back. Soon the gasoline gauge showed empty. Fish knew not even he could survive long in Greenland's waters. He rose to 5,000 feet, turned inland and set the plane down on a relatively smooth strip of snowfield. The frail craft shattered, but Fish and Shorty emerged merely battered, put on all their spare clothes, pocketed their charts, packed the iron rations and began walking.

For 10 days they slogged and slid across snow and ice. Their minds whirled. They saw things not there. After 100 miles they saw the fjord and scrambled down to the shore. Safe at last! But Hobbs' camp was on the other side. The men gathered drift wood, started their first fire, boiled some soup and, warmed inside, lay down and slept. After a while one awoke, looked out into the fjord. A canoe! Could it really be a canoe? He awoke his partner. Yes, it was a canoe, going up the fjord, toward the camp. The men shouted and jumped about and waved and threw wood on the fire. The canoe passed on, the paddles not even pausing. Fish and Shorty saw death near.

But the next day two small boats skimmed down the fjord bringing Hobbs' helpers who told Fish and Shorty that Eskimos coming to the camp said they had seen two crazy white men camping along the fjord. Hobbs assumed they were the long overdue fliers and dispatched the boats. The next supply plane returned the fliers to Rockford.

Hassell continued to preach the polar route as the sensible way to fly between continents but was content to wait for proper planes, airports and navigation aids. Not Shorty Cramer. He knew man would fly the polar route to Europe and he was going to be the first. His enthusiasm infected Gast. In May of 1929 Gast proposed to the Colonel that he and Shorty fly 4,750 miles from Chicago to Berlin in the *Bowler*. "My answer was an emphatic no," the Colonel recalled. "I told them The Tribune was not interested in adventure. But I was finally convinced that this distinguished company of fliers and the suitability of the plane would remove the element of adventure and it would prove of real value to the development of aviation." He could have added that the enterprise would make The Tribune better known around the world and, as years passed, would help establish Chicago, long the rail center for midwestern America, as the air center. Why, the Chicago airport might become the busiest in the world!

Gast and Cramer flew the *Bowler* to the Sikorsky factory to replace the passenger seats with three 100-gallon gasoline tanks and to strengthen the struts to withstand the strong winds expected in the Arctic. A young reporter, Robert Wood, was added to the crew, as "historian." "I am overwhelmed," he said. By the title, he meant. The three men flew the plane around the Chicago area and up to Milwaukee for lunch, proving, the Colonel said, that Milwaukee was now a Chicago suburb. This was an argument The Tribune was advancing as it sought readers and advertisers in that thriving Wisconsin city 80 miles distant. Each of the three bought an extra set of wool underwear, sox, shirt, chamois-lined leather helmet, parka, 16-inch-high moccasin boots, gloves, spikes to help when walking on ice, tools and spare parts for the plane, a flashlight, a .22 rifle to kill rabbits for the pot and a .303 to guard against hungry polar bears, a waterproof matchbox, pemmican and enough army iron rations for 30 days and ropes and pegs to anchor the plane during the night. Gast considered disposing of the wheels to save 500 pounds but decided to keep them for an emergency landing on land. On July 1st weathermen reported fog and mist over Labrador but thought the depression would move out into the Atlantic in the next day or so. The sun shone on Greenland night and day.

Late on July 2nd Gast flew the plane from Midway airport to the Grant Park beach and drew it up on the shore. Through the night police guarded it against souvenir hunters. In the morning eager helpers eased the craft into the water. At 8:30 Gast opened the throttle, Shorty tied down the key of the 50-watt transmitter that would send out continuously the plane's call letters, KHEJ,

Wood waved from a porthole. Fifty minutes later the *Bowler* landed off a Milwaukee pier. A boatman rowed the trio ashore, a driver took them up the bluff to lay a wreath at the statue of Leif Ericsson, then back to the plane. The 5,000 spectators wondered if they ever would see the three men again. At 10:51 the *Bowler* rattled across the water and in 10 seconds lifted itself into the sky. Its tanks held only enough gas to take the plane 300 miles to Sault Ste. Marie where they must land for Canadian customs inspection. The Canadian government had set aside 600 gallons of gas. The *Bowler* arrived at 1:35 but refueling was difficult and was not completed until about four o'clock. Gast had hoped to spend the night on Hudson Bay but put the plane down halfway, at Lake Remi, at 6:44. They had advanced 660 miles.

At 5:58 a.m. on Thursday, July 4th, they resumed the flight, hoping to reach Port Burwell at Cape Chidley on the Labrador strait, their planned second night destination, but Wood cautiously radioed: "Left for Great Whale. Will push on as far as possible." Forty-five minutes later the Tribune station at Elgin, Illinois, picked up a message from Cramer: "Visibility clear. Ceiling unlimited. Scattered clouds. All O.K." Then silence. Then a broken message from which engineers could pick out only "Eighty-five. . .eighty-five. Land." Had they landed or had they not? If so, where? Two weeks of worry and consternation had begun. At 3:10 another broken message was interpreted as indicating that the *Bowler* was well on the way to Port Burwell. The hard reality was that the trio, after enjoying clear weather for an hour to Rupert House on Hudson Bay, saw clouds ahead. Gast thought by flying low and keeping the coast always in sight he could reach the Hudson Bay company station on the Great Whale River where 600 gallons of gas awaited. However 100 miles short of the river, the crew met fog and turned back to Rupert House. They asked for fuel but only 32 gallons was available. So they flew north again to another Hudson Bay company station at Fort George. It had gas but refueling was finished only after midnight. The plane had advanced about 500 miles.

On Friday, July 5th, Gast decided to try to make up time by flying straight eastward from Fort George to Port Burwell, a distance of 600 miles. But within an hour, fog thickened. Gast turned northwest, found the Great Whale River and followed it to the company station and set down. The net advance for the day was only about 100 miles. Fog wrapped itself tightly around the plane and stayed fast through that day and the next, Satur-

300

day, July 6th. On Sunday, the 7th, the fog thinned. The *Bowler* set off at 8:30 and within an hour was in clear sky. In four hours the plane arrived at the coast. The compass had misbehaved, a condition that was to prove normal in the Labrador area of the magnetic North Pole, and Gast and Cramer met the same problem that had faced Cramer and Fish the previous year at Greenland. Should they turn north or south? Gast reckoned Port Burwell was north. A few distinctive islets soon proved he was correct. But the fog tightened and, when still 40 miles from the goal, the *Bowler* could safely go no farther. Below, big chunks of ice—growlers—tossed about on the rough water. The shore offered no haven, but just off shore was an islet and behind it the water was smooth and clear of ice. Gast landed there and drew the plane close to the rock. The men scrambled ashore, tied down the plane, found poor shelter and, on the evening that they had hoped to be feasting in Berlin, they chewed pemmican. Two thirds of the journey was still ahead. The tide came in. And in. And in. The men retreated, pulling the plane behind them. Never had they seen such a tide. Forty feet the tide rose that night. Then the water swept out, trying to take the plane with it. At mid-morning on Monday, the 8th, the men saw a gap in the fog, jumped into the plane and dashed toward Port Burwell and, they thought, safety. But after 45 minutes and 30 miles the fog again defeated them. They sought refuge in a small inlet and twice fought the tide for possession of the *Bowler*. On Tuesday the 9th, the fog persisted but Gast was becoming desperate in his contest with the tide for possession of the plane. The three boarded and Gast wove through the growlers until he saw a short open reach, then skipped into the air and, skimming the water at 80 miles an hour, barely fast enough to keep the craft aloft, he felt his way along the coast 10 miles to Port Burwell.

What did they find?

Four shacks! The station manager had been in bed four months with no medical care and no boat had come to Port Burwell since the previous August. Where's the harbor? A helper pointed to the inlet where the rare ship sometimes anchored. Gast taxied the plane there, but did not like the winds nor the growlers. He thought another inlet seemed less hazardous, taxied there and tied up. The station organized Eskimos to carry the gas in 10-gallon cans two miles from the storage shed to the plane.

The fog still held. Later Wood learned that three Canadian air force planes assigned to Port Burwell to study ice patterns along the Labrador coast had flown only 35 hours in a year and a half.

For three days the *Bowler* crew struggled with the tide. One day the ice was so thick and charging about so wildly that Gast started the motors and taxied about, twisting and turning to keep the plane in clear water. On July 13th a gale blew down from the north just as the tide was going out. It snatched the *Bowler* as though it were a child's kite, snapping her moorings, and drew her out to sea. Growlers gathered around her, crashed into the hull and tore open the thin metal. The *Bowler* sank.

Gast, Cramer and Wood made themselves useful about the station. After 18 days the Hudson Bay ship *Acadia* arrived, bringing a cook and supplies for a year. It took away the station manager and the fliers, struggled for a thousand miles through ice and gales around the northern tip of Labrador and down Hudson Bay to Churchill. The railroad delivered the thwarted polar-route fliers to Chicago on August 18th.

The Colonel bought another Sikorsky, christened it *'Arf Pint* and continued to go air cruising, but only in kind weather. Shorty Cramer set off again by himself, reached Iceland and flew on toward the Faroe Islands north of Scotland. He never was seen again.

* * * * *

On Greenland, snow covered the *Greater Rockford*. Some 30 years later a warm summer exposed it. A Norwegian military helicopter lifted in a score of men, including The Tribune's aviation editor Wayne Thomis, to dig out the broken plane, dismantle it and bring it home, eventually to the Rockford airport, where students of Rock Valley College set about restoring it. During his labors on the ice cap, Thomis saw high, high above, an airliner on its way to Europe. By then Chicago's airfield, O'Hare, was the busiest in the world. "So you see," Thomis reflected, "Fish and Shorty were right all the time."

* * * * *

Could *'Arf Pint* whisk the Colonel between Cantigny and Tribune Tower? Soon Fred Byington, of The Tribune's transportation department, was rowing into Lake Michigan to meet the amphibian flying in from a quiet stretch on the Fox River, five miles west of Cantigny. One day the Colonel pointed to a reach closer to Cantigny and told the pilot to land there. The pilot said the water was too shallow. "Let's try," the Colonel said. The pilot put down the plane tenderly with no problem but as the plane lost motion it settled onto the mud bottom. The Colonel stepped out into the river and waded ashore, calling back, "Told you we could land here. Ho. Ho. Ho." The pilot towed the plane free. There must be a better way to shorten the travel time.

Soon Eddie Edwards' farm crew was smoothing and packing a strip through a cornfield, chopping a path through a woods and sowing grass seed. Now the Colonel could fly from and to his doorstep although one day after a heavy rain the amphibian's little wheels dug into the softened earth and the plane flipped upside down. The next day the Colonel told his editorial writers: "I knew something was wrong and I'd better get out of there. I unfastened my seatbelt and fell on my head. Ho. Ho. Ho."

He tested the practicality of the autogyro, later called the helicopter. An autogyro deposited him on the Monticello hilltop in 1931 to preside over a memorial service for Thomas Jefferson, champion of a free press. Later a helicopter carried him to an elegant garden party at the Whitelaw Reids' Long Island estate. Gusts from the blades scattered everything everywhere, just as a generation later the presidential helicopter that delivered President Eisenhower to the opening of the St. Lawrence Seaway spread gray dust over Queen Elizabeth's gleaming yacht, *Britannia*. Did the Colonel apologize? Did the White House apologize to Buckingham Palace?

*   *   *   *   *

The Ford and Thompson suits had established the Colonel as a fierce fighter for a free press. It was not surprising that one day in 1927 the Colonel received an appeal from the publisher of a small weekly paper in Minneapolis which had printed hard things about public officials there. The paper was considered by most people to be a scandal sheet and public officials had persuaded a judge to order the cessation of publication. The big papers in Minnesota were glad to see the sheet closed. When the Colonel read copies of the paper, the Saturday Press, he could understand the big papers' attitude. The Saturday Press was indeed a scurrilous sheet, but if its reports that public officials were linked to criminals were true, the Saturday Press was justified completely in printing the accounts and the editor, Jay M. Near, deserved help. The Colonel's legal training and the preparations for the Ford and Thompson suits warned him that if he and The Tribune were to help the editor they must take on the Minnesota legislature and State Supreme Court.

Earlier in the 1920s another small-time Minnesota editor, John L. Morrison, sorely had tried the patience of quite a few people in Duluth with his weekly called the Rip Saw. Morrison, a puritan, suspected that a lot of people in and out of office were getting away with improper behavior because no one exposed their misdeeds. Morrison did not print gossip; he printed only accounts he was certain were true, a trait that may have made him an even greater danger. Various persons drew him into court on libel charges but he did not change his ways. Various persons thought he must be silenced. Three offended men, a state representative, a judge and a former mayor of Hibbing, persuaded the state legislature in 1925 to pass a law which authorized a judge, on application from a public prosecutor and without trial by jury, to stop publication of a periodical which had a record of printing material that is obscene, lewd and lascivious or scandalous and defamatory. The legislators reckoned such a publication had no more right to continue operation than a dairy which consistently sold bad milk should be able to continue selling milk which probably would be bad. As the sheriff went to arrest him, Morrison left town in an ambulance and crossed into Wisconsin. His critics accused him of running away from the law, but before the day ended Morrison died of a brain clot.

Two years passed before Near and Howard Guilford started the Saturday Press in Minneapolis. Unlike Morrison they were not puritans. The chief of police ordered that the first issue be removed from the streets even before it appeared. Soon County Attorney Floyd Olson asked Judge Mathias Baldwin for a temporary injunction under the 1925 law. A civic-minded lawyer, Thomas Latimer, dared defend the Saturday Press, claiming the gag law violated the Minnesota constitution which guaranteed freedom of the press. The Judge granted a temporary order but handed the case to the Minnesota Supreme Court to rule on the constitutionality of the law. Near asked the Colonel for legal help and money. The Colonel offered no money but, on persuasion of his chief lawyer, Weymouth Kirkland, entered the case. Kirkland filed a 377-page statement with the Minnesota Supreme Court.

305

Howard Ellis, a member of the Kirkland firm, appeared before the court.

On May 25, 1928, the Court unanimously upheld the law. The constitution, the Justices declared, guaranteed liberty, not license, and was not meant to protect persons purveying scandal and defamation without a good cause. Near was living off small earnings from writing for other papers. With his impatience showing he wrote bitterly to the Colonel, implying that Ellis deliberately lost in Minnesota so the case could be moved to Washington. That, he said, might be a good legal tactics but didn't help him earn a living.

The Colonel ignored the plea. He asked the American Newspaper Publishers Association if it would join in the appeal to the United States Supreme Court. The president, Harry Chandler of the Los Angeles Times, advised letting the matter rest in Minnesota, reasoning that if the appeal were lost, other states might well adopt the Minnesota gag law. The Colonel replied that unless the gag law were beaten, other states would adopt it. He asked that the publishers be polled. The Tribune, he added, would pay all costs of the appeal. All but five of the 259 publishers approved of the appeal, providing The Tribune paid the bill.

On January 30, 1931, Kirkland presented The Tribune's arguments in Washington. He admitted that the Saturday Press was defamatory but said the proper remedy for defamation is prosecution for libel. The Minnesota law, he said, imposed restraint prior to a deed and that is unconstitutional. Minnesota argued the law came into force only after a series of deeds. Justice Brandeis interrupted to say that the Near articles charged a "combination" between officials and criminals. "That is a privileged communication if there ever was one," he said. The Justices retired to read, think and consult.

In Minnesota Olson, now governor, proposed the gag law be repealed. The House of Representatives approved but the Senate declined. The Colonel rejoiced; repeal would have cancelled the Supreme Court appeal. He wanted a ruling which would deter future efforts by public officials and lawmakers to control the press.

The Justices announced their decision as the last act of the court term. The eight Justices divided four to four. The deciding vote came from the Chief Justice, Charles Evans Hughes, who assigned himself the task of writing the majority opinion. In it he saw "a primary need" for a "vigilant and courageous press."

"The fact that liberty of the press may be abused by miscreant purveyors of scandal does not make any less necessary the immunity of the press from previous restraint in dealing with official misconduct," he declared. The Chief Justice limited the decision to charges of defamation. He did not touch on the second part of the law's reason—obscenity—for shutting down a paper.

The full story of the Near case was told by Fred W. Friendly in his book, "Minnesota Rag," (Random House, 1981). He sums up: "Few could have predicted the impact the case would have on the half century that followed, particularly with the civil rights struggle and anti-war movement. No other nation has constitutional tradition against prior restraints comparable with those which sprang from Hughes' sweeping opinion. . .The Constitution is not a self executing document. The free press clause could have remained a benign exhortation but history, fate or whatever force it is that provides the unlikely champion or the subtle improbable turn of events that leaves its indelible stamp upon the course of human events, intervened. The landmark status of the Near case will continually be reread in the context of history. Whether its significance is to be upheld or eroded is a question whose answer lies chapters ahead in American law and liberty, in our newsrooms no less than in our courtrooms."

The Colonel saw any effort to restrict any part of a newspaper's operation as an attack on press liberty. Defending a suit brought in 1922 by the Chicago Journal of Commerce over circulation practices, the Colonel had gained from Judge Kenesaw Mountain Landis a ruling that a newspaper is a private enterprise, not a public utility. He refought that battle, again successfully, when the Truman administration almost 30 years later tried to have newspapers reclassified, bringing them under government regulations.

"Citizens should remember," the Colonel said, "that their precious liberties are never secure, even under the best of governments, if they fail to guard and to fight for those freedoms."

The Colonel recognized that rights carry responsibilities. A misbehaving newspaper can be sued for libel but, to the Colonel, a more important check was held by readers. "The press," he stated, "must constantly retain the confidence of its readers. Sensational falsehoods may pick up readers but not retain them. A book author or publisher is free of such restraints. He may hope to make such a killing in one book as not to need to write or publish another."

The Colonel quoted Medill: "Leading and influential journals like our own are watchmen on the walls, looking for the approach of danger. They have thrust upon them the duty, not always pleasant, of acting as conservators of the public good, often at the expense of their private interests."

The Colonel abhored censorship. He saw how British, French, German and Russian control over war news may have been tactically helpful in the short term by depriving the enemy of information but in the long term was damaging to the censoring nations themselves. "A nation that sets out to deceive," the Colonel argued, "winds up by deceiving itself."

Oswald Garrison Villard said The Tribune "kept alive the historic right of press dissent, even in wartime." The Colonel, he added, "has in his stubborn way steadfastly fought for the right of the press to live up in the fullest degree to that one of the four freedoms that pertains to it, a fight that several contemporaries forgot."

A biographer, Joseph Gies, commented: "If anyone doubted Colonel McCormick's willingness to go to jail to support freedom of the press, they did not know him."

Little did the Colonel guess that a Tribune news story would lead him to the gates of prison, accused by his enemies not of libel, but of treason in wartime.

17. "Neutral in Nothing; Independent in All"
1932—1935

In 1930 the Colonel was 50 years old. By breeding, birth and rearing he was a Republican, much in the manner that he was a Presbyterian. He accepted the creed of Grandfather Medill who on gaining sole control over The Tribune in 1871 stated:

"The Tribune will hereafter be an independent Republican journal. It will be the organ of no man, however high, no clique or ring however influential. While giving the Republican party and its principles hearty and generous support, The Tribune will criticize the actions of Republican leaders freely and fearlessly as in days of yore but it has seemed to me unwise for a great representative journal, for the purpose of correcting some alleged abuses of an administration, to desert its party organization and turn its guns on old friends and help into power the leaders of organizations whose political records and official conduct show they are insincere."

To continue Medill's independence, the Colonel drew added strength from his now-solid habit of solitude. Rarely was he tempted to choose words to please or protect a friend, colleague, or business associate.

The Colonel had been too busy at the Sanitary District, in Russia, in the army, directing the fast-spreading Tribune enterprises, playing polo, improving his country estate to take more than passing note of national politics. That had been the realm of his elder brother, the Senator, and the Senator's wife Ruth. The Colonel's main political interests lay in the city council and state legislature which levied taxes, regulated trade and distributed jobs and contracts. As a young alderman, McCormick had learned to expect government operations to result in high cost, low performance and graft. His aldermanic experience reinforced the opinion inherited from Grandfather Medill that the least government is the best government, although as president of the

309

Sanitary District he had acknowledged that at special times under special circumstances government must take on special jobs.

From Medill, too, came the Colonel's low regard for communism. As early as 1860 Medill had warned against the false attraction of communism as benefactor of the working man. "Decorate every lamp post with a communistic carcass," Medill had said. Less bloodily, the Colonel noted that the first American colony, Jamestown, was founded on the communist creed: "From each according to his abilities, to each according to his needs." Hard-working settlers saw results of their labor going to idlers and slowed their efforts. The colonies became self-supporting, he said, only after they adopted free enterprise. He warned Americans not to look to the army for protection against communism; an army developed to restrict communists could become an army supporting communists. He quoted Lincoln's idea of a true citizen: "As I would not be a slave, so also I would not be a master." The Colonel was convinced that the working man rarely could meet his employer on equal grounds and needed help against bad employers, help which could come from a union or the government. As a boy he had been little impressed by the march of Coxey's army on Washington, but in 1932 he thought the unemployed were justified in their mass march on the capital.

Over the years he often had gone to Washington to see his mother and aunt and to try to make peace between them, but he departed as quickly as was decently possible. In 1930 Washington was remote from the daily life of American citizens. The President was still something of a distant uncle, neither eager nor able to tell citizens how they must conduct themselves. President Hoover left to President Roosevelt a White House staff of 45. A half century later President Reagan employed 376, plus uncounted hordes in his executive office, his budget office and other supplementary bureaus. Until the 1930s Congress was careful when putting its hand into the people's pockets and did so usually to refill the pork barrel, not to redistribute incomes among rich and poor. At election time politicians and voters spoke hard words in loud voices but few voters really expected the election outcome to have much effect on their own lives. In 1932 the deepest national concerns grew out of the depression. A few candidates offered radical programs to bring back prosperity. The Colonel blamed the depression on high government spending. Hoover's 1928 budget collected $3,900,329,000 and spent

The McCormick Era

$2,961,245,000, leaving about one billion to reduce the national debt which, on his handing over the presidency to Roosevelt, had been cut to $19,487,002,000. The Colonel said for the country to prosper again the new President must spend less.

The second most pressing problem, the Colonel said, was prohibition. He blamed the 1919 amendment banning alcoholic drinks for the rise of gangsters who killed one another and innocent Chicagoans while providing illegal booze for the thirsty millions, including the Colonel.

Looking beyond the nation's borders the Colonel had moved sharply away from his grandfather's advocacy of making all of North America part of the Union, by arms if necessary. The derring-do of the Spanish American War with its easy victories over the exhausted, almost dead Spanish empire may have inspired young Bert, but the American army's fiasco at the Mexican border in 1915 had cooled immature desires for military adventure. He wanted all Mexicans to stay in Mexico. Let them in, he said, and they will undercut the American workman and complicate eventual assimilation of all immigrants into a unified nation. His weeks on the Russian front and his months in the trenches of France had sickened him with the terrible killing of citizens in the name of national honor and glory. He had followed the plea to make the world safe for democracy and found it to be a sham. During the years his father had been ambassador to three world powers he had seen how Europe had tormented itself generation after generation with war after war after war, all fought, in the Colonel's vision, to widen national territories. Europe had not changed its ways. Governments made alliances to suit the moment and broke them with no thought of honor. The United States, he advised, must not line up with any other government nor alliance of governments. It must mind its own business, as George Washington had advised, while maintaining an army and navy sufficiently strong to dissuade any European government from thinking it could ignore American rights. When a German submarine sank the *Lusitania* in 1915, The Tribune declared a mere breaking of diplomatic relations would "only impress the world with our futility and invite further aggression," philosophizing, "There is such a thing as a man being too proud to fight (as President Wilson said) but if we are too proud to fight, let us be too proud to talk as if we were ready to fight." After that war the Colonel had no faith in the League of Nations. "President Wilson," he said, was "trying to rise from head of a nation to

312

head of a group of nations," abandoning his own country.

*   *   *   *   *

Early in 1931 Amy's brother George, promoted to major general, was made commander of the 1st Division, the Colonel's outfit in World War I but died while turning over his earlier command in Panama. He was buried beside his father at West Point.

*   *   *   *   *

The Colonel offered four planks for the Republican 1932 platform: Bring back alcohol—the Colonel wondered why Christian clergymen should foist on a Christian nation a law decreed by Mohammed, cut government spending, stay out of foreign wars and, a parochial matter, complete the waterway between the Great Lakes and the Gulf of Mexico, a pet project since his canal building days at the Sanitary District.

The Republicans convened first and stayed with prohibition and Herbert Hoover who, four years earlier, had won with the slogan, "Dry Clean Al Smith with a Hoover." The Colonel accepted the decision but did not cheer. The Democrats were lining up behind Franklin Delano Roosevelt, governor of New York, assistant secretary of the navy during World War I, advocate of strong defense, no supporter of prohibition and a schoolmate at Groton.

Roosevelt, replying to a request from The Tribune to all presidential candidates, sent a telegram addressed personally to the Colonel. "A preliminary study," Roosevelt wrote, "leads me to believe federal expenditures can be cut 20 percent by eliminating many functions not absolutely essential and by complete reorganization of many departments." The Colonel replied: "Delighted you share these views although I doubt if there will be enough money in the country to meet the budget by inauguration day." He addressed the note to "Dear Frank," and signed it "Robert R. McCormick."

Roosevelt was nominated. The Colonel told the chief editorial writer, Clifford Raymond, to "treat Roosevelt nicely; I want the boy that I went to school with at Groton to know I wish him well in his career."

Roosevelt invited the Colonel to his home at Hyde Park. On re-

313

turn to Cantigny the Colonel, in his thank-you note, said he "enjoyed every minute" of the visit but added he subsequently had read a Roosevelt statement that the government, to spur recovery, should force corporations to disgorge surplus funds accumulated during the depression. The Colonel explained that before his time The Tribune distributed profits promptly to its stockholders and as a consequence he, on assuming control, lacked cash to meet serious problems and to pursue opportunities. He began building up cash and continued the policy. He added he was convinced that any businessman, smart or stupid, could run his business better than "any outsider"—the government. On election day the Colonel urged voters to reelect Hoover but described Roosevelt as "a high-minded man with desire to advance the well-being of American citizens." "No fair critics will doubt his intentions," he added.

Roosevelt invited the Colonel again to Hyde Park before the inauguration. The Colonel went and, in the thank-you note, drew from his war memories: "I feel you are going over the top and the least I can do is to wish you well."

The Colonel, like most American businessmen of the day, looked upon Roosevelt as a financial conservative. The Colonel was more concerned with the soundness of banks and the banking system than with any fiscal deed the new president might perpetrate. The Colonel had his own urgent problem. The final payment on a bond issue floated for the Canadian paper operation was coming due. The small print said the bonds were redeemable in gold, a customary phrase at the time. The Colonel had the necessary $800,000 on deposit but worried that the banks might close or the government might freeze gold. Already banks in Detroit and New Orleans had closed. D. M. Deininger, who had been so helpful at the Sanitary District and Red Oaks and now was Tribune comptroller, proposed withdrawing gold from the bank and putting it aside for payment day. The Colonel agreed. Deininger went to the First National Bank and presented a request for $800,000 in $20 gold coins. The bank put young officers—among them James Bourke, who long remembered the arduous day—to counting 40,000 coins weighing a ton and a quarter and to loading them into a Tribune delivery truck. Deininger took the gold to the Harris Bank, which was involved in the bond issue, and put the coins into a private strong room there. On payment day the Colonel told the bank to take the gold and pay the bonds. The bank declined to remove the gold from the private

315

strong room. Deininger did the longshoreman job himself. After the inauguration President Roosevelt ordered a banking moratorium and an embargo on gold and raised the gold price by 75 percent. The Colonel, his own cash flow problem beaten, publicly congratulated the new President on his admirable "promptness" and "reassuring firmness."

Two weeks before the inauguration, the Colonel had written to "Dear Frank" seeking his help in stopping negotiations between the United States and Canada for a treaty to limit use of Great Lakes water needed by the lakes-to-gulf waterway. Roosevelt did not reply but passed the note after the inauguration to his secretary of the interior, Harold Ickes, a former Tribune reporter with no love for the Colonel. Ickes passed it on to an aide who in time sent the Colonel a packet of government handouts. The Colonel had expected more from his Groton schoolmate.

The New Deal administration sent to an obedient, frightened Congress a deluge of proposals, many drawn from the Hoover files, updated and expanded. The Colonel accepted the creation of the Civilian Conservation Corps and the Public Works Administration to provide jobs on worthwhile but not commercially viable projects, and the Federal Emergency Relief Administration to help the desperately poor, but suspected that Roosevelt, in copying a social program Bismarck had introduced into Germany, was, like Bismarck, seeking votes from the masses. The Colonel, as a hobby farmer, disliked the creation of the Agricultural Adjustment Administration and denounced its orders to slaughter six million pigs and to let fertile fields revert to weeds. At Cantigny he planted Secretary of Agriculture Henry Wallace's new hybrid corn and rejoiced when his farmers reported Cantigny bins held more corn than ever before. He thought the Tennessee Valley Authority encroached too heavily on private enterprise although he had exercised equal powers and similar policies as president of the Sanitary District. He saw danger in the codes for fair competition written under the National Recovery Act which he looked upon as borrowed from Mussolini's corporate state. The NRA code for newspapers turned his suspicions into anger. Let bureaucrats tell editors how to run their papers? Preposterous! Besides, it's unconstitutional. Enough editors joined the Colonel to force the Congress to insert a clause stating that no NRA action would impinge on the constitutional right of free press.

The Colonel was temporarily ready to forgive the President for

316

all of his acts during his first 100 days in gratitude for ending prohibition. He invited the President to stay at Cantigny when he came to open the Chicago World's Fair in May. "It seems to me you are making very good weather in the storm," the Colonel wrote in his invitation. As things turned out, the President was too busy in Washington to come to Chicago, but in his thank-you note to "Dear Bert," he said, "Do let me know when you are coming to Washington." The Colonel dropped the invitation into a wastebasket.

* * * * *

By summer the honeymoon was over. The President was miffed by being forced to take a few steps backward on the newspaper code and the Colonel was beginning to suspect from the sweeping powers Congress was giving the President and from the outpouring of federal funds that Roosevelt deliberately had misled him in his telegram mentioning a 20 percent cut in spending. FDR, the Colonel said, was putting America on the road to dictatorship. Many people scoffed but the Colonel argued: Look at events in Germany; there, to ease economic and political problems, the Reichstag had given up so many of its rights that Hitler could no longer be deposed peacefully, and Hitler was behaving as have all powerful rulers through the ages and was tramping on critics with storm-trooper boots. Germany, the Colonel concluded, had willingly and blindly drifted into dictatorship. In America, the Colonel continued, Congress, to solve the nation's problems, was similarly giving up the citizens' right to control their own destiny. He quoted New Deal members and supporters who openly derided the Constitution as obsolete and preached economic and political revolution as necessary to bring back prosperity and produce social justice. Indeed, some boasted the revolution was already underway. When the Rhode Island legislature removed five Republican Supreme Court Judges, the Colonel decreed the state had removed itself from the Union and, to emphasize his verdict, he cut one star from the flag hanging in the Tribune lobby. A former law partner and advertising manager, Samuel E. Thomason who, despite a personal pledge, had bought a rival paper, informed the Federal Bureau of Investigation. It formally notified the Colonel that to mutilate the flag is to face imprisonment. The Colonel restored the star.

The Colonel's scorn often focused on Henry Wallace. "As a

317

business man," the Colonel said, "Secretary Wallace is a fit companion for Mr. Roosevelt the speculator in worthless German marks, Mr. Morgenthau the gentleman farmer made a financier by fiat, 'Honest' Harold Ickes the stock market sucker who had to be bailed out by his wife and those two professional spenders of other people's money Harry Hopkins and Madam Perkins. It is impossible to recall in American history an appointment of a person so completely incompetent to perform the duties of office or one whose appointment was more brazenly in discharge of a political debt to those bent upon destroying the American government and substituting for it the slavery of communism."

The majority of Americans preferred the New Deal to any visible alternative and did not share the Colonel's fear that dictatorship lay ahead. They went along with the President and voted their confidence in the 1934 congressional election. To the Colonel the election demonstrated the urgency for a more vigorous campaign to expose the New Deal's errors and to awaken the people to their peril. Of all American editors the Colonel was heard most widely and, as a consequence, he became the most frequent target for attack by the President, his administration and his supporters. The President was expert at using vicious ridicule to destroy a rival and the Colonel became famous and infamous. Foes dubbed him a reactionary with "the best mind of the fourteenth century." The barbs hurt but, just as a boxer expects pain when he enters the ring, the Colonel, hardened by 50 years as odd-boy-out, tried to ignore the agony produced by the critics, even those he considered unfair. The cause was worth the pain. Many men would have become silent under such a barrage. Not the Colonel. As did Grandfather Medill, he met shot with shot. He made Lincoln's dictum his own: "I have said nothing but what I am prepared to live by and, if it be the pleasure of Almighty God, to die by." Friend and enemy reached for The Tribune. The President read The Tribune in bed every morning, and The Tribune prospered. In 1935, the Supreme Court declared the AAA and the NRA acts unconstitutional. I told you so, said the Colonel, his hopes rising that the nation would see the truth as he saw it and refuse Roosevelt a second term.

* * * *

A Yale classmate, Joe Thomas, organized a fox-hunting club in the rolling countryside northeast of Nashville, Tennessee. The Colonel, eager to abandon Aiken, was a founding member, although most of the other members were Easterners. The club, called Grasslands, included a comfortable clubhouse with suites for members. Thomas brought a pack of hounds from England. The season began about Thanksgiving Day, two months earlier than in Aiken. Unlike Aiken's riders, those at Grasslands pursued the fox across country, through woods and over the many old stone fences.

The Colonel and Chauncey McCormick sent their horses there and used the clubhouse. Amy went also to Grasslands but after a short time continued on to Aiken, disturbed by a relationship developing between the Colonel and a member's wife. For the first time Amy was aware of the Colonel's interest in another woman. The Colonel commuted from Chicago to Grasslands in his plane, a three-hour flight, to give himself long weekends with her. The relationship continued for some time at Grasslands and in the East but never at Cantigny and never with the Colonel considering a change of wives. The Colonel broke off the relationship, acquaintances said, when he learned that her expectations went beyond his gifts to her. This kind of foray into feminine company cost the Colonel dearly.

For some time Amy and the Colonel had been finding less pleasure in each other's company. Now silence settled over the dining table when they were alone and spread through the house and through Cantigny and followed them wherever they went. Amy built on the southern edge of Cantigny, a mile from the house, a studio with a large northern window and passed long hours there painting. "Bois de Madame" she called her retreat. Now and then downtown galleries exhibited her work, the proceeds going to charities, such as Orphans of the Storm, an animal refuge. The wall around the Colonel which Amy had worked for years to erode again hardened, leaving little room within for Amy.

After two years the Easterners began pulling out of Grasslands, finding that Thomas' assessments to meet costs were exceeding his predictions and their expectations. The club went bankrupt. Amy purchased the hounds and brought them to Cantigny.

The Colonel considered joining the summer polo set on Long Island and sent his horses to the Drinkwater stables. The Midwesterner was not happy among the Easterners on Long Island. One summer was enough. Now and then on weekends the Colonel returned to Aiken. The polo had become rough and tough, almost vicious. Players did not check their drive to prevent injury to one another. One player was killed by the smash of an opponent's mallet against his head. The Colonel rode his ponies with no thought for his mount and if a poorly wielded mallet broke the horse's leg, he shot the horse. During one game a player charging hard toward the goal crashed his horse into that of the defending Colonel, toppling the Colonel from his saddle and shattering a shoulder. The shoulder never was the same and not again did the Colonel seriously play polo.

When riding in the Cantigny woods the Colonel often carried a pistol. Continuing his boyhood killing of stray dogs, he shot squirrel, raccoon, skunk. Late in life the Colonel said he had killed every kind of living creature in North America except buffalo (including one Texas cowhand.)

* * * * *

The Colonel's name dropped from The News masthead in 1933. The News remained a subsidiary of the Chicago Tribune and earned millions of dollars, enabling the Colonel to enhance The Tribune and expand its operations, but no paper ever more truly belonged to one man than did The News to Patterson. The News was Joe Patterson, with Mary King at his side, and Joe Patterson and Mary were The News. In his last years his sister Cissy asked him what he thought would happen to The News after he died. "Who cares?" he replied. "There won't be any News five years after I'm gone."

18. "A Fitting Monument"
1932—1935

In the heart of Cantigny was a swamp, smallish but powerful in production of mosquitoes. Trees grew in every direction, competing for sunshine. Giants that had died generations ago rested on branches of sturdier youngsters, giving the swamp a wild beauty. The Colonel, riding his land, often paused on a rise to watch the sun go down over the swamp turning the willows into gold. Here indeed was a place for a man to enjoy the world the way God made it, after a bit of human improvement here and there. Here the Colonel could be half a mile from everyone. The loudest exhaust from trucks rampaging along Roosevelt Road— Teddy Roosevelt Road—could not penetrate this far. Here he would build his home.

On July 4, 1932, his mother died of a heart attack at Versailles, outside Paris. She was 79. Services were held in Paris and on July 18th in the Astor Street house in Chicago with Chief Justice Hughes and General Summerall among the honorary pallbearers. She long ago had given her Washington house to her now deceased elder son, Senator Medill McCormick. She had restored the Colonel to her will and divided her Tribune stock rights between him and the heirs of her elder son.

With income to spare for the first time the Colonel began planning a new house, one with style and distinction that would qualify it for becoming a museum "for all of the Medills" after his death, joining Washington's Mount Vernon and Jefferson's Monticello in the nation's architectural heritage and serving as a proud western entrance to Chicago.

Amy spoke up against the project. Medill's house was beautiful, an architectural gem, albeit small in the catalog of mansions, providing more than enough room for the two of them. Why all the extra space? They never would have children; they never had long-staying guests. She might as well have spoken to the wind.

The Colonel took Edwards to the swamp and said, "We should have a lake here." His notes to the farm manager record the progress:

"Are you making the pools deep enough to let the fish live through the winter?"

"That muck you seem to have piled up as a dam will not hold water. To make a tight dam you should excavate down to the clay and then build the dam of clay all the way and pack it with either a roller or a tractor."

"There are two oak trees near your mud pie. The only one to cut down is the one with the dead top."

Again Amy spoke up. If you must have a new house, she said, build it on the southern edge of the estate, near her Bois. That position would be more convenient. The Colonel spurned the proposal, saying it would cost too much.

The Colonel marked the lines of his new house above the lake. Eddie built a swimming pool, drilled a well, raised a windmill to keep the lake filled during dry weather and buried a drain to carry off surplus water in wet periods. With the water level stabilized, the muddy shores dried, grasses and wild flowers flourished and mosquitoes moved on. The swamp became Swan Lake, with black and white swans cruising sedately.

All was now ready for the house to rise.

The Colonel wrote to Willis Irvin, the Augusta, Georgia, master of southern colonial architecture who had designed the McCormick house at Aiken, asking if he would design a new house at Cantigny. It should look over the new lake and be placed on the avenue of elms, giving it a vista and making it visible from both north and south. The architect should use fully the fine woodwork in Medill's house created by Architect Coolidge but spare no expense and reduce the peril of fire.

The Colonel was undecided about the future of the Medill house until a fire consumed a neighboring vacant house and convinced him the wooden building should come down. The foundations could be converted into a formal garden or be cleared away to open a view from Roosevelt Road. But the architect was reluctant to destroy the finely crafted old house, and gradually the Colonel considered saving it. Could Irvin add a wing with one big fireproof room at least 50 feet long and 28 feet wide with a high ceiling for his books, and another wing with ground floor bedrooms, also fireproof, for himself and his wife? Could his bedroom be on the southwest corner, sheltered from Roosevelt Road and the rising sun? Could the family porch be moved from the noisy east side to the quiet south side? The giant oak to the east, the smaller oaks and chestnuts to the south and the elms to the west must not be disturbed; about that the Colonel was adamant. Place the wings at an angle if you must, the Colonel said. Amy thought such an arrangement disharmonious but the Colonel said he had seen a house like that somewhere and "found it not objectionable."

Irvin dutifully proposed putting the library on the east and the bedrooms on the west, making the length of the house 160 feet, identical to that of the White House. He refined the Colonel's library slightly, cutting three feet from the width and making the height equal the width, paneled it in Brazilian butternut and placed at each end a fireplace so big it demanded logs four feet long. Jefferson installed at Monticello an elevator to bring wine from the basement; the Colonel installed at Cantigny an elevator rising from the library floor to bring logs loaded on carts efficiently engineered for ease and quiet in handling. Bookcases, recessed in the paneling, were to hold the Colonel's well-read 5,000 books, mostly about the Revolutionary and Civil War periods and world historical leaders. Pages are marked with bits of torn paper; lines are marked with pencil. One day long after the Colonel's death a casual reader came upon a lock of blond hair. Winston Churchill sent copies of his books after each stay with the Colonel. One set is inscribed: "With every good wish, and in the hope that the English-speaking peoples may increasingly write their history in common."

A finger pressed against two small carved rosebuds in the paneled wall opens two hidden doors to a sparkling art-deco bar. The doors cannot be opened from the inside. There is a story that someone once closed the doors not knowing that the Colonel and Churchill were in the bar. The story insists that neither man shouted for help. A brass plaque identifies the bar as the Winston Churchill room. Commendations to the 1st Division are carved into the library paneling and over the fireplaces. Blueprints identify the library as Liberty Hall although the Colonel usually referred to it as "my room." Everyone else called it simply "the big room."

The library opens onto a new east porch copied from Jefferson's portico at Monticello. "It must be an exact replica," the Colonel ordered, "or we'll tear it down and start over." At the top of a series of grassed terraces was a swimming pool kept fresh

323

with well water and heated only by the sun. Overflow water was carried to a double reflection pool on the lowest terrace. The Colonel disdained a swimming suit when no guests were at Cantigny and strode through the house swinging a towel but he disliked guests dripping water as they returned to their rooms so Architect Irvin provided dressing rooms under the Monticello porch.

Under the library Irvin placed an equally sized room, except for a lower ceiling, orginally dubbed the ratskeller but altered during planning into an art-deco movie theater. The ceiling glows with gold leaf applied over silver leaf for lightness. Murderous guillotine-like steel shutters suspended by a rope protected the Colonel and his guests from possible flash fire of the celluloid film in the projection room.

At the other end of the house the architect designed a much larger wing with, on the ground floor, bedroom, sitting room, bathroom and a dressing room walled with closets for the Colonel and, for his wife, a bedroom, bathroom, 2 x 4 closet and dressing room so small that one has to face sideways to raise arms; on the second floor six bedrooms and two bathrooms for servants; in the basement a new kitchen, butler's pantry, staff dining room and chauffeur's room, plus a new porch for the staff. Irvin achieved an architectural wonder by providing passage from almost any room to any other without going through a third and by giving each main floor suite its own outside door as an escape from fire.

During the construction an event tragically heightened the Colonel's fear of fire. On March 6, 1934, winter still gripped Cantigny. About one hour after midnight, Mrs. John Oswald was awakened by her crying baby. Smoke was drifting into their apartment in the stable loft. She aroused her husband. They wrapped the baby in blankets, grabbed coats for themselves and ran down the stairs. They heard the horses snorting and thrashing, trying to kick themselves free from the stout plank boxes. As Mrs. Oswald carried the baby into the frozen outdoors, Oswald opened the door to the stable. Heat and smoke burst out. The fire was raging along one end of the stable just inside the only door. If he could get past it, he could open the box doors and free the horses. Arm over face, he edged into the stable. The flames seared him. He retreated. Jack Kunde, the dairyman, who had been awakened by the crackling and flaring of the flames, ran from his house. Together he and Oswald decided they could not save the horses but they could save Mrs. McCormick's 25 prize

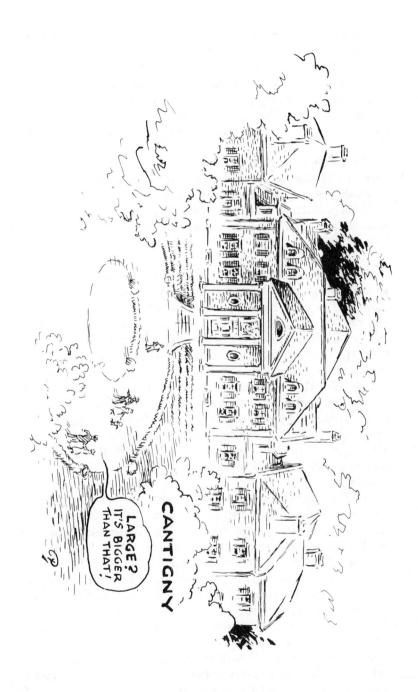

Guernsey cows in the nearby dairy barn. They opened the dairy barn doors; the cows catapulted out pursued by smoke.

In Winfield, a mile away, the fire bell clamored at the chief's home, calling out the volunteers. In about three minutes the chief, Herman Reiser, arrived with the truck. Firemen followed in their own cars. The flames already had swallowed the stable and were biting into an adjoining garage and licking the five cars there.

"It's goodbye to the stable and garage," the chief told the volunteers. "Maybe we can save the dairy and the Kunde house." The volunteers turned their hoses onto the house, known as the honeymoon cottage because it always was occupied by a newly-married couple. Its paint already was being blistered by the heat.

The Colonel hurried over from the big house. "Is everyone all right?" he asked. Kunde told him the Oswalds had escaped and added he was sorry he and Oswald were not able to save the horses. "That's all right," the Colonel said. "So long as no one was hurt, it's all right. Everything else can be replaced." Mrs. McCormick drove from the house and left her car near the garage. The fire chief told the Colonel some of the doomed horses in the stable were still alive and asked, "Is there a gun in the house?" The Colonel reached into his overcoat pocket, withdrew a .45 pistol and gave it to the chief. "Don't forget to bring it back," he said. The chief shot two horses still threshing about in agony. Now only the crackling of flames disturbed the cold night. The chief returned the gun. The Colonel said thank you and walked slowly back to the house. Mrs. McCormick, ashen-faced, remained.

The fire engine from Wheaton, three miles away, arrived and hooked its hoses to the barn water system, but the flames burned the power lines, cutting off the well pump. Hoses dried. The Winfield truck used the last of the water in its tanks. Then the firemen stood helpless, dry hoses in hand. Company 77 from Chicago, almost 20 miles away, clanged along Roosevelt Road and joined the spectators as gas tanks in the five cars exploded and the holocaust reached its peak.

By three o'clock the flames had eaten the stable, the garage with five cars and Mrs. McCormick's car nearby. The cow barn and cottage were safe. The firemen went home. Mrs. McCormick returned to bed, suffering over her horses' agony and determined such a thing would not happen again.

Embers smoldered and smoked through most of the next day. On the second day Joe Schmidt and other farm hands brought a team of horses from one of the outlying farms and a skid and loaded the blackened bloating mounds, all that remained of Mrs. McCormick's seven blue ribbon hunters including Fan Tan, grand champion at the recent Fort Sheridan show, two of the Colonel's polo ponies and two draft horses, and dragged them a quarter of a mile to a small clearing in the woods where the farmers had dynamited a long shallow pit in the frozen ground. They laid the mounds side by side in the pit, covered them with dirt and placed as a marker a large rock. Mrs. McCormick had a brass plaque made, inscribed: "To my beloved horses." And named them.

The Colonel set the monetary loss at $50,000. The Winfield department asked Mrs. McCormick for a $50 donation to replace a ladder broken at the fire. She refused. The Colonel, also thinking the village firemen inefficient, asked that Cantigny be transferred to the Wheaton fire district, offering to contribute $100 for each call. Winfield went to court to oppose the change. The volunteers admitted that the horses and cars were lost but said the fire was out of control when the firemen were called. They added that they had successfully put out seven other fires at Cantigny. The judge kept Cantigny in the Winfield district. A vote would have established the Colonel as Winfield's most unpopular citizen.

In the summer the Colonel built a new stable. He made a false start, having a foundation dug beside a woods before deciding to place the building far from anything that might burn. He asked the architect to design a stable with a sleeping quarters for a groom amidst the horses, doors on all four sides, a heating plant and storage room well away from the building and a 30,000 gallon underground water cistern. Chauncey McCormick admired the completed stable and built a duplicate on St. James Farm.

*   *   *   *   *

Irvin roofed the enlarged house with deep red shingle-like oversized tiles and wrapped the building with roughly textured pink brick made by hand in Aiken. Painters swabbed white paint over the brick but before the paint was dry everyone realized that was a mistake and workmen wirebrushed off as much paint as they could. As years passed areas exposed to the weather have been washed clean but protected areas are still mottled pink and white, giving the house the soft patina of a much older building.

On the library's exterior walls the Colonel carved the names of his special heroes, George Washington, Thomas Jefferson, Patrick Henry, George Mason, General Daniel Morgan and General George Rogers Clark, all in one way or another among the United States' founding fathers. The architect provided niches for statues of Washington and Jefferson beside the east portico. One day the Colonel asked young Joe Schmidt to climb into a niche so the Colonel could determine the best height for the statues. A short time later the Colonel saw an advertisement offering a cast iron statue of Washington precisely the right size. He ordered it. The statue arrived. It depicted Washington as a Roman Caesar, his right arm in the folds of a toga as though in a sling. The face was small and sharp. White enamel paint coated the entire figure. The statue was relegated to the darkest corner of the basement and wrought-iron flower baskets were placed in the niches.

The Colonel considered ways to improve Coolidge's breeze cooling system. He proposed installing large attic vents which when open at night would let the warm air escape into the sky and draw in fresh garden air, cooled as it passed through long large pipes deeply buried under the lawn. The system had one flaw: It demanded all windows be closed all night. The Colonel suspected that someone was bound to open a window. He abandoned the idea and chose to pipe well water—always 55 degrees through the hot water radiators. That too had a flaw: Moist air condensed on the radiators and trickled across the floors. In the end he installed a small version of the air conditioning plant which made Tribune Tower one of the earliest fully air conditioned office buildings. He did make use of the garden by building another reflection pool to cool freon gas from the compressor. Discoursing once on air conditioning he concluded: "This lesson is intended for men only, as I have never found a woman capable of taking it in."

During the rebuilding, spread over two years with frequent visits by the architect, the Colonel sometimes lived in a farmhouse and Amy in her Bois. Some neighbors criticized the Colonel for spending so much money on a mansion during the depression when so many people were short of cash. Others praised him for creating jobs. The Colonel stated his position in a one-page tract headed: "Why So Much House."

"When time had tired the wooden home of Joseph Medill beyond practicable repair, the problem arose how to provide a habitable dwelling place without destroying the old house or moving away from surroundings enriched by several lifetimes of landscaping. The plan adopted was to brick over the old house, continue to use the dining and living rooms and build one fireproof wing for sleeping quarters and another to safeguard books, pictures, and records not to be jeopardized by a careless cigarette.

"And with this determination came further planning. The old porch which once faced on a sleepy country road now looks upon a transcontinental highway. Groups that exchanged greetings with passing neighbors are deafened by raucous sirens and open cut-outs. To escape this annoyance it was decided to turn the house around and face it to the south, keeping the old New England portico as an entrance.

"The architecture of the Old Dominion had already been decided upon as appropriate in territory conquered by Virginia, when the opening of the fight to destroy the American Constitution suggested that the building be modeled into a shrine to human liberty.

"Accordingly, the style of Montpelier, the home of Madison, father of the Constitution, was selected for the southern entrance, and that of Monticello, seat of Jefferson, author of the Declaration of Independence, for the eastern view. Statues of Patrick Henry, as conqueror of the Northwest Territory and proponent of the Bill of Rights, (Henry gave way to Jefferson during the building) and of Washington, as victor of the Revolution and Father of his Country, will stand in niches above the stair terraces, looking into the morning in token that we will not allow their work to be destroyed.

"Wall space will be used in Liberty Hall, for so we call the east wing, to commemorate the builder of the old house, his family, and worthy men and their brave deeds, now passing from the minds of a busy people: The 8th Illinois Cavalry, raised in the county where the house stands, and William Medill, who commanded it in its most glorious days and who fell leading it in the last charge of the Gettysburg campaign, as he had led it in the first, and their gallant opponents, and soldiers of old wars which gave the world all it has of freedom.

"If the efforts of the designers and builders shall prove successful, the bricks piled here will remain awhile, a fitting monument at the western portal of the City. If not, they will soon give way to the eternal march of time."

For his sitting room the Colonel had made an oversized chaise lounge, so big that on tiring he could stretch out and nap. Within reach were his favorite bedtime books, Wodehouse and Conan Doyle. Coming home on chilly evenings, he lit the downstairs fireplaces, all 10 of them except the one in the room set aside for Amy. At dusk the valet or maid cranked shut the wooden shutters, pulled down a black shade, then a white shade, then drew together the thickly padded drapes. A second door, two and a half inches thick, shut out the sound of anyone or any dog pattering up and down the servants' concrete stairs. Even so, at times a muffled tap, tap, tap of heel or claw seeped into the room until the stairs were carpeted.

A small hallway connected the Colonel's bedroom with that designed for Amy but she returned to her bedroom and parlor upstairs in the old part of the house which the morning sun filled with light.

* * * * *

The minister of the First Presbyterian Church in Wheaton, the Rev. Dr. Robert Stewart, had free run of Cantigny and of Chauncey McCormick's adjoining St. James Farm as well. The six-foot, handsome New Englander, his bearing aristocratic, his speech Boston's best, arrived in Wheaton in a convertible with a wolfhound named Bruce and a gentleman's gentleman named Radford, who had buttled for the Gillette safety razor family. A bachelor, the minister lived in Wheaton with Jack and Yvonne Burt, until the Burts' young son bit the wolfhound on the nose. For the minister Wheaton was a big step down from his New York church. One Sunday before his arrival only 17 members had come to hear a five-dollar-a-sermon, fill-in preacher.

Chauncey McCormick was the most important member of the congregation. On the way to church he dropped off his wife and Amy at Wheaton's Episcopal Church if the two had not ridden their horses into town. Chauncey, president of the Chicago Art Institute, embellished the Presbyterian Church with a 16th century Spanish pulpit and some rococo pillars he found in the Institute basement and his wife ecumenically gave the Presbyterian

330

AMY'S
FAITHFUL
CRITICS—

331

church a 15th century Crusader iron cross and an equally old chest with elaborately carved panels of saints.

The congregation multiplied under the ministry of Doctor Bob. There was competition for places in the front pew and for dances with him at parties. At Cantigny he rivaled the Colonel in shouting out old songs although neither could carry a tune. He served his congregation faithfully. A lame girl, active in Sunday school, died while he was on a Canadian vacation; the minister flew home to conduct her funeral. Wheaton citizens, Presbyterian or not, sought his company and advice when shopping for antiques. He exercised his wolfhound by running it beside his top-down convertible as he drove through town. The congregation bought a house for him and then built a church. The Colonel paid for erecting a passageway between manse and church and sometimes took the minister on trips to Canada and Florida. The Rev. Dr. Stewart remained in Wheaton for the remainder of his life.

The Colonel rarely attended church. One hot summer evening after dinner at a Chicago Lake Shore apartment the minister and the Colonel chatted on the fire escape. Suddenly Stewart asked why he never had joined the church.

"No one ever asked me," the Colonel replied.

"Well, I'm asking you now," the minister said.

The next Sunday the Colonel was introduced as a new member and sat prominently in the front pew. No one ever saw him in that pew again although occasionally he slipped into the church as the service was beginning and sat in the rear pew beside Marion Duffield, who considered that place hers by prior right. He always left quietly just before the service ended.

19. Back to Work
1935—1937

The debilitating depression still gripped minds and company board rooms in 1935. Half of Canada's paper mills were closed or in default on loans. In all of North America only the Thorold plant was operating at full capacity. The price of newsprint had dropped to $40 a ton and some mills were offering it for $33. Plants cut wages but Thorold employees found their checks 50 percent above the new lower average for the community. Schmon, who had been given charge of the Thorold operation on the death of Curtis in 1930, had brought about so many improvements that production went up by a third and costs went down. The 3,000-ton ship wanted by Curtis was loading paper at Thorold and delivering it to The Tribune's new warehouse on the Chicago River close by the printing plant. With money cheap the Colonel turned in his eight percent Thorold securities and accepted notes at lower rates. The Tribune, in 1934, earned a profit of just over $3 million and its subsidiaries earned another $3 million.

The Colonel in 1935 saw signs that the worst was over. Manufacturers and retailers were placing more advertisements. People were buying more newspapers. The Tribune's circulation passed 800,000 and The News 1.5 million. The two papers together were using more paper than ever before and the Thorold mill could supply little more than half. Schmon told the Colonel that mills would begin edging up their prices as they cleared surplus stocks.

Is the time right to resume work on the North Shore? the Colonel asked. Schmon listed favorable trends: Good labor was available; manufacturers were eager for business and willing to make firm delivery dates; money was cheap; the Quebec government would look with delight on any project to provide jobs. Common sense had to conclude that yes, the time is right.

Common sense also dictated, Schmon told the Colonel, that a

new mill should make paper as well as pulp for the Thorold mill.

All right, the Colonel said, but to run a mill successfully up there, we will need a town, something much better than the log cabin settlement at Shelter Bay. "My own idea," he wrote Schmon, "is that we should encourage our employees to build their homes and own the land on which the homes are built. I don't believe too much in company ownership in the long pull. The best monument I can build will be a successful industry. It won't be successful if I load it down with too much capitalization."

"Be bold in designing the paper mill," the Colonel commanded. "We want the highest quality paper at the lowest price. Ask Ben Jones (the engineer at Thorold) what changes he would make if he could rebuild that mill today. Make your mistakes on paper. We will also need a ship to take the paper to the New York News and bring back coal. We will begin work in the spring as soon as the ice goes and finish in the third summer. Arthur Schmon will be the boss all the way."

Schmon's first decision concerned the width of the paper to be made. In the past each widening of the roll brought new production problems; however, a wide roll had an advantage over a narrow roll: It could be cut into a variety of widths to meet differing press needs.The Colonel opted for a wide roll, reckoning that production problems could be overcome but no one could improve on arithmetic.

Schmon's engineers proposed boosting the temperature at which pulp was cooked and enlarging up to 50 tons the steel rollers which compressed it into paper. To keep a constant watch on the porridge fed into the block-long machines chemists devised more accurate testing laboratories. The Colonel knew the proposals were risky but he told Schmon to order two machines. Tribune craftsmen made an accurately scaled model of the mill. In his office at Tribune Tower the Colonel shifted blocks representing the many pieces of machinery, seeking the most efficient layout. He liked best an arrangement by which the railroad entered the mill at one end, deposited equipment and supplies brought from the dock, moved on to pick up rolls of paper and went out the other end and back to the dock a mile away where ships waited.

Electric power would come from the Outardes, 12 miles to the west. For nine years engineers had debated how water could be brought from the dam to the yet unbuilt powerhouse a mile downstream. The up-and-down granite terrain ruled out a ditch and blasting a tunnel would drain the Colonel's treasury. A pipe was the only alternative but a pipe so big that a car could be driven through it. Pipes of such size had been made of concrete for sewers but supporting a concrete structure above ground would be as uneconomic as blasting a tunnel. Make the pipe of wood, the Colonel decided. Outardes had trees, trees everywhere, but none big enough to provide the strong, long, thick planks required for the biggest, longest wooden pipe ever built. Across the continent in British Columbia, firs grew tall and strong. Ships could carry the giant timbers down the west coast, through the Panama Canal, up the east coast, up the St. Lawrence to Outardes where workmen would form slightly tapered planks into a pipe bound every few inches with steel cables.

To carry logs to the mill from the Outardes and the bigger, lustier, more defiant Manicouagan, the Colonel approved construction of a round-bottomed flume, five feet wide—wide enough to reduce the likelihood of the four-foot-long logs jamming—and two and a half feet deep, made of wood as was the pipe, lined with sheet aluminum, perched on a single line of poles and held firm by guy wires on either side. Gravity, that often neglected gift of nature, moved water and logs at seven miles an hour. Between May and October the flume must bring enough wood to supply the mill all year.

The Colonel, always worried by fire, told Schmon to keep weeds away from the pipe and the flume. Schmon hired extra men. The Colonel, seeing a chance to cut costs, bought cattle, shipped them to the Outardes and told Schmon to graze them along the pipe and flume, eating weeds and also providing meat for the workmen. The cattle strayed. The crew resumed chopping weeds.

After conquering such challenging tasks, designing the power house and the transmission lines was Sunday afternoon entertainment.

In the decade and a half since the Colonel had watched the hulk of the *Wiley M. Egan* sink off Shelter Bay to provide the footings for a small dock, harbor engineers had learned how to overcome the St. Lawrence's riotous winds and waves. They designed for the new community an L-shaped concrete harbor, the short arm running out from a steep granite shore to the longer arm parallel to the shore. The basin could shelter six ships.

Every time the Colonel and Schmon looked at the swamp at the end of the bay they favored it less as a site for the town, and, lifting their eyes to the surrounding hills, decided to scatter houses along the lower slope of the tallest hill. The Colonel christened the town Baie Comeau for his woodsman hero, Napoleon Alexandre Comeau, and called the hill Mont Sec for one in France from which the 1st Division had so gallantly driven the German army during the last summer of the Great War.

Schmon brought to Baie Comeau from across the St. Lawrence an experienced lumber man, Arthur Sewell. The Colonel admired Sewell's war record—he had volunteered at 17 to fight with Canada's kilted Black Watch regiment—and enjoyed hearing about an ancestor who as Lord Chief Justice condemned to death Canada's last witch, but did not want to hear anything of another Sewell ancestor who had given the consecration address of the Old North Church in Boston. He was a Harvard man.

Schmon and Sewell took for granted that all houses in a model town must have water and sewer. To provide these facilities on Mont Sec, men had to blast 18 miles of five-foot-deep trenches out of the granite. One day the Colonel arrived from Chicago just as a string of dynamite charges went off.

"He blew up," Sewell recalled. "He said, 'My God, what fool persuaded me to build a town here. Shut it down. Shut it all down.'" Sewell's surprise showed.

"I mean it. Shut it all down," the Colonel repeated. He stomped to a shed used by Ben Jones, slammed the door and locked it. Foremen gathered and appointed Ed McGraw as emissary because the Colonel seemed to enjoy being with Ed.

McGraw knocked.

"Who's there?"

"Me. Ed McGraw."

"Come in."

McGraw entered. Before the door closed, Sewell heard the Colonel say, "I'm mad and I want to stay mad."

After an hour or so the Colonel called for a small boat and had it take him to the fishing cabin on the English River. For two days no work was done. Then the Colonel emerged and said, "All right, go ahead."

By midsummer 3,000 men were working in Baie Comeau and another 2,000 in the woods.

During the first winter at Baie Comeau men building the mill and town were locked into an icy wilderness. Barracks were primitive, families left behind, days short, nights long. The only way out was to run 100 miles behind the bi-weekly postal

dogsled. The Colonel forbade alcohol, but bootleggers had smuggled in a long winter's supply, cleverly cached it, and, as weeks passed, did much business. Men had a drink or two on Sunday, then four, then six. By midwinter they were drinking every night and waking every morning with hangovers. By late winter some men were waking up so drunk they could no longer perform their skilled tasks. Sewell telegraphed the Colonel in Chicago for permission to fire them and send them home on the first boat. "No," replied the Colonel. "But they can't do their jobs," Sewell persisted. The Colonel ordered: "Make jobs they can do." The men stayed, recovered during the summer as their families arrived and completed the project on time. Years later Sewell recollected that the Colonel recognized the pressures on the men, and, instead of blaming the men for cracking, blamed himself for having sent them to face such unanticipated conditions.

In the autumn a proud, happy Colonel invited Tribune directors to see the wonders that had been achieved. The propellor of the boat bringing them from Montreal became entangled in a discarded piece of cable while approaching the harbor. The captain tooted for help at each passing vessel and skippers politely tooted back. Late in the day the skipper of a French schooner did sidle over to ask if anything were wrong and agreed to take the passengers ashore. By then the tide had gone out and the little French boat bobbed at the base of a slimy 20-foot ladder fastened to the wharf timbers. The Colonel fairly bounded up but the wharf crew tied life lines around other waists. The directors toured the project and applauded.

The Colonel told department heads he would give them collectively $5,000 for each day they could cut from the schedule date for starting the paper machines. The first paper came off the first machine in January of 1938. The Colonel gladly paid, Sewell remembers, $240,000.

For the formal opening, July 11, 1938, steamers brought 200 guests. A band played in the small park. Quebec Premier Maurice Duplessis boasted the project was the largest in Canada since the start of the depression but warned other American publishers that they could not expect to take away Quebec's forests. The Colonel said he hoped Baie Comeau would become an important community and reminded the Premier that he had spent $180 million in Canada for wages, supplies, royalties and taxes since 1912. Schmon said Baie Comeau had cost in two years $13 million and another $17 million would be needed to complete the project, big sums as the depression lingered on in 1938.

"Nature does not smile on human endeavor in the North Shore wilderness," Schmon commented. "Baie Comeau has demanded persistence, hard work and the almighty dollar."

Each year saw more houses rise at Baie Comeau. More merchants established shops. The residents, urged by the Colonel, reluctantly formed a city council, began levying taxes, elected Sewell mayor and kept reelecting him until he was transferred to Thorold 12 years later. Schmon showed the Colonel plans for a house—a chalet, he called it—which he planned to build for the Colonel's use. The Colonel approved, but that night he told Mrs. McCormick, "Arthur wants to build a house for himself." The Colonel continued to sleep at the fishing camp where the phone hung on a tree and could be safely ignored. When the church rectory burned, the priest moved into the chalet until the rectory could be rebuilt. Then the chalet became the home of Jim Lane, the manager.

* * * * *

In a further move of innovative independence the Colonel set about establishing his own shipping line to transport the products of his mills and his forests. Tribune craftsmen made for the Colonel a model of a ship to carry paper down the St. Lawrence and along the Atlantic coast to New York City. Its plates would be welded to eliminate damage to paper rolls caused by rivets although no welded ship that big ever had been built. In the model the Colonel shifted little wooden cylinders representing rolls of paper until he found an arrangement to make best use of the space in the holds.

The ship was built in Britain, christened the *Joseph Medill*, loaded with Scottish anthracite and dispatched to Canada. In mid-Atlantic she met a gale and disappeared. A court of inquiry considered that the welds might have broken in the storm or that the ship might have run into an iceberg. The Colonel thought neither explanation made sense. The radio operator had sent no SOS call. Why? Probably because he lacked time before the ship sank. Broken welds or an iceberg were unlikely to bring such a quick end so the fault must lie with coal carried as ballast and loaded into the hold without partitions. As the ship rolled heavily in the gale, the coal must have shifted, disturbing the ship's balance so radically that on one deep roll the ship did not right

339

itself but continued rolling over onto her side, turned bottom up and sank. The Colonel was so certain of the explanation he ordered a duplicate ship built. She, the *Franquelin*, crossed the Atlantic the next year with a ballast of unshiftable clay and became queen of the St. Lawrence.

* * * * *

Depression and drought tormented midwestern farmers, testing their faith. The Colonel, with a deep trust in the good earth of Illinois as a generous provider of food, bought several farms, establishing a tenant or manager on each and setting aside grassed strips for his plane so he could make quick, frequent inspection visits on his way downtown from Cantigny. "Keep the engine running," he sometimes told the pilot before striding about, looking, looking, rarely speaking to anyone, then returning to the plane and, airborne, scribbling notes to the tenant or manager. "The Colonel was a plain-speaking man," one of the farmers, Herbert Dalton, recalled a half century later. "He knew what should be done and he made sure it was done."

The Colonel was reluctant to abandon horses for tractors. Horses provided a built-in, year-long market for produce of the farm whereas tractors ran up enormous bills at the gasoline station. On a farm bordering the Fox River, where the soil was very heavy, the tenant and his two helpers arose at 4 a.m. to curry the 12 horses and hitch them to a mammoth disc that seemed to reach from fence to fence. Men and horses were in the fields by 6 a.m. During the harvest, the work continued until sundown with an hour and a half break for men and animals at 11:30 a.m.

The Colonel was intensely interested in trees. In Canada he cut hundreds of thousands each year to feed his mills but at Cantigny only black cherry trees could be cut without his specific permission. If the cherry tree leaves fell into a pond, he said, and cattle drank from it they died. He walked the estate with his tree expert, L. F. Irvine, or Tribune farm editors in all kinds of weather. He would ask, what kind of tree is that? Or what is wrong with that tree? Richard Orr, on his first walking inspection after being appointed farm editor, told the Colonel he knew very little about trees but no one ever disregarded a question from the Colonel. Orr noted them all, sought people who knew the answers and reported back.

A neighbor, Joy Morton, builder of a salt fortune and son of

340

the founder of Arbor Day, developed an arboretum on his 1,500 acres five miles east of Cantigny, brought trees from many parts of the world and established a research station. The Colonel, challenged, began buying rare trees by ones and twos and planting them on the lawn between his house and Roosevelt Road, sheltering the house and providing himself with his own library of trees on his own doorstep. A small brass identifying plaque hung from each tree. If on visits to Baie Comeau he noted a fine young tree he had woodsmen dig it out, plant it in a stout wooden box and send it on the next paper boat to Chicago. Three oaks and two chestnuts boldly stood close to the Madison verandah, blocking the best view down the long avenue. To a visitor's question of why he didn't cut them down he'd reply, "They were here first," or "It takes a hundred years to grow an oak; 30 minutes to cut it down."

One day the Colonel, sitting on the Madison verandah, sent for Edwards and told him, "Eddie, we need a couple of willows out there beyond the reflection pool." Edwards studied the terrain. The pool rested on a broad ridge that fell off steeply on both sides. The drop was small, only 10 feet to the west, 20 to the east, but enough, he knew, to drain the ridge.

"Willows won't grow there, Colonel," he said. "Willows need lots of water. They should be planted in low ground."

The Colonel looked out with new eyes. Yes, the pool was on high ground. Yes, willows do need much water. He had to agree with Eddie's recitation of the facts. He raised his brown eyes which so awed many employees and strangers.

"Eddie," he said, "let's put our minds to it."

Eddie took himself to a quiet spot and matched needs against possibilities. He told himself, "The Colonel wants it done; it must be done." After completing his tabulations he added, "It can be done." He fetched two farmhands, two horses and a scoop. The team dug a hole big enough to hold the foundation of an ordinary house. In the center the men piled large broken rock into a pyramid. They filled the hole with silt brought from the swamp, ran a pipe from a well pump to the pyramid to keep the soil wet and covered it all with black dirt and sod. The next time Eddie saw the Colonel on the porch he said: "Colonel, we're ready to plant the willows." The Colonel made certain he had his pocket knife. The two walked to his favorite willow by the stables. The Colonel chose two small branches, whacked them off cleanly. He and Edwards walked to the chosen spot. The Colonel thrust one branch into the ground and then, 20 feet away, the second.

"Now, Eddie," he said, "that wasn't very difficult, was it?"

The willows prospered in the hilltop swamp made just for them and daily waved their thanks.

Cartoonist John McCutcheon wrote in his memoirs that he constantly was amazed at the Colonel's attention to detail. Nowhere was that trait more closely revealed than at Cantigny, as a glance at notes from the Colonel to Edwards testifies:

"Have you sprayed the apples?"

"There is water in the holes where you dug out the evergreens. They breed mosquitoes."

"Three or four posts on the Roosevelt Road fence near the gate seem to be broken."

"We must find a suitable place to plant sunflowers next year. They are both ornamental and valuable." And two weeks later: "I want to raise a considerable amount of sunflowers next year. Where do you suggest, and are there more than one kind?"

"Please collect catalpa and evergreen seeds. I will tell you later where to plant them."

"The red maple looks sort of punk."

"If we have any poison on the farm, see that it is locked up and only one man has the key to it."

"I think it might be a good idea to put some martin boxes in the vicinity of our pond next year. They would reduce the bug population."

The Colonel strove to have the farm pay for itself. It never did, even though the accountant sent from The Tribune was instructed not to include labor nor a charge for the land.

The Colonel's firm Tribune policy against accepting gifts did not prevail at Cantigny. He happily accepted use of a new tractor, reckoning that Cantigny was doing the maker a favor by testing the machine. The same thinking let him accept on payment of $1,000 a bull that would bring $5,000 in the stockyards auction.

The Colonel chose crops and animals not for their market value but for the pleasure of watching them grow and of trying something new. To accommodate his wide variety of crops the fields were divided into plots too small to be economic. Cattlemen seeking profit had Black Angus or Hereford beef herds; a Shorthorn herd was a status symbol. The Colonel bought Shorthorns and specified they be white. He had little trouble concentrating on white chickens, white turkeys, white, or whitish, hogs and sheep

342

and white geese, but he had to accept multi-colored pheasants, guinea hens, quail, peacocks. Cantigny's most powerful work-horses, Bill and Bob, were black with a white diamond on the forehead. A herd of black Karakul sheep was developed from one ram and three ewes. The Colonel did not kill the lambs at or before birth when the fur is most tightly knotted, but let them live to old age to try to learn why Karakul are more hardy than European sheep. He did earn some money by clipping them and selling wool to makers of an unusual kind of oriental carpet. At butchering time a Karakul or two found its way onto Cantigny tables and the Colonel pronounced the meat tasty. A University of Minnesota professor brought to Cantigny a new type of South-down ram with a fearlessness not expected in sheep and placed him in a small pen with a big Alsatian. The two creatures stood nose to nose. The dog was first to back off. The professor started to talk about the ram but the Colonel's eyes were on the cow-ardly dog. "Tell me about the dog," he said. He did not try to in-still boldness in Cantigny sheep but he did try hormones hoping to bring the ewes into heat twice a year, and he did feed pigs arti-ficial milk. Double failure! He bought miniature horses, smaller and more stylish than Shetland ponies, but soon saw no future in them. He was tempted to develop a herd of Brahman cattle but was discouraged by their reputation for fierceness until he read that a Texas breeder tamed Brahmans by having children comb them daily for six months when young. He bought three heifers, guaranteed by the breeder to have been so coddled. The day they arrived Edwards and two farmhands climbed into the corral. The heifers charged with a ferocity that would have brought cheers from a Madrid bull ring crowd. The three men fled over the rails to safety two snorts ahead of the heifers. The Colonel complained to the breeder who replied the heifers merely were being playful and advised if they behaved like that again Edwards should wait until they came into reach and then gently tap each on the nose with a piece of rope. The Colonel did not put Edwards to the test but moved on to Herefords, all chosen for exceptionally white faces.

In the fields the Colonel tested new varieties of standard mid-western crops and defied nature by trying to grow cotton, pea-nuts and other southern crops. When the Japanese conquest of the Philippines cut off the supply of hemp needed by the navy for hawsers, the Colonel acquired seed, planted it and encouraged other farmers to join him in helping the navy. The young plants thrived until government narcotics inspectors descended on Cantigny and pulled them all up. The plant is also the source of marijuana. The navy had to manage without Cantigny.

The Colonel looked after the beef herd, sheep, woods, fields, machinery; Amy ran the dairy herd, the chickens, the vegetable and flower gardens and lawns. They shared responsibility for the horses. Amy was the preferred employer. She paid better and was more considerate. "She was a soft touch," old timers said. She retained a hard-drinking chauffeur out of consideration for his wife and baby girl and taught farm children how to ride and gave them treats. During heavy work periods she hired extra hands as soon as the Colonel went on a trip and told them to hide if the Colonel came back unexpectedly, even if they had to crawl into the hay. The Colonel told farmers to use the horses instead of the new tractors and thereby save gas but Amy said to use the tractors if the machines eased labor. On hot afternoons Amy brought jugs of iced lemonade to men working in the fields. Amy loved Cantigny and everyone at Cantigny loved Amy. Well, almost everyone. Coming one day upon an uninvited guest known for loose conduct, Amy told her sharply, "Get out of my house, you whore," and made certain she left quickly.

The Colonel experimented with introducing a Tribune time-card system, each workman recording the hours and minutes devoted to each task daily. The sheep man, Pop Rawlings, crossly scribbled: "Worked 24 hours. Worked every day." The experiment ended.

The Colonel enjoyed watching pheasants. To make them more readily visible he fed them and provided shelter boxes near the house. Amy complained they dirtied the lawn and damaged the gardens. Her head gardener, John Wallner, agreed. "Pheasants will draw rats," he told her. The next day the Colonel sought out the gardener and demanded, "John, have you seen any rats about?" The gardener did not know how to reply. The Colonel said, "It seems there are a lot of rats around here," and returned to the house. A few days later the pheasants were moved to the woods. "Mrs. McCormick usually had her way although it might take a while," Joe Schmidt, who worked for both the Colonel and Amy at different times, remembered. Peacocks roamed the lawn and slept on the roof behind the big chimneys.

Each farmer had special tasks. Kunde looked after Amy's Guernsey cows, a herd so immaculately tended that the milk was bought unpasteurized by hospitals and so productive that the cows were milked three times a day. The Swedish cook, Elizabeth Johnson, churned creamy butter and ice cream. One farmer cared for turkeys, chickens, geese, ducks; another the beef animals; another the pigs; another the horses. The families gathered berries and nuts by the bushel for the house and themselves, made elderberry wine, jam and jelly, canned fruit, tended their vegetable gardens and kept flocks of their choice and perhaps a pig or two. Bees produced honey eaten directly from the comb; the pond yielded frog legs. Farmers with children drew milk by the gallon from the dairy. Elizabeth insisted vegetables be fresh daily, especially on Sundays when the Colonel was home for lunch. The garden boys learned that Saturday's vegetables looked fresh on Sunday if kept in the well pit overnight and sprinkled in the morning. The greenhouse supplied roses for the house all year. Each spring Amy cut washtubs full of lilacs and peonies and had her driver deliver them to hospitals.

The Colonel insisted that everything be tidy, fences unbroken and painted, yards neat, hedges trimmed, horses carefully clipped, farmhouses well heated, flower boxes at windows, hedge apples at basement windows to keep spiders away. Everyone made do with material at hand. The farmers cut trees and split them into fence rails. A saw mill supplied rough timber.

When Frank Zeier's wife burned herself on the wood stove, the Colonel installed an oil furnace. The sand road running the length of the estate was kept graded and dry so horses could be exercised there when the weather made woodland trails soggy.

The Colonel registered Cantigny as a wildlife preserve and, by erecting four miles of fence, lowered his tax rate and improved his privacy. Deer, mink, raccoon, possum, weasel, groundhogs, rabbits, squirrels, quail, wild turkeys, beaver thrived. Pheasant, both wild and farmyard raised, strolled the riding trails with the confidence of an emperor on parade. Birds sang all day challenging the knowledgeable to listen for their song and to locate them high in the trees. People who knew birds counted more than 70 species in one morning of enchanted bird-watching. In spring and autumn, ponds sheltered migrating ducks and geese, some staying long enough to hatch and tutor their young. Guinea hens thrived in the dry season but once taken into a farmyard would not return to the wild. One day the Colonel thought he saw an Hungarian pheasant, a bird he had shot in Europe. Edwards surmised the strange bird was one of the female pheasants he had just released which had lost her tail feathers. The Colonel considered squirrel and raccoon delicacies for his dinner table.

Over the years he acquired a small but fine collection of guns, ancient and modern, handguns, rifles, shotguns, including a rare piece with three barrels that fired in sequence from one trigger. He bought a powerful shotgun and took it into the fields to test fire. The recoil almost knocked him flat. He never fired it again but locked it into one of the three bookcases in his library from which he removed books to display the guns. During a hunt on a neighboring farm a gun used by Henry Hooper, husband of Maryland Hooper, exploded, tearing off two fingers. Cantigny farmers thought the Colonel blamed himself for the accident. Hooper was to suffer a greater loss to Cantigny.

One summer crows held a national convention at Cantigny, stripping fields. The Colonel organized a hunt. Big businessmen, expensively camouflaged, took up positions in opposing fields and blasted away, their barrages driving the crows back and forth over no-man's-land. The Colonel, who did not join, opined that someone should invent a special crow-hunting gun, firing a shell which would burst after 100 yards and spread shot in all directions. Another summer when fox gathered, the big businessmen came again, formed a long line and, in perfect World War I formation of soldiers going over the top, advanced through the woods. They met not one fox. Another summer the Colonel saw dogs running wild in the woods. He had Orr write a piece saying if the DuPage sheriff were not concerned about protecting the citizens from rabies, the county should have a new sheriff. The next day a sheriff's armed posse cleansed the woods of wild dogs. The Colonel widened his protective arm to include all Illinois citizens, having Orr harass the state legislature until it decreed all Illinois dogs must be innoculated against rabies annually and carry a tag.

The Colonel was proud of Cantigny. In the orchard he, dipping into childhood grammar, asked a schoolboy picking cherries, "Are them cherries ripe?" "They're good," said the boy, his face red with cherry stain. "Everything at Cantigny is good," the Colonel replied. At dinner one evening he passed up vegetables until the butler told him they were grown on the farm. For several years fields testing new crops were open to the public. Everyone was welcome at pulling contests when pairs of horses and oxen took turns tugging at a heavily loaded pickup truck. The winning pair pulled a load of 3,400 pounds.

Amy and the Colonel both liked Alsatians. Amy named hers Diana and Sheila and the Colonel called his Lotta because she had a lot of pups—the Colonel was dismayed by the practice of spaying. The dogs added security. One day a neighborhood boy, on a dare, crawled through the fence, darted through the grounds and made himself comfortable on the Madison porch where the Colonel came upon him. "What are you doing here?" the Colonel asked. "Just looking around," the boy said. "All right," the Colonel said, "but watch out for the big dogs." The boy skedaddled. The dare never was repeated.

One day Emil took Lotta for a walk. She ran away. Emil chased her to the estate boundary and beyond before losing sight of her. The Colonel called out everyone at Cantigny, the Winfield police, the sheriff and his deputies, the state patrol. In time Lotta came home on her own.

The Colonel was jealous of Lotta. One day when walking with the Colonel, Lotta saw Emil some distance away and ran toward him. The Colonel angrily shouted at her to return. Farmers said they could hear him a mile away.

"Don't do that! Lotta is my dog," the Colonel snapped at a young dinner guest, Louise Brydon, when she joined him in dropping choice bits of meat to the dog lying between them. Lotta rose, walked defiantly to the other side of Louise and settled there. The guest giggled and very obviously chose a piece of meat and lowered it to Lotta. "Come back, Lotta!" the Colonel commanded sternly. The dog returned to her place. Louise, still giggling, leaned down and patted Lotta. She and the Colonel took turns feeding Lotta for the remainder of the dinner, and at a great many more dinners following drag hunts during which Louise, whenever tossed onto her head, jumped up, brushed herself, collected her horse and rode on. Because of her fair hair and blithe, bright ways her fellow riders, including the Colonel and Amy, called her Blondie. In time Louise became almost a daughter to the Colonel and Amy. The Colonel liked to hear Blondie, skilled with and devoted to horses, tell and retell how as a small child in Virginia she left home at 4 a.m. to ride five miles through the darkened woods to attend a meet. One evening the Colonel asked her, "Why don't you call me RR?"—a term of address invented by Amy and, until then, used only by her.

Cantigny farm children took over Swan Lake. Boys built rafts and lay in the shade of the willows, fishing and seeking turtles to take home as pets or frogs as a dinner table delicacy. They swam

348

in the pool although Lucille Zeier, born at Cantigny, learned to swim in the pond when her brothers threw her from the raft. A Zeier boy caught a baby skunk and kept it as a pet even after the teacher sent him home to change his clothes. Most children made pets of rabbits or raccoons. Every family had its pet dogs and cats. Lucille's dog, Teddy, frequently escaped by tunneling under wire fences. "He's no dog," the Colonel told her. "He's a groundhog." The children learned to detour around the unfriendly peacocks that presided over the lawns.

Wheaton boys going swimming in nearby Herrick's Lake on summer days made a shortcut through Cantigny. Often they paused at the stable to pet the horses. Sometimes the stable hands let them help shovel manure and rewarded them with candy from the refrigerator, or 12 cents, the admission price of the local movie, or let them sit on a horse being exercised in a meadow. If the Colonel happened to be at the stable, he might give the boys pieces of red candy he carried in a pocket. If noon were near he might invite the boys to come back to "the big house" with him for a sandwich on the south verandah. He asked each new boy his name. He did not always remember the Christian name but he did remember the father's name. "You're the Hadley boy," he'd say, or "You're the Young boy." Sometimes he'd sit for quite a while with the boys, telling them about animals and circuses before dismissing them with "You boys better get along home now," sometimes suggesting they pick a sack of apples on the way. Forty years later, David Young remembered the afternoon that the Colonel asked, "Would you like some milk and cookies?" He led him into the basement kitchen, found the cookie jar, and, wonder of wonders, opened a heavy plank door and walked into a refrigerator as big as a room and came out with a pail of milk fresh from the Cantigny dairy. As boys became fathers and grandfathers, they became aware that the Colonel had been a very lonely man.

One April 1st, Cantigny children wrote "April Fool" on note paper, put it in a large purse, placed the bag on the highway and hid in the bushes. A car shrieked to a halt, the driver ran to the purse, picked it up, opened it, read the note and disgustedly threw it all down. The children replaced the note and the game went on. In winter the children ice-skated on the pond, roasting themselves beside flaring bonfires. The farmers hitched workhorses to a bobsled to take the children part way to school. The McCormicks rode a sleigh with thin curved runners drawn by a reproachful hunter. The Colonel tramped the estate on snow-shoes, visiting the farms and petting the animals. One morning the farmers ordered their children to stay out of a certain woods. They would not say why, but news does get about: A stranger had been found hanging by the neck from a tree. He was a Chicago bootlegger who had double-crossed the gang. "We kids had the best of all worlds growing up at Cantigny," Lucille Zeier recalled.

* * * * *

Each May or June veterans of the 1st Division gathered at Cantigny. One year the young hero of Peking, Charles Summerall, now a general, was a special guest. The admiring Colonel put a brass plaque on the door of the bedroom where his hero slept. In 1932 George Marshall, operations officer at the battle of Cantigny and now on his way to becoming chief of staff, joined in the baseball game. He had been sent to Chicago against his will to try to improve the Illinois National Guard, then under the Colonel's sharp attack as incompetent. The Colonel thought the ambitious Marshall judged the task to be taking him off the promotion ladder. The Colonel did not post another plaque and years later fiercely denounced Marshall for taking a horseback ride on the morning the Japs bombed Pearl Harbor and, after the war, for "giving China to the Reds."

The French government rebuilt the village of Cantigny and in 1937 invited the Colonel to dedicate a monument in the village square to the 1st Division. General Pershing was there. On the Colonel's return home he had his own eloquent speech written in gold letters on the floor of his new library.

* * * * *

Cissy Patterson had begun thinking in her late forties about what she should do with her life. As the only granddaughter of Joseph Medill, sister of the publisher of The News and cousin of the publisher of The Tribune, she naturally considered building a newspaper career for herself. Of course she would start at the top. Her Tribune stock rights inherited from Grandfather Medill gave her an income of more than $100,000 a year.

Arthur Brisbane, daily mentor of some 25 million people who read his "Today" column in the Hearst papers and others, was her obvious adviser. Hearst owned a faltering evening paper in Washington, The Herald. Could she buy it? Brisbane asked

Hearst; he said no. She turned to another Washington morning paper, The Post, which had been important and profitable when owned by John McLean, who had moved into Washington from Cincinnati where he had The Enquirer, one of the most highly respected papers in the Ohio Valley. Under his son Edward The Post became politically bankrupt. Cissy asked her brother Joe if she should buy The Post. "Don't be crazy," Joe said. "You'll lose everything."

Brisbane went again to Hearst and persuaded him to hire Cissy at $10,000 a year to run The Herald. She moved to Washington and ran The Herald as though it were a circus. Joe told her a publisher must have dignity. "I'd rather raise hell than vegetables," she replied. Circulation grew and Hearst raised her pay to $15,000. The Herald continued to lose money. Hearst's debts were mounting toward $125 million. He was 73 and losing also his appetite for adventure. His Washington problem deepened when in 1933 Eugene Meyer, a millionaire 50 times over from Wall Street operations, bought The Post. Meyer threw into it most of and in some years more than his million-dollar income. Meyer did not accept the continued losses happily, each profit and loss statement convincing him that Washington could not support two morning papers. One would have to go. He offered Hearst $650,000 for The Herald, intending to fold it into the Post. Hearst was tempted to sell; Cissy was not. To save The Herald and her new career she borrowed a million dollars against her Tribune stock, lent the million to Hearst and enticed him into leasing the paper to her. After 18 months she borrowed another half million, bought The Herald and two years later added Hearst's evening Times. After losing a third million Cissy merged the two papers, giving The Times-Herald the largest circulation in the capital.

*   *   *   *   *

Alice Higinbotham Patterson, after more than 20 years of separation, offered to give Joe a long-sought divorce if he would give each of their three daughters $20,000 a year for life and on his death transfer to them blocks of Tribune stock held for him in trust. He accepted the terms. He and Mary King married.

*   *   *   *   *

The Colonel's niece Katrina, eldest child of Ruth and Medill McCormick and named for Kate's lost daughter, brought her husband, Courtlandt Barnes, to Cantigny. She had been at Cantigny only once before and through the years had just one serious discussion with the Colonel. Katrina, like her father's cousin, Joe Patterson, believed the United States must change its ways, approved of Franklin Roosevelt's social program and was disgusted by The Tribune's bitter attacks on the New Deal.

"It was a dreadful evening," Mrs. Barnes recalled. "The Colonel had a strange little cell, little more than a linen closet and did not come down to dinner. Amy made light of his absence. We came to a parting of the ways and that was that."

Katrina decided to sell The Tribune stock rights she had inherited from her father, but trust restrictions prevented her offering the stock on the open market. She told the Colonel of her decision. "He asked me not to sell," Katrina said later. "When I insisted, he turned hard as nails." The Colonel offered to buy as much stock as he could raise the cash for and arrange with the Tribune-News employees trust to buy the remainder. Katrina asked the Colonel to put a value on the stock. The Colonel replied, "I want you to get a good lawyer. I don't want anyone to say I skinned my niece." After the sale Katrina, not wanting to profit from an operation that she considered evil, gave the money she received for the stock to charities active in civil and social reform, permanently removing herself and her family from all consideration for places in The Tribune's future.

* * * * *

Baie Comeau quickly grew into a mixed community with a small Protestant minority and a large Catholic majority. Father Gagne, the Catholic priest at Shelter Bay, transferred to Baie Comeau and within weeks was blasting trenches for the foundation of a church halfway up Mont Sec. The small Protestant community began building a tiny Anglican chapel. Most Canadian Catholics were of French descent and spoke French although after 200 years of physical separation from France with an accent that was far from Parisian. Most Protestants were of British descent and spoke English. The Colonel when in Baie Comeau spoke the French he had learned at Versailles as a boy. Company business was conducted in English. He'd stop a boy or girl on the street, say "Bon jour," and, if the answer were in English, the Colonel would say, "You must learn French." He ended speeches in French to employees and their families with the admonition in English: "To those of you who did not understand what I said, there"—pointing—"is the school." He ordered the inscription on mail boxes to be changed from "Letters" to "Lettres." Each community wanted its own school. The Colonel obliged, insisting that French schools teach English and English schools teach French.

The Colonel's requirement that everything at Baie Comeau be first class or better produced a luxurious inn in the Manoir. After a fire it was rebuilt as one of Canada's 5-star hotels. A hospital rose not far from the two churches, and the library so eagerly sought by Alice Lane, wife of the mill manager. The company encouraged individuals and companies to come to Baie Comeau to open shops and provide services.

The Colonel enjoyed talking with Father Gagne. On one of Amy's infrequent visits to Baie Comeau the priest said he must leave to make a round of parishioners. "Father Gagne gets about on foot," the Colonel told Amy. "Why don't you give him a car?" She wrote a check.

In two years the priest completed only the basement of his church. The Colonel urged him to finish the job. "As soon as we get more money," Father Gagne said. The Colonel asked how much would be needed. The priest said $75,000. "The paper company will give you $5,000 a year for 10 years," the Colonel said. The parish raised the balance and work speeded. The $75,000 provided only a stark structure. The Colonel donated three stained glass windows for the altar wall. In Montreal he saw a new church alive with frescos painted by an Italian artist, Guido Nincheri. The Colonel brought the artist to Baie Comeau. The artist made small paintings of scenes that, enlarged, would cover all walls and the barreled ceiling. He strolled about town seeking faces for his 32 angels. In an earlier church project he had painted the devil; for that face he chose his own. He enlarged each scene into a full size drawing and each morning chose the section to be completed that day. At dawn the plasterer applied the final coat to a small area. The artist laid over the fresh plaster the pertinent section of his drawing—he had pricked the outline with a pin—and patted the drawing with a small bag filled with lamp black, producing on the fresh plaster an outline of black dots. The artist worked fast filling in the outlines. The wet plaster absorbed the colors, making the fresco permanent. Often the artist worked late into the night, knowing that the next morning the plaster would be dry and not usable.

In August of 1939 Britain and France went to war with Germany. When Italy came into the fight on the German side, Canada took the artist from the church and locked him in a concentration camp as a dangerous enemy alien. After two years he was freed and returned to the church. The scaffolding was still in place. He resumed his work. In another year and a half the frescos were complete. The church became a Canadian art treasure.

The Colonel did not forget the Protestants. He provided their chapel with its altar window. The artist chose the always popular scene of baby Jesus in the manger, but at Baie Comeau a moose, not a lamb, looks lovingly at the cherished child.

*   *   *   *   *

The young farm manager, Eddie Edwards, long remembered the final McCormick departure from Aiken. He and his Winfield, Illinois, fiancee, Florence, the previous autumn had set their wedding for May 22nd. The Colonel had built a cottage for them next to Amy's studio. The spring of 1937 was late in coming to Chicago but Aiken's beautiful April weather, best time of the year there, continued into May. Amy was reluctant to leave the prolonged spring at Aiken for the prolonged winter near Chicago and put off her departure. Florence became nervous. Go ahead with the marriage; get a proxy to stand in for me, Edwards proposed. Florence wouldn't hear of it. Just in time, Amy said, "Take the horses home tomorrow, Eddie."

The departure was permanent. The Colonel gave Whitehall to the Citadel, the military academy in Charleston, as a residence for General Summerall, then commandant.

354

20. "The Wrath of God"
1937—1939

Amy for some time had tired easily. During the summer she was found to have cancer. Carefully she prepared for the autumn hunting season, giving no indication that she was ill, never speaking of pain. She rode only a few times during the late summer with Cantigny horseman Peter Jensen, a former trooper in Denmark's Royal Hussars, but every morning she, usually favoring a French beret, went to the stable to visit her horses. "She loved them all," Jensen observed. When the Colonel was home, Jensen prepared Kickapoo, the Colonel's favorite polo pony. The Colonel walked over from the house and rode off alone into the woods, the trails bright with wild flowers he and Amy had sown on their many early rides together.

In October Amy was operated on at Passavant Hospital in Chicago for "chronic appendicitis," an euphemism of the day for cancer. She came home to Cantigny with a hospital staff nurse, Margaret Lacey, chosen by Dr. Irving Cutter for her fine expertise and character. Cutter was dean of Northwestern University's medical department, author of a health column in The Tribune and the McCormick family doctor. The Colonel and Amy, not wanting to call the nurse by her first name as were the cook, the two maids and the butler, or by the last name as were the chauffeur, the riding master, the grooms, the valet and the farming staff, softened Miss Lacey into Slacey. The nurse was assigned the Colonel's former bedroom on the second floor in the old house next to Amy's suite. Marie, Amy's French maid, made Amy's satin and lace robes and night gowns as well as her satin sheets, which were changed every other day. One morning Amy told Slacey, "I hope some day I will be rich enough to have fresh sheets every night." Amy liked country-style outfits for daytime and simple dresses for evening. She so admired a $20 black dress with epaulets which Slacey bought for herself that Amy had Marie

355

duplicate it in three colors for her. Every day, indoors or in the gardens or woods, Amy wore some of the pearls the Colonel bought at the time of their wedding with his mother's $50,000 bribe. Slacey thought Amy must have had them duplicated in paste and wore the fakes. Many pearl owners might have done so. Not Amy. These pearls had a value beyond money.

Gradually Slacey realized Cantigny was two domains one centering on the Colonel, the other on Amy. Slacey never did learn the cause of the division nor did she ever hear spoken one word about Grasslands nor the name of its siren. On most mornings Slacey breakfasted with the staff in the downstairs kitchen and then had a riding lesson from Jensen. Amy breakfasted alone in her room, going through The Tribune diligently and chatting for hours on the telephone with friends. The Colonel awoke about seven, rang for Elizabeth to send up coffee and unbuttered toast. The last edition of The Tribune was at his bedside. The Colonel read it, line by line, tearing out paragraphs on which he scribbled notes. The coffee cooled, the toast dried, the Colonel didn't notice. About nine or 10 he bathed, shaved still with his old straight-edge razor, dressed in clothes laid out by the valet and left for town, sometimes looking in on Amy.

Late in the morning Amy walked about the estate with her Alsatians. Slacey changed for lunch with Amy on the Madison verandah if the weather were fine, or in the small sitting room which had been Joe Medill's library. Then Corbin, the chauffeur, brought the Packard convertible and drove Amy and Slacey around the farms, talking with families, looking at crops and animals. At the dairy barn Corbin honked and the cowmen came running with the day's news of the Guernsey herd and milk production figures. If there were a new calf, Amy entered the barn. Over each stall was the name of the cow, in bronze, and a record of its daily consumption of feed and its production of milk. At the stable she lingered long with every new colt and watched closely as Jensen demonstrated progress in the training of new or troublesome horses. Sometimes these days she was easily roused. She honked crossly when she saw Dorothy Kunde's bicycle lying on the front porch of the Kunde home. "Put it away," she would call out to the girl. Amy demanded that the Kundes dry their washing out of sight in a high fenced yard far removed from the drive. Families noted that Amy was becoming "testy." Some afternoons Corbin drove her and Slacey to Arlington Park for the races. Amy did not bet. She was content to study the beautiful horses and to watch them move, so gracefully, so powerfully, giving their all.

Back at the house Amy rested while Slacey read or chatted with the staff. As day turned night, the two, in long dresses, came down to the library. The bar door was open. Amy had a scotch and soda in a tall glass and introduced Slacey to sherry. The Colonel on coming home changed into a comfortable jacket and joined them. He too liked scotch in a tall glass. At dinner the Colonel sat at one end of the eight foot long table, Amy at the other. Slacey was at the Colonel's right where she could look out into the long avenue of elms. On fine summer evenings the Colonel preferred the smaller table on the verandah. The talk was spasmodic and concerned mostly the day's events at Cantigny. Never did Slacey hear the Colonel orate about any political doings or person or discuss Tribune matters although Amy told him about the day's features she liked and disliked. The Colonel ate sparsely and quickly and soon disappeared into the library with the first edition of the next day's Tribune which had been brought from Chicago personally by the conductor of the evening interurban express. The paper was handed at the Winfield halt to young Joe Schmidt, who was paid an extra 50 cents a day to meet this train. Amy and Slacey retreated to Amy's sitting room and passed the evening playing backgammon. On evenings when Ed Prendergast and Corpening were visiting, they joined Amy and Slacey at bridge.

Friday evenings were an exception. That was movie night in the art-deco theater. Often on movie night the Colonel and Amy had guests for dinner; then they greeted more guests coming to the movie. A neighbor once invited to a movie was welcome to come at his pleasure, the men in tuxedos, the women in long gowns. Staff and farm families also could come to any showing. The Colonel, Amy and their guests sank into deep, down-filled chairs and sofas while staff and farm families perched on little gold cane chairs at the back. The show began precisely at eight, the moment the pay began for the projector operator, a union member. After the show Elizabeth produced snacks and the butler served drinks but usually the Colonel had disappeared with his Tribune before the lights came on.

* * * * *

The Colonel rarely saw his nephew John, only son of his

357

brother and Ruth Hanna. For birthdays and Christmas the books and toys he sent were often unsuited to a boy of John's age. As a teenager John went to South America with a scientific expedition and sent a few reports to The Tribune but he had no inclination to become a newspaperman. As a student at Columbia University he wrote essays and short stories and began to hope for a career as a novelist although he did not consider his student efforts good enough to be submitted for publication. His hobby was rock climbing. On a trip to Europe he mastered the Matterhorn. In June of 1938 he and a friend, Richard Witmer, ventured into the small but jagged Sandia Mountains near Albuquerque. A thunderstorm burst over the mountains. Lightning bolts struck the peaks. The two young men did not come home that night. The next day a search party found their car in a ravine and Witmer's body on the ledge several hundred feet below a knifelike ridge. Six days later shepherds walking along the opposite side of the ridge found John's body. Film in his camera showed the two young men standing on the three-foot wide ridge. Climbers surmised that soon after the pictures were taken a lightning bolt stunned the young men, toppling John in one direction and Richard in the other.

The Colonel was in the Tribune newsroom when the word of the nephew's death was telephoned from New Mexico. The Colonel listened, put down the phone, looked off into space and said to himself but loudly enough to be heard at adjoining desks, "Now everything will go to Joe's boy." His shock at the death of the only male McCormick who could carry the Medill heritage into the fourth generation remained in memories of Cantigny farm families many years later.

*   *   *   *   *

That autumn Chauncey's eldest son Deering joined Amy as joint master of the hunt. On its big day of the year, riders were invited from other hunts. Everyone knew it might be Amy's last hunt, Jensen recalled. As things turned out, it was also Cantigny's last big hunt. The day was perfect. The hunt's scribe Blondie—Louise Brydon—wrote: "Sun kindly glowing, Wind softly blowing, Leaves gently falling, Hounds gladly calling. Ladies, all side-saddled, in small bowlers and veils." As the hunt gathered Amy sat mounted on "steady Ashmore" looking, the scribe wrote, "rightfully ready to lead her field if only the doc-

358

tors would permit. To see her up gives us that certain something of strength and feeling to really carry on."

The Colonel did not ride. Among those riding but not jumping were Slacey, Chauncey's wife Marion, and Mrs. Maryland Hooper. Jensen was on Marmint, a pure white Irish-bred horse which Amy had told him no one dared to ride, owned by one of Amy's good friends, Dancer Irene Castle.

The scribe noted: "The DuPage representatives outdid themselves in giving the entire field a rallying lead. Jimmie Simpson muttered loudly and continuously on the subject of people who oil reins just before a hunt. Mr. Johnny Pirie's chestnut tucked his toes into a chicken-coop and went end over end to land firmly and flatly on the unfortunate Mr. Pirie and his high silk hat thereby producing the only casualty. . ."

Of Amy, Louise recorded: "She makes the whole hunt possible. We thank her for the happiness she has given us." Louise's comment about the Colonel was tart: "Have you ever watched a small boy pout at not getting his way and then stand silently all alone feeling thoroughly miserable, afraid to let himself get back into the spirit of the game? One wonders whether he deserves pity or spanking."

Amy continued gallantly, hiding the illness, although close friends did note that she was physically dwindling and slowly reducing her activities. Looking back in later years, some friends wondered if Amy brought to Cantigny, to the Astor Street house and to Florida, people who might make up for her increasing disability and who might add interest to the Colonel's life after she was gone. Maryland Hooper was a frequent overnight guest. On the opening night in Chicago of "The Great Waltz," Amy gave a midnight dinner party for the star, Marion Claire. The soprano, who never had met the Colonel, remembered the night as awkward. Amy met her at the door, took into the party, introduced her to the Colonel and seated her on his right. Ms. Claire was awed by the stiff figure at her side.

On Christmas eve at Cantigny the Colonel and Amy staged a Yule spectacular with touches of Bracebridge Hall and Dingley Dell. The fun began in the afternoon with a party for all farm children in the movie theater. Santa Claus, chauffeur Gene Corbin, gave toys to the young children and to each of the older girls a beautiful dress, all selected by Amy. Parents received cash. Elizabeth offered homemade ice cream, cakes and other delicacies. Amy chatted with the children. Standing tall over all was the Colonel, smiling, benign, quiet but not at all at ease doing his duty as squire. As evening neared, a bonfire crackled in the circle drive before the house. Small lights winked on eight evergreens standing guard on the porch. Just inside the door the Colonel, in hunting pink, welcomed the guests, 40 or so, holding out to each the three-handled silver cup given to Amy and him on their wedding by Yale's Scroll and Key, now filled with strong wassail. Guests moved to the library. The bar was open. Buffets, each presided over by a boar's head, awaited in Medill's dining room and in the art-deco theater. Small tables were set in several rooms. After dining, guests returned to the library. Lights dimmed.

Marion Claire, in the most ravishing gown of her latest WGN production, entered and curtsied. The Colonel led her to the floor-to-ceiling tree. She sang "O Little Town of Bethlehem." Eddie and Peter, wearing their bright hunt gear, brought up on the wood elevator the Yule log, cut from the woods and brilliantly wrapped in Christmas paper. With a flourish they heaved it into the fireplace opposite the tree. The Colonel gave Ed Hurley's daughter Jeannette a foot-long match and asked her to light the log. "You are our Yule maiden," he announced. Everyone sang songs, favorites which the Colonel had collected into a booklet already serving as the McCormick Christmas card. There were Christmas songs, comic songs such as "My Love Works in a Greenhouse," songs from the World War and the Civil War. That was the moment for all to look up at the portrait of Great Uncle Willie and sing the Civil War tribute to the hero that begins, "We shall meet but we shall miss him. There will be one vacant chair" and relates, "Often will the bosom swell At remembrance of how our noble Willie fell, How he strove to bear our banner Through the thickest of the fight And upheld our country's honor In the strength of manhood's might."

It may have been after "In the Gloaming" that the Colonel reminisced to Ed Hurley's sister, Helen Ryan, who had a summer home on the adjoining Hurley estate. "Long before I was married," the Colonel said, "I went with a girl I thought the most beautiful I ever saw. I was crazy about her. A couple of days ago I saw her again. Oh! she must weigh a ton!" Marion Claire remembers that the final song was the one the Colonel liked best, "Annie Laurie." It tugged at the Colonel's deep down, strong, romantic Scottish sentiment.

The Colonel concluded the evening with a dig at President

Roosevelt, who had decreed that Thanksgiving should be celebrated no longer on the last Thursday of November but on the
fourth Thursday of the month. "Anyone can set Thanksgiving
forward but it takes Someone to move Christmas," the Colonel
said.

In a Christmas radio talk, the Colonel took a smack at mon-
archs. In feudal times, he recalled, each household was expected
to protect itself and to seek its own vengeance on robbers. To
permit safe travel at special times the king decreed that for eight
days during Christmas, Easter, Pentecost and at coronations an
offense against any citizen was an offense against the king.
"Alas," the Colonel commented, "royalty seldom escapes its oc-
cupational disease, which is avarice," and said that after a time
the king instructed his agents to collect money from offenders
against the king's peace and give the money not to the victim but
to the king.

Soon after Christmas Corbin drove Amy and Slacey to Florida.
Marie and Elizabeth Johnson followed with the dogs and suitcases. The Colonel flew in and out. Amy and Slacey fished from
the Colonel's boat. One day each caught a sailfish. A few days
later the Colonel gave Slacey an Abercrombie and Fitch jewel
case nesting a brooch fashioned like a sailfish with 40 small pearls
as scales, a ruby for an eye and a blue enameled fin.

Amy soldiered on through the spring and summer of 1939. In
August she was absent from Cantigny for several days. On the
morning of the 14th the Colonel telephoned Louise Brydon and
told her, "I have lost Amy. Can you come to the farm and walk
with me?" Louise came quickly from her honeymoon cottage in
Wayne, 20 miles away. The Colonel, she remembered, seemed in a
daze. She took his arm. They walked into the woods, saying
nothing. After she left, the Colonel walked alone to the stables.
"Mrs. McCormick has died," he said. Amy had gone to Passavant
hospital for an operation considered minor but pneumonia developed.

The Colonel asked Slacey if Amy ever had mentioned where
she would like to be buried. "At Cantigny," the nurse said, "in
pink chiffon," adding, "she also said she would like to have a military funeral." "Why?" the Colonel asked. "Because," the nurse
said, "she drove an ambulance in France during the war." "I
never knew that," the Colonel said. A message to the Episcopal
bishop of Chicago led to the quick consecration of a plot below
the house as a cemetery and another call won the army's consent

for a full military funeral. A chauffeur brought Amy's Red Cross uniform from the Astor Street house and Marie added swatches of pink chiffon. Was the Colonel, maybe unconsciously, trying to make amends for past omissions and sins? Slacey thinks not. "He was merely trying to do what Amy wanted," she judged. Louise saw the Colonel as "a lost soul." He had taken Amy for granted. The loss was overpowering. She had been mother, sister, wife. Now, suddenly, she no longer was there.

Chauncey McCormick assumed responsibility for details of the funeral service. In the evening he telephoned to a Wheaton carpenter, Frank Mittman, asking that he come quickly, met him at Cantigny's front door, told him the Colonel's wife had died and asked him to build an altar shaped like a horseshoe in a sheltered retreat just below the ancient oak. Lumberman Ralph Wheaton was roused from his bed to supply the lumber. Mittman and a helper returned to Cantigny at dawn. As they worked, the Colonel walked past on the way to the woods. On returning he stopped, introduced himself, shook hands and told Mittman, "You might as well stay for the service."

The Cantigny flag was lowered to half mast. Amy's prize dahlias were banked high against the altar. Hussar, the only black among her horses, stood patiently, his saddle empty and Amy's boots reversed in the stirrups, Jensen holding his bridle. "She was a creator of beauty which can come only from beauty," said the Rev. Frank Hobart Millet of Trinity Episcopal church in Wheaton. The minister and his wife had been Amy's frequent dinner guests when the Colonel was away. The Rev. John Evans, an Episcopalian and The Tribune's religion editor, conducted the service. Presbyterian Doctor Bob Stewart spoke a prayer. A string quartet from WGN played and an octet sang. Dr. Cutter read his poetic tribute later inscribed on the memorial:

> Peace, dear heart, the bugle has blown,
> Life's music has faded away;
> But there echo still those joyous airs
> That you would have us play.
>
> Yes! Play and keep on playing,
> Our spirits blithe and gay,
> For you loved life and its living,
> With nature in full panoply.
>
> We hear you say, "Let no one mourn;

For me let no one weep.
The wind is in the tree tops—
Hark! It has gone—let me sleep."

Everyone sang Amy's favorite hymn:
  He who'd valiant be 'gainst all disaster,
Let him in constancy follow the Master
There's no discouragement
Shall make him once relent
  . . .to be a pilgrim.

An honor guard from Fort Sheridan fired a salute. A bugler sounded taps. The Colonel's plane circled overhead, dropping rose petals—"like rain," said Jensen. The active pallbearers were Cantigny employees: Eddie Edwards, Frank Zeier, Peter Jensen, Jack Kunde, Gene Corbin, Carl Henderson, John Wallner and Emil Hawkinson. The coffin was lowered temporarily into a grave near the oak tree until a memorial and tomb could be built. Among the mourners were Amy's sister Ida and her husband, Dr. Small, Henry and Maryland Hooper who had come home from a fishing trip in Michigan and Louise.

That evening Louise came into the house and found the Colonel sitting alone on the big sofa in the library. She gave him her customary girlish greeting, "Hi." She started to speak but choked and turned away. The Colonel reached for her hand and drew her down beside him. He was crying. Tears came too from Louise. A few other friends came into the room. Louise started to rise. The Colonel, still holding her hand, kept her next to him. They sat there for quite a while, he holding her hand, both crying, neither saying anything. "He sensed that I loved Amy," Louise recalled, "and that I too had lost someone precious."

After all had gone except Slacey, the Colonel walked to the grave. He sat there all night. In the morning he came into the house looking, Slacey recalled, as though he had been hit by the wrath of God.

A few days later as Slacey packed to leave Cantigny, the Colonel told her that if she wanted to become a doctor he would see her through medical school. He said she should speak with Dr. Cutter about entering Northwestern University's medical school. She did and found Cutter bitterly antagonistic toward women doctors. "Hen medics" he called them and offered no help. Slacey joined The Tribune as head nurse. The Colonel dropped into her office now and then, unannounced, and asked for a rub although the nurse thought that he really came for a friendly chat. When America entered the war she told him she planned to volunteer for the army nursing service. "Is that what you really want?" he asked. She said yes. The Colonel, taken aback, bellowed, "Then go," and walked out. She did volunteer and was sent to Europe for the invasion of Italy. The Colonel asked Tribune war correspondents to seek her out and buy her the best dinner available.

Before Miss Lacey left Cantigny the Colonel asked her what she thought of a painting of a green parrot by Marie Laurencin which Amy had bought in Paris and hung over a fireplace in a guest bedroom. "I like it very much," the nurse said. "Take it," the Colonel said. "I'm tired of having those eyes always following me." Was it the cry of a puritan with a guilty conscience? After the war Miss Lacey married. The Colonel came to her home and saw the painting. "You still have it?" he asked with a touch of surprise. "I wouldn't part with it for anything," she said. The Colonel obviously was pleased.

In her will filed August 29th Amy, signing herself as Amie, left her Lake Forest house and most of her personal property estimated in press reports at $850,000 to her sister Ida rather than to the Colonel who, she said, "did not need it." She did will the Colonel the impressionist paintings she had bought over the years from a Chicago dealer, including a Picasso, a Cezanne, a Degas, two Raoul Dufys, an Utrillo, a Modigliani, a Matisse, a Rousseau, a Gauguin, her cars, her books, her herd of Guernseys, her Bois de Madame including hounds and studio. The Colonel gave most of the paintings to the Art Institute. He gave the hounds to the Wayne Hunt with which Amy's hunt amalgamated, and sold or gave away most of the horses, his as well as hers. He opened Amy's closets to her friends and told them, "Take anything you like."

Amy willed her furs and jewelry, apart from the pearls, to her sister. The pearls acquired under such challenging circumstances were given into the keeping of her brother-in-law Dr. Small and the Northern Trust Company to be sold and the proceeds added to her residuary trust for the lifetime use of her sister and brother-in-law and then her niece and nephews. "The pearls shall not be sold at a sacrifice," Amy demanded. She said the pearls had been valued at $215,000. However Small and the bank sold the pearls to the Colonel for much less. He divided the pearls into three strands and gave one each to Maryland Hooper, Frances Crawford and Ann Bryant, all of whom had been friends of

Amy for a long time. Mrs. Hooper subsequently gave her strand to her daughter Alice. Amy's executors paid $137,544.38 in federal estate tax and $81,484.98 in Illinois estate tax.

For months the grave was not marked. One day Elizabeth the cook told the Colonel she considered the lack of a stone disgraceful and disrespectful. The Colonel had an architect design a small temporary marker to serve until a proper memorial could be built for Amy and himself. The marker carried Amy's name and birth and death dates. The Colonel, shown the drawing, erased the birth date, 1872, and inserted 1880, his own birth year. He asked his architect friend, Andrew Rebori, the Prendergast in-law, to design a permanent monument. Make it a friendly place, the Colonel said, a place where people can sit and talk just as did the Greeks meeting in a glade to discuss Pericles' latest decrees. The Greeks called such a place an exedra. Rebori drew design after design. None satisfied. A dozen years passed before Rebori saw in a technical magazine a drawing of a machine in which sugar cane was crushed between two cylinders, a smaller one inside a larger, the two coming together at the base. "You've got it," the Colonel wrote. So Rebori drew a tall-backed circular bench, wide at the opening and narrowing to nothing at the far end to provide space for a cross. Three wide curved steps completing the circle would lead into the exedra. The two graves would be side by side in the center, one engraved "Amy Irwin McCormick, wife of R. R. McCormick, 1880-1939. Buried with Full Military Honors;" the other, "Colonel Robert R. McCormick, 1880—, Buried with Full Military Honors." Cut into the floor would be Jesus' promise, "I go to prepare a place for you. In my Father's house are many mansions." The exedra would face east, making the north bench a warm refuge on sunny winter days and the south a shaded cool place on hot summer days. On the exterior would be engraved the poem composed by Dr. Cutter for Amy's funeral and the Colonel's military citation. One day when driving through Lincoln Park the Colonel noted the bas relief winged lions flanking the entrance to a memorial to the assassinated president.

"Let's have wings," he told Edgar Miller, chosen by Rebori to do the sculpturing. "And cut Lotta and Sheila in stone and place one at the head of each grave. We've got to have the dogs. They are the only friends I've got."

Miller made a two-foot model of the exedra. Too small, the Colonel said. Miller doubled the size. Still too small. So a carpenter from nearby Warrenville, George Heller, made a full-size model in wood, cloth and plaster. Rebori and Miller placed it in a little hollow to the southeast of the house. Not impressive, the Colonel said. So the architect and sculptor moved the model from place to place. One day they put it in the midst of the avenue of trees that reaches for a mile. They were relieved when the Colonel said no. In the end the Colonel chose the original site. He said the entire monument must be made of the most enduring of stones— granite—and only the whitest granite in all America, that quarried at Mount Airy in North Carolina. To produce the steps in one piece a flawless 64-ton block would have to be broken from the mountain. A construction company that did much work for The Tribune was given the overall contract at a fixed price of $160,000 but without a starting date. When the Colonel died, Amy's 16-year-old grave still was marked only with Elizabeth's temporary stone.

At Baie Comeau the new church was to be named for St. Jean Eudes, a 17th century French missionary, teacher and founder of a congregation of secular priests. Father Gagne proposed the church be dedicated to the memory of Amy and have as its patron Sainte Amelie, the name nearest Amie in the roster of saints.

21. Patriot or Traitor?
1940—1942

For 10 years international affairs had played little part in American politics. The big governments were behaving as though the Great War really had made the world safe for democracy even though the Senate had kept the United States out of the League of Nations. The Colonel saw little loss from American absence. The League, he said, was "a fickle, futile, false brotherhood." For the United States to join, he said, could be equated with an American heiress marrying an impoverished duke, a situation he knew first hand from Cousin Cissy. He thought the United States was stupid to sink warships to bring its navy into line with the navies of Britain and Japan. The sinking, he argued, opened the Orient to Japanese ambitions which had been cooled only temporarily by the peace agreement President Theodore Roosevelt had thrust upon Japan to end the war with Russia a generation earlier. Japan had not withdrawn from Manchuria, its contested region with Russia, but instead, in 1931, had set up the puppet state of Manchoukuo and soon began forays into China. Beware, America, the Colonel said, Japan's long-term plan includes war with us. He urged the United States to give independence to the Philippines and bring home the few marines in China, thereby reducing the risk of being involved in a Far Eastern war. He wanted the United States to build a navy large enough to protect both shores but not so big as to encourage admirals to fight in foreign waters. Big navies and big armies, he said, are always dangerous to the rights of the public, encouraging admirals and generals to seize power. He said the nation should protect itself against such military men by having more troops in the National Guard, controlled by states, than in the federal army. The Colonel regarded Britain as a tough competitor for trade and an all-too-clever rival in international affairs. American diplomats, he declared repeatedly, were so busy seeking social position in foreign capitals that they were "completely hypnotized" and did not speak up nor work for America, and the State Department had been infiltrated by homosexuals and communists. He thought Britain and France should pay their wartime debts to America. If Britain could not supply the cash, it could hand over battleships or western Atlantic and Caribbean islands which the United States could incorporate into an offshore first line defense for the east coast and the vital Panama Canal. He shared with Winston Churchill, his houseguest in the 1930s, a belief in "my country right or wrong" and differed only on the identity of the country.

The real European threat, he said, was the Soviet Union. Russians, he said, are Asiatics who "came out of the woods" long after the Europeans and therefore lack the Roman tradition of law and morality. To him communism was a step backward for civilization. He was irate when in 1933 President Roosevelt established diplomatic relations with Stalin. The Colonel early despised Mussolini for his high-handed treatment of citizens and early predicted—he was in Germany the day Hindenberg died— that Hitler would receive from the German Reichstag further powers putting him beyond challenge. Hitler's moves against German Jews were a war on all Jews, the Colonel said. He suspected that the two dictators were using the Spanish Civil War to test new weapons and tactics in preparation for renewing their own national wars of expansion. The Colonel was the first editor to send a correspondent to Ethiopia to report the invasion and conquest by 250,000 of Mussolini's new Roman legions. The reporter, Wilfred Barber, died of malaria, was buried in Addis Ababa and posthumously given the Pulitzer prize.

The Colonel commented that Mussolini was "shaking the peace of Europe" but was not surprised when the League was unable to halt the invasion. He shared a rising American worry when the Berlin-Rome partnership expanded informally to Tokyo. He was not at all comforted by President Roosevelt's advice to the nation "to avoid the small acts that lead to war." However the issue of war or peace did not prominently enter the 1936 election.

The Colonel entered that election year with an editorial headed, "Turn the Rascals Out," accusing the administration of "breaking faith, being false to their words, untrue to their promises, dishonest with the American people." He looked for a Republican who might defeat Roosevelt. Briefly he considered offering himself but put down the temptation. When Cyrus

McCormick earlier had been equally tempted, Nettie had warned him off diplomatically: "They only want your money. You have an enviable place. I ask you to be content with that." Frank Knox, former Hearst man and the new owner of the Chicago Daily News, did offer himself and gradually earned a considerable following. The Colonel spotted Kansas Governor Alf Landon, sent reporters to interview him, gave much space to his speeches, offered him use of WGN radio, donated thousands of dollars, organized women volunteers. The Republicans nominated Landon and gave the vice presidential place to Knox.

The Colonel believed Landon would win, certainly in Chicago, although his former Sanitary District foreman Ed Kelly, now mayor, told him Roosevelt would win Chicago by a half million and sweep the nation. Kelly was right. Sixteen million voters wanted Landon but 27 million wanted Roosevelt to continue in the White House. The tremendous victory emboldened the President. Within three months he asked Congress to increase the Supreme Court members from nine to 15. The Colonel was enraged by the obvious attempt to bypass and devalue the Constitution. So many other Americans protested that Roosevelt withdrew. But as second best he set New Deal bureaucrats and lawyers to rewriting the voided measures to bring them within the constitutionality as seen by the Justices until the older conservative Jurists died and could be replaced with men sharing the President's goal of remodeling America.

In mid-1937 Japanese armies fighting their way through China sank an American gunboat in the Yangtze. The Colonel again advised America to get out of China, to give independence to the Philippines and to ignore Japanese threats to British Singapore and French Indo-China. Joe Patterson, who had applauded Roosevelt from the first inaugural day, was welcomed at the White House and suggested as he and the President cruised the Potomac that the navy organize a Pacific Ocean defense line from Alaska to Hawaii to Australia to Singapore. Secretary of Interior Ickes recorded his belief that war with Japan was inevitable.

In the autumn the President came to Chicago to dedicate a bridge on the Outer Drive and surprised the holiday-mood crowd by making a serious speech about world affairs. He said dictatorship is an infectious disease and will spread unless isolated—unless quarantined. The oceans, he said, as had the Colonel, did not bless the United States with immunity, but then, leaving the Colonel behind, said the United States had a duty to help nations attacked by aggressors. To the Colonel the speech was proof that Roosevelt was leading the nation into war against Hitler. To stop Roosevelt, the Colonel suggested the budget for the navy be cut. He defended British Prime Minister Neville Chamberlain's bowing to Hitler over Czechoslovakia, "a jigsaw nation," and thought the easy Nazi conquest of that country would lead Hitler into invading Russia. He did not expect Germany to attack Britain. In the summer of 1939 The Tribune predicted Stalin and Hitler would join forces. They did so in August, each pledging no war on the other. Germany promptly invaded Poland. France and England went to Poland's aid and The Tribune declared: "Europe's War Is On." The editorial stated flatly, "This is not our war." The Colonel argued the new war was merely a continuation of the ageless struggle among rival European governments for territory. But his regard for family tradition came uppermost when he asked William Wood Prince, who was at Cantigny riding, "Why aren't you in France?" The question was a reminder to the young man of his cousin, Norman Prince, who had founded the Lafayette Escadrille before America entered World War I and had lost his life flying for France.

Germany and Russia divided Poland. When Russia then moved against Finland, the Colonel proposed Britain, France and Germany call off their war and together attack Russia, the natural enemy of all three. The United States, he repeated, must stay out of the war. Soon Germany moved into Norway to overcome, in the Colonel's view, Britain's mining of Norwegian waters. The subsequent German blitz through France eliminated, in the Colonel's mind, need of dispatching American troops to Europe. The German invasion of Russia hardened his conviction this war was being fought for territory. He noted that the American Communist Party, which had been against entering the war when Hitler and Stalin were comrades in arms, now screamed for war against Germany. The Colonel said the United States could beat Germany but at a cost of 20 million conscripts of whom a million would die, and $400 billion. He advised Britain to negotiate a peace with Germany. He saw American proposals for lend-lease to Britain and the embargo on war material for Japan as steps to war.

Americans who wanted America to help Britain and France and to stop Hitler argued that sooner or later America would be drawn into the war. The question was, they said, should we jump, or let ourselves be pushed? They were a small minority. A somewhat larger minority said America should improve and enlarge its navy and army. The Colonel quoted the judgment of America's hero Colonel Lindbergh who, after an inspection of German forces, said the American army and navy were not capable of challenging rearmed Germany. The Colonel pointed to the 1940 German blitz through the lowlands and France as proof of superior German battlefield power. Maxwell Corpening, sent on a tour of American military camps, found Americans poorly trained, badly equipped and undisciplined, and predicted that if they were sent against German troops they would be "slaughtered like sheep."

Gradually Americans became convinced America inevitably would be drawn into the war. That must not happen, the Colonel said. As the 1940 conventions neared Roosevelt added two Republicans, Knox as secretary of the navy and Henry Stimson as secretary of war, to his cabinet in a bid for Republican support. The Colonel surmised the President would break tradition and seek a third term and would have his party make a show of drafting him. "Draft him and he'll draft you," a Tribune cartoon quipped. The President persuaded Vice President John Garner, who had broken with him over a third term, to urge Southern Democratic supporters to vote for Democrats but Garner did not mention the name Roosevelt.

The Colonel chose as his candidate a political newcomer, Wendell Willkie. In New York, Easterners with clout formed the Century Club to work for American entry into the war—"a strange partnership of millionaires and communists!" the Colonel called it. They bought a page advertisement in The Tribune to spread their message in Chicago. Chicagoans with clout formed the Emergency Committee to Defend America First bringing together a wide variety of persons—Ambassador to Britain Joseph Kennedy, University of Chicago President Robert Hutchins, World War I hero Eddie Rickenbacker, CIO President John L. Lewis, Sears Roebuck President Gen. Robert Wood, Gen. Hugh Johnson of NRA fame. Colonel Lindbergh became a spokesman. Willkie added his voice to the American First accusation that Roosevelt was plotting to bring America into the war. The Colonel was not a founding member but his voice soon became one of the most strident. "What else would you expect from a man who hates Britain?" the pro-war faction snapped. The Colonel replied: "I have never had Anglophobia. The empire has deserved a great deal of criticism. Britons do not like it and attribute

372

my criticism to Anglophobia." Despite his explanation "anti-British" became a prefix to his name.

The President announced he had obtained from Britain the right to use British islands in the western Atlantic and Caribbean as bases in return for the loan to the British navy of 40 old American destroyers. The Colonel congratulated him. For almost 20 years the Colonel had wanted an offshore defense line in the Atlantic and for him the acquisition of the bases more than outweighed the danger of bringing the war closer to America. Two hundred 1st Division veterans gathered at Cantigny for their annual picnic and shouted approval when the Colonel said the United States must stay out of the war.

As the election approached the President declared there was no secret treaty with Britain, no obligation, no understanding to involve America in the war. "I tell you again and again and again," he said, "your boys will not be sent to die on foreign soil." He's lying, the Colonel reckoned. Publicly he stated the President hoped to win votes just as Wilson did in 1916 with his slogan "He kept us out of war."

In September Japan formally became an ally of Germany and Italy. "The Japanese can now start the war whenever it suits their purpose," the Colonel said.

Distrust of Roosevelt's intention about the war, New Deal blunders, quadrupled federal spending and disregard of the two-term tradition cut into Roosevelt's support. Willkie increased the Republican vote to 45 percent—not enough. He immediately offered to help the third-term President in any way, confirming old-time Republicans' feelings that Willkie's pre-election support of the party platform was merely a passing position demanded of him if he were to reach the White House. Roosevelt sent him on a short mission to Britain and then let him disappear into the populace.

Events moved swiftly in 1941. The Colonel, called to testify before a Senate committee considering lend-lease, said Britain could survive without our help and Germany and Italy could not invade North America but he would fight to keep the Axis from seizing the British western-Atlantic bases newly acquired by the United States. He advised America to extend the Atlantic offshore defense line by sending troops into the Azores and if Hitler tried to block the landing there or tried later to drive out the troops America should fight. He was certain the British fleet would not be given into Axis hands. "I have known Winston

Churchill for 25 years," he said. "A more thoroughly honorable man never lived. He would not have made the promise not to surrender the fleet if he had not intended to keep it." As for the Germans, "They are not so tough. I have been up against them and there is no use being scared of them."

The Colonel accepted the dispatch of American troops to Iceland to free British soldiers there, but he warned that the Germans properly could interpret the move as an act of war. Polls indicated seven out of 10 Americans still opposed going to war against Germany. At the end of November the Colonel again said the President, in proposing an embargo on oil and other war materials to Japan, courted war on two fronts. On December 3rd Managing Editor J. Loy Maloney showed the Colonel a joint army-navy chief of staff study that Senator Burton Wheeler had given to a Tribune Washington reporter, Chesly Manly. The study, prepared at the the President's request, listed measures necessary for total war in Europe, Asia and Africa. The report predicted the forces would need 10 million American men, half of them abroad. The date for a landing in western Europe was set for July 1, 1943. Maloney accepted that the report was genuine but questioned if using it might be a breach of national security. "Print it," the Colonel said. The headline was: "FDR's War Plans." Secretary of War Stimson confessed that the account was true but asked, What would you think of any military leaders and government who did not prepare contingency plans, and what would you think of any man who would reveal those plans to the enemy? The President remained silent. The same day a new paper, The Sun, appeared in Chicago, financed by Marshall Field III at the urging of Roosevelt supporters who thought the administration's cause was not being presented boldly enough in Chicago nor was the Colonel being attacked with sufficient skill and ferocity. Marshall Field, a name honored for three generations in Chicago, became an anathema to the Colonel.

Three days later Japan bombed Pearl Harbor. The Tribune headline was "US and Japs at war." The editorial, printed two columns wide at the top of the front page, said:

"War has been forced on America by an insane clique of Japanese militarists who apparently see the desperate conflict into which they have led their country as the only thing that can prolong their power. Thus the thing that we have all feared, that so many of us have worked with all our hearts to avert, has happened. That is all that counts. It has happened. America faces

war through no violation of any American. Recriminations are useless and we doubt that they will be indulged in. Certainly not by us. All that matters today is that we are in the war and the nation must face that simple fact. All of us, from this day forth, have only one task. That is to strike with all our might to protect and preserve the American freedom that we all hold dear."

The Colonel went to bed that night certain that within hours Germany and Italy would be in the war and the United States would, as he had warned a week earlier, have to fight on two fronts. He was also as certain as anyone outside the immediate center of power in Washington could be that Roosevelt had engineered the whole thing. The Colonel did not share the general American anger aroused by the surprise attack. He later explained that the Japanese navy had been trained by the British navy and had adopted British tactics and precepts, including striking without declaring war. The Japanese, he went on, were therefore "entirely unprepared" for the angry American public response.

The Colonel asked the Chicago police department for extra protection. For three weeks a patrolman was always on duty at the Astor Street house. The nights were icy and because there was no heat in the McCormick vestibule the policeman sheltered in the entry of the John Paul Welling home across the street, a building never entered by the Colonel. Welling had not forgiven the Colonel for, in his mind, stealing Amy from Ed Adams, the uncle of Welling's good friend, Cyrus Adams II. Welling had boycotted the Colonel ever since the marriage to Amy.

The day after the Japanese attack, Joe Patterson appeared at the White House. The meeting had been arranged by a New York Daily News reporter and a White House aide. Patterson thought Roosevelt had sent for him to offer him a high war job while the President thought Patterson had asked for the meeting to apologize for having objected to lend-lease. President Roosevelt kept Patterson waiting in the outer office and then standing before his desk. He did all of the talking. Patterson emerged livid. He told his driver to take him to the nearest public phone. He called the Colonel.

"He made me stand there like some naughty schoolboy," Patterson said, his anger coming through the words. "After 15 minutes he said he wished I would do him a favor. I should go back to New York and read The News editorials and think how they put back the war effort six months and will cost a lot of American lives. 'And, Joe,' he said, 'tell that son-of-a-bitch cousin of yours. . .'"

Patterson told the Colonel he had changed his mind about Roosevelt. "Until today The News has been for Roosevelt," he said. "Starting tomorrow we are against him. He lied to me." He repeated the account to his sister, Cissy Patterson. Her paper, the Washington Times-Herald, had followed The News in supporting the President. It too now went against him. In one short interview the President had lost support of two major newspapers permanently. The President and the Colonel went through the war as, at best, co-belligerents against Germany, Japan and Italy. No editor more diligently used his staff to report the war but he did not lessen his attacks on New Deal agencies nor could he say anything good about Roosevelt. Editorial Writer Leon Stolz proposed praising the President's plan to build 50,000 planes in 12 months. The Colonel "bit Stolz' head off." No editor probed more deeply into the events leading up to the Japanese bombing of Pearl Harbor. Many sources were closed but the findings of Editorial Writer George Morgenstern supported the Colonel's suspicion that Roosevelt had worked to bring America into the war. The opening of wartime documents 25 years later confirmed that for two years Roosevelt and Churchill had cooperated secretly. For Churchill December 7, 1941, was the best day of the war. Until then he had not been able to see how Britain could win the war. After Pearl Harbor victory was only a matter of time.

When rivals accused the Colonel of hurting the war effort he could recall that Grandfather Medill, similarly condemned for criticizing the failures of General Fremont, responded: "We need not say that The Tribune, whatever its other faults, has that of timidity nor that in time of war more than in days of security and peace it refuses to be true to its honest convictions and patriotic duty. We know of no reason that exempts military men from criticism and, if necessary, vigorous denunciation. We hold it to be a duty to denounce all who'd stand in the way of the triumph of the good cause and it matters little to us whether those who impede are of our own faith and party or belong to the enemy. We bid our contemporaries who would rather be victorious over The Tribune than over Jeff Davis howl on. We can afford to be honest and fearless and to wait."

The Colonel appeared to be open to a charge of treason by The Tribune's printing as part of its report of the navy's victory in the Battle of Midway a list of Japanese ships involved. The navy surmised the Japanese would deduce from the report that the American navy had broken the Japanese code and could read radio messages between its ships. The war correspondent who supplied the list, Stanley Johnston, a survivor of the sunken carrier *Lexington*, told the navy he had composed the list from his studies and from conversations with officers on the long voyage home and did not know the code had been broken. As days passed and the Japanese continued to use the code, the navy realized the report had done no harm and decided to drop the investigation. To bring a charge would give the Japanese information they had failed to deduce. However the President would not pass up an opportunity to discredit The Tribune and the Colonel and ordered the attorney general to bring the matter before a federal grand jury in Chicago. For the Colonel the three days of the hearings were the most anxious of his life. He angrily stalked Cantigny lawns and woods with a riding whip, whacking off any weed that dared raise its head. The jurors found no cause for a charge. At The Tribune when the Colonel walked into the news room, editors and reporters stood and cheered.

Tribune reporters and governmental bureaucrats joined in the contest between publisher and President. Tribune reporters as a group worked more diligently to find stories to discredit the administration than to praise it but when a Washington staff member proposed doing a story on the then little-known continuing romance between Roosevelt and Lucy Mercer, the Colonel brusquely said, "No, The Tribune does not fight that way."

One day the Colonel said the army had asked him to give General Motors a blast for falling behind in army truck deliveries. "I don't think I'll run that story," the Colonel said. "It wouldn't produce more trucks. It would only give comfort to the enemy." On their side, Washington bureaucrats used their powers to make life difficult for The Tribune. The War Production Board ordered all newspapers to reduce their use of paper by 15 percent but made special allocations, often to FDR supporters including the Chicago Sun. The WPB, after a public hearing, declared that the Sun knowingly and willfully used more paper than its extended quota. The Sun appealed. At a private WPB hearing the finding was erased. The Colonel's neighbor, Ed Hurley, head of the Thor Washing Machine Co., told the Colonel his company was having trouble with the War Labor Board. "You put it down and we will print it," the Colonel said. Hurley declined the offer, thinking the publication would push the Labor Board to greater efforts against him. "I don't know of anyone who had a tougher time in Washington than the Colonel," said Hurley's daughter, Jeannette Reuben.

Governmental harassment reached into Canada. There the government requisitioned five of The Tribune's eight ships. The Colonel thought this order "extra severe." Canadian manager Arthur Schmon continued paper deliveries to New York and Chicago with the remaining ships by arranging to haul bauxite and coal on the return journeys. Government-ordered power cuts stilled three of Thorold's five paper machines. To discourage a total cutoff of power the mill began making yeast and 600,000 gallons a year of alcohol to supply synthetic rubber factories. The Colonel commented Grandfather Medill, a campaigner against alcohol, must be turning in his grave. The Baie Comeau mill was exempt from power rationing because it provided its own hydropower and no other user was at hand. Baie Comeau woodsmen cut timber for Britain at a loss and made pulp for army cartons, also at a loss. Baie Comeau shared its paper with Canadian newspapers at less than cost but Canadian publishers denounced the Colonel as anti-British. When they called Schmon's younger son a draft dodger, although he was just 16, the Colonel suspended visiting Canada. Schmon's elder son Richard became an officer in the American army and was killed in action with Patton's army. Seventeen other Baie Comeau employees gave their lives.

Towards the end of the war the Colonel publicly listed acts of harassment. He included a heavy customs charge suddenly imposed on newsprint brought from Canada to Chicago. He did not tell the full story. The incident had begun one day in 1938 with the surprise visit of customs inspectors to The Tribune's paper warehouse on the Chicago River. They took away samples of paper recently brought by boat from the Canadian mill. In a few days the customs office reported the paper did not fit the specifications laid down by the Congress in 1914 when it removed the duty on newsprint. The report was correct. Elbert Antrim, The Tribune's business manager, for some time had been asking the mills to improve the whiteness of the paper. Schmon and his engineers discovered that a better whiteness could be obtained if calcium carbonate were added to the pulp. Seeing no legal infraction they changed the formula. The Tribune reported how much of the improved paper had been received and customs sent a bill for $172,000. The Tribune paid and the mill returned to the old mix. Tribune lawyer Kirkland thought nothing could be done but asked a new member of the firm, Hammond Chaffetz, assigned to the law firm's Washington office, to look into the matter. Chaffetz arranged a series of meetings with the commissioner of customs and found him to be a veteran civil servant who had served under several administrations and did not bend his actions to please any incumbent government. Chaffetz argued that the 1914 specifications were those used by the industry at the time and the Congress in quoting them in the law did not intend to prevent improvements in the product certain to follow. The commissioner accepted the position, rewrote the specifications to permit betterment and to the astonishment of Chaffetz made the rule retroactive to 1914. Chaffetz next called on the assistant secretaray of the treasury who wrote a check refunding all but $5,000 of the $172,000 payment. The astounded Colonel cashed the check but did so with a tinge of disappointment. He no longer could protest that everyone in New Deal Washington harassed The Tribune. He referred to Chaffetz as "the New Dealer in our Washington office" and marveled at his clout. The Colonel gave the law firm a $50,000 bonus. None was passed on to the young lawyer. Nor did the Colonel ever write him a note of commendation. By 1944 the Colonel spoke only of the $172,000 bill, not the $167,000 refund.

* * * * *

In Washington Cissy Patterson's paper, The Times-Herald, steadily gathered readers and advertisers and in 1943 earned its first profit, $44,156. Cissy distributed the money among employees.

That summer Cissy became ill. She was only 62 but questioned her stamina. She asked her brother Joe if he would buy The Times-Herald. He declined. She offered it to Joe's daughter Alicia. She declined; she was busy with her own paper on Long Island, Newsday. Cissy offered The Times-Herald to the Colonel. He declined. Cissy persevered.

* * * * *

Nature mishandled by man almost cut short the life of Canada's community at Baie Comeau. Less rain than usual fell in the summer of 1942. One July evening a family picnicking along

JOE &
CISSY

The New York Daily News

The Washington Times-Herald

the Manicouagan River failed to put out their fire. A brisk wind from the west fanned the embers into flame which spread to nearby dried brush. Soon flames were advancing through the forest on a three-mile-wide front. Sewell called out every man from the mill, rounded up volunteers from stores, brought in men from the woods, flew in men from the South Shore. The evening plane about to leave Quebec unloaded its passengers and brought pumps and hose. The effort was no match for the wind. On the second day the flames approached the flume carrying logs to the mill from the Manicouagan and the Outardes. If the flume burned, the mill would not have enough wood to carry it through the winter. Sewell sent teams to dam the flume and spill water onto the grass ahead of the fire. The grass steamed but did not burn as the fire leaped from tree top to tree top. On the sixth day the fire neared the town. Schmon advised women to carry their most valuable possessions to the dock where a barge waited. One wife was content to save only the family photo albums; all else could be replaced. When the town seemed doomed nature repented. The wind changed to the east and blew the fire back upon itself. Before the embers cooled the Colonel arrived from Chicago. The loss was serious but not catastrophic. Most of the trees useful for paper already had been harvested from the burned area and in 10 years the charred landscape would be green again. Nature had demonstrated to the pioneers the lesson the Indians early learned and always heeded: Do not challenge nature; misuse her and your most valiant efforts are as puny as a bucket is useless in draining the ocean.

Insure, insure, insure, the Colonel told Schmon and Sewell, remembering how Chicago's great fire of 1871 had burned down the new Tribune building, uninsured because it was considered to be fireproof. One day lightning struck an iron manhole cover in Baie Comeau, traveled along a buried pipe and surfaced in a woodpile, setting it alight. The insurers paid.

The Colonel was not put off by challenge nor by risk but he was not foolhardy. In the early days of Baie Comeau the staff bridled and saddled a workhorse to take the Colonel through the forest to the Outardes dam site. The Colonel looked at the horse that was unhappy over the unfamiliar saddle and bridle, patted the horse's head, asked its name, stepped back, studied the pawing animal and said, "Let's go back to town."

During the war the Canadian government sent German prisoners into the woods as laborers. Their physical fitness impressed the Colonel. "I don't know what Hitler put into their minds," he commented, "but I never saw such consistently splendidly scaled men." German sailors rescued by the British navy after their corvette was sunk built a model of their ship and gave it to the Colonel. Encased in glass it stands on the fireplace mantel in Medill's library at Cantigny. Most prisoners worked well. Nazi stormtroopers did not, and Baie Comeau foremen quickly returned them to prison compounds.

22. Nationwide, Every Saturday Night, Live
1939—1955

Singer Marion Claire proposed to the Colonel in 1939 that WGN present each week a one-hour synopsis of an opera, light opera or musical comedy, sung in English of course. The show would be aired when the audience was largest, on Saturday evening. About half way through the Colonel would talk about anything and everything. A transcript of his talk would appear in the Sunday Tribune. The Colonel liked the idea and told Ms. Claire and Henry Weber, musical director and her husband, to start production.

The show, the Chicago Theater of the Air, was carried by 300 stations coast to coast and became the longest running, one-hour music program in radio history. So many listeners asked to attend that the show was moved to the 4,000 seat Medinah Temple. In 1944 fans bought a half million dollars in war bonds to get tickets for "Naughty Marietta." The Colonel's most dedicated listeners included political conservatives who hated Franklin Roosevelt, the New Deal and foreign entanglements or armchair strategists who soaked up his precise assessments of military situations. Many talks were written by WGN's Francis Coughlin, an ultra liberal. The Colonel's memory of detail was encyclopedic. Carl Wiegman, an editorial writer, disappeared into libraries to write an assigned talk on the Battle of New Orleans. "How about the chain?" the Colonel asked after reading the script. Wiegman returned to the libraries and found a footnote that Andrew Jackson had put a chain across the river but it had proved of no consequence. The Colonel's radio recollections of his youth and his formative years, lightened with deadpan humor, provide the best insight into the young McCormick.

His voice once heard never was mistaken. Briefly he took speech lessons; a silken-voiced friend, Judge Julius Miner, also coached him, but the Colonel continued to speak with little change of pace, volume and key. Quite a few listeners timed coffee-making with his talk. When he was out of Chicago, his talk was carried into Chicago by radio or telephone and fitted into the program.

The Colonel devoted several broadcasts a year to stories of his heroes: Admiral Marc Mitscher, who ordered every ship in his task force to turn on all lights to guide home carrier planes lost in the Pacific's black night; General MacArthur, "the greatest soldier since Grant and the greatest statesman since Lincoln"; Senator Henry Cabot Lodge, "the great patriot"; Okichi Saito, inspiration for Madame Butterfly; Benjamin Franklin, "the most versatile man of all time"; the captain of the steamboat Robert E. Lee, who raced 1,120 miles from New Orleans to St. Louis in three days, 18 hours, 30 minutes—the Colonel installed the ship's whistle in The Tribune boiler room; Sir Walter Scott, who for his last seven years wrote almost night and day to pay off a huge debt brought by failure of a publishing firm as he was building his house, Abbotsford; James Madison; Thomas Jefferson; Patrick Henry; Nathan Hale; George Washington, the Indian Tibasse, Thaddeus Kosciuszko, Polish patriot; all of the fliers of Torpedo Squadron Eight; the captain of Old Ironsides; Andrew Jackson, who as President cut taxes and paid off the public debt; John Paul Jones; Sergeant John Basilone, marine machine gunner on Guadalcanal; Alberto Gainza Paz, fighter for a free press in Buenos Aires.

The Colonel choked with emotion as he told how Butch O'Hare, a young Chicago flier, attacked a Japanese battleship. He repeatedly read the Declaration of Independence, the Constitution, Patrick Henry's speech, Lincoln's brief talk at Gettysburg, George Washington's farewell address and Jefferson's inaugural, his own speech at the Cantigny memorial dedication in France. On Christmas Day of 1944 the Colonel read a letter Lincoln wrote to a mother of five sons killed in the Civil War reflecting on "your solemn pride to have laid so costly a sacrifice on the altar of freedom."

The Colonel frequently commented on Britain, sometimes favorably, more often not:

"In science, England ranks among the highest."

"The lower classes, long held down, are revengeful and intent on destroying their superiors."

"Having grown up in England, I learned how to browbeat the lower classes."

"English common law reached its height in the time of Elizabeth when courts told her she could not give monopolies to her lovers."

"The aristocracy has served England well. Even in decline, they have run the American State Department for 50 years."

"The English army, by taking officers from the lower classes, has become impotent."

"The English language has wonderful sonority. Fortunately it does not lend itself to the vituperation achieved by Hitler in the German tongue. We did well to keep the English language."

"England is still as Joseph Medill found it, with the richest people on earth and the most paupers. Ancestry is more important than accomplishment. The arrogance of the nobles pervades the nation."

"English statesmen are, when compared to others, almost humane."

The Colonel praised the British soldiers who fired on American colonials at Boston. The massacre, he said, happened only in the minds of rebellious propagandists. He also praised a British fleet which, at a tense moment in Manila Bay, maneuvered itself between a threatening German flotilla and Admiral Dewey's ships and allowed the Americans to put marines ashore unmolested. In time the Colonel realized that he gained nothing in protesting charges of being anti-British. Sometimes when asked why he hated the British he would say, "If your ancestors had been scalped by the Indians while the English stood by doing nothing to help, you wouldn't like the English."

Six months after the Pearl Harbor attack, the Colonel declared: "It is now plain to all that America will win this war." He expanded the theme month by month:

—"Our form of government based on equality produces young people capable of absorbing training. So whatever the initial mistakes and calculations we will find that the government of the people, by the people and for the people cannot perish from this earth."

—"Japan will meet her fate at the hands of the great American republic."

—"American inventiveness, enterprise and, above all, courage, will win this war."

—"Japan made several mistakes—by attacking us, by not hitting hard enough, by not attacking Panama or taking Midway, by not putting enough men on Guadalcanal."

—"Conquerors always overreach themselves. Hitler's empire will crumble like a pack of cards."

After the D-Day invasion of Normandy—"I don't know which way our forces will move, but I do know we will win."

Coming out of the studio one day, the Colonel remarked to Ward Quaal, later WGN president, "I don't know how much longer the people will stand me, but I am proud that we are giving them quality music. Always remember, Ward, quality pays dividends."

Marion Claire recalled many years later that the artists had to adjust their final act to fit the time the Colonel left to them. The Colonel, impeccable in evening dress, was servant of no stop watch, not even a clock. One Saturday just before show time Marion Schroeder, WGN librarian who served as program manager, scanned the Colonel's text and told him his talk would take not the allotted 15 minutes but 21. "That's your problem," the Colonel said.

The Colonel left the choice of the music and the performers to Ms. Claire and to Weber and not once in 15 years did he ask that any performer be fired or hired. Mary Garden, Scottish-born opera diva and a favorite in Chicago, said Henry Weber and Marion Claire made Chicago a world music center. In no other city, she said, did so many young performers begin their careers. The program costing a million dollars a year went off the air soon after the Colonel's death in 1955.

* * * * *

Throughout World War II Press Wireless, outgrowth of the Atlantic radio beam originated by the Colonel in the first days after World War I, sent operators and transportable transmitters to the battlefields. From tents, battered barns or other accommodation not already requisitioned by military forces, Prewi crews let American newspapers tell the people at home in detail never before imagined about the progress of the war and the welfare of their young men and women in uniform.

The rapid growth of radio had demanded ever more and bigger studios and more powerful equipment but the larger audiences brought increased earnings. WGN made its first profit in 1934. The Colonel asked architects to design a building incorporating the most advanced techniques, providing adequate space for audiences, called guests in those days, and doing justice to the high quality of the artists, the programs, WGN and The Tribune. The Colonel proudly declared that the resulting five-story structure adjoining Tribune Tower was the most beautiful broadcasting building in the world. The largest of the six studios could accommodate a symphony orchestra, an opera chorus and an audience of 600. The pipe organ studio rose two stories to capture the richness of the pipes. All studios floated on hydraulic cushions. Everything was air conditioned. On the stone exterior McCormick embedded rocks from the Coliseum, the Great Pyramid and the Great Wall of China. But in just 10 years, the coming of television demanded a new kind of studio.

Radio reception tended to fade. Engineers said a new method called frequency modulation cured the trouble. In 1940 WGN added an FM channel, first in Chicago, that sometimes borrowed programs from WGN, sometimes created its own. WGN abandoned FM in 1953.

When the Associated Press had begun carrying photographs

over wire, the Colonel wondered if someday entire newspapers could be distributed over the air. Subscribers would switch on a receiver and out would come The Tribune. Think of the saving! No more presses! No more delivery boys! In the late 1930s WGN engineers found a way to bring about the miracle but at a cost too high to be practical. During the war WGN opened its facsimile transmission to the Federal Bureau of Investigation to transmit fingerprints and other documents and to the military to make instant delivery of vital contracts and drawings. Development continued slowly through the war. In May of 1946 a four page facsimile edition of The Tribune was beamed by WGN 30 miles to a receiver at Cantigny. It was a technical breakthrough. The Colonel saw much work still must be done before a newspaper could be distributed by radio or wire but warned: "Newspapers will be well advised to keep in touch with these processes and be ready to adopt them at any time they may threaten to supersede the older processes of news dissemination."

Another electronic development was more productive. In 1944, 18 years after WGN engineers had exhibited a three inch circular glass screen on which pictures moved, the Colonel ordered WGN's first television transmitter. Broadcasts began April 5, 1948, from studios in the Chicago Daily News building that had been used by the Civic Opera cast for rehearsal.

The Colonel commented: "A pioneer has always felt that in casting off the old he was adventuring toward something more splendid and more spacious. He marked out the trail, not only for himself but for others. He went among the first and there was high adventuring in his going. It is this feeling of adventuring that I would communicate to you. In television we have embarked upon another of America's adventures. Come along with us! Let us share the adventure together. We are going as far as we are able. Our partners are the American people."

23. New Opportunities
1942—1946

The Colonel continued as a duty the New Year's Day party for Tribune families. Everything in the Tower including the Colonel's office was open, buffets waited in strategic places, clowns entertained children, the Colonel greeted everyone, sometimes picking up children and hugging them. Lotta lay at his feet. "He wants protection," carping critics falsely sniped.

Wives, widows, divorcees and spinsters sought his company, hoping for marriage. Their success varied. To part with one North Shore horsewoman, he set up a trust fund, with Corpening acting as go-between, bypassing the Colonel's lawyers. The Colonel did enjoy the presence of pretty, lively women. Cissy Patterson introduced him to Hedda Hopper. The Colonel found her doubly delightful; she was beautiful and she throbbed with Hollywood's newest gossip, soon incorporated into a column for The Tribune and its syndicate. The Colonel laughed at her tales and advised her to be careful. She brought Hollywood people into his acquaintance. Singer Grace Moore enchanted him.

One day Rebecca West, the clever English writer, called on Tribune Literary Editor Fanny Butcher and told her she and the Colonel some years earlier had crossed the Atlantic on the same liner. Miss West's account led Fanny to believe a considerable shipboard romance had developed. "The last thing he said," Miss West recounted, "was that if I ever came to Chicago I should call him." Fanny telephoned the Colonel and told him Miss West was in her office. "Bring her up," the Colonel said. The Colonel greeted Miss West, whom Fanny remembers as a striking beauty with a keen mind. She and the Colonel gossiped for some time about people and things, neither mentioning the ocean crossing. They said farewell. As soon as the door closed behind her Miss West laughed. "It's funny, really funny," she said. "I never laid eyes on that man before. I wonder who my ship companion really was?" Fanny joined in the laughter.

The Colonel began dropping in at the Lake Forest home of Henry Weber and Marion Claire for Sunday luncheon. He gave the Webers a Doberman that WGN had bought to guard a remote transmitter but, loving people, proved incapable of the role. The Webers named her Diva and took her to the studio with them. Gossips said Ms. Claire became the Colonel's mistress, not knowing that Ms. Claire's mother was usually present during his visits. The mother and the Colonel were compatible. She laughed long when the Colonel, asked by the maid if he would like some cherries jubilee, said he would have only the jubilee, and he laughed long when she mistook his scotch for her gingerale, drank thirstily and, choking, grabbed her throat. He was there on December 7, 1941. Ms. Claire's mother said, "Isn't it awful what the Japs are doing in Hawaii?" The Colonel ran from the house to his car without recovering his coat and hat. At The Tribune he ordered a new editorial pledging The Tribune's full help in winning the war he had seen coming and tried to prevent. In mid-afternoon he telephoned WGN and asked announcer Ward Quaal, "Who is learning how to pronounce all those strange names? Who is studying the geography of the Far East?" Then, carrying an armful of snapdragons, Maryland Hooper's favorite flowers, he drove to her apartment. She had expected him for luncheon. The Tribune had telephoned her asking that the Colonel telephone his office instantly on arrival. The Colonel, handing Mrs. Hooper the flowers, told her he had been driving around the countryside. Given the message he telephoned the Tower, listened a minute, said, "The Japs are bombing Hawaii," and hurried away.

Maryland Hooper had entered the Cantigny circle through the Chicago Golf Club 15 years earlier and for a dozen years had been one of Amy's best friends although 26 years younger. Amy had painted her portrait—it now hangs at Cantigny. One evening Rebori told Mrs. Hooper, "You are a little vixen. You know what you want and you make sure you get it." She and Henry Hooper had married February 10, 1923, and had two daughters, Alice and Anne. Hooper was president of the North Shore Fuel Company. His father, a New Englander, had practiced medicine in Chicago for many years. Isaac N. Arnold, his grandfather and friend of Joseph Medill, was a notable Chicago citizen, friend of Lincoln, congressman and bibliophile. The Hoopers separated in May of 1943, he moving from their Lake Shore apartment to the Lake

390

Shore Club. One day as the Colonel and Mrs. Hooper rode through the Cantigny woods the pair paused in a glade. The Colonel asked if she would marry him. She was not surprised but could not remember later exactly how he phrased the question nor how she phrased her acceptance. Subsequently he gave her a framed color photograph of the romantic stretch of bridle path.

*   *   *   *   *

The 1944 election brought Dewey against Roosevelt. The Colonel was cool on Dewey who echoed administration policies so often that the Colonel referred to him as Me-Too Dewey. The Colonel was not distraught by Dewey's defeat.

*   *   *   *   *

In November of 1944 Mrs. Hooper went to Mexico City, settled in a hotel and asked the court for a divorce, charging her husband with drunkenness. A long-time acquaintance whose wife had just died arrived in Mexico City and called on Mrs. Hooper. The Colonel heard about his visit, telephoned her and angrily demanded how the man knew she was in Mexico City and what he was up to. Mrs. Hooper said she had written him a note of condolence on hotel stationery and he was up to nothing. "Bert was a very jealous man," she commented many years later, recalling also that once she returned from a few days in Washington to find that the Colonel had replaced in her room an autographed photograph given to her by Errol Flynn with one of the Catholic Bishop of Quebec.

Hooper did not contest the divorce. The decree granted, Mrs. Hooper telephoned the Colonel and suggested he meet her in Texas and they marry there. The Colonel declined. He said they would marry in Chicago and because the Mexican divorce might not be recognized in Illinois he wanted no repetition of the furor that followed Amy's divorce. She should come home and get a divorce in Chicago. She came, her lawyer filed a petition and, the next morning, Judge John A. Shabaro called a hearing at 8 a.m., long before the normal hour for starting court business. The Judge said he set the early hour because he was suffering from sinus trouble and was hurrying south. Mrs. Hooper testified that her husband struck her two days in a row without cause. She waived alimony. Hooper's attorney waived Hooper's legal rights.

391

The Judge granted the divorce. The Colonel later said he paid for the divorce, just as he had paid for Amy's 30 years earlier.

The Colonel wanted the wedding plans to be kept secret. Mrs. Hooper found a refuge from prying reporters and gossipy people in the home of Tribune Lawyer Howard Ellis and his wife Maude. Mrs. Ellis bought the wedding ring, an elegant platinum band. The day before the engagement announcement was to be made, the Tribune guard on the 24th floor told the Colonel that Mrs. Hooper had arrived. The beaming Colonel hurried out to meet her and found a stranger. "I'm Miss Hooper," the stranger said. "I would like to talk to you about a matter affecting one of my clients." Miss Frances Hooper, head of her own advertising firm, meeting the Colonel for the first time, never forgot how "suddenly the Colonel's face dropped," the smile yielding to puzzlement. He invited her into his office, listened to the client's problem, promised it would be corrected and courteously said goodbye. Shortly afterward Mrs. Hooper arrived. "The damndest thing just happened," he told her. Miss Hooper's rating with her client shot off the top of the charts. Imagine having an agent who had the ear of the Colonel! Miss Hooper, not one to discount good luck, never explained. The next morning she opened The Tribune and saw the announcement of the Colonel's engagement to Maryland Hooper.

Richard Daley, county clerk and soon to become the famous mayor of Chicago, drove to the Ellis home with Weymouth Kirkland, the Colonel's lawyer, taking an unnumbered wedding license application, an expediency used by Cook county clerks to help favorites who wished to keep secret from the press the issuance of a marriage license. The Colonel and Mrs. Hooper filled it out. "That's two dollars," Daley said. The Colonel made a show of searching all of his pockets for money. Kirkland produced two rumpled bills, "the dirtiest pieces of money I've ever seen," the bride-to-be noted.

The couple married the day before Christmas in the Lake Shore apartment of Chauncey McCormick with Joe Patterson as best man and, in the Colonel's lapel, the badge of the 1st Division. Wheaton's Presbyterian minister, the Rev. Dr. Stewart, officiated before about a dozen relatives and friends. The Colonel gave the bride a circle of diamonds to be followed over the years with a dazzling array of rubies, emeralds, diamonds and pearls. The wedding photograph presents a glowingly happy Colonel, his smile speaking of the joy he expected to come from a loving companion drawing him at last from his cocoon. A news photographer carried away in his camera bag highly valuable Napoleon goblets but returned them the next day with a note that he had been the unwitting butt of a colleague's prank. Daley belatedly entered the license in the register, giving it a half number. The newlyweds drove to Cantigny where the staff had lit a huge bonfire, tramped a heart into the snow and tied red satin ribbons to the collars of the dogs. The Colonel was 64, the bride 47. Mrs. McCormick occupied the first floor bedroom in the new west wing that Amy had shunned. The two Hooper daughters, Alice, then 21, and Anne, 19, a student nurse, came to live at Cantigny, given rooms on the second floor in the main old house. The girls, acquainted as children with the Colonel and Amy and later on visits to Cantigny during vacations from their convent school in Montreal, long had called the Colonel Uncle Bert and continued to do so. Jensen gave them riding lessons. Anne enjoyed the sport and the peril of taking a horse over a fence but Alice was not happy and pulled on the horse as he approached a jump. Jensen stopped her lessons. Why? the mother asked. "Because she's ruining the horse," the riding master said. The mother agreed that Alice and the horses should part.

At Cantigny life resumed at a slower pace, the Colonel and Maryland using it mainly as a summer place. The polo ponies had gone and the polo field had been planted with crops. The yield was high, which farm families told one another should be expected, considering how the Colonel had, for polo, "fertilized the field with vast quantities of ten dollar bills." The hunt was only a memory. Corpening had married and become a property developer. Ed Prendergast had become ill with cancer. "Will you take care of me?" he asked. "Of course," the Colonel said. Prendergast died in 1946. The Colonel paid for his funeral.

The new Mrs. McCormick reorganized the staff. Elizabeth stayed as cook, a bit testy with the new lady of the manor. From Japan came a valet, the first Japanese to receive an American immigration visa after the war, as the Colonel's Washington bureau staff proudly declared. The English butler, Emil, stayed on. The Colonel delighted in telling the editorial writers he had bought a new brand of scotch and told Emil he didn't know its quality. "It's a lot better than what we have been drinking," Emil replied. One night Emil tipped a tray of roast beef, potatoes and vegetables, all thick with gravy, over a meticulously groomed woman guest. "Good God," the Colonel said, arose and departed, leaving

393

his wife to cool down and clean up the guest, a testing task.

Mrs. McCormick also presided over the Astor Street house, an apartment in Washington, the house at Boynton Beach and a tower suite in the New York Waldorf Astoria. Staff moved from place to place as needed for the Colonel's comfort.

At 65 the Colonel still could wear his World War I uniform. He weighed himself every morning on an accurate balance scale. If it showed 211 he ate less until the scale returned to 210. He was a meat and potatoes man but ate anything put before him. At his plate for every lunch or dinner at Cantigny Elizabeth placed a menu card so the Colonel could pace himself, eating less of an early dish in order to have more of subsequent dishes he liked better.

Mrs. McCormick introduced dachshunds, Pekinese and an English bulldog, Buster Boo. When Lotta died at 14, Mrs. McCormick bought for the Colonel an Alsatian named Lisa. Remembering Lotta's frequent littering she had Lisa spayed. Too late she learned that the Colonel disapproved of such mutilation. The Colonel adopted Buster Boo and left Lisa to Maryland.

Buster Boo was unforgettable when Marcia Winn, star reporter, was married in the Colonel's Astor Street house. Attracted by the scent of the wartime leg makeup the bride wore in the absence of silk stockings, Buster Boo followed her down the stairs, where the Colonel awaited, and followed them both into the library. The Colonel left Marcia beside the bridegroom, Editorial Writer George Morgenstern, and stepped back. Buster Boo did not. As the minister asked the questions and the bride and bridegroom made their pledges Buster Boo happily and noisily licked away the makeup. Marcia kept her eyes on the minister and the bridegroom and twitched not even a toe, such being the upbringing of a fine Southern young lady.

Lisa also was unforgettable at a dinner party honoring the mayor, Martin Kennelly, a proper bachelor. Seated next to him was a widow, beautiful, lively and correct. During the main course each began to look at the other quizzically. Soon each was leaning away from the other. By dessert she had nudged her chair away from him and he had shifted his away from her. Then out from under the table came Lisa. The mayor and the widow suddenly brightened. It was Lisa who had been so busily rubbing alternately against the mayor and the widow.

One summer day the Colonel strolled to the swimming pool off the east porch. As usual when no women were on hand, he was wearing nothing. He paused by the pool to look at some very large carp his gardener had placed there after learning that fish eat larvae and thus reduce the mosquito population. A little frog hopped onto the rim beside the Colonel, paused, then jumped into the pool. Before it hit the water a big carp rose, mouth open, and swallowed the poor frog whole. "Did you see that?" the Colonel asked Dr. Theodore Van Dellen, who was sitting beside the pool. "I'm not going in there without my pants." He didn't.

* * * * *

Maryland was not interested in the farming operations. She urged the Colonel to cut down the three oaks and two chestnuts that spoiled the view of the avenue of trees from the Madison porch but could not dent his steadfastness. One summer she told the Colonel the leaves of an oak were curling. "It's oak wilt," she said, pretending to have expert knowledge. "Now you will have to take it down." The Colonel sent for his tree expert who diagnosed merely a split limb. The limb went, the oak stayed. But after a little time someone buried salt around the tree and the oak really died. The trunk of one obstructive chestnut mysteriously split while the Colonel was away. On returning he saw the tree was doomed and asked Eddie Edwards to chop it down. Farm hands told one another that on a dark night a Cantigny hand had on instructions hitched a tractor chain to the tree and pulled it apart.

Mrs. McCormick set about completing the furnishing of the new wings. For the library she found a lawn-sized oriental carpet, two sturdy massive oak refectory tables, a handsome French desk. The Colonel, hearing that William Randolph Hearst was short of spending money, told him: "I'll have a couple of chests off you, Bill," and brought in a 15th century Gothic chest that once held vestments in a cathedral somewhere in Europe, and a low walnut chest softly and deeply carved with cherubs and big enough to hold his sword collection. The great fireplaces, served by the elevator, brought the library alive. WGN sent the newest radio-phonograph but the Colonel rarely played it. Long low carved oak benches served well, holding the Colonel's current books, papers and glass. Craftsmen made three oversized sofas. Ordinary-sized mortals had to sit either at the front of the sofa with no support for the back but with feet on the floor or well back in the deep down cushions with legs straight out. Miniature cannon, all capable of being fired, covered one table and his collection of watches the other. The Colonel assigned to his wife the smaller and more elegant sitting room. After a visitor caught her slipper heel in a loose strand of one of Amy's Aubusson carpets and fell, Maryland gave the aged carpets to the Art Institute, getting a $30,000 tax deduction. "I should send you downtown to run The Tribune," the Colonel said. She happily repeated the remark to executives. Some took it seriously.

*   *   *   *   *

On April 12, 1945, President Roosevelt died. "The whole nation is plunged into mourning; those who opposed him in politics no less than those who followed him," the Colonel's editorial commented. "History will appraise his work. For the moment we can only express the deep sorrow all Americans feel at the passing of their chosen leader." Some friends were coming to dinner that evening. "Don't serve champagne," the Colonel told Maryland. "I don't want anyone to say we are celebrating." The Colonel had flags half-lowered at the Tower and at Cantigny. "I don't know of anyone," he said, "for whom I'd rather do this."

The Tribune commented that President Truman "inherits an immense task at this difficult hour" and promised Truman "will receive the loyal support of all of us." Not many days passed before it became apparent that to the Colonel "loyal support" did not mean blind support nor even perhaps fair treatment. The barrages between the White House and Tribune Tower continued. The surrender of Germany and of Japan brought deep national relief which quieted many critical voices but not the Colonel's. He spoke a long-smothered certainty that Roosevelt, remembering how the blowing up of the Maine led to war with Spain, "operated by stealth" and provoked the Japanese attack on Pearl Harbor "to bring the nation into war while cloaking his actions as trappings of defense and peace and later, in signing the Yalta agreement, betrayed the American people."

*   *   *   *   *

When American troops were about to enter Vienna, the Colonel asked Maj. Gen. Stafford LeRoy Irwin, commander of the 5th Division and Amy's nephew, to find Margaret Prendergast who, after World War I, had married in Paris a retired Austrian army

396

officer, Major Alois Frimmel. The Frimmels lived in Vienna during the Nazi occupation and the war. As the American convoy approached, Margaret ran along it, holding high her American passport, and identified herself. General Irwin arranged for the pair to go to Munich where Frimmel entered a sanitarium for treatment of the last stages of tuberculosis. Margaret made army broadcasts and worked in an army post exchange. After Frimmel's death, Margaret came to Chicago and did a variety of small jobs before entering an Episcopalian retirement home. There, at 92, she recalled the dark days in Vienna and the Colonel's help. "He was a fine man," she said.

The General, like his Aunt Amy and his father, Maj. Gen. George LeRoy Irwin, had grown up in the army. At West Point, he, already dubbed Red, entertained cadets with his cartoons and impressed them by dropping to his knees every night at bedtime to say his prayers. He was with the 11th Cavalry at the Mexican border but was kept home in 1917-18 to teach artillery. In the World War II as artillery commander of the 9th Division, he stopped Rommel's Afrika Corps in Kasserine Pass and as commander of the 5th Division waded ashore in Normandy, plugged the southern gap in the Battle of the Bulge, raced through Bavaria into Austria and Czechoslovakia to meet the Russians. After the war a heart attack cut short his command as lieutenant general of American occupation forces in Austria and let him finally achieve his desire since his youth to paint water colors.

* * * * *

Bazy was three when her father died and 10 when her mother married Congressman Simms and moved to the Arizona ranch. A dog and a horse became Bazy's companions. No ranch pony could maintain the pace the girl required. At a polo match her mother saw a tough little gray mare, three quarters Arabian, dance and prance about the field, chukker after chukker, without pause. Her name, Little Joe, was tattooed on a hip. Mrs. Simms told the owner, "I have a daughter who rides all day. I must have Little Joe for her." The owner sold and Bazy began an eternal love affair with Arabian horses which was to enrich her life. Bazy was a junior at Foxcroft the summer her brother John was killed on the mountain. During summer vacations from school she worked on her mother's paper in Rockford and met a young reporter, Peter Miller. He went away to the war, returned and married Bazy.

The couple bought the two newspapers in the twin cities of Peru and LaSalle and combined them into The News-Tribune. Bazy was responsible for a local news column which she called "The Starter," a pressroom term applied to the last plate to be placed on the presses before the starter button is pushed. Without warning Miller began suffering occasional bouts of epilepsy. Bazy gave more time, thought and energy to the treatment of that disease than to her career.

Occasionally the Colonel took Bazy to The Tribune. "This will be good for you," he said. The remark was the closest he ever came to reminding Bazy that she might one day run The Tribune or have a major voice in Tribune affairs.

* * * * *

Joe Patterson died suddenly in May of 1946. He was 67. Mary King continued as woman's editor and took over some of his positions on Tribune boards. At one meeting a News executive, Jack Flynn, seated himself opposite the Colonel in the chair that Joe had occupied. "Uncle Bert blew up," Bazy recalled. Flynn moved and Patterson's chair remained vacant. Cissy proposed that Joe's place on the McCormick-Patterson trust, which held voting control of The Tribune Company, be given to Joe's daughter Alicia, who in founding and operating Newsday had proven that Great Grandfather Medill's journalistic genes had settled in her. But the Colonel refused to bring Alicia into any part of the Tribune operations. Why? Jealousy, some said; she was a Patterson, not a McCormick. The Colonel assumed Joe's rights. Cissy continued her advocacy of Alicia in private and public and the McCormick-Patterson feud carried on so long by Kate and Nellie but carefully avoided by Bert and Joe now flared anew. Cissy's challenge to the Colonel's dominance was noisy but ineffective, like that of a French poodle snapping at the hooves of a Percheron. Joe's two other daughters had taken themselves from the Tribune orbit, apart from collecting dividends. The eldest, Elinor, after a career as an actress starring in Max Reinhardt's American production of "The Miracle" and making a movie, married stockbroker Donald Baker. The youngest, Josephine, married the artist Ivan Albright who grew up in Warrenville, Illinois, a few miles from Cantigny. Joe and Mary's son, Jimmy Patterson, was a potential heir but Mary did not push him and the Colonel did not object when Jimmy, after being graduated from West Point, became an army officer.

24. My America, First, Last and Always
1945—1952

The Colonel declared that the war was won by America. "Of that there can be no doubt," he said. He was proud the atom first was split in Chicago and believed the atom bomb would lead to wide peacetime benefits. "It is time that all Americans hold their heads high with pride," the Colonel announced. "It is time for hyphenated Americans to be silent, for schools to stop decrying everything American, for the literary world to show some patriotism and for the New York stage to stop being positively anti-American."

The Colonel was not surprised that the Soviet government continued its long-term campaign to make the whole world communist. "Stalin will take all of Europe if he can," the Colonel said, and advised America not to disarm as it had in 1920. "Because our last three wars were fought far from our shores," he said, "people have come to think total immunity to the consequences of war is a kind of national privilege. It is not so." He reckoned the United Nations would be no more effective in maintaining peace than had been the League of Nations. Americans who helped organize the United Nations had, in the Colonel's mind, "sought to rise to international status by betraying their own country." The only American to "achieve immortality as an internationalist," he recalled, was Benedict Arnold, who received $30,000 in British gold for selling out his country. The Colonel pointed out that in the UN, Britain would have seven votes, Russia five and the United States just one, a split that made certain the United States would achieve, by joining the UN, not world leadership but American subservience to foreign interests. He said a stamp issued by the United States post office placing the UN flag above the Stars and Stripes correctly demonstrated the subordinate position to which UN supporters relegated the United States. He saw a danger that wishful thinking about the

UN's ability to prevent war—"It's a pipe dream"—might induce Americans into reducing our military preparedness and another danger that communists present at the UN as members of delegations or employees of the UN might become "enemies within our borders."

The Colonel saw more bad than good for America coming from the North Atlantic Alliance. He said the treaty "perilously increased America's territorial responsibilities." He argued that the United States would station in Europe a force too small to be able to defend itself but big enough to guarantee that the United States would be involved in any new European war from the first shot. Thus, he said, the NATO treaty was "a harbinger of disaster" and opened the United States to the possibility of another Pearl Harbor surprise attack.

The Colonel argued also that as a member of NATO the United States would "bleed ourselves white to defend nations that won't defend each other." America, he declared, does not need the assistance of any country to stop Russian aggression. As for the Europeans, he asked, why are they so afraid of the Russians? Neither side, he said, could afford to invade the other. He considered the American monopoly of the atom bomb to be temporary. "What we have done with our bomb they can do to us," he warned. Despite skepticism and ridicule, he had a paper storage room in the deepest of the three basements at the Tower strengthened to serve as an atom bomb shelter and stocked it with canned pineapple, then recommended as the best aid for radiation burns. At Cantigny the only window of a basement dressing room for swimmers was closed with reinforced concrete so that room could be a refuge. He considered a person would be safe in either shelter for 24 hours after a bomb burst. He believed development of the bomb would not prevent future wars but it would "measure the potential of every nation to keep the peace or wage unbelievable total war." He wrote off missiles as "too far in the future to be taken into consideration now."

America's security, he declared, lay in being so strong that no nation could attack. By strength, he did not mean merely number or quality of weapons. Strength implied much more. He quoted Joseph Medill: "What constitutes the bulwark of our liberty and independence? Not our settlements, our seacoasts, our warships, our army. Our reliance is the love of liberty which God has planted in our bosoms." He also quoted Lincoln: "Let us have faith that right makes might." To the Colonel lack of unity within a nation is more dangerous than aggression from any outside nation. The South lost the war between the states, he summed up, more from lack of support—100,000 Confederate soldiers deserted in 1864—than on the battlefield, and Napoleon was beaten at Waterloo because of discontent among the French people and threat of sedition among the leaders. "I have no sympathy and little patience with people who blame all the evils of the world on my country," the Colonel said. "If they are foreigners, their attitude may be natural. If they are American citizens, their conduct is unnatural." Certain truths do not change, the Colonel argued, again quoting Lincoln: "Human nature does not alter. We will always have the weak and the strong, the silly and the wise, the good and the bad." The Colonel saw hope that American science and industry, which created the military force that beat the Germans and the Japanese, "may well be the key by which men of good will can enter upon a finer and fairer world."

The Colonel was opposed to the Marshall aid program. He said the American goal—to stop the spread of communism by helping Europe regain prosperity— was correct but he claimed that the way in which aid was being handled deprived America of a proper return on its investment. Why, he asked, should Americans work hard for 40 hours a week to support Britons who won't work more than 32?

* * * * *

The Second World War had grounded the Colonel. His latest plane had been one of 345 taken into government service. After the war the military asked what recompense he wanted. "Another plane," the Colonel replied. The military delivered a Lockheed Lodestar, a twin-engined, 185 mph, unpressurized, 14-passenger craft which had been equipped most comfortably for use by a general. The Colonel was delighted with its long settee. So was Buster Boo, his drooling English bulldog. However, the Lockheed lacked instruments for blind flights, limiting its use for commuting between Chicago and often foggy Baie Comeau. American Airlines serviced the plane at its Midway airport shops and provided two pilots, Howard West and George Marks, full time, the Colonel giving them a bonus on top of their airline pay and expense money when out of Chicago. West and Marks flew the Colonel and Maryland around Central America. Marks re-

401

turned to the airline after a year but West remained with the Colonel until a motorcycle crash grounded him. The Colonel bought a surplus navy training plane for use around Chicago. Wayne Thomis, a Tribune reporter who had been a navy flyer, took off each autumn Saturday with three Tribune photographers, delivered them to the most important Big Ten football games, waited for each to get good action shots, returned to Chicago and dropped the films in watertight bags to a reporter waiting not far from The Tribune on a spit of wasteland protruding into Lake Michigan, a remnant of the 1933 World's Fair. Exclusive photos, The Tribune boasted.

*　*　*　*　*

As the 1948 election year neared, Dewey, the front-running Republican, approved support of NATO and the Marshall aid program, again earning the Colonel's title of "Me-Too Dewey." Senator Robert Taft of Ohio pleased the Colonel when he said the Marshall Plan would cost so much money it would disrupt the already weak American economy. However, the Colonel continued to be fascinated by Gen. Douglas MacArthur, his longtime military hero earning new praise for his administration of Japan.

The Colonel and Mrs. McCormick flew to Tokyo to be guests of the General. The flights being too long for the Colonel's plane, he reluctantly turned himself over to Pan American Airways. The Tribune's Tokyo correspondent, Walter Simmons, sent his seven-foot bed to the United States embassy to guarantee the Colonel a good night's rest.

The Colonel was not able to convince the General he should become a Republican candidate but after leaving wrote to MacArthur saying that he would continue to seek his nomination. The General appeared to Simmons as apprehensive that support from the Colonel would be more harmful than helpful, so continuous had been the denunciation of the Colonel as an ultra right wing crackpot. Other politically minded people, both Republican and Democratic, were trying to enlist Gen. Dwight Eisenhower, busy organizing the North Atlantic Treaty command and forces.

The Colonel called on Emperor Hirohito, who told him of his gratitude for MacArthur's efforts to rebuild Japan and said he anticipated many years of good relations between Japan and the United States. The Colonel lectured Japanese newspapermen on their need to maintain the press freedom given them by General

MacArthur. The Emperor assigned the royal railroad coach to the Colonel for a side trip to Kyoto. At bedtime Mrs. McCormick called the steward to ask him to turn down the heat. She spoke no Japanese and the American occupation was not yet old enough to give the Imperial steward an awareness of American speech. Mrs. McCormick patted the bed, put her hands beside her head and closed her eyes in an effort to tell him she was retiring. He seemed to understand. But he was bewildered by her stating repeatedly, "Hot, hot, hot, turn down the heat, turn down. . .the heat." She grasped the lapels of her kimono and flapped them in and out. The steward stared. He paled. He shook his head rapidly. He fled. To this day, Mrs. McCormick said a generation later, the steward must be going around Japan telling everyone about the American wife who, as soon as her husband had gone to his bed, tried to get the steward into her bed.

The Colonel made his Saturday night broadcast from Tokyo using neither text nor notes. Radio Tokyo's Japanese technician told him, "Very sorry, reception at San Francisco no good." A new circuit was opened and the Colonel made another talk on a completely different subject. One night after dinner he spoke about the problem of growing old. "All my friends are dead," he said.

The Colonel asked to inspect a racially integrated army unit. The Tribune had just published a series of reports by Carl Wiegman on Negro progress and problems in the South, the first by any Chicago paper. The Colonel told the soldiers: "I ask that on your return home you will join with me and others who look upon all Americans as Americans regardless of race to develop a solid and cohesive United States of America."

*　*　*　*　*

While the Colonel was in Tokyo, linotype operators at all five Chicago newspapers struck, demanding changes in the new Taft-Hartley law which curtailed union rights. Union leaders assumed that without typesetters the papers could not publish and the fat strike fund would see the operators through a short strike. The Colonel was flabbergasted. His printers strike? The boys with whom he had played late-night poker? By themselves, Tribune men might not have walked out, but at other papers only one in 10 opposed the strike. The Tribune recruited 60 of its secretaries and stenographers to type copy which was then photo-engraved, a slow process. The first evening the Tribune was cut to 30 pages but by the second day the paper was up to 80 pages. As weeks passed the appearance improved but deadlines for advertisements and features were counted in days rather than in hours and urgent news in hours rather than in minutes. After 22 months the union called off the strike but by then the strike had led to one of the darkest nights in The Tribune's 101 years.

*　　*　　*　　*　　*

In Shanghai Mrs. McCormick became ill. The mayor, K. C. Wu, wartime Minister of Information for Chiang Kai-shek's Nationalist government, supplied doctors and medicine and began a friendship that was to give the childless Colonel deep contentment and to decorate Cantigny with teenage laughter and romance. Mrs. McCormick found a more immediate decoration for Cantigny when she saw in a Shanghai artist's studio a glorious mural some 80 feet long, done in blue and white watercolors with delicate Chinese hunting figures in oil. She borrowed one panel filled with horses and the next morning asked the Colonel what he thought about putting the mural in the Cantigny dining room. The Colonel's eye was drawn to a horse departing the scene. "Oh, I don't know," the Colonel said, "if every evening at dinner I want to look at a picture of President Truman." Mrs. McCormick bought the mural. It runs all the way around the room. Invariably dinner guests mentioned the painting. "Isn't it strange," the Colonel would ask, "that a Chinese painter would put in his picture a portrait of our President?" The guests would search the small figures for a likeness. "Where?" one would ask eventually. "There," the Colonel would say, shooting a pointed finger at the retreating horse. An equal source of fun was the portrait of Nell Gwyn by Sir Peter Lely brought by the Colonel's mother from London and hanging in the sitting room. London's Drury Lane theater actress and mistress of Charles II wears a gown with a low exposing neckline. To one old friend asking the Colonel the name of the lady he replied, "That is Mrs. Bretherton. She runs a dairy in Chicago."

In the Philippines, the U. S. air force commander gave the Colonel a ride in a B-17 Flying Fortress bomber that had been converted for his personal use. The plane's four engines and long range charmed the Colonel. The General told him the United States was disposing of surplus B-17s and the Colonel might be

405

able to buy one for a low price. On his return to Chicago the Colonel asked Thomis to see if a plane could be bought and converted. Thomis found an air force parking lot filled with planes flown only from the factory to the storage field. He bought one for $7,500. The air force threw in four extra engines. Thomis flew the plane to California for conversion. Gasoline pumped from its long-range tanks more than paid delivery costs. In the bomb bay engineers installed two bunks, a desk with a disappearing globe, a half dozen large chairs, a pantry and toilet. The lower half of the glass-nosed double-decked cockpit became, with the addition of two huge spongy chairs, a spectacular perch in the sky. To reach this delightful eyrie, the passenger lay flat and wriggled through a tight tunnel for 10 feet or more. This the Colonel would not do, nor would Maryland McCormick. The imperial box seats thus became available to traveling companions. The unpressurized plane's best traveling altitude, 8,000 feet, was ideal for watching the world go by. American Airlines maintained that plane in its hangars at Midway and supplied the crew led by Captain West. Crossing the Atlantic in the B-17, the Colonel boasted, was less dangerous than walking across Michigan Avenue in front of Tribune Tower or across Broadway in New York City or taking a taxi anywhere in any city. Late one evening in Florida the Colonel asked Captain West to take him to Chicago. The Colonel arrived at the West Palm Beach airport in pajamas and robe, carrying a book. He greeted the crew and tucked himself into a bunk, pulling the curtain. The crew completed its pre-flight task, took off, climbed to 8,000 feet, trimmed the controls, turned on the automatic pilot. West asked the co-pilot to see if the Colonel would like a cup of coffee. In 10 seconds the co-pilot was back. The Colonel was not there! Did he look in the toilet? Yes, not there either! Good God, West said, we've left the Colonel behind. He put the plane into a tight face-about turn and set a new speed record for bringing a plane from runway to the private plane passenger lounge. Out came the Colonel, carrying a newspaper. West met him at the plane steps. "You went off without me, Ho Ho Ho," the Colonel said. He reported that soon after going to bed he reached for a newspaper, remembered he had left it in the lounge, went back to fetch it and saw the plane fly away. He said he knew West would return, in time.

* * * * *

During the early months of 1948, Cissy felt death near. To

make sure The Times-Herald did not fall to the Colonel after her death, Cissy wrote a will giving the paper to seven executives and passing by her only daughter Felicia and Drew Pearson, Washington's most-talked about columnist who had been married for a time to Felicia. Soon Cissy had second thoughts and decided to give the executives money with which they could buy The Times-Herald if they wished. On the afternoon of July 24, 1948, before she signed the new will, her butler found her dead in bed. A doctor blamed Cissy's mixture of sleeping pills and liquor but Washington gossips suspected poison and murder. The tale strengthened when her former treasurer jumped to his death and her former social secretary died of an overdose of sleeping pills. The gossip troubled the Colonel and was later to govern his own actions when he saw his own death approach.

The executives lacked cash needed for inheritance taxes, overdue mechanical improvements and working capital. Personal differences arose. Eugene Meyer again offered to buy The Times-Herald and also Cissy's 202½ non-voting shares in the Tribune Company. The Colonel was alarmed. He had no regrets about the possible removal of The Times-Herald from the family but he did not want Tribune stock to spread. He authorized Wood to negotiate with the heirs, offering to buy The Times-Herald for $4.5 million, the figure offered by Meyer. The Colonel would buy 45 shares of Cissy's stock rights and The Tribune and the employee trusts would buy the 157½. Wood, Willis Nance, a member of the Kirkland law firm, and the heirs agreed on terms. Then Wood asked the heirs to remain until he could report to the Colonel. He and Nance sought security in the National Art Gallery— "the last place anyone would look," Wood remembered.

The Colonel gathered the directors in Chicago without telling them the reason, and flew them to a delightful camp in Tribune woodlands on Manitoulin island near the north shore of Lake Huron where they too would be invisible. Within 10 minutes of landing Canadian police arrived and told the Colonel, his directors and crew that all were under arrest for entering Canada illegally, pointing out that the island strip was not a port of entry. The Colonel telephoned his lawyer in Canada, Terry Flahiff, who sought help from Canada's Secretary of State for External Affairs Lester Pearson. While the pair tried to find some way to free the Colonel, Weymouth Kirkland forwarded Wood's report that the heirs were ready to complete the deal. The Colonel herded his guests into the plane and flew away before the police realized what was happening. A few minutes later Pearson phoned the police to tell them the Canadian government had declared the strip to have become at dawn an international airport and would remain so for 24 hours. How long did the Colonel intend to stay? "He's already gone," the police replied. "Good God," Pearson said, "we didn't mean to drive him out of the country."

The seven heirs accepted the offer, modifying it only to let each man buy at least 10 shares of Cissy's Tribune stock at $35,000 a share. Frank Waldrop, Cissy's editor, who had continued in that position as one of the seven heirs, assumed the Colonel would make him editor-in-chief.

Tribune company directors met at Baie Comeau to approve formally the purchase of The Times-Herald. Jack Flynn whispered to Bazy that she and her husband, Peter Miller, should go to Washington to run the paper. Bazy's "Scottish intuition" told her Jack already had made the suggestion to the Colonel. She asked Peter how he would look upon the appointment. He was agreeable. Bazy told him she would accept only if the move were good for Peter. The Colonel said nothing that day but the next day he told her, "I want you and Peter to go to Washington." "Fine," Bazy said. "We'd love it there." Bazy was 28. She knew little of Washington and national politics.

The Colonel took them to Washington for the announcement of the purchase and the appointment of Bazy as publisher. Miller was assigned to the mechanical side. Peter's brother took over the Peru-LaSalle paper. Cissy's editor, Waldrop, felt betrayed.

*　*　*　*　*

General MacArthur removed himself from the 1948 presidential race. The Colonel adopted Taft as did Illinois voters in the primary. For the vice presidency the Colonel proposed Harold Stassen. The Minnesotan declined, hoping for the top place, unwittingly encouraging Illinois Gov. Dwight Green's own hopes to be given the second place. The party had chosen Green as keynote speaker, a strategic position for winning delegates' support. On the eve of the convention, the Colonel and Mrs. McCormick gave a dinner for Taft and his wife at the Astor Street house. Taft sat on Mrs. McCormick's right. Guests numbered about 20. The next day in Philadelphia Taft invited the McCormicks to a reception. Toward the end Taft asked the Colonel and a few others to come to his suite for a private discussion. The Colonel turned to Mrs. McCormick and said, "Come along, darling." Taft seemed surprised. "She's my wife," the Colonel said. "Oh!" said Taft, "I thought she was your stenographer."

"Taft may have made a good president," Mrs. McCormick said later, "but he lacked the social graces necessary to win a national election."

As delegates gathered in Philadelphia, it became evident that Taft would lose to Dewey. The Colonel, in a final effort, instructed his political writers from Washington, Springfield and Chicago to watch for dirty tricks by Dewey's Eastern banker supporters to snatch Taft votes. George Tagge, The Tribune's state political editor, heard from Illinois delegates that Governor Green was urging them to shift their votes from Taft to Dewey, hoping to entice the Dewey group into supporting Green for the vice presidency. The delegates said that Don Maxwell, the Tribune city editor who led the paper's editorial team at the convention, personally and privately encouraged Green. Tagge thought Green and Maxwell were not following the Colonel, The Tribune and the Illinois primary voters.

Robert McCormick Adams, a member of the Illinois delegation and a relative of Amy McCormick's first husband, told Mrs. McCormick about Green's maneuver. She asked Mary Brooks, wife of Illinois Senator C. Wayland Brooks, if the report were true. Mrs. Brooks asked her husband who confirmed the report. Mrs. McCormick then told the Colonel. He was irate and sent word to Maxwell to have Tagge come to his suite in the Warwick Hotel at once. Maxwell saw personal disaster ahead. He and Walter Trohan, second in command of the Washington bureau, decided that Trohan should go to the Colonel instead of Tagge. Trohan in his memoirs said Maxwell told Tagge to "get lost" although Tagge had no memory of any message and, indeed, learned of the Colonel's request to see him only from Trohan's memoirs. Trohan went to the Colonel, explained he had come because he and Maxwell had been unable to find Tagge and, asked about the maneuver, said the report was untrue. He repeated the denial to Mrs. McCormick. She believed him, thinking that Trohan, reporting the national scene, was not aware of the maneuver in the state delegation, Tagge's preserve. The Colonel was not convinced. He did not, however, ask again to talk with Tagge. Why? Tagge thinks the Colonel did not want to know the unpleasant truth. Mrs. McCormick agrees and further thinks that the Colonel did not chastise Maxwell on the spot because he did not want to make a public spectacle of such disloyalty within The Tribune. Green's keynote speech to a half-empty hall aroused no enthusiasm. His aspirations melted. Tagge was not surprised. He considered Green's chances of becoming Dewey's running mate even poorer than those of Taft in getting the top place.

McCormick remained faithful to Taft. After Dewey achieved a majority of votes and the chairman, as is customary, asked the convention to make the nomination unanimous, the disgruntled Colonel left the hall, letting his alternate give that distasteful vote to Dewey. The second place went to California Gov. Earl Warren.

Worse was to come. Polls indicated Dewey would win the November election. Even Chicago's most sanguine Democratic politician, Jake Arvey, thought Truman would lose. He liked Ike, General Eisenhower. The Colonel doubted the accuracy of the polls and asked Wayne Thomis to take time off from an aviation errand in New York City and look into the political situation there. Thomis knew little of politics and nothing of New York politics. The city Republican headquarters loaded him with reports proving Dewey would sweep the city but Thomis, making a round of precinct offices, found the Republicans lackadaisical and confident whereas Democrats were working hard. He reported to the Colonel the Democrats probably would sweep the city. The report did not appear in the paper.

In November the linotype operators were still on strike. The production department had beaten mechanical problems and again was putting out a full paper but the early editorial deadlines remained. Pat Maloney, the managing editor, saw the early deadlines as a serious challenge. Each evening The Tribune printed a series of country editions timed to meet trains and trucks departing on all-night runs. Maloney knew that distant readers on opening The Tribune in the morning would want to know who won, but only skimpy results would be received by the new early first country edition deadline. Maloney encouraged Washington bureau chief Arthur Sears Henning to chart previous election returns. Most of the early results come from heavily Democratic city precincts but during the night the Democratic lead shrinks as Republican areas report. The speed with which the lead narrows indicates whether the lines will cross and give the Republicans the victory.

True to form the first results gave the Democrats a lead but not of such size that could not be overcome during the night. Henning, encouraged to believe in his own and other polls, wrote the lead story headlined flatly: "Dewey Defeats Truman." Maloney ordered the pressmen to print the first country edition.

The Colonel and Mrs. McCormick had been invited to a dinner party and then to an election night party at WGN studios. The Colonel told Mrs. McCormick he felt a cold coming on and would stay at the Astor Street house and go to bed early. Deprived of his candidate, he did not care which nominee won. As Mrs. McCormick said goodnight the Colonel commented ambiguously that the "early returns are significant." He was neither elated nor depressed. The Colonel had a direct phone line to The Tribune from his bedside but whether he used it during the night no one now knows.

About 11 p.m. Maloney went home. By then reports were not giving Republicans the gains needed to bring them a victory. Maxwell stopped the presses and substituted a new lead story concentrating on state and local races. The new headline was: "Democrats Make Sweep of State Offices." By then 35,000 copies of the wrong story had been printed.

At the WGN party Henning told anyone who asked, "Everything will come out all right." Whether he was speaking about Dewey or himself no one is certain.

In the morning President Truman held up with rare glee for the cameras of the world a copy of the "Dewey wins" edition. Foes of the Colonel's blamed him personally for the wrong story and headline proving, they said, that the Colonel ran The Tribune on prejudice with no respect for truth. That evening a guard heard a gunshot in the Colonel's office. He ran in and saw the Colonel put a revolver into a drawer. The bullet had pierced the ceiling. The Colonel said not a word of explanation and the guard left without a word of questioning.

Tribune employees waited for the Colonel's ax but nothing happened. The Colonel wrote a note to Thomis: "Thank you for your accurate reports." Henning continued to head the Washington bureau and was followed by Trohan. Maloney continued as managing editor but he had lost confidence in himself. He became depressed. A prostate operation was followed by severe hemorrhages. He told the Colonel he could no longer do his work properly and asked to resign. The Colonel told him to take a year off and then "come up to the 24th floor with me." The Colonel forgave Maxwell his convention disloyalty and when Maloney became ill appointed Maxwell to be managing editor. As his own health deteriorated, he named Maxwell in his will as one of five trustees, leading to Maxwell's succeeding the Colonel as editor of the Chicago Tribune.

People who did not know the Colonel were surprised by the Colonel's steadfastness toward his executives. Not Mrs. McCormick. "Bert," she commented years later, "was never one to cry over spilled milk."

* * * * *

After the communists took over Shanghai, Mayor Wu, who had helped Mrs. McCormick defeat a fever during the Far Eastern tour, wrote the Colonel that he and his wife were planning to move to Formosa with Chiang's government but he did not know what to do with his two daughters. Wu, a Christian, had had the girls baptized and had given each an English as well as a Chinese name. The elder, 18, was Eileen and Hsiu Yung, the name of a variety of geranium. Edith, a year younger, was Hsiu Hwei, a variety of orchid.

The Colonel, without consulting his wife, cabled Wu: "Send the girls to me." The girls arrived, each with a small suitcase into which had been tightly folded 100 silk Chinese dresses. The girls, pretty as their names and so tiny that Mrs. McCormick said they could be hung on a Christmas tree, charmed the Colonel. He made them his legal wards. They spoke little English but the Colonel persuaded Roscoe "Rocky" Miller, president of Northwestern University, to enroll them. Within a few weeks the girls were fluent in English and ended the year near the top of their class.

The sisters lived during the week in a university dormitory and came home to the Colonel at Cantigny or Astor Street or Boynton Beach for weekends and vacation. Their gaiety brought a lightness into the household. Every night each chose a long Chinese dress for dinner. One of light green silk delicately embroidered became a favorite with the Colonel. He summoned a Tribune photographer and put Edith's picture in the paper. He repeated the process whenever either girl produced a new dress he thought exceptional. The girls called the McCormicks uncle and aunt; the Colonel delighted in the unaccustomed role. Boys and girls came and went. "It's like Grand Central Station around

413

here," he told Eileen one day. The voice was gruff, as always, but Eileen sensed his kindness and pleasure.

On Chinese Nationalist Day at Northwestern, Eileen met a young Chinese engineer, Yi Yuan Yu, completing a doctorate. He came to call at Cantigny. The Colonel opened the door. "Who are you?" he demanded of the stranger. "I'm Yu," the visitor said. "What?" the startled Colonel asked. "I'm Yu," the visitor repeated. The Colonel was silent for a moment and then laughed, "Ho Ho Ho!"—31 years later Eileen produced a faithful facsimile of the Colonel's laugh—"You must be Eileen's beau." In the spring Yu did not return to China but joined the faculty of George Washington University in St. Louis, continued courting Eileen by telephone, mail and visits and proposed marriage. Eileen asked permission of her father who had become governor of Formosa. He did not like the prospect of her dropping out of university at 20 but asked the Colonel what sort of man Yu is. The Colonel replied: "He looks you straight in the eye," a considerable feat for a man who barely reached the Colonel's shoulder. The father relented and the mother came to Chicago bringing a regal dress, white, rich with embroidery, a train that swirled around the tiny feet.

The bride asked the Colonel to give her away and the bridegroom asked the British consul-general, Sir Berkeley Gage, who had become a friend of the Wus when he was in the diplomatic service in China, to be best man. The bride wanted a Christian wedding. The Colonel asked the Rev. Dr. Stewart to grant her the wish. There was one small problem. The groom had not been baptised. Doctor Bob took care of that the day before the wedding, christening him Rutherford Berkeley Yu. The bridegroom answered to the name at the wedding service but never again, the Colonel addressing him subsequently as YY. After the wedding in the Cantigny garden the Colonel cut the cake using a long thin ceremonial sword. He also provided the champagne. Yu remembered a generation later that the 200 guests drank 44 bottles.

Reporters and photographers were everywhere. Henry Luce, long-time foe of the Colonel, sent a squad from Time and Life, encouraging the Colonel to tell Eileen, "For the first time, Henry and I are at peace." As she said goodbye, the Colonel sadly told her, "Everyone is leaving me, even my Eileen," Not much later her parents came to the United States, settling in Atlanta, the younger daughter joining them there. Cantigny lost its girlish laughter.

The B-17 let the Colonel fly the world but could not shorten his most frequent journey—between Cantigny and Tribune Tower. Wayne Thomis told the Colonel one day that the strip of wasteland in Lake Michigan off the Loop created for the 1933 World's Fair could be developed into a landing field only a few hundred yards from Tribune Tower. During the war, he said, he had flown from strips a lot shorter. "If you think you can get a field, go ahead," the Colonel said. Thomis began writing pieces for the paper and speaking to important people in city hall and at the Federal Aviation Authority about the advantages a downtown field would bring Chicago, although at the time he saw few regular users other than the Colonel. The park district declared the project impossible, but Thomis persisted until the FAA gave its approval for a 4,000 foot runway and contributed $8 million. The field was built. "It will be called McCormick airport," Thomis reported to the Colonel. He was pleased. But after a minute or so he suggested that it be named instead for Merrill Meigs, publisher of the Sunday supplement, coast to coast, for the rival Hearst newspapers and a flying enthusiast who accompanied the Colonel on several short hops. The Colonel never explained why he wanted a name other than his but Thomis, after years of thought, speculated that the Colonel suspected his name on the field would provoke snorts from critics that he had used public money to make his life easier. "The Colonel was a fox," Thomis reflected.

The Colonel was much more deeply disturbed by reports that important Democrats were about to name Chicago's big new airport, becoming the busiest in the world, for General Marshall. The Colonel's objections were not political, even though the former chief of staff had become out of favor with him. The Colonel was appalled that thousands of travelers daily would speak the name of the rival publisher of The Sun, Marshall Field. The Colonel announced the airport must carry the name of a Chicago hero. He remembered Butch O'Hare and his one-plane attack on a Japanese battleship. It is his name that tens of thousands of travelers daily speak.

For the short hop between home and work, Thomis chose an Aero-Commander after proving its reliability by flying it on one engine from the factory in Oklahoma to Washington. The Colonel found the seating cramped until Thomis installed one large overstuffed chair.

The Colonel often worked until after dark. On such evenings

Thomis used lights from cars on Chicago's Outer Drive to guide him in and out of unlighted Meigs Field. On one such evening at Cantigny, Farm Foreman Henderson drove his car with its lights on to one end of the strip. The plane arrived, passed over the strip and circled. Thomis radioed Tribune Tower, asking at which end of the strip was the car. The Tower telephoned Cantigny. Henderson brought a second car for the other end. As days shortened, the Colonel installed a strong light at each end, wired from his house. One Monday before flying to Washington, the Colonel told Edwards, "We need some lights." He returned Friday to a still unlighted field and asked Eddie, "Where are my lights?" Eddie said he had brought in engineers who told him that lights would cost $8,000. The Colonel said, "Eddie, I did not ask you how much lights would cost. I said we needed lights." Cantigny got lights. The Colonel sometimes said the runway should be paved but Howard Wood, who wrote the checks, always found some reason to defer that very costly project.

Pilots urged that a venerable oak near one end of the strip be taken down. The Colonel abided by his rule that no Cantigny tree be cut so long as it put out one green leaf until one gusty day the tree's outstretched arms almost clutched the plane. "Cut it," Colonel said. Eddie went at dawn with ax and saw. The tree resisted. Years earlier the Colonel had strengthened it with a solid core of concrete. It yielded only to a husky charge of dynamite.

On one Atlantic crossing, using the great circle route penetrated by the *'Untin' Bowler*, the Colonel detoured across Labrador to see Hamilton Falls. It lived up to his expectations as a mighty source of power, but he concluded it was "too far from civilization" to permit economic development. After his death, world need for iron ore put the Falls to work. Coming into Iceland to refuel, the Colonel found the thick fog that defeated the *Bowler* now was centered on the airport although the remainder of the island was clear. The plane circled for two hours waiting for the fog to rise to 200 feet and let Captain West bring it in. Icelanders, proud of having the first parliament in the world, took the Colonel to a natural amphitheater where the meetings had been held centuries earlier. The Colonel was more impressed with a nearby pond into which, he was told, Vikings threw unfaithful wives.

* * * * *

The Colonel flew into Canada at any time of day or night and expected customs and immigration officers to be on hand, causing problems for his executives. Coming home from Europe one year, Captain West landed at Gander, Newfoundland, about 2 a.m. to refuel. The ground crew told West the plane must wait until the day shift came to work. West demurred. Loud voices, American and Canadian, awakened the Colonel. He came to the plane steps in dressing gown and pajamas. Told of the problem, the Colonel loudly proclaimed, "What else can you expect from a batch of inbred bastards!" Only a direct order from Canada's minister of transport, aroused by Lawyer Flahiff from his bed, produced fuel.

On a self-assignment to Argentina as part of a Latin American tour, the Colonel and Mrs. McCormick were invited by the Perons to their country place. Peron wore his gaucho outfit, trousers tucked into low boots. The Perons were charming. Mrs. McCormick came away thinking their romance was one of the great love stories. On return to Buenos Aires the Colonel, a guest of Dr. Alberto Gainza Paz, South America's most effective publisher and a political foe of Peron, began relating to Gainza Paz some of Peron's achievements. "But, Colonel, he is a dictator," the Argentinian said. "Argentina is not ready for democracy," the Colonel persisted. Gainza Paz poured out a list of Peron's abuses. The Colonel would not accept them. Finally the Argentinian said, "Colonel, don't you know Peron's model is Franklin Roosevelt?" The Colonel's rebuttal ceased.

The State Department asked the Colonel, while passing through Cuba, to meet with Baptista. The Cuban dictator set the meeting for midnight, long after the Colonel's usual bedtime. The Colonel made the call and came away with a deep dislike. "He's an awful man," the Colonel reported. The State Department asked the Colonel to call again on Baptista during a later trip. "Never," the Colonel said.

*   *   *   *   *

In the summer of 1950 communist North Korea invaded South Korea. President Truman authorized General MacArthur to use American military forces in Japan to support the South Koreans. The Colonel accused the President of usurping the powers of Congress and making an illegal declaration of war but tempered his charges as American forces under MacArthur drove the North Korean army back to the border with China. North Korea did not seek peace as MacArthur expected. Instead com-

417

munist China sent 300,000 soldiers across the Yalu River into North Korea. The 105,000 Americans retreated, fast. MacArthur asked permission to bomb Chinese bases across the border. Truman refused. The Colonel accused the President of adopting a no-win policy and demanded he resign. The President fired MacArthur. The Colonel exploded. He demanded Congress impeach the President. "America," he said, "is led by a fool surrounded by knaves." General MacArthur came home to a hero's welcome, reviving the Colonel's hope for the General's being nominated in 1952, but the cause died from lack of support.

The Colonel flew to Europe to visit General Eisenhower at his headquarters outside Paris as commander-in-chief of NATO forces. Quite a few Americans, both Republican and Democrat, again were urging Eisenhower to become their candidate. The Colonel was only mildly warm. He called the General I-too-Ike. He still preferred Senator Taft and on returning home he gave a luncheon for Taft on the Cantigny lawn. One of Mrs. McCormick's women friends found President Herbert Hoover, a guest, very personable. "Marry him," Mrs. McCormick teased, "and I'll give you the linen from my former marriage (to Henry Hooper). It's already embroidered HH." At the convention Hoover persuaded Mrs. McCormick to tell Taft he was not as popular as the Colonel and Taft himself reckoned and he should step aside in favor of General Eisenhower. She went to Taft's hotel suite. Taft was aghast. "Stassen has promised to stay with me until the third ballot," he said. Eisenhower won on the first ballot. The Colonel suggested that Republicans and Democrats who wanted a change in policies vote for candidates of either party who would provide it and produced a partial list of such men but there was no response. General Eisenhower became the president. The Colonel was pleased by Eisenhower's ending the Korean War which, no cheap victory as Truman first predicted, cost 20,000 American lives. He approved also of Eisenhower's taking the American fleet out of Formosan waters, ending wage controls and endorsing the completion of the St. Lawrence Seaway, making Chicago a world port. The Colonel could relax. The administration was finally on course—well, almost on course. "All of us fervently hope," the Colonel said, "to see a rebirth of Americanism."

25. Seventy—Time for Bold New Projects
1950—1952

For the Colonel's 70th birthday in 1950 Maryland McCormick arranged a spectacular party at Cantigny. The July evening was perfect. In late afternoon as the 350 guests gathered, soft clouds slowly floated by, dappling the lawn and making redundant the large striped tent raised beyond Madison's Montpelier porch to shelter the satin-covered tables. As twilight faded, a full moon, right on schedule, spread its soft light over the gardens and for a quarter of an hour turned into shining gold the highest leaves on the great elms planted by the Colonel 30 years earlier. Hundreds of Chinese lanterns came alight. "Bert must have led a good life to get a night like this," Mrs. McCormick said.

The Colonel and Mrs. McCormick welcomed the guests as they arrived at Architect Coolidge's Grecian pillared front porch. A plane swooped out of the sky with the William Randolph Hearsts and the Jack Knights. Waiters by the platoon brought treat after treat. For this special night, Elizabeth's simple menu card was replaced by a large eight-page souvenir booklet offering:

Cocktails   *Hors d'oeuvres*

Grande Romaine Salmon   *Golden Lemon*

Relishes   *Cheeses and wafers*   *Fresh vegetables*

Assorted Fruits

Chopped Chicken Liver Pineapple Mold

Potato Aspic Salad Mold

Molded Chicken Salad   *Molded Lobster Salad*

Hot and Cold Decorated Baked Virginia Smithfield Hams

Hot and Cold Garnished Roast Vermont Tom Turkeys

Hot and Cold Decorated Baked Sugar Cured Hams

Lobster a la Newburg in Flaming Dish

Creamed Parsley Potato Balls

Steamed Wild Rice with Mushrooms

Baked Sweet Potatoes a la Roxy

Dr. Stewart gave the invocation. Everyone sang the "Star Spangled Banner" and "Happy Birthday." Lawyer Kirkland called for the toast to long life and good health. Bazy read the good wishes of the board of directors and presented a bulldog puppy the directors already had christened Tribby to join Buster Boo. A handsome black Arabian horse, gift of King Saud, was skittish after six weeks at sea and a long rail journey. The Colonel passed the gift on to Bazy, already a leading breeder of Arabian horses. General MacArthur telegraphed: "May your shadow never decrease." The Colonel, already studying how Cantigny could be preserved, promised: "Those left behind me will see that Cantigny, family home of all the Medills, is maintained."

There was dancing. The Colonel led Cartoonist Joe Parrish's wife Ludean, in her new blue taffeta dress, to a canoe floating on the swiming pool. He handed her into the fragile, tipsy craft, stepped in, knelt Indian fashion behind her and paddled around the pool. Something always happened to Ludean at Cantigny parties. At another the Colonel asked if any woman could milk a cow. Only Ludean and Dr. Cutter's wife could boast of the skill. Up came a cowman with two Guernseys and two white stools. "Prove it," the Colonel said. They did.

*   *   *   *   *

Often when flying over the tumultuous Manicouagan River, the Colonel considered how its mighty torrents could be put to work. Many other pioneers had had similar thoughts but all had put them aside reasoning that the cost of mastering the river would exceed the value of the power. For a dozen years the Manicouagan had served the Colonel helping to bring logs out of the wilderness. One day the Colonel had Sewell drive him to the river. He stood for a long time looking into the torrent. He returned to the car. "Arthur," he said, "I am going to tame this river." He had good reason. The Outardes turbines were using all of the water brought through the wooden pipe, and the Baie Comeau mill and town were using all of the power the turbines could produce. If one turbine failed, the mill must close until the turbine could be repaired. The Baie Comeau and Thorold mills operated night and day but together they could provide only three-fourths of the paper used by The Tribune and The News— a half million tons a year, one-twelfth of all paper used by all American newspapers. Without more power the Baie Comeau mill could not be expanded and Baie Comeau was condemned to continue as a one-company town, a community too small to justify an all-weather airport, a paved road from Quebec, television, sports. Baie Comeau could achieve its destiny only if the Colonel found a way to master the Manicouagan.

For the Colonel 45 years dropped away. Once again he was wresting power from the Chicago River reversed to flow not into Lake Michigan but uphill into the Mississippi. Learning how to put the placid canal to work had been his kindergarten course; the Manicouagan would be his doctorate.

If a river flows out of a vast lake as does the Niagara and plunges over a cliff as does the Niagara, man need only carve a powerhouse into the foot of the falls and divert water through a steep tunnel into the powerhouse. The lake maintains a steady flow of water all year. If a river flows through a deep canyon as does the Colorado, man need only dam the canyon and let the water back up, providing both storage and a drop to the turbines.

The Manicouagan had no lake, no canyon. In early summer as the snow melted, the Manicouagan was more forceful than the Niagara but in mid-winter it was little more than a creek. As the river approached the end of the wooded plateau it passed through a tilted saucer with chips in its rim before falling 100 feet to the St. Lawrence. In winter water dribbled through the chips and trickled down the steep rocky face. In summer water flooded over the edge of the saucer and jumped and raced and bounced and tumbled in a broad cascade.

Engineers debated for months how best to turn the saucer into a storage lake big enough to hold water needed in winter for the turbines and to retain logs until they could be flumed to the Baie Comeau mill. Ten proposals dropped into the Colonel's waste basket. Then 10 more. Number 24 looked good, 25 was almost right. The Colonel studied plan 26. This was it!

The Colonel opened an office in Montreal under Schmon to place orders and hire men. He sent Traffic Manager Fred Byington to organize delivery of 140,000 tons of equipment and supplies, enough—The Tribune's North Shore historian Carl Wiegman reckoned—to fill a railroad train 43 miles long.

As soon as the ice began breaking up in the river just before Easter, a boat set off from Montreal with a housekeeping crew to open the nine tarpaper shanties that had served the Outardes dam workmen nine years earlier and to have a hot meal ready for the construction crews on their arrival. On Easter Monday the first work crews came ashore in small boats and found the shacks deserted; the housekeepers were locked in a fog somewhere on the St. Lawrence. The crews built a ramp to receive barges bringing supplies. The housekeepers arrived. Bulldozers began hacking out the site for the mill and roads. Houses fairly popped up out of the rock.

Frequently the Colonel left Chicago by train for Montreal, met with Byington over a buffalo steak at The Ritz and said "Goodnight, Fred. Get me a crock." In the morning the Colonel rode the Atlantic Limited train along the South Shore to Rimouski and then took the overnight boat to Baie Comeau, the captain providing one of the boat's two cabins. The Colonel was on deck when the ship arrived before dawn. He had a sailor hose him down on deck or dived into the river never far above freezing. If the boat stayed overnight to unload, he slept aboard. If it left, he rode a converted sailboat five miles to the English River fishing camp where Ludger Boudreault acted as a perfect servant to the seigneur.

To drain the saucer, miners carved a tunnel 1,000 feet long and 35 feet in diameter sloping downward from a low part within the saucer to the St. Lawrence, leaving a plug at each end. They packed four tons of explosives into the lower plug and 14 tons into the upper one. Early in December, the Colonel and Maryland flew to Baie Comeau. On a platform three-quarters of a mile away, Mrs. McCormick pressed a golden button. The river growled as small charges burst deep within the rocks, shattering the granite. Then the main charge brought a sharp crack. Rock erupted into a 300-foot-high gray fountain. Before the dust settled, engineers ran to the wound torn in the rock. They looked. They cheered. The blast had cleared away the lower plug. Again Mrs. McCormick pressed the button and again the earth roared like an angry lion prodded a second time. Then a crack like that of a bolt of summer lightning. From the saucer bed, boulders floated up and up and up, some as high as 700 feet, before falling back to earth in a gentle curve and a final smack. The blast gathered water into a wall 30 feet high and rolled it across the saucer in a fan-shaped tidal wave. As the power spent itself, water flowed back, swirled into a great whirlpool and dived into the sloping tunnel to the St. Lawrence.

Before darkness settled over the forest, workmen began erecting forms around the chipped rim of the now-dry saucer. They knew the rim must be patched and raised before the ice broke in the spring and brought into the saucer more water than the tunnel could carry. Arctic rampages did not stop the work and men removed the last forms one week before the spring thaw. By then other crews had built a powerhouse beside the St. Lawrence and miners had dug two more tunnels to bring water into the turbines from the heightened, enlarged saucer.

Everyone concerned agreed on a name for the structure—McCormick Dam.

During the summer the saucer became a lake five miles wide and 11 miles long, guaranteeing an all-year supply four times the flow needed for the two turbines. The powerhouse and the mill could be expanded to meet every foreseeable need. Baie Comeau was now ready to move into its second chapter.

"My work is done," the Colonel said. "Other enterprises will come to Baie Comeau after I am gone from this world."

*   *   *   *   *

The meeting of the American Newspaper Publishers' Association in Chicago and the 1952 Republican convention were reasons for more parties at Cantigny. The GOP guests included Hedda Hopper, her hat announcing her support for Taft, Irene Dunne playing safe with an uncommitted elephant on her hat, movie producer Cecil B. DeMille, John Wayne, Clare Boothe Luce and, out of the long past, Alice Roosevelt Longworth, and, from the war, General Wedemeyer. The Colonel missed the party. He had just undergone a prostate operation and dark memories of the 1948 double debacle were still too fresh to make renewal of political acquaintances a welcome prospect.

There were occasional small dinner parties. Sometimes the gold dinner service was brought to Cantigny from the Astor Street house although the insurance lapsed when the pieces left the supposed security of downtown Chicago for the assumed lawlessness of the countryside. One evening the Colonel sat at the side of the table. "Why aren't you at the head?" Frederick William Specht, chairman of Armour and a new neighbor, asked. The Colonel answered, "Where MacGregor sits is head of the table."

For one party the Colonel had moose meat flown from Canada. A report in the social columns alerted officials on both sides of the border, who notified the Colonel that moose meat must not be taken out of Canada nor brought into the United States. The Colonel paid the fines.

The Colonel delighted in exhibiting Cantigny's beauties and innovations to visitors, especially those from abroad. He assumed that the prime minister of newly independent, poorly fed, non-alcoholic Moslem Pakistan would be interested in ways to increase farm production. The Colonel had Edwards line up the newest equipment and arrange displays to show how Cantigny earned bonuses from its fields and herds. "We'll come out right after lunch," the Colonel said. At 5 p.m. Eddie sent a messenger asking if he could let the men start on their evening chores. "Put the men to work," the Colonel replied. "All the son of a bitch wants to do is drink."

* * * * *

Bazy thrived in Washington. Looking back, Bazy said the Colonel found her hard to handle. "The situation was like that of a father with a precocious child," Bazy recalled. One day she learned that Secretary of State Dean Acheson and Alger Hiss walked together most mornings. She sent a photographer to waylay them and ran the photo. The Colonel carried the clipping for days and showed it around proudly. But if someone else told him about something outstanding Bazy had done he replied: "She's getting too big for her britches."

On the Colonel's instructions Bazy kept Waldrop as editor. He resented being second in command and began undermining the Colonel's confidence in Bazy. Small differences also developed between Bazy and the Colonel. "I didn't know how to step down," Bazy recalled. "I lacked experience." A big difference arose when Bazy developed a special friendship with a reporter, Garvin Tankersley. The romance revived Washington gossip about Cissy and her affairs. Bazy divorced Peter, giving him her share of the LaSalle-Peru paper and custody of their children. Tankersley divorced his wife, she receiving a quarter of a million dollars. The Colonel, displeased, brought Garvin Tankersley to Chicago hoping to cool the romance, just as 40 years earlier his mother had hoped to break the Colonel's desire for Amie by sending him to Russia. He had no more success than had his mother.

424

In April of 1951 the Colonel asked Bazy, after less than two years in Washington, to come to Chicago for a discussion. She found Maloney and Tribune Lawyer Kirkland in the office with the Colonel. She knew Maryland McCormick for some time had carried Washington gossip to the Colonel. Bazy was confident she could have "cited chapter and verse to disprove the allegations but had not done so knowing that such acts would set the Colonel against Maryland."

The Colonel asked abruptly: "Are you going to marry Tankersley?"

"That question does not concern the paper," Bazy replied. "It concerns only me personally."

"It does concern the paper," the Colonel said. "If you marry Tankersley, you will have to leave the paper."

"I don't see why," Bazy said. "I am divorced. Tank is divorced. We are free to marry whomever we choose."

The Colonel repeated that she would have to leave the paper if she married Tankersley.

"I see nothing wrong," she said. "You married two divorced women."

"The difference," the Colonel said sharply, "is that they got the divorces."

Bazy sensed that the Colonel would not change his position.

"Well," she said, "may I buy the paper?"

The proposition surprised the Colonel but after only a brief delay he said, "All right." He told Kirkland, "You and Bazy go into the next room and see what you can work out."

Bazy and the lawyer left but before they could get down to critical details, Maloney came in.

"The Colonel says no," he reported.

Bazy knew the word was final. Without speaking again to the Colonel—"I sensed he could not tell me no to my face"—she left The Tribune, returned to Washington, resigned from The Times-Herald, married Tankersley and devoted herself to "doing what I enjoy most—raising Arabian horses." She did continue to be a director of Tribune Company and at board meetings continued to sit on the Colonel's left with Mary King Patterson next to her.

The Colonel assumed direction of The Times-Herald, sent executives from Chicago and made the paper a weak copy of The Tribune. The Colonel and Mrs. McCormick rented a Washington apartment. Mrs. McCormick, with the prospect of becoming a leading capital hostess, urged the Colonel to rent or buy a large

425

house. He refused but he spent $4 million on a new printing plant. The paper flopped about and lost a half million dollars a year. The Colonel's long-standing distaste for Washington and the tax spenders grew. He hated the days he had to be there and saw no good future for The Times-Herald.

* * * * *

The Colonel flew across North Africa to India where Jawaharlal Nehru told him the Colonel's editorials about the British empire had fed his aspirations for independence. The Colonel flew to Central and South America and confirmed his belief that control of the Panama Canal was vital to America's future. In a bar at Belem he studied a painting of an Amazon warrior and asked why her right breast had been cut off. "To eliminate an impediment to her use of the bow," he was told. Finally the Colonel's curiosity took him to Africa, from governor-general's palace to governor-general's palace on invitation of British Colonial Secretary Oliver Lyttelton. Two staff foreign correspondents —Veysey, who had made the arrangements, and Gwen Morgan— were to join the party at Roberts Field, a former American air base in Liberia. In the Colonel's party coming from the United States were Mrs. McCormick, his secretary Dorothy Murray and his Japanese valet Shin. Captain West's crew included co-pilot and navigator. The South Atlantic flight required so much gasoline that Captain West worried about getting the overloaded plane off the runway at Recife, Brazil, but the stout plane met the challenge. At 8,000 feet Captain West trimmed the controls, turned on the automatic pilot and set course for Africa. Well on his way he reached for the ship's papers. They were gone. He searched the cockpit. No papers! Where had he last seen them? At the tower in Recife. West told the Colonel they must return. They could refuel and start again immediately or wait until the next day. The Colonel said they would stay overnight.

West now faced a very serious problem. He would arrive at Recife with much more gasoline than was recommended for a safe landing. The plane had no ability to dump gas. Either he could fly circles for several hours until the fuel was used or he could take a chance. He did not put the question to the Colonel. He flew straight into Recife and landed most gently. He never did tell the Colonel.

The Tribune's Latin American correspondent, Jules Dubois, had guided the Colonel through Central America. After saying goodbye to the party at Recife, Dubois settled his nerves in a hotel bar. He was startled by the Colonel's reappearance. Miss Murray later asked the Colonel, "Did you notice that Jules was stinking drunk?" The Colonel, who knew of the strain his presence imposed on some correspondents, answered, "I'd have done the same thing myself."

The remainder of the trip followed the schedule, more or less, but before every flight when West came into the cabin and said, "We're ready to go, Colonel," the Colonel asked, "Got the ship's papers, Howard?"

At Kampala in Uganda a British Comet, the world's first jet passenger plane, zipped in on a tropical test, landing near the Flying Fortress. The Comet pilot proudly said he had come from London at 450 miles an hour. The B-17 was plowing along at 170. Times indeed were changing. The Colonel was being outrun 3 to 1 by the British! Perhaps he too should move ahead.

Preparing to land on coming home into Chicago the Colonel, cleaning out his desk on the plane for customs examination, found a parcel. "What's this?" he asked. "Miss Murray's girdle," Mrs. McCormick quickly replied. The Colonel dropped the parcel "as though it were a hot cake." The Customs also ignored the parcel, fortunately, because in it were egret feathers Mrs. McCormick had been given. Importation into the United States was forbidden by law.

In four years the Colonel had flown 265,000 miles. "I have flown my last long journey," the Colonel reported but added, "Or have I?"

A thorough inspection of the B-17 revealed corrosion in the wings. Thomis already had noted a tendency of the engines to run away, a mishap which could break a propellor and wreck the plane. He recommended that the Colonel trade the B-17 for a Convair, hardly a jet-age craft and no globe girder but efficient for fast movement within America. The Colonel agreed. A mapping company bought the B-17. An engine did run away while the plane was mapping the Arizona desert, a propellor blade did break and did smack into the plane, cutting the fuel line. Spilled gas caught fire. The pilot ordered the co-pilot and photographer to jump, stayed at the controls until the pair were safely in the air, then jumped. His chute did not open. The B-17, one of the hardiest planes ever built, circled slowly on three engines gradually descending. The fire burned itself out and the plane brought itself to earth gently, skidding through the soft desert. No pilot ever made a better belly landing than did the pilotless B-17.

* * * * *

From the moment the Colonel saw the Wright brothers magically rise into the sky no one ever heard him say a harsh word about a plane or a pilot. Woe to any car or train or ship or horse that did not start on command and arrive on schedule but in the air neither fog, rain, wind nor snow disturbed him. Three times the Colonel had walked away unhurt from a crashed plane. Companions might turn white with fright as the plane tossed and slewed in a rainstorm but the Colonel sat there, confidently reading a book. A typhoon flooded and darkened the Manila airport the night the Colonel was ending his Philippine visit but for two hours the Colonel sat in ankle-deep water waiting for the storm to abate and the Pan American plane to land. He opened a small leather case he called "the jewel box," from it lifted three large decanters of scotch and passed them out into the darkness to other intrepid souls. The flasks came back empty along with a chorus of thanks. Flying was for him immune from human criticism. Perhaps the Colonel reckoned that man was not meant to fly and that in becoming free of the earth human beings achieved the miraculous powers the ancient Greeks ascribed only to their gods.

* * * * *

The Yale-Harvard football game annually enticed the Colonel. Now and then he yielded. In 1953 the game coincided with the 50th reunion of his class. He flew to New York, rented a private railroad car and invited classmates to join in the pilgrimage for what he labeled their trignitaquinquennial. He had Marion Schroeder, WGN librarian, put together a booklet of old college songs. "Next week I am going to be 50 years younger for a few days," he told Marion. He signed the book "From Rubberfoot," and recalled collegiate names of other classmates. Coffey had been Demitasse; Barber, Doc; Marshall, Chief Justice; Lamb, Ba; Van Dyke, Dutch.

The gray and balding alumni, translated back to Mory's for a day, left New York singing old class songs:

"There's nineteen two and nineteen four, There's bound

428

*to be a lot of nineteens more, But nineteen three is the best
company That ever came to the university."*
and:

*"Well, here we are: well, here we are! Just watch us roll-
ling up a score! We'll leave those fellows behind so far, They
won't want to play us anymore! We've hope and faith in Eli
Yale: to win we cannot fail! Well, a Boola Boo, Boola Boola,
Boo, Boola Boo, Boola Boola Boo."*

At New Haven the railroad parked the car in a noisy part of
the yards eliciting some hard words from the Colonel until Fred
Byington, the Colonel's ever-helpful traffic manager, persuaded
the railroad to shift the car to a less noisy place. Police restored
high spirits by providing a non-stop escort to the Yale Bowl with
sirens and alums in full voice.

* * * *

In 1954 Kent Cooper, the Colonel's long-time friend who since
retiring as head of the Associated Press had lived in a grace and
favor house on the Colonel's Florida estate, sent a note on his
own initiative to Eugene Meyer at the Washington Post telling
him he thought the Colonel would sell The Times-Herald if he
could recover the purchase price and the cost of the new plant.
Meyer, more certain than ever that his Post would thrive only if
it were the sole morning paper, told Cooper he would pay that
price but nothing must be said until the deal was signed. Cooper
reported to the Colonel who sent Wood and Nance to work out
details with Meyer's son-in-law, Philip Graham. The Colonel
called a Tribune board meeting at The Times-Herald without explaining the purpose. Bazy was present as a major stockholder
and director.

The Colonel asked Wood if he had an announcement. Wood reported the proposal worked out with Graham. The Colonel asked
directors for opinions on whether The Tribune should sell to
Meyer. The directors, starting on the Colonel's right, each said he
thought the sale a good idea until Mary King's turn came. She
said she did not like the idea at all but would go along with the
sale if all of the others wanted it. Bazy was last. She said she was
appalled at the prospect of giving the leftish Post a morning monopoly in Washington. The Tribune, she said, was abdicating its
conservative political responsibilities and ignoring the fate of the
Times-Herald employees. The paper, she said, had turned a

corner and had become financially sound. "The paper is doing well," Bazy said. "I think we should keep it."

"But I have decided to sell," the Colonel said sharply.

Bazy asked if she could buy the paper and save it.

"No," the Colonel said flatly.

Mary King spoke up. "I think," she said slowly but firmly, "we have a moral responsibility to Bazy and to the staff and should give her an opportunity to buy it and keep it from being swallowed up."

The Colonel relented. He told Bazy he would give her 48 hours to raise the money, cautioning her not to tell anyone of Meyer's offer nor the reason for her effort. Bazy tried to call Jesse Jones. He was ill. She talked briefly with Jones' nephew but could not explain the situation. The nephew reported that Jones was not interested. The deadline passed. Meyer got the paper. The Times-Herald disappeared and The Post became dominant in the Capital and rich. Later The Times-Herald advertising manager, Frank Gatewood, told Bazy that The Post's advertising manager had told him that before the purchase The Post was "on the ropes" and about to fold. Jesse Jones told Bazy that had he known the facts he would have supplied the money. Bazy's bitterness was sharpest against Cooper.

"I felt terrible," Bazy recalled. "I had never wanted to be in the newspaper business but The Times-Herald had become for me a living thing. The staff had a fine spirit. To sell out to the competition, their enemy, was unbelievable."

Bazy immersed herself in her Arabian horse farm, eight miles from the Capital. She made the herd one of the finest in America. She and Tankersley moved to Arizona, where the horses winter near Tucson and summer on a ranch 7,000 feet high.

26. How to Be a Successful Editor
1920—1955

Coming home from World War I, the Colonel had given considerable thought to how The Tribune should be managed. He concluded the organization was "infinitely too large" to be run by one person and that only by having "the many parts of a highly complex machine work together harmoniously" could The Tribune be "indestructible, unassailable and increase in profit, power and value to the community."

His first task was to work out an harmonious arrangement with his cousin Joe, an equal heir. Since childhood, he had seen how the continuous feud between their mothers had created problems for The Tribune and cost everyone opportunities. The two men, repeating the Cyrus and Nettie pact, composed their own "Iron Bound Agreement," pledging themselves to act together in all things, that should they disagree they would submit the matter to a third person and would abide by his decision. Each locked his copy of the pact, written on fragments torn from the top of a newspaper page, into his strongest strongbox to lie unseen, untouched and unbreached until death.

The Colonel, setting forth in a 1928 guidebook his ideas of a good editor, drew upon advice of Grandfather Medill who on acquiring sole control declared: "There must be an executive head of a newspaper whose decisions are supreme although he shall consult his associates. All experience shows the soundness of this view." The Colonel put it this way: "The task of the editor cannot be handled by one man no matter how remarkable he might be. He must delegate authority but there can be only one supreme will, one general policy if the paper is to be powerful and successful. The editor cannot be in 20 places at one time, so subordinates must enforce his will for him. This does not mean they become mouthpieces. They must exercise judgment, create ideas, start something new. They must be sovereign in their own realms, handling problems with as much decision and finality as would the editor."

Editorials, the Colonel said, must be "timely, accurate in fact and intelligent in opinion, easily and quickly read. Today's newspaper reader is becoming more able to think for himself. He wants news rather than another's interpretation of that news. A newspaper must be sensitive to the pleasures, hopes and fears of all people. When the editor is sympathetic with the interests of every honest person, from ditchdigger to multimillionaire, his paper will be truly great." The Colonel again was reflecting the principles of his grandfather who described The Tribune as "a business newspaper taken and read by all classes of people who have something to buy or sell. The Tribune circulation is not the back alley sort nor dependent upon occasional sensational or scandalous attacks. Readers in the slums and back alleys who occasionally invest a nickel in a scandalous newspaper are not of the class whom advertisers wish to reach." "Of what value is high circulation," Medill asked, "if standards are low?"

The Colonel set six goals for The Tribune:

1. Make Chicago the first city of the world.
2. Build a seaway from the St. Lawrence to the Gulf of Mexico.
3. Electrify the railroads.
4. Abolish smoke from Chicago.
5. Build safe streets and highways.
6. Reestablish constitutional government.

A paper, the Colonel said, must be "brightened with humor." He inherited a cartoonist, John McCutcheon, with a subtle sense of humor, a quality that helped make the daily front-page cartoon one of the most popular features with both Democrats and Republicans. The bright quality was maintained by Carey Orr, Joseph Parrish and Daniel E. Holland—"the terrible three from Tennessee," the Colonel called them. A 1950s Parrish cartoon provoked by rough language used by President Truman to the press depicted a grandmother hurrying away two little boys, her hands over their ears. It became the President's favorite and now hangs in the Truman Library at Independence, Missouri. Truman wrote to Parrish, "If I said half the things that are quoted to me, I too would be closing ears of children."

The Colonel's own deadpan humor was often barbed. He spoke a quip with firmness as though announcing a new principle of physics. Of New York Mayor Fiorello LaGuardia's protest about being photographed while eating, the Colonel said, "His remedy is not a libel suit but a course in table manners." The Colonel owned quite a few Rolls Royce cars over the years. "A Rolls Royce is a good car," he explained. "It will take a politician anywhere except to the White House." At a New Year's party for Tribune exployees and their families, a guest who carefully had composed a compliment began, "Colonel, you may not know what I really think about you." The Colonel cut him short, "Probably just as well." One Saturday morning a veteran editorial writer was absent. "What's the matter?" the Colonel asked the faithful. "Doesn't he want to get ahead?" Cartoonist McCutcheon noted in his memoirs, "Drawn from Life," the Colonel's observation that people who ride the nine o'clock train do catch the nine o'clock, but those who come on the 10:10 frequently miss the 12:00. Sunday Editor Mike Kennedy, apologizing for the clutter that covered his desk, biggest in the Tower, told the Colonel someday he would clear it. "Don't do that," the Colonel said. "It proves someone around here does some work."

One day the Colonel sent for Howard Wood, then financial editor, held out an item he had torn from a newspaper and said, "Howard, I know you collect unusual headlines. This is one you cannot have." He put the slip on the desk and placed a thumb firmly on one corner. The story reported plans for the March of Dimes dinners and dances organized to raise money for polio research and to mark President Roosevelt's birthday. The headline was: "President's Balls Come Off Tonight." The Colonel looked closely at Wood. "I suppose," he reflected, "that is too much to hope for."

The Colonel augmented portraits of British military heroes hanging at the Chicago Club with gifts from his own collection of British generals and admirals who, starting with Cornwallis, had surrendered to American commanders. Of his cousin Joe the Colonel said, "The Pattersons were Scotch cattle thieves before they came to America." Of his own side of the family he said, "All of the McCormicks were crazy."

The Colonel liked the story of a boy who asked President Hoover for three autographs. "Why three?" the President questioned. The boy explained that a chum had two autographs of Babe Ruth and might be persuaded to trade one Ruth for two Hoovers. Opera, the Colonel said, is attended by the privileged few and appreciated by the still fewer. He liked a Baie Comeau

433

account of how Circulation Manager Louie Rose, told that proto-col demanded certain dinner arrangements, exclaimed: "Who is this guy Protocol anyway?" The Colonel ended a long discussion of inventions with: "This talk is intended for the benefit of young clergymen and students of economics who don't know how to produce anything." He happily related how one day at the front in France he asked, "Where is my horse?" and was told, "You ate him at dinner last night." He supplied the Overset Club, his luncheon gathering of Tribune executives, with birds shot at Cantigny and afterwards said, "Now you have eaten crow." After a trip through Africa he reported he had learned that Africans, too, have rights—men have the right to ride bicycles and women have the right to carry burdens on their heads. Invited to give a speech at a formal dinner away from Chicago he realized, while dressing, that he had left his valet behind and he did not know how to knot his bow tie. He went into the hotel hall, knocked on the door of the adjoining room and asked the man there if he could tie the tie. The man, a bit surprised, invited the Colonel into the room and told him to lie on the bed. The Colonel, sur-prised in his turn, lay down. The man made a perfect bow knot. The Colonel rose, thanked the man and asked, "Why did you want me to lie down?" "That's the only way I can do the bow tie," he replied. "I'm an undertaker."

* * * * *

The Colonel brought from World War I a strong impression gained from experience on the battlefield that the best units are those in which officers are promoted from within. He chiseled that principle into the foundation of The Tribune organization. Chesser Campbell began as a classified ad salesman, Howard Wood as a suburban reporter, Don Maxwell as a police beat leg man. All three rose position by position. The Colonel made them his executors and entrusted to them the management of The Tribune and Cantigny. The Colonel liked to think that anyone who "joined the Tribune," as he put it, was capable of rising to its presidency.

In making promotions, the Colonel rewarded exceptional per-formance. Wood was marked for high office after an event on the eve of Franklin Roosevelt's inauguration in 1932. The banking system was near collapse. Wood, then financial editor, assigned one of his reporters, Thomas Furlong, to cover a meeting of the

Federal Reserve Board in Chicago. Late in the evening the board chairman, James Simpson, left the room, saw Furlong and whispered to him that he should meet him in the men's washroom in a few minutes. There the chairman told Furlong: "Tell my friend Howard Wood that the New York and Chicago banks will not open in the morning." Other Chicago papers never did get the story. The New York Times caught up after five hours. As Wood advanced to the very top, Furlong followed.

Having "joined" The Tribune, men and women were expected —and most of them expected—to remain at The Tribune all their professional lives. Arthur Sears Henning came to The Tribune as a 23-year-old cub reporter in 1899, was moved to the Washington bureau after 10 years, in another five years became chief of that difficult, demanding bureau and remained for 34 years, retiring at 73. Schmon, the English literature graduate from Princeton, whom the Colonel made his Canadian right hand man, had confessed he didn't know a fir from a balsam. The Colonel saw no reason why Traffic Manager Fred Byington, who directed movement of supplies and people between Chicago and the Canadian woods and mills—as well as getting the Colonel's watch repaired and having flat wheels replaced on Cissy Patterson's private railroad car in Mexico City—should not be a good judge of the merits and demerits of a proposal to enlarge locks to let ocean-going ships travel between the St. Lawrence and the Great Lakes. The Chicago Association of Commerce led by railroad officials strongly opposed it. At the Colonel's request, Byington wrote three long articles which concluded that the Seaway should be built. Later, the Commerce Association reversed its position. The Seaway was built.

The Colonel expected all employees to work together. He never criticized one in the presence of another and would not listen to one employee complain about another. He gave employees his loyalty and assumed they gave him theirs. A liquor company offered Artist McCutcheon $100,000 a year for a series of cartoons. "I wish your work would not appear elsewhere," the Colonel told him. McCutcheon sent the liquor makers his regrets. The Colonel delivered to Historian Herma Clark a trunkful of his mother's letters with a note: "If you come across some family skeletons, I know you will protect me."

A Tribune reporter, John Boettiger, who achieved prominence during the search for the gangland killer of another Tribune reporter, Jake Lingle, was, as reward, assigned to the 1932 Franklin

Roosevelt campaign train. He met Roosevelt's daughter, Anna. Two years later they decided to marry. Boettiger mailed in his resignation. The Colonel replied that Boettiger's personal affairs did not concern The Tribune, but he saw that Boettiger's position as a presidential son-in-law working for the leading opposition paper would be intolerable in Washington. If Boettiger wished to come to Chicago, he could have an administrative position. If Boettiger stood by his resignation, "God be with you and may every happiness and success attend you."

When the only son of India Edwards, who had left The Tribune for Washington and become Democratic national committee vice chairman, was killed in the war, the Colonel invited her to return to The Tribune on her terms, "if doing so would help you overcome your grief."

To the Colonel, good manners were mandatory. Philemon McKinnon, a Baie Comeau mill employee, never forgot the cold morning when he, as a young man, and his wife came upon the Colonel walking along the dock. The Colonel whipped off his hat, greeted them and remained bareheaded while chatting, acknowledging the presence of Mrs. McKinnon.

The Colonel set down his business philosophy in a speech he wrote for an anniversary celebration of the Canadian operation: "The history of our company reminds me that people who talk about soulless and impersonal corporations are talking nonsense. Our company was organized and brought to greatness by men who worked against great obstacles. Often we tried something and it didn't work. We tried again and again and finally it did work and we were able to offer more jobs. I am proud of you and the work we did together."

In one of his last letters to Schmon, he wrote: "Looking at the motto of the 1st Division in my house, I thought what a priceless experience it was for us to serve in that division. I have no doubt that the determination we learned helped us all through life." The motto, carved over the fireplace, is: "No mission too difficult, no sacrifice too great."

From two military commanders the Colonel adopted principles for good administration. Thomas Truxtun, captain of the *Constellation* two centuries ago, drew up what he called "Common sense rules for success: Practice often, care well for your men, see that each person understands his duties, demand instant obedience, oversee everything." The Captain backed the principles with a technical innovation: Warships then were most effec-

436

tive if guns were fired at the instant the rolling ship was precisely upright. On the *Constellation*, the gun master watched a pendulum. As it swung into the upright position, he struck a gong, signaling gunners to fire. McCormick, too, always looked for new technology. He directed a reporter to ask the owner of a large dairy why milk was not delivered in paper cartons instead of bottles, and the president of a railroad why commuter trains could not be run backward in one direction, eliminating the need of disconnecting the engine and turning it around after each run. Dairyman and railroader sent back the identical reply: "That's the craziest idea I ever heard."

The second commander whom the Colonel drafted as his business mentor was General Bullard, first commander of the 1st Division in France. Soon after the Division entered the trenches, headquarters ordered a raid. Explosives needed to blow a gap in the barbed wire in no-man's-land did not arrive and a colonel called off the raid. An angry GHQ demanded to know the name of the officer who failed to produce the explosive. General Bullard replied: "I am in command of the 1st Division, all of it. I am responsible for everything that happens in the Division. I am responsible for this failure. If GHQ wants to blame someone, blame me." As editor, the Colonel accepted personal responsibility for every word, every picture, every cartoon, even every advertisement that appeared in The Tribune.

He liked to pick photographs, particularly those for the roto section. Mike Kennedy early learned that an actress could wear a dress cut low but not so low as to expose a nipple. "Don't show the pink," the Colonel ordered. However, with Asian and African girls, the less clothing, the bigger the space allotted the photograph. Bali maidens frequently danced across Tribune roto pages. The Colonel insisted that no picture show a woman's bare feet. Feet are ugly, he explained. But he did not explain why he insisted that an artist paint boots on a photograph of captured German officers being marched barefoot through the snow by their Russian guards.

Over the years The Tribune staff learned that the paper was published for just one reader, the Colonel. Most tried, in his or her way, to win the Colonel's attention, some by placing emphasis on his dictum that the paper must have one general policy and trying to fit their actions into that policy, others on his seemingly contradictory decree that subordinates must not be mouthpieces. Good reporters sought facts and wrote stories straight, although a reporter would need a head of solid bone not to know that a story presenting President Roosevelt or almost any Democrat, diplomat or bureaucrat, in bad light had a good chance of ending up on page one whereas a story casting a favorable glow on such individuals quickly might rest in a wastebasket. Too many reporters yielded to the temptation to gain page-one position and, they hoped, favorable recognition from the Colonel. They did no service to The Tribune and the Colonel nor did they bring honor to themselves. Slippage was perhaps the greatest in the Washington bureau. "It was sickening," wrote India Edwards, "to see so many men trying to anticipate the Colonel's wants. So many times they were completely wrong."

Earlier as the Tribune woman's editor, India Edwards wrote a positive account of Chicagoans' Bundles for Britain efforts which brought a note from the Colonel saying: "I wonder if the women's pages do not have the same editorial policy as the rest of the paper?" India replied, "We have the policy of reporting the news as faithfully and fully as possible. If you want us to do otherwise, please notify us." She heard no more. She ignored the Colonel's suggestion she write about the inefficiencies of the Red Cross, an organization she respected. When the managing editor told her he was removing a flattering photograph of Mrs. Roosevelt, India said, "Do that and you can look for a replacement for me in the morning." The picture stayed. So did India, flaunting her big Roosevelt button during every campaign. Lawyer Kirkland asked the Colonel how he could stand having such a rabid Democrat on his staff. The Colonel said India was a Southerner and therefore by nature a Democrat, and added, "If she can stand me, I can stand her."

During the World's Fair, a new teenage social reporter, Eleanor Page, brought in a story about Paul McNutt, the Democratic governor of Indiana, "having a gay time" at the Fair's Streets of Paris spots. McNutt, seeing the piece as McCormick's personal vengeance, sued, asserting he had not been in the Fair fun places. The Colonel, who knew nothing about the piece until it appeared, told Managing Editor Beck to order India to fire Eleanor. India said she, not Eleanor, should take the punishment. Beck proposed that India fire Eleanor and quietly hire her back in a couple of weeks. India did fire Eleanor and when Beck withheld permission to rehire, India personally gave Eleanor money to go to Indianapolis and tell McNutt the full story. The Democrat telephoned the Colonel, told him he was dropping the suit and asked that no one suffer from the story. The Colonel told India to rehire Eleanor. In time, Ms. Page became society editor.

The first time Wood reached a position qualifying him to attend the Tuesday morning meeting of department heads in the Colonel's office, he sat in the last row of little gold chairs lined up before the Colonel's big marble table desk. "Where's Howard?" the Colonel asked. "Here, sir." "Howard, I want you always to sit in the front row. I always want to see a no man." Years later after retiring as publisher of The Tribune and chairman of Tribune Company, Wood reminisced, "I don't think I ever actually said no to the Colonel. When I thought he was wrong, I said something like 'Colonel, have you considered. . .' or 'Colonel, here is a report that. . .' " Byington couched his no in "I'll work on it, Colonel." The Colonel's lawyer, Kirkland, advised anyone calling on the Colonel: "Be frank and give him all the facts you know."

The first note the Colonel sent Veysey in London related that Managing Editor Pat Maloney, just returned from England, had told him the postwar socialist government had taken over hospitals in a manner helpful personally to cabinet members. Veysey replied, after three days of hard thought, "Sir: Somebody must have given Mr. Maloney the wrong information. This story is not true." He sent a copy to Maloney and began looking for an early ship home, presuming that if the Colonel did not fire him, Maloney would. Maloney sent a note saying: "That Colonel, give him the time of day and he asks for your watch!" Veysey heard nothing from the Colonel but from then on, each note from the Colonel came as a question—Who is. . .Why is. . .What is. . .Veysey remained head of the London bureau for 26 years.

The Colonel was aware of the reluctance of subordinates to challenge his words. In his book about General Grant, the Colonel related how Grant listened carefully as President Lincoln proposed a strategy to defeat Lee's forces outside Richmond. The General, realizing that the plan would bring disaster to his own army, remained quiet and soon launched a completely different offensive. The Colonel took for his own Grant's policy of giving a subordinate a goal and letting him work out the tactics. Equally he agreed with Grant's belief that the only acceptable reason a subordinate can give for violating an order is to make his alternative succeed. "That takes a genius," the Colonel warned.

Probably no Tribune person was in a tighter political spot than the Colonel's niece, Bazy, after he promoted her from writing a column for a small town newspaper to publishing the Washington Times-Herald. Unknowing persons looked upon her as the Colonel's errand girl, but he gave her, on departure for the Capital, only two commandments: She must print any Tribune editorial forwarded to Washington with the word "must" and she must never, never become a friend of any advertiser. In Washington, she received three editorial assignments:

1. "Find out the secret government." She telegraphed back, "Frankfurter."

2. After India Edwards became the Democratic committee vice chairman: "Find someone as good as India or better to be vice chairman of the Republican committee." Bazy went to Senator Owen Brewster and asked whom he had in mind for the job. He said he favored Bertha Adkins. Bazy had her reporters write a memo on Ms. Adkins. It was favorable. Ms. Adkins got the job and the Colonel was pleased.

3. "Beat Tydings." "That took a little longer," Bazy commented.

Old-timers on The Tribune warned newcomers that a summons to the Colonel's office meant disaster. The first time Mike Kennedy received such a call, he cleaned his desk. The Colonel's secretary escorted him to his executioner. The Colonel arose. "Mike," he said, "I'm going to the Art Institute and I want you to come along. They have some Remington paintings of the old west and I want you to tell me if any are of use to The Tribune." Richard Orr swears that he was appointed farm editor and thus became a frequent visitor to Cantigny only because everyone else feared such close contact with the Colonel. India swears that the Colonel protected her from irate social matrons ignored in the society columns and angry fathers of brides not pictured in the paper despite, once, an offer of $5,000. George Tagge assumes politicians must have protested to the Colonel about some of his pieces but no complaint ever was handed down to him. Tagge's code name for the Colonel was "Mister Longfellow." George Morgenstern, long-time editorial writer, concluded that the Colonel ran The Tribune "as a benevolent autocracy with a touch of noblesse oblige."

For the Colonel the editorial conference was the happiest hour of the day. "He used us to think out loud, to express his joys and his worries, to unburden himself," recalled Editorial Writer Carl Wiegman. Some mornings the Colonel talked only of farm happenings at Cantigny. Frequently the Colonel was indiscreet but trusted writers never to carry his words beyond office walls.

To deal with proposals from the Colonel they considered unwise or even silly, the writers developed two courses of evasive action. In the first, a writer would compose the piece, have it set in type and put the proof on the Colonel's desk where it would rest for several days until the Colonel, thinking it had been published, discarded it. In the second course, two writers staged a debate before the Colonel, one presenting the Colonel's position, the other arguing against it. Usually the Colonel decided the opposition view was the more sound, dropped his proposal and the writers heard no more of it. But two days after one such debate in which the writers were certain Leon Stolz, the chief writer, had thoroughly demolished the Colonel's case as presented by Reuben Cahn, the expert on economic affairs, the writers were surprised to see the subject presented in a front-page news story from the Washington bureau. The Colonel had used Walter Trohan to make an end run.

The Colonel's manner toward the writers, as with others, was crusty and his words of praise were few. The writers considered symbolic the cactus plants which decorated their offices. Clifford Raymond, the only writer who called the Colonel Bert—Raymond predated the Colonel on The Tribune and occasionally was known to have exclaimed "Don't be a goddamn fool, Bert"—suggested that the department adopt as its theme song, "Where seldom is heard an encouraging word." A rare note did go to Gwen Morgan in London. She, sharing the Colonel's enthusiasm for history, used the coronation of Elizabeth II to review happily all English coronations since 1066. The series ran for weeks. Her report of the coronation itself filled three columns, astounding those readers who erroneously thought the Colonel detested all things British. The Colonel wrote:

"Dear Gwen:

Your articles about the coronation are excellent.

Most sincerely,"

With a flourish he signed it "McC."

When WGN engineers confused recordings from a GOP convention, the Colonel demanded by telephone: "Doesn't anyone down there know how to put on a phonograph record?"

Stuart List, sent to Chicago by William Randolph Hearst to be publisher of his dwindling paper, The American, early called on the Colonel at his office. The Colonel greeted him, "Young man, do you realize the serious situation into which you have been thrust?" List said he did. The Colonel promised no help but his subsequent steady support convinced List that the Colonel wanted The American to survive if only to be a problem for The Tribune's most dangerous competition, the Chicago Daily News. Some years after the Colonel's death, Joe's daughter, Alicia Patterson, who of all the fourth generation Medills was the most dedicated and talented as a publisher, gave a dinner for visiting publishers and editors. A guest told a cruel story about the Colonel. Alicia, sorely troubled, whispered to Maxwell's wife Marjorie, "I'm very disturbed whenever anyone says anything bad about Cousin Bert. I don't know how I could have managed except for him and Father."

Sunday Editor Kennedy was convinced the Colonel permitted everyone one goof. Advertising executive Fred Nichols agreed. Early in the strike by linotype operators which disrupted press schedules, Nichols accepted seven color advertisements for the next day's paper. The already harassed pressmen ended up 100,000 copies short. Circulation Manager Louie Rose was irate. Nichols was called in to explain his action. He found the Colonel seated at his marble desk, right hand outstretched. Nichols took the hand, shook it and suddenly realized the Colonel's hand had been reaching not for Nichols' hand but for the report. Nichols put the report on the desk. The Colonel read it, looked up and said softly, "We are all learning more every day about how to handle our new problems. We won't book seven color ads again, will we, Fred?" "No sir," Nichols said. Nothing more was said and Nichols continued his rise to the Tribune presidency.

Certain errors could be fatal in the early days. One hot summer day during the middle 1920s, the Colonel entered Hyatt's drug store in Wheaton and saw Red Grange, then on his way at the University of Illinois to becoming football's first superstar. Grange was reading a magazine and drinking pop between his ice route rounds. The Colonel called to him: "Come here, Grange. I want to tell you that when you were in high school here, I asked my football man to look at you and tell me how good you were because if you were really good, I wanted to get you for Yale. Well, my football man told me you would never make it in college. Grange, I want to tell you that man does not work for me anymore."

Advertising men were not allowed on the editorial floor. Paul Fulton, who rose to be advertising director, could recall only twice when advertisers asked him if he could arrange for offending articles to be left out of the paper. Fulton did not pass on

443

either request. The Colonel told Fulton one day, "Paul, I have a decision to make. I know that Sears is your most important client and General Wood (its chairman) is a good friend of yours. He phoned me that Such-and-Such wants to write a Republican party news letter. The General asked me to give $1,500. Paul, I do not care for Such-and-Such but I don't want to disturb your relations with the General and with Sears. What should I do?"

Paul replied, "Colonel, you know we sell advertising only on the basis of the return it will bring the advertiser. There is no need to consider anything else in this case."

"I'm glad to hear you say that, Paul," the Colonel said. "Thank you for coming."

Fulton never did learn if the Colonel gave the $1,500 nor could he decide if the Colonel wanted his advice or if he were testing Fulton's integrity.

In early 1941 when the Colonel was a leading advocate of staying out of the war, two large Jewish-owned department stores withdrew their advertising in protest. The Colonel did not mute one word. In a few weeks the advertising returned. At 2 a.m one night, the Colonel appeared at the home of a Cantigny farm manager, Carl Henderson. The Colonel himself had been awakened by a phone call from his night editor reporting that the Jewish Anti-Defamation League was threatening to take all Jewish advertising from the paper unless the Colonel personally stopped the presses and removed a story the league found offensive. The Colonel refused and wanted to clear his mind. As a listener, he chose a farmer, a man with common sense.

The Tribune advertising men were the most aggressive in town, also the best informed about the advertiser's business and the most helpful, offering such services as Tribune artist Charles Killgore to redesign and decorate the store, or in tipping off one merchant that a large wall clock reminded customers the day was growing late and they had better break off their shopping and move on. Periodically the Colonel summoned all ad men and reminded them they worked for The World's Greatest Newspaper, they were the best ad men in America and they had behind them the most comprehensive, most accurate consumer research service. "So get out there and sell," he ended, "and if when you finish the guy still won't buy the ad, say goodbye and walk out. As you leave, give them this"—he sounded a raspberry. "They need The Tribune more than we need them and if they can't see that they are stupid."

THE LASTING FRIENDSHIP —

MAYOR ED KELLY OF CHICAGO

The Colonel instructed labor negotiators to be generous in dealing with unions and in return to ask only for a fair deal. He was personally offended when his linotype operators walked out in response to a union official's call for a city-wide strike. Tribune pay for non-union members exceeded union scale and was best in town. Editorial members were deaf to appeals to organizers of the Newspaper Guild. The Colonel rewarded special effort. After one year of tremendous progress, the Colonel split a million dollars among four top executives. The Colonel signed a million-dollar contract for Sidney Smith's highly popular Andy Gump strip. One day the Colonel asked Chester Gould, creator of Dick Tracy, if he would do a special Tracy cartoon for use in a Tribune promotion. Gould drew the feature. A few days later the Colonel asked Gould to walk with him to the Tribune garage. Part of the building had been walled off with paper. Through the flimsy partition burst a Rolls Royce. "It's yours," the Colonel said.

Employees shared profits and were encouraged to save. Tribune people traveled first class, stayed in first class hotels, ate in first class restaurants, never accepted gifts more persuasive than a box of candy. A travel editor was fired for asking resort advertisers for a free vacation. Single employees enlisting in the military forces during the Second World War received $250 a month to supplement their small military pay and married employees were given two-thirds of their Tribune pay. When Literary Editor Fanny Butcher became ill with pneumonia, the Colonel sent a note telling her the job would be held open and her pay would continue, for six months if necessary. He later extended the protection to all employees and added a second six months of half pay. During an African assignment, Veysey was taken to a remote hospital with a broken and displaced neck after a car wreck. The Colonel cabled Veysey's wife in London to fly immediately to Africa, see that her husband had the best care available, bring him to London when able to travel and send all bills to the Colonel. The Midwest's most prominent neurological surgeon, Dr. Loyal Davis, who was to become father-in-law to President Reagan, appeared at the hospital bedside of State Political Editor George Tagge, felled by a puzzling ailment. "I'm taking over your case," Dr. Davis announced. The Colonel had sent him. The Colonel gave a home at Cantigny to the police horse that for years patrolled Michigan Avenue in front of the Tribune. Returning to the Tower from an outdoor ceremony one cold day, the Colonel summoned Managing Editor Maloney. "I saw our re-

446

porter Marcia Winn there," the Colonel reported. "She didn't have a coat. Something must be done." Maloney asked Marcia what kind of coat she would like as a gift. Marcia, proud Southerner, was irate. She could, and would, buy her own coats, thank you very much. "People can say blah-blah-blah about the Colonel," said Lucille Zeier Regnier, born and reared in a Cantigny farmhouse, "but I say the Colonel always made sure no one at Cantigny ever went hungry." As the depression set in, the Colonel sent a note to all department heads: "I do not think it's fair to discharge any employee" and proposed that all accept a 10 percent cut in pay. After the Second World War not one wartime addition to the staff was fired to make room for returning employees restored to the staff.

With the Colonel's generosity went a careful use of money. Employees were expected to file precise expense accounts. Floyd Gibbons, a famous war reporter, came into disfavor when he asked to be reimbursed for hiring an entire caravan to take him into the North African desert. The Colonel told Emil, his English butler, to have a bill for an operation sent to him but was surprised at the size of the doctor's charge—$3,500. The Colonel asked Dr. Van Dellen if the sum were right. Van Dellen called the doctor who sent an amended bill for $350. Visiting the company store at Franquelin on the North Shore of the St. Lawrence, the Colonel bought a pair of cotton gloves. "How much?" "Thirty-five cents." "Too much. I'll give you a quarter." Dropping in on a sale of work by the Baie Comeau Women's Guild, he chose a small piece of beautifully woven silk but found it too small to make a cravat. He asked the woman if she could weave a larger piece. Yes, she said, if she had more thread. The Colonel said the company would supply the money for the thread. Two years later he returned, sought out the woman and asked if she had the cloth. She did. Why did the Colonel send an office boy to collect a dime from reporter Clay Gowran, who had stepped on one of the Colonel's shoes in a crowded elevator?

The Colonel rarely carried money. Walking with Flahiff down a busy Montreal street, the Colonel strode into the city's foremost department store, chose a pair of the best gloves and liked them so much that he asked for a dozen. The clerk wrapped them elegantly as a gift. The Colonel picked up the parcel and walked from the store. The clerk signaled the security man who hurried after the Colonel. Flahiff intercepted him and paid the bill. The next day the Colonel bought another dozen and again went

447

through the little scene, this time invoking knowing smiles. After boarding a train in Florida with Campbell, then business manager, and Maxwell, then managing editor, the restless Colonel went for a walk in the station, not bothering to check the time. The train pulled out. The Colonel summoned a taxi and told the driver to take him to the first stop 70 miles up the line before the train got there. The driver did so. "That'll be $70," he announced. The Colonel said he had no money. The driver sought a policeman. The train arrived. Campbell and Maxwell jumped from the train while the Colonel, ignoring the hubbub, blithely mounted the train steps, knowing Campbell would pay the driver and add a tip large enough to wash away his anger and maybe give something to the policeman. The Colonel invited Maryland Hooper to go with him to the lilac festival in Lombard, not far from Wheaton. The gatekeeper held out two tickets. "Twenty five cents each," he said. The Colonel asked Mrs. Hooper if she had some cash. "I never carry money when I am with a gentleman," Mrs. Hooper said. The Colonel told the gatekeeper, "I will mail the money. I am Colonel McCormick." The gatekeeper replied, "Yes and I'm Napoleon." The Colonel and Mrs. Hooper did not see the festival.

The Colonel liked to help young people get started, especially someone who had been in the artillery. On a train from Wheaton to town he chanced to sit next to the county highway superintendent, whose freshly graduated son hoped to enter advertising. Tell him to see So-and-So in classified, the Colonel said. The son did and was given the lowliest task. Years later, when Charles Gates was rising fast in the organization, So-and-So gave him the note the Colonel had sent down: "If young Gates comes in, hire him. If after two months he's no good, fire him." Coming home to Cantigny one evening, the Colonel told his driver, Eugene Corbin, that if Corbin's son, about to graduate from high school, wanted a newspaper career, the Colonel would help him through journalism college. Corbin reported the next day the son did not know what he wanted to do. "Tell him," the Colonel said acidly, "to go out into the world and learn the value of the dollar." The offer never was repeated. Paul McVicker, a veteran of the battle of Cantigny and a Tribune guard, remembered the Colonel's instructions to him that any war veteran asking to see the Colonel should be taken immediately to the Colonel's office. "They always came away with something," McVicker said.

The Colonel had entered Chicago journalism in a robust era.

Cocky reporters made a virtue of not lifting their hats to anyone on any occasion. The Colonel did not despair of journalistic brashness but held himself aloof. One evening he was guest of honor at an American Legion convention banquet. As entertainment the committee provided a naked dancer. The Colonel told the chairman, "I am sorry but the editor of The Tribune cannot be seen at such a thing," and left.

The Colonel did despair of ignorance.

In 1921 he was one of the founders of the Medill School of Journalism at Northwestern University. The school offered a four-year afternoon and evening course at the downtown campus for working journalists and a two-year course as part of a four-year Bachelor of Science degree study in the School of Commerce at the main campus at Evanston. University President Walter Dill Scott spoke of the "vital importance of journalism in influencing public opinion and improving minds and character of mankind." The Colonel hoped the school would "perpetuate the ideals" of its namesake, his grandfather. Joe Patterson later commented: "They took our money but not our advice."

Medill had believed in education and also supported Northwestern University, founded in 1851, four years before he came to Chicago. He spoke up firmly for Professor of Economics Robert Sheppard rumored to have used university funds—he was also Northwestern's treasurer—to build a fine house which would befit his standing when, he hoped, he became president of the university replacing Henry W. Rogers. The latter was in difficulty for opposing American annexation of the Philippines, for admitting so many women students that they equaled men in number and for not gathering in enough bequests and gifts. Abruptly, Sheppard resigned. Evanston lore relates that Medill, shocked at learning that his faith in the professor was unjustified, reimbursed the university for losses. University archives contain no evidence of any wrongdoing by the professor nor recompense from Medill, only the resignation. "In those days," an archivist says, "universities did not wash dirty linen in public." Charles "Call me Charlie" Dawes bought the Sheppard house and today it is the home of the Evanston Historical Society.

The Colonel could be inconsiderate. He did not show up at a formal dinner with London publishers at which he was guest of honor. On train journeys he assumed that the center stateroom would be his and sat there, the door open, reading the papers and discarding them, on by one, into the corridor for the untipped

449

porter to pick up. Schmon arranged an elaborate birthday party for the Colonel at a magical lake deep in the Canadian forest. Schmon flew in the chef, maitre d' and a royal feast from The Ritz in Montreal. He flew in tents, china, tables, chairs, flowers. He sprayed the region for mosquitoes and flies. He chartered a large flying boat to bring guests. At Baie Comeau the day dawned gray and misty. "Let's have the party here," the Colonel said. They did. When meeting both Schmon, a captain in World War I and head of the Canadian operation, and Flahiff, his junior by a generation but a general in World War II, he first greeted Flahiff, "Good morning, General," and then turned to the elder, senior Schmon, "Good morning, Captain."

After Schmon had completed delicate negotiations in Wales for construction of two new-design paper-carrying ships, the Colonel curtly telegraphed: "We don't need no boats." The flabbergasted Schmon returned to Canada but before the year was out, the Colonel ordered the boats.

The Colonel dictated a piece for the farm column saying that Cantigny's lawns were poor that summer because his current farm manager did not know how to maintain them properly. He scolded Jack Flynn, editor of the New York News, for putting up as collateral Tribune stock rights the Colonel had given him as a bonus.

Individuals who crossed the Colonel, wittingly or not, received the fierce force of meanness. One disgruntled businessman described the Colonel as a "spherical son of a bitch." Asked what he meant, he said, "Anyway you look at him, he's a son of a bitch."

Strangers found him blunt, austere, aristocratic, haughty, arrogant. "In fact he was shy," Wood said. "He was uneasy with people he did not know. What people took to be coolness was his way of covering up." "He was the most shy man I ever knew," said Louise Brydon. "I loved him." "He was the nicest man I ever worked for," said Diva Marion Claire. "He was shy and sweet," recalled caustic Music Critic Claudia Cassidy, not known for a gentle tongue. Andrew Rebori, friend and architect, summed up the Colonel this way: "With all the success in the world and money to boot, he was a lonely man, shy by nature. He preferred solitude rather than the company of people of lackluster interest. He made few personal friends, but those few cherished and respected him. Once crossed by those he considered wrong or culpable, he could be a rugged adversary with no holds barred."

Staff members often told one another the Colonel walked past them without speaking and put it down as arrogance, but Fanny Butcher had another explanation: "He was so tall that he looked right over people." Also, the Colonel may not have been wearing his spectacles, often letting them hang from one ear. Pat Maloney told India Edwards that when he spoke to the Colonel, the Colonel sometimes answered and sometimes didn't. "He's so arrogant," Pat said. "He's not arrogant at all," India rebutted. "He's deaf. He doesn't know you are talking to him if he is not looking at you." Maryland McCormick arranged for a specialist to fit the Colonel with a hearing aid, but before the specialist reached the elevator, the Colonel had filed the aid in the waste basket. Was it vanity? Pride? Or was it he just couldn't be bothered?

No one became familiar with the Colonel twice. Reuben Cahn, favored, prized editorial writer, made a joking remark about the Colonel at a party. "Rube," the Colonel said, "that's the way you earn severance pay."

The Colonel's curiosity was boundless. Reading old books during a voyage through the Great Lakes and down the St. Lawrence, the Colonel came upon a statement that in the era before the discovery of gunpowder, armies used as a catapult trigger either the sinew taken from the neck of a bull or hair from the head of a woman. Why not hair from men? he asked. He did not accept that the male custom of cutting hair short was an answer. In those days of serfdom, he argued, rulers could order men to grow hair to a length that made it useful to makers of catapults. He never did find an answer. No Tribune member ever learned how to anticipate his questions. The first time the Colonel sent for Maxwell, newly appointed sports editor, the Colonel asked, "Don, how far is it from Moscow to Vladivostok?" "Colonel, that's one of the things I don't know, but I'll know it in ten minutes," Don replied. The Colonel said thanks and Maxwell found his way to an atlas, wondering if he had passed a test.

The Colonel looked upon himself as a conscientious reporter. He remembered the advice given him by Richard Harding Davis, the foremost reporter of the earlier generation, that when reporting on travels abroad, he should begin each trip with an account of the preparations and tell how he, or she, moved from place to place so readers and listeners can travel along. The Colonel advised everyone to travel, quoting Dr. Johnson: "The principal use of travel is to regulate the imagination with reality."

The Colonel often summed up a nation, city or people in one sentence:

"Panama is the most important spot in the world."

"Puerto Rico is not ready for self-government."

"In South America dishonesty and ignorance make communism the greatest danger."

"Why all the outcry against Peron? I do not know. He has a clear majority of the people and his domestic policies closely approximate those of the New Deal."

"The Japanese cannot support themselves but, being savage people, make excellent soldiers."

"We must withdraw from Korea (this in 1947) even though the Russians will find an excuse to move in."

"The Chinese never could play football. Teamwork is alien to them. The Chinese army has just about only thieves. The Chinese Reds want to live by violence and divide up what little is left."

"Europe is deceived about American opinion because European reporters seldom go beyond the Hudson River."

"There is little hope England can ever support herself again."

"The fine houses in Edinburgh show that spinning and weaving are highly profitable."

"The total collapse of the French civilization cannot be far away."

"Spain and Portugal are far from any modern government."

"Popular government is not suited to Italians."

"Denmark is closer to Moscow than to America."

"Russians never had any rights."

"Tangiers, like the United Nations, partakes in the vices of all of its constituent peoples and in the virtures of none."

During a Caribbean visit, the Colonel was guest of honor at a diplomatic dinner given by the American ambassador. As dinner ended, he signaled Maryland that he wanted to leave quickly. She made her apologies. As the Colonel hurried her to the car, she asked what was wrong. He said he had the scoop of the year and he must telephone The Tribune. What's the story? she asked. He said the ambassador's wife, his dinner companion, had whispered to him that President Truman had taken a mistress on a boat trip and she had shot him in the arm. Mrs. McCormick suggested they return to the party and ask the ambassador's wife for further details. They returned. The ambassador's wife began, "Our president went out on his boat. . ." Mrs. McCormick interrupted. "Our president? Do you mean Mr. Truman?" "Oh no," the wife said. "Our president here in Santo Domingo, Mr. Tru-

jillo." The Colonel was deeply disappointed.

Trivial incidents gathered gaudy ornamentation as they passed from mouth to mouth. One day when about to set off for a hunt, he saw visitors on the verandah. Wanting to show them his new horse, he had the groom drive the horse van onto the lawn. The Colonel, dressed in his pink hunting coat and hard hat, mounted the horse and paraded it for the guests. Then off he and the van went. Long after the Colonel's death, the incident was told in this manner: The Colonel invited staff members to Cantigny, saying he had a surprise for them. The employees assumed he would announce a bonus. Instead up came a truck, the doors were flung open, down came a ramp and out rode the Colonel in his World War I uniform. That was his surprise. Snicker, snicker, snicker.

For several years, the Colonel had two secretaries, Genevieve Burke and Dorothy Murray. Miss Burke, the senior by many years, presided over a room designed for the secretary while Miss Murray was allocated a desk in a waiting room. Each room had its own entrance. The two women rarely spoke and never consulted. The Colonel, on arriving, gave to one his brief cases with scribblings made in bed or in the car or plane on the way downtown. The secretary tried to decipher the jottings, typed her interpretation on a half sheet of paper, ignoring spelling, grammar and punctuation, and added the Colonel's initials. Sometimes the Colonel scrawled his initials over the typed letters but rarely read the message. The Colonel addressed his notes by the Christian name of the intended recipient with the result that a note intended for one Arthur might be delivered to another Arthur on a different continent. Often the recipient puzzled long over the message the Colonel intended to convey but always he dropped everything and set out to seek the information he thought the Colonel might want. Pat Maloney explained: "When the Colonel asks for a glass of water, we turn on the fire hose."

The Colonel, returning from an Asian trip, wrote a thank-you note to Percy Wood, the Asian correspondent who had traveled through the continent with him. The Colonel recalled that Percy had told him about a weird drink called a suffering bastard dispensed at the bar in Shepheard's hotel in Cairo and asked what the drink contained. Percy flew from Delhi to Cairo, checked into Shepheard's, settled solidly at the bar and ordered a suffering bastard. The ancient barman tipped this bottle and that. Percy sipped the drink. "Good," he said. "What's in it?" The barman tapped his forehead. "My secret," he said. Percy dutifully ordered another and another and another, each time noting which bottles the barman drew from and the amount. When confident he had mastered the contents, he zig-zagged to the cable office, dispatched the secret recipe to the Colonel and flew back to Delhi. The recipe: Put one shot of gin, one shot of brandy and a dash of Angostura bitters into a tall glass filled with cracked ice, stir well, fill with ginger ale, add a sprig of mint.

The secretaries were equally unhelpful in passing on verbal messages. Miss Murray telephoned Walter Simmons, the Far Eastern correspondent, while on home leave in South Dakota, telling him the Colonel wanted to see him urgently. Walter packed his bag, rode the first train to Chicago and a taxi to the Astor Street house and found the Colonel, recuperating from a prostate operation, in a roughly hewn bed and reading the paper. "Good morning, Walter," the Colonel said, "I have been wondering when you plan to return to Tokyo." Walter gave him the date. "Thank you, Walter," the Colonel said and turned his attention back to the paper. Simmons asked the Colonel about the bed. The Colonel said it was made from fence rails split by Abraham Lincoln. "A fine tale!" Mrs. McCormick exclaimed later.

Tribune staff members, honored with the Colonel's notes, cables and phone messages, frequently asked one another why he put up with such inefficient, no, such trouble-making secretaries. Only Mrs. McCormick put the question to him. He did not reply. It is probable he was unaware the women were causing problems and making him look silly and assumed that because he personally had chosen them they must be the best secretaries in the whole world.

The Colonel asked no favors. George Halas, owner of the Chicago Bears professional football team, sent him two season tickets at a time when such tickets were highly prized. The Colonel returned them. His cars bore no special license numbers nor markings, his drivers were instructed to obey all laws, even not to park in the crosswalk at the entrance to Tribune Tower. An interim driver was fired for installing a siren and using it to blast through traffic when alone. The Colonel's political clout was more apparent than real. When a lawyer was appointed a federal judge, the Colonel told him, "I had nothing at all to do with the appointment." The mayor of Wheaton, the town adjoining Cantigny, urged the Colonel to ask the state to install a traffic light at a busy crossing on the state-maintained highway that goes through the town and along the northern edge of Cantigny.

455

Nothing happened. But sometime later, a boy rode his bicycle out of the cross street into the side of the Colonel's passing car. The boy was not hurt but the bike was demolished. The Colonel bought the boy a new bike. Two days later a state crew installed lights. The Colonel asked the mayor to order a resident to lower the hedge around his corner house and improve visibility for drivers; the resident declined and the hedge remained uncut. In the late 1920s the state paved the highway from Chicago as far as the entrance of Cantigny. Later the state planned to widen the highway to four lanes; the Colonel asked that the road be diverted to spare Cantigny from the increased traffic noise; the state widened it in place. The Colonel erected as a sound barrier a seven-foot-high solid one-mile-long wooden fence; the state complained that the fence shaded the road, worsening icing conditions, and asked him to remove it; "You move the road," the Colonel replied. The fence stayed. The ugly fence enraged neighbors, who vented their fury on the boards. Every Monday a Cantigny farm hand repaired damaged wood and painted out smears. The Colonel failed to persuade the Congress to remove legal protection for seagulls and the Illinois legislature to end a ban which prevented him from blasting away with a shotgun from his bedroom at the mourning doves which awakened him, but he did get the post office to print a stamp honoring all birds. He was influential in advancing Dwight Green, prosecutor of Al Capone, to the Illinois governorship, and C. Wayland Brooks, prosecutor of the gang killer of Tribune reporter Jake Lingle, to the United States Senate, but he never could turn FDR out of the White House although he claimed with the election of General Eisenhower that "we pulled down the New Deal after an unrelenting fight of 20 years." Twenty-five years passed before the state and city governments approved the construction of a vast exhibition hall posthumously named for him, but Flahiff, his Canadian lawyer, guided 34 pieces of legislation helpful to Tribune Canadian operations through the Canadian and Quebec Parliaments. There is a story that on a certain election day the Colonel appeared at the polling station in Winfield, a village bordering Cantigny, where the officers, all Democrats, pretended not to recognize him and questioned his right to vote. The Colonel stamped out in a rage and arranged for Cantigny residents to vote in Republican Wheaton. No records verify this account.

The Colonel, so busy handing out verbal clouts, learned early to take knocks. He repeated a comment by President Lincoln: "If

I were to read, much less answer, all the attacks made upon me, this shop might as well be closed for any other business. I do the very best I can. If the end brings me out all right, what is said against me will amount to nothing. If I am wrong, ten angels swearing I was right will make no difference." On a day when Time magazine did a hard job on the Colonel, the editorial writers assumed he would be angry, but when they entered his office for the morning conference, he happily held up the magazine with its caricature of him on the cover and asked, "How is that for free national publicity?" He framed and hung in his office a cartoon by the English master, Low, ridiculing him. One night he and his cousins, Cissy and Joe Patterson, met in an airport operations shack at Montreal. Cissy was angry over uncomplimentary Saturday Evening Post stories concerning her. She said she would sue. "Don't be a goddamn fool, Cissy," her brother Joe said. "Don't you realize in a couple of weeks nobody will remember those stories? Keep your damn mouth shut." Whenever an author sent the Colonel the script of a proposed article about him or The Tribune, the Colonel returned it unopened. To read a script, he said, could be mistaken for approval. He was bothered by frequent accusations of being anti-Semitic, a term never applied to him by anyone close to him. For years his chief editorial writer was Leon Stolz, son of a rabbi. One day the Colonel instructed State Political Editor Tagge to shun the use of Jake, the popular nickname for the very powerful Democratic politician, Jacob Arvey. "Call him Jack," the Colonel said.

Asked shortly before his death how long he thought The Tribune would survive unchanged, he guessed about 15 years. "Changes must continue," he said. "A dead hand cannot run The Tribune."

Twenty-five years after the Colonel's death, Mrs. McCormick found in a Chinese leather and gold chest a clipping, creamy and crumbling with age from an unidentified east coast newspaper. The publisher obviously was well known to the Colonel, perhaps a fellow member of the Associated Press board of directors, on which the Colonel had served for 28 years, much of the time as chairman of the Freedom of the Press committee. This was its summation of the Colonel:

"Everyone will agree that Colonel Robert R. McCormick, editor and part owner of the Chicago Tribune, was a man of great influence in national affairs. Here in the East, many detested him and ascribed to him motives and attitudes little short of malevo-

457

lent. Because of his antipathy, few hereabouts made any real attempt to understand him.

"To our thinking, he was a man of great simplicity. He saw the world as sharply divided between what was good and what was evil. He never doubted that what he personally called evil was in fact evil and he was therefore against it with all the powers at his disposal. He regarded himself, with justice, as a pure patriot and his patriotism was as uncomplicated as his ethics. It involved a deep conviction that the United States could live and prosper apart from the rest of the world of which it is a part and hence all 'entanglements' were bad.

"This simple view of life and its problems, so honestly held and so effectively expressed, was made to order for millions of Americans and was, indeed, the real source of the Colonel's influence. Moreover, his sincerity of purpose was as evident as his patriotism. His tall figure with its proud bearing, his benevolent manner, his sympathy with the oppressed, all these emphasized his disinterestedness. Add his learning, particularly in the field of American military history, and his ability to quote chapter and verse to bolster his theses, and a better understanding of the man and his power emerges."

27. To Preserve a Treasure, Give it Away
1953—1955

As a boy and a youth the Colonel was often ill, almost a sickly child. As a young man he had "weak lungs"and doctors recommended outdoor exercise. Scarlet fever kept him home from Cuba. As an army officer in France he almost died in the 1918 influenza epidemic which took more American lives than guns, bombs and gas together. In 1926 jaundice racked him, impairing the liver and bringing problems in later life. He worked at keeping fit. Polo, riding and long hikes through the Canadian wilderness, often on snowshoes, demanded more than normal exercise for a desk man. On some days when at The Tribune he dressed for polo after lunch, mounted a wooden horse perched amid the Gothic buttresses atop the tower and drove a polo ball with vigor into a net which, with help of a sloping floor, returned the ball to him at a decent speed. When he was 72 his wife asked a doctor at what age a man abandons sex. "Sometimes at 90," the doctor said. She replied, "Good God!"

Joseph Medill's constant campaign against alcohol was one of his grandfather's policies which the Colonel did not continue. Scotch was his drink although never during working hours. Careful preparation laying in a stock and quiet supplementary purchases over America's dry years freed the Colonel from abstinence demanded by the 18th Amendment. As he reached 60, sleep eluded him. Many things were on his mind. Harsh things said by his political enemies led by President Roosevelt troubled him and chased sleep out of his head. The injustice and cruelty of the barbs gnawed. The prospect of war and a repetition of the killing of millions he had seen in World War I appalled him. The most effective sedatives were a book and a bottle of scotch. He probably never finished the book before sleep overcame him but he frequently finished the bottle. He awoke with a clear head. One day he told the doctor, "The only man I know who can drink

459

more liquor and hold it better than I can is Winston Churchill."

The steady consumption of alcohol slowly hardened and shrunk the liver and subsequently the bladder, bringing discomfort and pain. At 65 his appetite faded. Often even a light meal produced flatulence. He lost weight. His wife persuaded him to call in a local Wheaton doctor, Clarence Wyngarden. "We will send a limousine," the secretary said. In a few minutes the biggest, blackest car the doctor ever had seen stopped in front of his small home. The doctor found the Colonel's general health good, his heart strong, circulation excellent, brain clear. The problem was alcohol. Dr. Wyngarden, an abstainer, was certain that anyone who drank more than three or four ounces of scotch every day for several years was an alcoholic doomed to a shortened life. The liver could not be restored although death could be moved back by giving up alcohol. The doctor's gentle suggestion of a change in habits did not impress the Colonel and for several years thereafter, Dr. Wyngarden was summoned only when the Colonel had a cold.

"The Colonel, like so many rich men, suffered from a plethora of specialists," Dr. Van Dellen once philosophized. Shortly after the Colonel's 70th birthday, a variety of doctors diagnosed an enlarged prostate gland and suggested that an operation cutting away part of the gland would remove the partial blockage. The operation loosened control over the bladder. The Colonel's driver noted which filling stations between Cantigny and the Tower had clean toilets.

The prostate operation was repeated. The next morning the Colonel announced he was leaving the hospital and going home. Doctors conferred and, knowing the Colonel would go home with or without their approval, acceded but recommended that a Tribune nurse be at Cantigny at all hours. Send for the Tribune ambulance, the Colonel commanded. The Tribune dispatched a station wagon. The Colonel was carried on a stretcher from the hospital and shoved into the vehicle. He was too long; the door would not close. Let's go, the Colonel commanded. The driver paused for a second or maybe two to consider whether the city rule that a red flag must be hung on any load protruding from a moving vehicle should be observed in this instance. He gave himself the wise answer: No. The Colonel rode the 30 miles to Cantigny with his feet hanging out. The second prostate operation also failed. The Colonel said the Bible was correct: A man was all right for three score 10 years and then he started falling apart.

Dr. Wyngarden became the on-the-spot doctor. One day he repeated his recommendation to give up scotch as the only way to halt deterioration of the liver. "Young man," the Colonel said, "everyone of us has his idiosyncrasy. Scotch is one of the few pleasures in my life. I will determine when I give it up." The doctor did not insist. "Nobody ever ordered the Colonel about," he recalled. "You suggested and advised but you did not command."

The doctor was convinced the nightly bottle slowly was killing the Colonel, but also it was permitting him to become calm after busy, trying days, to sleep deeply and to awaken each morning refreshed, restored, ready to resume battle. Wyngarden reasoned that without sound sleep the Colonel easily might become, in street terms, a nervous wreck. And what was the alternative? The habit was so deeply ingrained that to break it the Colonel would need long treatment in a hospital. His pride would not permit him to accept such treatment.

The Colonel's remedy was to send for the Tribune building superintendent, who brought a crew to Cantigny and, during a few days while the Colonel was out of town, bricked off part of the south porch to provide a washroom only four steps from the Colonel's favorite soft sofa in his library.

The Colonel went to Europe in 1953, telling none of his hosts about his ailment. He paid for his pride with pain that developed while being honored at a dinner or taking the salute at a 1st Division parade in Germany. The weather was icy and, although the Colonel had brought a thick coat with a wide fur collar, he became chilled. A fever developed. In Copenhagen, final stop on his itinerary, doctors diagnosed pneumonia and proposed he enter a hospital. The Colonel flew home, cabling ahead: "Have some Arabian horses lined up or some American ponies if any still exist. They must of course be gentle, sound, don't stumble, with good mouths and gaits, preferably, I guess, from eight to 10 years old to make them steady." He arrived looking haggard. He developed a dangerous skin infection. The bladder problem became more demanding. Doctors worried about cancer and suggested he go to the Mayo Clinic in Rochester, Minnesota. No cancer, the doctors there said.

"I have been much sicker than they have given out," the Colonel told Louie Rose. "We might call it strike two. I had strike one in Denmark. Strike three and it will be all over, which brings to mind I have not accomplished the reoganization I boasted so much about. I have got to go to Florida for an indefinite period,

461

which really begins my retirement in all but name." As part of the reorganization the Colonel proposed that Rose retire after 43 years. "The new crowd is never kind," he added. Rose retired.

* * * * *

The Colonel had long pondered how he could preserve The Tribune, its subsidiaries and Cantigny after his death. He recognized that no person would have the financial control gained by his grandfather, Joseph Medill, and preserved into the third generation by himself and Joe Patterson under a trust created by Medill and, on its expiration, rolled into a new trust, the McCormick-Patterson Trust, to continue until 20 years after the death of the last surviving Medill grandchild. The trust arrangements discouraged the heirs from selling The Tribune and reduced their inheritance taxes. Each Medill daughter divided her half interest equally among the children, Medill and Robert McCormick and Joe and Cissy Patterson. Under the Colonel and Patterson the Tribune Company paid low dividends, using most of its large earnings to expand resources and operations. To widen his own holdings, the Colonel had bought as much as he could afford of stock coming available from members of the family or Medill partner heirs, sometimes selling Cantigny land or borrowing. Stock beyond his financial reach was bought by the employees trust which subsequently, on the Colonel's instruction, sold the non-voting right to favored employees at a price worked out in accordance with a formula drawn by Tribune lawyers and based on dividends. Sometimes the rights were given to very special executives as a bonus. The price hovered around $35,000 a share, or $2,187 for one-sixteenth. The trust was administered by a committee of employees chosen by the Colonel. The committee gave its proxies to the Colonel which, when combined with the 54 1/3 shares he owned outright and his right to 327½ shares in the McCormick-Patterson Trust, gave him control of the company. The Pattersons and the Medill partner heirs might have been able to combine against him but never did so.

The Colonel worried that each death in the family could dilute the family control. His brother, Medill McCormick, willed his interests to his widow, Ruth Hanna, and their children, Katrina, John and Bazy. On John's fall from a mountain his share was divided among his mother and sisters. Ruth Hanna left an incomplete will and her stock right passed to her second husband, Con-

462

gressman Simms, the first non-family member to become a new major stockholder. The transfer alarmed the Colonel. However Simms wanted to build an office structure in Albuquerque and, to get money, sold the stock right to the Colonel and the employees trust.

The Colonel similarly purchased Katrina's stock right when she decided to part completely from him and The Tribune, and from Cissy's heirs.

Joe Patterson gave his first wife Alice right to 65 5/8 shares as a part of divorce settlement and pledged that two-thirds of his remaining stock right—about 165 shares—would be divided among their three daughters on his death. Patterson divided the final third between his second wife Mary King and their son Jimmy.

As the Colonel advanced toward his mid-seventies he had to meet a problem more difficult than keeping control in one hand. To whom would that control pass? The usual rich person divides his or her fortune, powers and responsibilities among the children, with secondary provision for spouse and others of that generation. Such a distribution almost always breaks up the personal empire; often the children refuse to work together, prefer cash and sell their inheritance. The childless Colonel had no such worry. Equally his life of isolation, of seclusion, his preference of solitaire to any game involving partners, freed him of personal attachments that should be rewarded. There was one exception, Maryland McCormick.

Tribune executives speculated that she, a highly intelligent, strong-willed person blessed with much common sense and drive, was urging the Colonel to give her a large block of stock and name her as his successor as publisher and company president or at least make her a director of the company. He did give her Katrina's stock right, but before the transfer was completed the Colonel changed his mind, saying his lawyer, Kirkland, had reminded him that Maryland was much younger than he and might marry again and leave her stock right to her next husband as had Ruth Hanna. Mrs. McCormick recovered the transfer certificate from her bank vault and delivered it to the Colonel. As for wanting to become publisher and president, nonsense, she said later; she couldn't begin to run The Tribune nor did she want to. Nevertheless strong rivalries did arise between Mrs. McCormick and the executives, who gossiped that the Colonel was talking about a divorce, and between executives of The Tribune in Chicago and the executives of The News in New York. The Colonel had also to consider the minority stockholders. One of the biggest, Alfred "Bob" Cowles, told Howard Wood if the Colonel gave power to the current management, he would continue his support at directors' meetings. In his last months the Colonel wrote to Katrina, "I'm awfully sorry you came to dislike me and I do not know why." Katrina crumpled the note but on reflection smoothed it. A friend told her, "No matter how you feel, the Colonel deserves a reply."

*   *   *   *   *

The Colonel wanted Cantigny to survive him. He had seen too many beautiful estates cut up, too many fine houses hacked about, abandoned or demolished. He once offered to give the estate to Bazy but she said she didn't want "to live in a mausoleum." He considered giving the estate to the City of Wheaton, to Chicago, to DuPage County, to the State of Illinois, to some federal agency. He had studies made of how estates given to such bodies had fared. Invariably the recipient body sooner or later had ignored the donor's wishes.

For a while he considered giving the estate to a community association being formed to build and operate a hospital, the home to be the nucleus. One day the Colonel put the question to Judge Win Knoch, a neighbor with a lifetime experience in probate. The best thing to do, Judge Knoch quickly told him, would be to set up a tax-free trust, give to it the estate and enough capital to maintain the estate properly and to operate it as a public park and museum, and name the men to run the trust and to pick their successors. "Win, you haven't even stopped to think about it," the Colonel protested. "I don't have to," the Judge said. "I've just been through the same thing with Joy Morton." Knoch was referring to the salt heir who turned his 1,500-acre estate six miles from Cantigny into a now famous arboretum.

*   *   *   *   *

The Colonel rated Tribune nurses as the best in town. For years he dropped in on the medical department to report some ache or to have his back rubbed. Often he asked for Iola Mayer. During his illness in the late summer of 1954 Iola was brought a week at a time to Cantigny. The Colonel told her she had free run of the estate and she could use the swimming pool but only if someone else were present for safety's sake. Mrs. McCormick provided a suit. Nurse Mayer breakfasted in the kitchen and took the dogs for a long morning walk. Often she and the Colonel lunched alone on the porch. The Colonel asked her about herself. She delighted him with a story about the day a bear walked into a hotel lobby in Duluth, Minnesota, her home town. They talked of history but never of current politics. On some days editorial writers or Tribune executives came on business and stayed for lunch. Iola sensed that being with men he considered to be his friends acted as therapy. No business was talked at lunch. After lunch the Colonel told Iola that he had arranged that So-and-So would show her something on the estate. Then the Colonel returned to the business matters. One day the Colonel told Iola that his plane was bringing Mrs. McCormick from town. "Have you ever flown?" he asked. She said no. When the plane arrived, he had the pilot give her a long joy ride. The executive who was to have flown back to town was sent by car. If someone dropped in unexpectedly during the evening, the Colonel welcomed him but soon excused himself and left the nurse to entertain the visitor. One night Iola was awakened by the Colonel's buzzer. The nurse, her hair in curlers, hurried to the Colonel. The sight startled him but he said nothing. On nights when he couldn't sleep she made cocoa. He was touched.

As months passed the Colonel weakened. By autumn his digestion could accept only mushy foods—cereal, jello, ice cream, custard. His body shrank; his energy lessened; his interests wandered, although he continued to go to the Tower almost every day, even on days when a chill or a fever should have kept him at home. Scotch became nauseating and the nightly bottle disappeared from the bedside. Specialists came and went. One mentioned the possibililty of melancholia. The remark deeply disturbed the Colonel who remembered that in 1899 some doctors blamed melancholia for the death of Grandfather Medill.

Lawyers also came and went. The Colonel told no one of his discussions with them.

Members of the Wheaton Presbyterian congregation heard that the Colonel offered to leave enough money to replace the outgrown church and that the minister, Doctor Bob, wanted to name the church for the Colonel. The entire congregation welcomed the prospect of getting the money, but a few important members refused to carve into the corner stone the name of a man who rarely attended service. The suggestion was heard no more.

On December 18, 1954, the Colonel signed his will and on January 3rd he added a codicil, both acts known only to his lawyers. Neither Mrs. McCormick nor Tribune executives knew the contents. Mrs. McCormick continued urging the Colonel to favor her. Kirkland summoned Wyngarden and other doctors to his law office to state in writing that the Colonel was of sound mind.

In January a specialist suggested that the basic problem was adhesions to the bladder and proposed surgery. Dr. Van Dellen and Dr. Wyngarden both thought the operation unnecessary, but it was carried out January 19th at Passavant Hospital in Chicago. No adhesions were found. A nurse came upon the Colonel walking down the hospital corridor toward the elevator carrying a saline bottle and dragging tubes. She coaxed him back to bed. Doctors agreed to let him move to his apartment nearby at 209 East Lake Shore Drive, a fine-looking, solid, very costly 1920s apartment building with large rooms and an exciting view over the lake front and cars gliding noiselessly along the Outer Drive. Not an apartment habitue, he referred to the building as "the tenement." The Colonel had given the Astor Street house to Northwestern University Medical School.

The Colonel asked that someone from The Tribune be with him at all times, day and night. He was disturbed by the uncertainties surrounding the deaths of his cousin Cissy and William Randolph Hearst. He was aware that dying persons had, while dozing, signed wills and other papers put before them. He asked Wood to organize The Night Watch, assigning to it Stanley Johnston, the happy, outgoing, former war correspondent; Wayne Thomis, the Colonel's long-time pilot; Eddie Johnson, the ebullient director of the color photography studio and Frank Schreiber, head of WGN. All had in the course of their work been with the Colonel for considerable periods. He was easy in their company. They took turns daily. Gottfried Hintersdorf who had become the Colonel's "man" in 1915 and served him 32 years until he was 72 came to call. "We'll get to the farm and walk in the grass," the Colonel told him.

The Colonel resumed going to the office on January 29th, The Tribune reporting the surgery had brought about remarkable restoration of health. General MacArthur and General Summerall sent congratulatory notes. Campbell, Wood, and Maxwell jointly gave the Colonel a large ring which he wore flamboyantly and made a point of showing. He told Wood, "I have been going around giving the impression of being a successful gambler which, after all, is what the newspaper business is, anyway."

One Saturday morning he did not sit at his desk when the editorial writers came into his office but lay on the big leather sofa. Morgenstern sat as usual in a high-backed chair near the desk. The Colonel asked him to "come over here where I can see you." The editorials for Sunday were worked out. Usually when the task was done writers left without any greeting, but this Saturday each came up to the Colonel, shook his hand and said, "Goodbye, Colonel." Morgenstern added, "Good luck." They sensed they would not see him there again.

On February 5th the Colonel flew to Florida. The two-year-old bladder problem seemed solved. Forever, the Colonel told himself optimistically. The Tribune plane brought milk and eggs from Cantigny as well as Tribune executives, some summoned for business, others for companionship.

The Colonel had leather-covered booklets lettered in gold made for his "Watchers of the Night," and for Van Dellen and the Colonel's Japanese valet. To the list of night watchers Johnston added Buster Boo and had the bulldog certify his nightly presence with a paw print. The certification was difficult. Buster Boo liked the flavor of the ink and licked his paw clean before Johnston could apply paw to paper.

The Colonel sent to a jeweler for four gold watches, had them inscribed, "In appreciation of my recovery" and gave one each to Campbell, Wood and Maxwell. A fourth was intended for Van Dellen but the Colonel merely told a secretary, "Give it to the doctor," and she handed it to a local doctor who had been brought in to assist on a day that Van Dellen was in Chicago. After the Colonel's death The Tribune began giving a watch to each employee upon completion of 30 years with the paper.

The Boynton Beach home bought by the Colonel for $650,000 was chilly, built in the days when Florida was considered immune from winter. The room arrangement was inconvenient, all bedrooms opening off the living room. So many people walked unsuspectingly into a patio pool that the Colonel had it filled in. The house stood on a long, narrow sand island separated from the mainland by the inland waterway, the beach extending for a half mile in each direction, the only access road crossing through marsh and scrub. The Colonel sent for Wood, on vacation at Sanibel Island, and told him he had decided to sell the Boynton

Beach property. "You fellows," he said, "will have enough trouble running The Tribune without having to worry about Florida real estate. You fellows will have more clout than I did because you will have the entire income from my fortune. I have had to pay taxes up to 80 percent." He asked Wood to drive him to a real estate office to sign the transfer papers. The price for the residence and the mile of beach was $581,000. The Colonel reserved the right for Kent Cooper to live out his life in the fine house the Colonel had built for him.

Executives and friends, Dr. Stewart among them, came to call for a few hours or a few days. One evening the Colonel, in pajamas and bathrobe, came from his bedroom into the living room where Campbell, Wood and Maxwell were playing gin rummy, their favorite card game. The Colonel said he was hungry, found a banana, peeled it and watched the three. After some time he said, "This is a hell of a way to run a newspaper." In the middle of one night he awoke with a yen for ice cream. Stanley Johnston could find none in the freezer so he fetched some from an all-night drug store. In the morning Elizabeth was angry. "You should have awakened me," the cook scolded. "I would have made some ice cream. He likes mine best." One Saturday evening Buster Boo lay under the desk while the Colonel read his radio speech. The microphone picked up the bulldog's naturally hard breathing. Listeners wrote saying they were sorry the Colonel was ill and hoped his breathing soon would return to normal.

The pain returned. The Colonel weakened. His face seemed to shrivel day by day. He seemed to lose interest. He sent his plane to bring Wood from Chicago. Wood found the Colonel weak, trying futilely to put on a green silk shirt. He lay down on the bed, took Howard's hands, closed his eyes. "Howard," he said, "there are two things. First, please give my regards to your charming wife. Second, go back and tell the boys at The Tribune I've got the company set up the way I want it. This is the way it will be. My mind is at peace."

The Colonel ordered a wheelchair and used it to move about the house. One day he asked Dr. Van Dellen to roll him onto the beach. Maxwell went along. For some time the Colonel looked out at the ocean, saying nothing. Out of the beach grass wriggled a snake, a big one, seven or eight feet long. Its path would take it directly to the Colonel. Maxwell started to shout a warning. Van Dellen put a finger to his lips. Shhh! The snake arrived at the chair, wriggled under it, out the other side and went on its way.

Later Maxwell asked Van Dellen why he had exposed the Colonel to the danger of the snake. It was better not to disturb him, the doctor said.

Another afternoon, again on the beach, the Colonel saw a ship with four funnels pass. "I've never seen anything like that," he said. "Get Miss Vydra." The secretary came. He dictated a note to Arthur Schmon in Canada: "A four-funnel ship just passed." His executives wondered why he sent the note. Perhaps, they surmised, he and Schmon long ago had talked about ships and discussed why ships had more than one funnel.

One day he dictated a note to Veysey in London saying that when he was a boy in Britain his favorite book concerned a ship which could travel on the water, under the water and in the air. That was all. An ad in The Times of London produced the title and the name of the author. The London library service, which never discards any British book, produced a copy that went off to the Colonel. Another ad located in a bookstore a copy to fill the gap on the library shelf.

Early in March Sunday Editor Mike Kennedy came to Boynton Beach, sleeping in a motel and coming daily to the house. Van Dellen also came. "Why should you be doing this?" the Colonel asked. "You have a hell of a hard job in Chicago writing a column six days a week. Get the best man in the country and ask him to come." Mrs. McCormick asked Kennedy to summon a popular doctor in Chicago but the doctor said the Colonel should come to him.

Van Dellen was now certain that the long-term liver problem was nearing its final stages and in a short time the kidneys would cease functioning and death would follow. The bladder drained at will, causing the Colonel deep embarrassment. He refused to have a catheter. Dr. Van Dellen recommended that a procedure to stretch the bladder be carried out. The Colonel flew to Chicago on March 10th. The expansion was done at Passavant hospital. Van Dellen phoned Bazy in Washington. "Has Mrs. McCormick told you," he asked, "that the Colonel is in the hospital? He has had another operation. He is quite ill." Bazy said no one had told her. "The Colonel wants to see you," the doctor continued. "He said he treated you outrageously over The Times-Herald and wants to ask your forgiveness before he dies." In five minutes Bazy was in a car to Chicago. Claustrophobia kept her out of planes. At the hospital she found the Colonel half awake. She bent over him and kissed him, took his hand and, holding it,

469

sat beside the bed for some time. Neither said a word. When the Colonel dozed off she left the hospital and walked to the jewelry store at the Drake Hotel. Seeking something that would tell the Colonel all recriminations were ended, she bought a gold fishing knife and had it engraved with a line from the "Three Musketeers," "All for one, one for all. Love, Bazy." She did not see the Colonel again. At the funeral Dr. Van Dellen told her the Colonel kept the knife within reach until he died.

A week after the operation the Colonel was taken from the apartment to Cantigny. He was very weak, rarely moved through the house and lay for long periods on a large sofa in the library. Bess Vydra daily brought the mail and messages from downtown. Mike Kennedy brought pictures for selection. The Colonel gave him two picture books. "These may be some use to you at the paper," he said. The Colonel's sitting room was cleared of furniture and a hospital bed installed. Dr. Wyngarden came every morning and often stayed until midnight. The doctors considered giving the Colonel morphine but decided against that course. Mrs. McCormick, asked her opinion, said the Colonel should not be drugged nor should artificial means of continuing life be used. Dr. Wyngarden agreed, advising that the Colonel be permitted to die in dignity. Stanley Johnston was always on hand, at the bedside when the Colonel awoke from a fitful sleep, talking to him, telling him stories about his boyhood in Australia, his gold mining in New Guinea, his war days. His voice seemed to soothe the Colonel.

Mrs. Wu, mother of Cantigny's only bride, came to say goodbye. The Colonel asked about Eileen. Told that she was well and her husband was rising in the university world, the Colonel asked, "How many children does she have? It's been three years." None, the mother replied. Distress tightened the Colonel's face. "Tell Eileen," he commanded fiercely, "that she must have children." The mother passed the order to Eileen. The words burned into the young woman's memory and were still vivid nearly 30 years later when she and her husband made a sentimental return to Cantigny. The words, she reflected, were a cry from the heart, exposing the Colonel's own long-submerged sorrow over not having children of his own to carry the Medill-McCormick Tribune dynasty into the fourth generation and beyond.

Eileen and YY did have children, their first daughter after seven years of marriage, the second two years later. The elder was graduated from Massachusetts Institute of Technology, the other from Harvard. YY became dean of engineering at the New Jersey Institute of Technology and a consultant to the post-Mao Chinese government on reopening of the universities Mao had closed, depriving a generation of young Chinese of the higher education so essential to the welfare of their country.

* * * * *

The Colonel planned to fly to Baie Comeau for his 75th birthday in July. As its gift to him the town engaged a sculptor, Wheeler Williams, to create a bronze statue. Williams, shunning the conventional standing or seated figure, sketched the Colonel kneeling in a canoe, white man's fashion, toes bent forward, paddling along a rippling river. "We can't have that," some townspeople said, "Kids will climb all over the canoe. They won't show the Colonel proper respect." The Colonel differed. "I do not find that prospect distasteful," he said. The sculptor placed in the canoe a map of the St. Lawrence, a rifle, a woodman's hatchet and the Colonel's Mexican border campaign hat with its broad stiff brim that could support a net and keep flies from the face.

Mrs. McCormick asked Dr. Van Dellen to bring a young man knowledgeable in medical care to stay with the Colonel at night and to relieve Johnston. Van Dellen recruited one of his second year medical students. "He chose me, I decided later," Dr. Jack Kronfield said, "because I was the tallest member of the class."

He was six feet two, almost able to look the Colonel in the eye. Kronfield was a San Franciscan and knew nothing about the Colonel. He arrived at Cantigny in early evening after dinner and helped the Colonel change into pajamas. The Colonel walked toward the door. The young man stopped him and told him, much as a father speaks to a young son, "Colonel, you must go to bed now. You need to rest." The Colonel, startled, halted, looked slightly down on the student and said, "My boy, no one has ever spoken to me like that."

For a short time the two stood, eye to eye.

Then the Colonel turned, walked to his hospital bed and lay down. "I tucked him in," Dr. Kronfield recalled.

"Where are you living?" the Colonel asked.

"On the top floor," the student replied.

"I won't be using my bed," the Colonel said. "When you finish your studies, come down and sleep in my room."

The young medical student did so. Only rarely did the Colonel

471

call him during the night. "He gave no trouble," said Dr. Kronfield a quarter of a century later, now a San Francisco specialist. "Other people were surprised. They said the Colonel was willful and cantankerous. I did not find him so."

Each day the Colonel seemed less attentive. At times it was hard to tell if he were awake and resting or sleeping or in a partial coma. At other times the Colonel walked around the house. One day he ventured into the theater in the basement. "Where's my Indian?" he demanded. Mrs. McCormick had given the wooden cigar store statue to Maxwell who had placed it in his basement recreation room where he took out his frustrations on a set of drums, day or night. Maxwell returned the Indian quickly.

One afternoon the Colonel walked into the library to find Dr. Wyngarden holding a plain brown Toby jug. The doctor said Mrs. McCormick had told him he could have it to add to his collection. "I cannot give that away," the Colonel said. "I drank ale from it at Yale." The doctor put the jug back on the library table.

Each day the Colonel became weaker. As March dragged on, the Colonel could no longer rise from his bed. His stomach would accept nothing but an occasional sip of water. To ease the final days the doctors sedated him. As March entered its last week the Colonel's mind seemed to drift away. He spoke fewer words and on the 29th became silent and entered a coma. Despite his earlier admonitions the doctors inserted a catheter to keep the bed dry and prevent infection. But they continued to carry out his demand that his body always be covered, even when doctors were examining him.

Through the final three months Dr. Wyngarden had watched the Colonel fight off death but refuse to talk of death. Rather he spoke often of plans to enlarge the Cantigny airfield so he could bring in a big plane and fly non-stop to Japan. "He seemed to fear dying," the doctor reflected years later. "He had no conception of eternal life. To him, death was final. You died; everything was over. The Colonel did not want life to be over but he knew his life was ending and at that time of need he had nothing to lean on. I was very sorry for him."

On March 29th the Colonel's breathing became weak, his pulse irregular. He was worse the next day and the following. The evening of the 31st, about 10 o'clock, Johnston said he would not leave the Colonel during the night. Johnston's wife Barbara who had come to Cantigny to be with her husband, Mrs. Horace Wetmore who had come during the day to see the Colonel and Mrs. McCormick's daughter Anne visiting from California, all went to bed. Dr. Wyngarden gave Mrs. McCormick a sleeping draft. During the evening large trucks carried away furnishings promised to the Presbyterian church and to others.

About two o'clock on the morning of April 1st, 45 years after Robert Patterson died in Philadelphia, Johnston thought the Colonel's breathing might have stopped. Dr. Wyngarden felt the pulse and found no beat. Johnston called Van Dellen at his home in Chicago but did not try to awaken Mrs. McCormick from her sedated sleep. Van Dellen came. He said death had been caused by a myocardial insufficiency due to arteriosclerotic heart condition and cirrhosis of the liver.

Johnston called the funeral home where for a year an oversized coffin chosen by the Colonel had been stored. The Colonel had been appalled by stories that sometimes an undertaker cut the feet off a tall man to make the body fit the coffin. The undertaker said he would bring the coffin in the morning. "Bring it now," Johnston demanded. The undertaker came. The body was placed in the coffin. Johnston closed the lid. In the morning when Mrs. McCormick's sleeping draft wore off, Johnston told her the Colonel had died. He said he had closed the coffin because the Colonel's face had become so shrunken and yellowed he thought no one should be haunted by his grim image in death but rather remember the Colonel as he was in life. Mrs. McCormick said the decision was wise. Van Dellen explained the cause of death and asked if she wished to have an autopsy to confirm the finding. She said she thought such an investigation unnecessary.

The Colonel wanted to be buried at Cantigny, beside Amy, in the gardens, 100 steps from the house, below a low ridge, in the monument long-planned but not yet built. Mrs. McCormick asked that the service be private and that no flowers be sent. A dozen telegrams were sent to persons thought to be specially concerned. Bazy and Katrina came. The closed coffin was wheeled into the library before the double French doors. Dr. Stewart conducted the short Presbyterian burial service. Eight soldiers from the 1st Division carried the coffin across the Jefferson verandah, down the stairs under the great oak and into the avenue of trees the Colonel had planted so long ago, past the swimming pool to a newly dug grave beside that of Amy. Soldiers fired a final salute. Two days later, a memorial service was held in the Fourth Presbyterian Church downtown. The Rev. Harrison Ray Anderson read from the Scriptures. About 1,500 people attended. A clipping service collected 5,786 accounts of the death.

The 25-page will made Campbell, Wood and Maxwell his executors "because their very long association with me has given them especial knowledge of the ideals and principles which have guided me in the management of The Tribune." He said the three executors with Schmon and Bazy should take over the voting rights of his half of the McCormick-Patterson Trust. Patterson heirs had chosen Mary King Patterson, Jack Flynn and News Editor Richard Clarke to assume Joe's rights. The Trust would continue until 1975. Outsiders expected that the Chicago and New York sections would compete for mastery of the company but Bazy and Mary King urged reason. So did the largest stock-owning heirs of Joseph Medill's partners. The directors chose Campbell as president and chief executive officer of the company and publisher of The Tribune, Wood as general manager, and Maxwell as editor, and maintained Flynn as publisher of The News and Schmon as head of the Canadian paper, power and ship operations. The will also set up the tax-free Robert R. McCormick Charitable Trust and gave to it the Colonel's Tribune stock right and named as trustees Campbell, Wood, Maxwell, Schmon and Assistant Editor Stewart Owen. When a trustee died or became 75, the other four must name, first, Production Manager Harold Grumhaus and then Advertising Executive Walter Kurz. Subsequently trustees could choose anyone but preferably someone who shared the Colonel's philosophy. After expenses, annuities and bequests were paid, all income was to be given to charitable organizations.

To a second trust, the Cantigny Trust, he gave the estate and one million dollars, eventually paid by the executors in 28 shares of Tribune stock valued at $980,000 plus $20,000 in cash and directed the income be used to pay maintenance costs which the Colonel had estimated at $50,000 a year. The estate was to be opened to the public as a park and the architecturally fine house as a museum and operated by the trustees for the "instruction, recreation and welfare of the people of Illinois."

Mrs. McCormick stated that the Colonel had told her he would make her a Tribune director. She considered contesting the will under which she would receive the Lake Shore apartment and a million dollars, tax paid, to be given $100,000 annually for 10 years and subsequently $100,000 a year, taxable, for life. She could remain at Cantigny with or without the farms as long as

474

she wished, paying all expenses. She could retain for herself or dispose of any of the furnishings and the Colonel's personal belongings except his father's Paris cufflinks which were to go to Chauncey McCormick's son Brooks, and then to Brooks' son "when he is old enough to appreciate and preserve them." A portrait of the Colonel's mother was given to the Art Institute and a portrait of his father to the federal government to be hung with paintings of other ambassadors in the embassy in Paris. The Colonel already had given Amy's collection of French Impressionist paintings to the Art Institute, his Aiken, South Carolina, winter estate to the Citadel for the use of his World War I commander, General Summerall, his Astor Street house to Northwestern University and use of part of his Florida beach estate to Kent Cooper, retired head of the Associated Press. The wooden case with the charming paintings of the 1893 Columbian Exposition, unopened all the years, was abandoned in the attic but the paintings in time decorated the Cantigny offices when not on public display. The Colonel gave $1,000 each to 40 executives, four lawyers, an old friend, Thomas Gowenlock, a relative, Isabelle Morris, and the butler Emil; $10,000 to each of his secretaries, Bess Vydra and Dorothy Murray. Some Cantigny employees said Dorothy had told them they would receive $1,000 for each year of employment and when they were unmentioned in the will unjustly blamed Mrs. McCormick for the omission. At Johnston's recommendation the trustees gave the Florida fishing boat to the long-time chauffeur, Gene Corbin. He sold it and used the money to buy a house.

The Colonel asked that help be given Tribune employees, past and present, in need because of illness or unable to provide university education for their children. He proposed assistance for needy widows and children of Illinois officers of the 1st Division. The Internal Revenue Service overruled these provisions as not conforming to charitable trust requirements.

The Colonel asked that Bazy's son Mark Miller "be given an opportunity of employment" and be considered later as a trustee. "I hope he will carry on the great newspaper tradition of Joseph Medill," the Colonel said. That was not to be.

The codicil gave $10,000 a year each to Mrs. McCormick's daughters Alice and Anne and $600 a year to a cousin Eleanor Jewell Lundberg, the Tribune's art critic.

The will directed the trustees to build the exedra within five years at a cost not to exceed the original estimate of $160,000.

475

The task was completed in two years for $153,206.90 and the bodies of Amy and the Colonel were moved into their permanent memorial.

After six months Mrs. McCormick moved to Washington and Cantigny passed into the hands of the Cantigny Trust. The residence became the Robert R. McCormick Museum. Guides began conducting tours. In time Sunday afternoon chamber music concerts, flower shows, art shows, seminars brought a new kind of life to the Georgian-style structure as the Colonel had envisaged when he added the wings. The farm animals were sold and lands rented to a tenant farmer. The Colonel's last horse, Clockwork, was boarded with Brooks McCormick at neighboring St. James Farm.

At Schmon's urging the trustees spent one million dollars to convert the stables into a museum telling something of the story of the men of the 1st Division in the two World Wars and, at the urging of Stewart Owen's wife Garry, a gardening enthusiast, engaged Landscape Architect Franz Lipp to convert part of the Colonel's airfield into 10 acres of formal gardens. An oak grove was opened to youth organizations for camping and 200 acres of woodlands, including Swan Lake, for hikes, making altogether a 500-acre green oasis amid the ever-consuming western suburbs of Chicago. Cantigny, as the Colonel wished, became "a show place because of its sheer beauty" and began providing without charge quiet pleasure for a quarter of a million visitors a year.

On the Colonel's 75th birthday Baie Comeau dedicated its gift, the bronze statue. The Catholic Bishop of the North Shore, Napoleon Alexandre Labrie, said, "In his frail bark, the Colonel moved into the unknown." The Bishop told the pioneers that the lesson the Colonel left for them was simple and direct: "Slacken not your paddle; be not halted by obstacles."

Today a handsome, young, undaunted Colonel, alone in his canoe, paddles eagerly up the St. Lawrence, looking for a better tomorrow.

Acknowledgments

Colonel McCormick's newspaper career is documented thoroughly in the Chicago Tribune's official histories, by the Colonel himself on the 75th anniversary, by Philip Kinsley on the 100th and by Lloyd Wendt minutely and massively on the 135th. Carl Wiegman tells the story of the Canadian operations, with Paul Provencher adding details of forest life and Harvey Smith of life in the pioneer settlement. John Fink relates the WGN story. John Chapman and Leo McGivena add sparkle to the New York News' official history. Military histories give the facts of the First Division in "the Great War" but an understanding of life in the trenches comes from a score of once popular books and personal tracts by Lieutenants Evarts and Boyd and Sergeant Empey. Kay Lawrence and Emily Bull are faithful reporters of the horsey set in Aiken. Fred Friendly supplies the definitive account of the struggle for a free press. Paul Healy, Alice Hoge and Ralph Martin bare Cissy. Frank Waldrop and Joseph Gies interpret the Colonel. Dozens of other books and the files and reference staffs of the Chicago Historical Society, the Chicago Sanitary District, Tom Dyba and his Lincoln files at Illinois Benedictine College and the Wheaton, Glen Ellyn, Naperville and Chicago Public Libraries, plus our own notebooks, add bits and pieces.

The fullest published accounts of the Colonel's personal life and ideas can be found in his hundreds of radio talks, scores of addresses, dozens of booklets and books and the Tribune editorial pages.

But for us, the Colonel came alive during hundreds of hours of conversations with people engaged in or knowledgeable about his first love, The Tribune —Howard Wood, Fred Nichols, Paul Fulton, Mike Kennedy, Fred Byington, India Edwards, Fanny Butcher, George Tagge, Marion Claire and Henry Weber, George Morgenstern, Carl Wiegman, Wayne Thomis, Stanley Rose, Ward Quaal, Walter Simmons, Fred Shafer, Terry and Francoise Flahiff, Arthur Sewell, Bazy Tankersley, the Colonel's namesake Robert McCormick Schmon, Hammond Chaffetz, Carl Lloyd, Polly Goodwin, Ludean and Joseph Parrish, Mrs. Weymouth

479

Kirkland, Howard Donaldson, Ben and Mary Jones, Marjorie Maxwell, Richard Orr, Eleanor Page, Tom Curran, Ed Freckelton, Byron Campbell, Joseph Cerutti and Claudia Cassidy. His other love, Cantigny, and his life away from The Tribune were fleshed out by Mrs. Maryland McCormick, Louise Brydon Coffin, Doctors Ted Van Dellen, Harold Method, Clarence Wyngarden and Jack Kronfield. Nurses Margaret Lacey and Iola Mayer, Barbara Johnston Wood, Eddie and Florence Edwards, Lucille Zeier, Jack and Yvonne Burt, Richard Carlson, Jeannette Hurley Reuben, Katrina McCormick Barnes, Helen Hurley Spencer, Eileen Wu, Dorothy and Jimmy Patterson, Mrs. Willis Nance, Dorothy Kunde, Joe Schmidt, Judge William Atten, William Wood Prince, Mrs. John Paul Welling, Brooks McCormick, Judge Win Knoch, Gottfried Hintersdorf, his mind still clear at 107, Margaret Prendergast Frimmel, Naneen Rebori, Ruth Roberts, Lucy Miller, Mary Ann Crawford, Richard Crabb, Mary Christmas Piper, Grace Corpening, Alice Hooper af Petersens, Peter Jensen, Elinor Patterson Baker, Felicia Gizycka Magruder, John Gamon, Red Grange, Eugene Corbin, Edgar Miller, John Caldwell, Mrs. John T. Bourke, James and Zifforah Snydacker, Cyrus and Harriet Adams, Corwith and Joan Hamill and scores more whose paths crossed that of the Colonel.

For reading parts or all of this manuscript we thank Howard and Barbara Wood, George Tagge, Carl Wiegman, Walter Simmons, Lee Major, Ann Bechly, Fanny Butcher, Anne Cummings, Ruth Hughes, D. Ray Wilson, Daniel Crombie, Alice McCoy and Betsy Jager Saltzstein.

For the title we thank Betty Davis MacKinnon.

Bibliography

Abbott, John S.C., *The History of the Civil War in America* . Gurdon Bill, Springfield, Massachusetts, 1866.

Bairnsfather, Bruce, *Bullets & Billets*. G.P. Putnam's Sons, New York, 1917.

Bairnsfather, Bruce, *More Fragments from France (Parts V-VIII)*. G.P. Putnam's Sons, New York, 1918.

Beadle, Muriel, *The Fortnightly of Chicago*. Henry Regnery Company, Chicago, Illinois, 1973.

Beale, Howard K., *Theodore Roosevelt and the Rise of America to World Power*. Johns Hopkins Press, Baltimore, Maryland, 1956.

Beard, Charles A. and William C. Bagley, *The History of the American People*. Rev. ed., Macmillan, New York, 1923.

Becker, Stephen, *Marshall Field III*. Simon and Schuster, New York, 1964.

Bowen, Ezra, *Knights of the Air*. Time-Life Books, Alexandria, Virginia, 1980.

Bull, Emily L., *Eulalie*. Kalmia Press, Aiken, South Carolina, 1973.

Butcher, Fanny, *Many Lives—One Love*. Harper & Row, New York, 1972.

Butler, Alban B., *Happy Days!* Society of the First Division, Washington D.C., 1928.

Casey, Robert J., *Such Interesting People*. Bobbs-Merrill Company, Indianapolis, Indiana, 1943.

A Century of Tribune Editorials. The Tribune Company, Chicago, Illinois, 1947.

Chapman, John, *Tell It to Sweeney*. Doubleday & Company, Inc., Garden City, New York, 1961.

Chicago Golf Club Diamond Jubilee booklet, 1892-1967.

The Chicago Tribune, *The WGN*. The Tribune Company, Chicago, Illinois, 1922.

Chicago Tribune booklet, *Joseph Medill, A Brief Biography and Appreciation*. The Chicago Tribune, Chicago, Illinois, 1947.

Churchill, The Rt. Hon. Winston S., C.H., M.P., *Great Contemporaries*. G.P. Putnam's Sons, New York, 1937.

Churchill, The Rt. Hon. Winston S., K.G., O.M., C.H., M.P., *Painting as a Pasttime*, Cornerstone Library, New York, 1965.

Clark, Herma, *The Elegant Eighties*. A.C. McClurg & Company, Chicago, Illinois, 1941.

Crane, Stephen, *The Red Badge of Courage*. D. Appleton and Company, New York, 1896.

Croly, Herbert, *Marcus Alonza Hanna*. Archon Books, Hamden, Connecticutt, 1965.

Cromie, Robert, *The Great Chicago Fire*. McGraw-Hill Book Company, Inc., New York/Toronto/London, 1958.

Dedmon, Emmett, *Fabulous Chicago*. Random House, New York, 1953.

Drury, John, *Midwest Heritage*. A.A. Wyn, Inc., New York, 1948.

Dunne, Hon. Edward F., *Illinois*. 5 Vols., Lewis Publishing Company, Chicago/New York, 1933.

Dyba, Thomas J., *Seventeen Years at Eighth and Jackson*. Illinois Benedictine College Publications, Lisle, Illinois, 1982.

481

Edwards, India, *Pulling No Punches.* G.P. Putnam's Sons, New York, 1977.

Edwards, Jerome E., *The Foreign Policy of Col. McCormick's Tribune 1929-1941.* University of Nevada Press, Reno, Nevada, 1971.

Empey, Arthur Guy. *Over the Top.* G.P. Putnam's Sons, New York, 1917.

Evarts, Jeremiah M., *Cantigny.* Privately printed, 1938.

Farr, Finis, *Chicago.* Arlington House, New Rochelle, New York, 1973.

Ferris, Paul, *The House of Northcliffe.* Weidenfeld and Nicolson, London, 1971.

Fink, John, *WGN—A Pictorial History.* WGN Company, 1961.

Flammer, Philip M., *The Vivid Air.* University of Georgia Press, Athens, 1981.

Friendly, Fred W., *Minnesota Rag.* Random House, New York, 1981.

Fyfe, Hamilton, *Northcliffe.* The Macmillan Company, New York, 1930.

Gibbons, Floyd, *And They Thought We Wouldn't Fight.* George H. Doran Company, New York, 1918.

Gies, Joseph, *The Colonel of Chicago.* E.P. Dutton, New York, 1979.

Gwynn, Stephen, editor, *The Letters and Friendships of Sir Cecil Spring Rice.* Vol. I and II. Houghton Mifflin Company, The Riverside Press, Cambridge, 1929.

Hale, Edward E., *The Man Without a Country.* Roberts Brothers, Boston, 1889.

Hanna, Charles A., *The Scotch-Irish Vol. I.* G.P. Putnam's Sons, New York, 1902.

Hannah, Barbara, *Jung, His Life and Work.* G.P. Putnam's Sons, New York, 1976.

Harbord, James G., *The American Army in France 1917-1919.* Little Brown and Company, Boston, 1936.

Healy, Paul F., *Cissy.* Doubleday & Company, Inc., New York, 1966.

Hecht, Ben, *Charlie, The Improbable Life and Times of Charles MacArthur.* Harper and Brothers, New York, 1957.

History of the First Division During the World War, 1917-1919. The John C. Winston Company, Philadelphia, Pennsylvania, 1922.

History of the Chicago Tribune. Published in commemoration of its seventy-fifth birthday. Chicago Tribune, Chicago, Illinois, 1922.

Hoge, Alice Albright, *Cissy Patterson.* Random House, New York, 1966.

Hurley, Maj. Alfred F., *Billy Mitchell, Crusader for Air Power.* Franklin Watts Inc., New York, 1964.

Hurley, Edward, *The Bridge to France.* J.B. Lippincott Company, Philadelphia/London, 1927.

The International Competition for a New Administration Building for the Chicago Tribune, MCMXXII. Rizzoli International, New York, 1980.

Keller, Albert Galloway, and Maurice R. Davie, *Essays of William Graham Sumner, Vol. I.* Yale University Press, New Haven, 1934.

Kinsley, Philip, *The Chicago Tribune, Vols. 1, 2, 3.* Alfred A. Knopf, New York, 1943.

Knickerbocker, H.R., et al, *Danger Forward.* Society of the First Division, Washington D.C., 1947.

Kogan, Herman, and Rick Kogan, *Yesterday's Chicago.* E.A. Seemann Publishing Inc., Miami, Florida, 1976.

Kogan, Herman, and Lloyd Wendt, *Chicago.* Bonanza Books, New York, 1958.

Lawrence, Kay, *Heroes, Horses and High Society: Aiken from 1540.* The R.L. Bryan Company, Columbia, South Carolina, 1971.

Lawrence, Kay, *Horse Tales.* State Printing Company, Columbia, South Carolina, 1976.

Linn, James Weber, *James Keeley, Newspaperman.* The Bobbs-Merrill Company, Indianapolis/New York, Inc., 1937.

Leslie's Photographic Review of the Great War, Leslie-Judge Company, New York, 1919.

Leslie, Shane, *Long Shadows.* John Murray, London, 1966.

Levine, Isaac Don, *Mitchell, Pioneer of Air Power.* Duell, Sloan and Pearce, New York, 1943.

McCutcheon, John T., *Drawn from Memory.* The Bobbs-Merrill Company, Inc., Indianapolis/New York, 1950.

McFeely, William S., *Grant, A Biography.* W.W. Norton & Company, New York, 1981.

McGivena, Leo, and others, *The News.* News Syndicate Company, Inc., 1969.

McCormick, Robert R., *Addresses: History of the Chicago Tribune 1847-1922.* The Chicago Tribune, Chicago, Illinois, 1922.

McCormick, Robert R., *The American Empire,* The Tribune Company, Chicago, Illinois, 1952.

McCormick, Robert R., *The American Revolution and Its Influence on World Civilization.* The Chicago Tribune, Chicago, Illinois, 1945.

McCormick, Robert R., *The Army of 1918.* Harcourt, Brace and Howe, New York, 1920.

McCormick, Robert R., *How We Acquired Our National Territory.* The Chicago Tribune, Chicago, Illinois 1942.

McCormick, Robert R., *The Freedom of the Press.* D. Appleton-Century Company, Inc., New York/London, 1936.

McCormick, Robert R., *Ulysseys S. Grant: The Great Soldier of America.* D. Appleton-Century Company, New York, 1934.

McCormick, Robert R., *The War Without Grant.* The Bond Wheelwright Company, New York, 1950.

McCormick, Robert R., *With the Russian Army.* The Macmillan Company, New York, 1915.

McCullough, David, *Mornings on Horseback.* Simon and Schuster, New York, 1981.

Martin, Ralph G., *Cissy.* Simon and Schuster, New York, 1979.

Mason, Jr., Herbert Molloy, *The Great Pursuit.* Random House, New York, 1970.

Meeker, Arthur, *Chicago with Love.* Alfred A. Knopf, New York, 1955.

The Monticello Papers, Number One. The Thomas Jefferson Memorial Foundation, National Headquarters, New York, 1924.

Moore, William E., and James C. Russell, *U.S. Official Pictures of the World Wars.* Washington D.C., 1920.

Morgan, H. Wayne, *William McKinley and His America.* Syracuse University Press, 1963.

Morris, Edmund, *The Rise of Theodore Roosevelt.* Coward, McCann and Geoghegen, Inc., New York, 1979.

Munson, Jr., Lester E., *The Chicago Tribune Fights World War II.* Princeton University, New Jersey, 1962.

Murray, George, *The Madhouse on Madison Street.* Follett Publishing Company, Chicago, Illinois, 1965.

The News: The First Fifty Years of New York's Picture Newspaper. News Syndicate Company, Inc., New York, 1969.

Nicholson, Nigel, *Mary Curzon.* Harper and Row, New York, 1977.

Pierce, Bessie Louise, *A History of Chicago, Vol. III, The Rise of a Modern City, 1871-1893.* University of Chicago Press, Chicago/London, 1957, Alfred A. Knopf, New York, 1957.

Patterson, Joseph Medill, *A Little Brother of the Rich.* The Reilly & Britton Company, Chicago, Illinois, 1908.

Patterson, Joseph Medill, *Rebellion.* The Reilly and Britton Company, Chicago, Illinois, 1911.

Pringle, Henry F., *Theodore Roosevelt: A Biography.* Harcourt, Brace and Company, New York, 1931.

Provencher, Paul, *I Live in the Woods.* Brunswick Press Limited, Fredericton, 1953.

Ralphson, George H., *Over There with Pershing's Heroes at Cantigny.* M.A. Donohue and Company, Chicago, Illinois, 1919.

Reischauer, Edwin O., *The United States and Japan.* Harvard University Press, Cambridge, 1950.

Roberts, Chalmers M., *The Washington Post.* Houghton Mifflin Company, Boston, 1977.

Roderick, Stella, *Nettie Fowler McCormick.* Richard R. Smith Publisher, Inc., Rindge, New Hampshire, 1956.

Rose, Kenneth, *Superior Person.* Weybright and Tally, New York, 1969.

Sirotek, Robert L., *The Wayne-DuPage Hunt.* The Wayne-DuPage Hunt Publishers, Broadview, Illinois, 1980.

Sixth Regiment Field Artillery: A History of the Sixth Regiment Field Artillery, First Division, United States Army. The Editors: Capt. Ralph T. Heard, editor and manager, Ransbach, Westerwald, Germany, 1919.

Sixth Regiment Field Artillery, Official History of. Telegraph Press, Harrisburg, Pennsylvania, 1933.

Smith, Alson J., *Chicago's Left Bank.* Henry Regnery Company, Chicago, Illinois, 1953.

Smith, Harvey H., *Shelter Bay, Tales of the Quebec North Shore.* McClelland and Stewart Limited, Toronto, Canada, 1964.

Society of the First Division, *History of the First Division.* The John C. Winston Company, Philadelphia, Pennsylvania, 1931.

Spanke, Louise, *Winfield's Good Old Days.* Winfield Public Library, Winfield, Illinois, 1978.

Stewart, Kenneth, and John Tebbel, *Makers of Modern Journalism.* Prentice-Hall, Inc., New York, 1952.

Tebbel, John, *An American Dynasty.* Doubleday, New York, 1947.

Waldrop, Frank C., *McCormick of Chicago.* Prentice-Hall, Inc., Englewood Cliffs, New Jersey, 1966.

Wendt, Lloyd and Herman Kogan, *Bet a Million! The Story of John W. Gates.* The Bobbs-Merrill Company, Indianapolis/New York, 1948.

Wendt, Lloyd, *Chicago Tribune, The Rise of a Great American Newspaper.* Rand McNally & Company, Chicago/New York/San Francisco, 1979.

Wendt, Lloyd and Herman Kogan, *Give the Lady What She Wants!* Rand McNally & Company, Chicago/New York/San Francisco, 1952.

Whitehouse, Arch, *Legion of the Lafayette.* Doubleday and Company, Garden City, New York, 1962.

Wiegman, Carl, *Trees to News.* McClelland & Stewart Ltd., 1953.

Winkler, John K., *William Randolph Hearst.* Hastings House, New York, 1955.

Index

486

487

489

490

Marshall, George C., 212, 215-217, 350, 415
Martyn, Edward and Mrs. Martyn, 69-70
Martyn, Hazel, see Lady Lavery
Mason, George, 35, 273, 328
Massachusetts Institute of Technology, 113, 259
Mata Hari, 182
Mathias, Baldwin, 304
Matisse, 364
Maugeuge, 151
Maxim, Hiram, 168
Maxwell, Marjorie, 443
Maxwell, W. D. (Don), 409-412, 434, 448, 451, 466-468, 472, 474
Mayer, Iola, 464-465
Means, Gaston, 279
Medill, Elinor (Nellie), see Elinor Medill Patterson
Medill, James, 16-20
Medill, Joseph Meharry, ancestors, 11-12; birth, 13; youth, 14-15; Coshocton, Cleveland, 15-17; marriage, 15-17; to Chicago, 17-19; Lincoln, 19-21; mayor, 22; majority owner, 22; creed, 24-28; simplified spelling, 28; builds house, 29, considers selling, 31; supports fair, 32; Thomasville, 37; buys Red Oaks farm, 39; builds country home, 39; dies, 46, 49, 51-53; Medill trust, 462; quoted, 61, 71-72; 76, 85, 93, 98, 100, 102-103; 109, 131, 135, 230, 308, 309, 310, 318, 377, 385, 400, 431, 459, 475
Medill, Josephine, 3, 12, 21
Medill, Katharine (Kate), see Katharine Medill McCormick
Medill, Katharine Patrick (Mrs. Joseph), 3, 15-18; 21-22; 27, 29, 33, 34
Medill, Margaret Corbet (Mrs. William), 13
Medill, Samuel, 18
Medill, William, 13
Medill, William (hero), 13-18; 20, 46-50; 110, 170, 175, 329, 360
Meigs Field, 415-416
Meigs, Merrill, 415
Menier, Henri, 240
Mercer, Lucy, 279, 378

Meyer, Eugene, 351, 407, 429-430
Meyer, George, 81-82
Meyers, Carl, 288
Middle Creek, Illinois, 232, 263
Miller, Edgar, 365
Miller, Mark, 475
Miller, Peter, 398, 408
Miller, Roscoe (Rocky), 413, 424
Miller, Ruth Elizabeth McCormick, see Ruth Elizabeth McCormick Tankersley
Millet, Frank Hobert, 362
Milwaukee, Wisconsin, 298, 299
Miner, Edward, 233
Miner, Julius, 383
Minneapolis, Minnesota, 303, 304
Minnesota State Legislature, 306
Minnesota Supreme Court, 304, 305
Mitchell, William (Billy), 186
Mitscher, Marc, 384
Mittman, Frank, 362
Modigliano, 364
Montdidier, 206
Monticello, 303, 321, 322, 330
Montpelier, 329
Mont Sec, 336, 352
Moore, Grace, 279
Morgan, Daniel, 328
Morgan, Gwen, 70, 426, 442
Morgenstern, George, 377, 394, 441, 467
Morgenthau, Henry, 318
Morode, Cleo de, 12
Morris, Ira Nelson, 155
Morris, Isabelle, 475
Morrison, John L. 304
Morton, Joy, 340, 464
Mory's, 56
Moseley, George Van Horn, 166, 187
Mount Airy, N.C., 366
Mount Vernon, 321
Mull, Island of, 110
Munsey, Frank, 104
Murray, Dorothy, 426-427, 454, 475
Museum of Science and Industry, 32
Mussolini, Benito, 256, 316, 368
Mutual Network, 287

Nance, Willis, 407, 429

495

496

498

499

Winn, Marcia (Mrs. George
  Morgenstern), 394, 447
Wisner, George, 90, 92, 106, 113,
  118
Witmer, Richard, 358
"With the Russian Army," 156
  157
Wodehouse, P. G., 330
Wolf, Otto, 284
Wood, J. Howard, 269, 407, 416,
  429, 433-435, 440, 450, 466-
  468, 474
Wood, Leonard, 67, 175, 184
Wood, Percy, 454
Wood, Robert, 298-302
Wood, Robert, 372, 444
Woolworth, F. W., 259
World Court, 256
World Eucharistic Congress, 255
World Series, 254
World War I, see McCormick,
  Robert R.
World War II, see McCormick,
  Robert R.
World's Fair (1893), 12, 30, 31,
  259

World's Fair (1933), 261, 317
"World's Greatest Newspaper,"
  115, 253, 258, 444
Wright Brothers, 107, 428
Wright, Frank Lloyd, 259
Wrigley, William, 258, 262
Wu, Edith, 413-414
Wu, Eileen, 413-414, 470
Wu, K. C., 405, 413, 414, 470
Wu, Mrs. K. C., 405, 413, 414,
  470
Wyngarden, Clarence, 460-461,
  466, 470-473

Yale, 6, 43, 55-60, 76, 89, 98,
  104, 108, 134-135, 203, 221,
  262, 428
Young, David, 349
Yu, Y. Yuan, 414, 470

Zalinski, E. L., 7
Zeier, Frank, 346, 363
Zeier, Lucille (Mrs. Regnier),
  349, 350, 447
Zenith, 253

501